THE SINO-INDIAN RIVALRY

Implications for Global Order

ŠUMIT GANGULY

Indiana University Bloomington

MANJEET S. PARDESI

Victoria University of Wellington

WILLIAM R. THOMPSON

Indiana University Bloomington

T0384750

CAMBRIDGE
UNIVERSITY PRESS

Shaftesbury Road, Cambridge CB2 8EA, United Kingdom

One Liberty Plaza, 20th Floor, New York, NY 10006, USA

477 Williamstown Road, Port Melbourne, VIC 3207, Australia

314–321, 3rd Floor, Plot 3, Splendor Forum, Jasola District Centre, New Delhi – 110025, India

103 Penang Road, #05–06/07, Visioncrest Commercial, Singapore 238467

Cambridge University Press is part of Cambridge University Press & Assessment, a department of the University of Cambridge.

We share the University's mission to contribute to society through the pursuit of education, learning and research at the highest international levels of excellence.

www.cambridge.org
Information on this title: www.cambridge.org/9781009193535

DOI: 10.1017/9781009193542

First published 2023

A catalogue record for this publication is available from the British Library.

A Cataloging-in-Publication data record for this book is available from the Library of Congress

ISBN 978-1-009-19353-5 Hardback
ISBN 978-1-009-19352-8 Paperback

Contents

vi　　　　　　　　　　*Contents*

Figures and Maps

vii

Tables

Acknowledgments

Šumit Ganguly wishes to acknowledge the support that he received from the Rabindranath Tagore Chair at Indiana University, Bloomington, for the production of the maps for this volume. Manjeet S. Pardesi thanks Victoria University of Wellington for a grant to cover the cost of the maps.

*

Šumit Ganguly dedicates this book to his wife, Traci.

Manjeet S. Pardesi dedicates this book to his father, Inderjit, and to the memory of his mother, Harjeet.

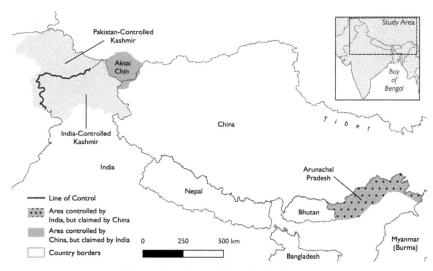

Map 1   The disputed Sino-Indian frontier

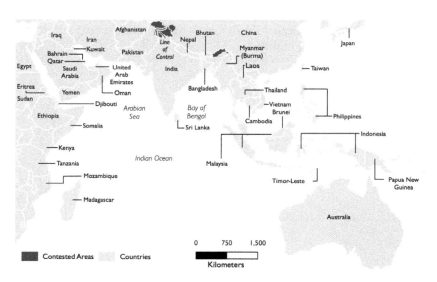

Map 2   China and India in the Indo-Pacific region

PART I

Introduction

CHAPTER I

Introduction

As the United States' "unipolar moment" wanes, Asia is witnessing the simultaneous rise of two powers, China and India. While the polarity of the emerging international system is a matter of considerable scholarly debate, most agree that China is in a separate league compared to other rising powers.[1] Indeed, China's phenomenal rise poses a significant challenge to America's "systemic leadership" as the lead economy and the center for technological/energy innovation.[2] China's asymmetric ascent vis-à-vis India – as it began growing earlier than India and continued to grow/innovate faster – has meant that International Relations scholarship has focused on the US–China strategic rivalry to understand the propensity for conflict in Asia and its implications for the international system.[3] However, the China–India strategic rivalry, which is equally consequential for the Asian and global order, has been relatively ignored in the academic scholarship even though there is recognition in the policy community that the "rise of multiple powers [in Asia] – particularly China and India – could spark increased rivalries."[4]

---

[1] In spite of this, China has not yet caught up with the United States. See Stephen G. Brooks and William C. Wohlforth, "The Rise and Fall of the Great Powers in the Twenty-First Century: China's Rise and the Fate of America's Global Position," *International Security* 40.3 (2015/16): 7–53.

[2] William R. Thompson, *America's Global Pre-eminence: The Development and Erosion of Systemic Leadership* (Oxford: Oxford University Press, 2022).

[3] There is vast literature on these issues. Notable contributions include Steve Chan, *Thucydides's Trap? Historical Interpretation, Logic of Inquiry, and the Future of Sino-American Relations* (Ann Arbor: University of Michigan Press, 2020); Asle Toje (ed.), *Will China's Rise Be Peaceful? Security, Stability, and Legitimacy* (Oxford: Oxford University Press, 2018); John J. Mearsheimer, "Bound to Fail: The Rise and Fall of the Liberal International Order," *International Security* 43.4 (2019): 7–50; Avery Goldstein, "US-China Rivalry in the Twenty-First Century: Déjà Vu and Cold War II," *China International Strategy Review* 2 (2020): 48–62; Khong Yuen Foong, "Power as Prestige in World Politics," *International Affairs* 95.1 (2019): 119–142; Aaron Friedberg, "Competing with China," *Survival* 60.3 (2018): 7–64; and Graham Allison, *Destined for War? Can America and China Escape Thucydides' Trap* (Boston: Harcourt, 2018).

[4] United States National Intelligence Council, *Global Trends 2030: Alternative Worlds*, Office of the Director of National Intelligence Council, December 2012, 103. www.dni.gov/files/documents/GlobalTrends_2030.pdf.

The aim of this book is threefold. First, we describe and analyze the Sino-Indian strategic rivalry and its implications for rivalry escalation. While previous studies have certainly not ignored describing the grievances of the rivalry participants (as discussed in the following chapters), they tend to list the various foci of the dispute without considering how they correspond to what we know about the general behavior of actors in "strategic rivalries."[5] Furthermore, there is a strong tendency to focus too much on the *spatial* (or territorial) dimension of the Sino-Indian rivalry while ignoring its *positional* dimension. However, we know that spatial and positional rivalries are different not only in terms of their causation but also in their propensity to escalate, to persist, and to terminate.[6]

Second, the Sino-Indian rivalry is also characterized by material and cognitive *asymmetries*.[7] As shown in Chapters 2 and 6, the material power gap between China and India is substantial, and it has widened in recent years. Additionally, Indian elites regard China as their *principal* rival, ranked above Pakistan, while China's elites regard India as a *lesser* rival, ranked below its other rivals, the United States and Japan, which are perceived as its peers.[8] Consequently, not only do we analyze the conflict dynamics in the Sino-Indian contest using the framework of strategic rivalries but we also pay attention to the spatial and positional contests that characterize their rivalry. Additionally, we examine how their asymmetries are shaping their conflict behavior as they are novel and deserve special attention. We demonstrate that, these differences notwithstanding, China has in fact begun to pay more attention to India in recent years.

Third, we show that the Sino-Indian rivalry is crucial for the regional order in Asia and for the global order. An inordinate focus on US–China rivalry has drawn attention away from the Sino-Indian rivalry and its very significant ramifications for the prospects of war and peace in twenty-first-century Asia. Our analysis is informed by our understanding of the evolution of global warfare and the tendency in the academic literature to highlight clashes between declining global leaders and rising regional leaders. Although this "global-regional" clash is important, warfare usually

---

[5] Michael P. Colaresi, Karen Rasler, and William R. Thompson, *Strategic Rivalries in World Politics: Position, Space, and Conflict Escalation* (Cambridge: Cambridge University Press, 2007).

[6] Karen A. Rasler, William R. Thompson, and Sumit Ganguly, *How Rivalries End* (Philadelphia: University of Pennsylvania Press, 2013); and David R. Dreyer, "Foundations of Rivalry Research," in William R. Thompson (ed.), *The Oxford Encyclopedia of Empirical International Relations Theory, Volume 2* (Oxford: Oxford University Press, 2018), 65–80.

[7] Manjeet S. Pardesi, "Explaining the Asymmetry in the Sino-Indian Strategic Rivalry," *Australian Journal of International Affairs* 75.3 (2021): 341–365.

[8] William R. Thompson, "Principal Rivalries," *Journal of Conflict Resolution* 39.2 (1995): 195–223.

breaks out because of conflict between the rising regional leader and other actors in the neighborhood.[9]

In the contemporary international system, Asia is the most likely venue for war between regional powers.[10] Accordingly, we argue that it is dangerous to overemphasize global-regional rivalry at the expense of regional rivalries that may be more critical to conflict escalation. In this context, we think that much more attention needs to be devoted to the Sino-Indian rivalry than currently being given, especially because several observers tend to dismiss it as a peripheral issue. For example, the Center for Preventive Action's annual Preventive Priorities Survey ranked a potential clash between China and India as a Tier III concern (which only deserved a "low" priority) in 2019, while dropping it altogether from its three-tiered list of concerns in 2020. However, the clash was raised to a Tier II conflict of "moderate" concern in 2021 and 2022.[11]

The rest of this introductory chapter is divided into three sections that explain the core features of our argument and the layout of the book. The next section provides a brief introduction to strategic rivalries and the conflict dynamic thereof, while also focusing on asymmetries that impact the behavior of the antagonists. The following section provides a description of our analytic approach that focuses on the China–India rivalry as well as its interaction with the US–China rivalry, and our emphasis on relying on history as well as general theories of war, great power transitions, and escalation/de-escalation dynamics of strategic rivalries. The third section provides an outline of our various chapters and our arguments related to the specific themes and issues in the Sino-Indian contest. Finally, we conclude by arguing that the Sino-Indian rivalry should be taken more seriously given its implications for the regional order in Asia and the wider world.

Strategic Rivalries

States interact with other states in various ways. A fundamental difference in international politics is the categorical distinction made between friends and

---

[9] William R. Thompson, *On Global War: Historical-Structural Approaches to World Politics* (Columbia: University of South Carolina Press, 1988); and George Modelski and William R. Thompson, *Leading Sectors and World Powers: The Coevolution of Global Politics and Economics* (Columbia: University of South Carolina Press, 1996).

[10] Sumit Ganguly and William R. Thompson, "Conflict Propensities in Asian Rivalries," in Sumit Ganguly and William R. Thompson (eds.), *Asian Rivalries: Conflict, Escalation, and Limitations on Two-Level Games* (Stanford: Stanford University Press, 2011), 1.

[11] These surveys are available online at Preventive Priorities Survey, Council on Foreign Relations, www.cfr.org/preventive-priorities-survey.

enemies.[12] Friends are not threatening. Interaction between friends or allies, therefore, is usually fairly cooperative. Enemies may be quite threatening although the levels of threat may vary over time. Interaction between enemies, as a consequence, is usually conflictual. But there is also a hierarchical element that needs to be considered.[13] Very strong and very weak states can regard one another as enemies but there may not be much that the weaker parties can do about their grievances (without assistance from other stronger states) because weaker states are simply not sufficiently competitive with the kind of resources their stronger enemies can draw upon.

Rivalries are relationships in which the adversary has been assigned the category of a threatening enemy and is operating in the same competitive league (at least as far as the issues under contention are concerned).[14] The term "rivalry," of course, is quite a familiar one in international relations discourse. Yet it is only recently that we have begun to deal with its implications in an explicit and theoretical fashion. In doing so, we have discovered that rivalries are not so numerous that they cannot be inventoried and dated for life cycles (origin and termination) and outcomes.[15] They can also be categorized by grievances that fuel them. *Positional* rivalries are about competitions over which state will benefit from possessing greater influence in a given global or regional locale. *Spatial* rivalries pit two states in a contest over the exclusive control of a specific territory. *Ideological* rivalries characterize interstate feuds over whose version of doctrine is superior. *Interventionary* rivalries are scaled-down type of positional rivalries in which one state claims

[12] David James Finlay, Richard R. Fagen, and Ole R. Holsti, *Enemies in Politics* (Chicago: Rand McNally, 1967); and Charles A. Kupchan, *How Enemies Become Friends: The Sources of Stable Peace* (Princeton: Princeton University Press, 2010).

[13] David A. Lake, "Great Power Hierarchies and Strategies in Twenty-First Century World Politics," in Walter Carlsnaes, Thomas Risse, and Beth A. Simmons (eds.), *Handbook of International Relations*, 2nd ed. (Los Angeles: SAGE, 2013), 555–577; and Ayse Zarakol (ed.), *Hierarchies in World Politics* (Cambridge: Cambridge University Press, 2017).

[14] Manjeet S. Pardesi, "Image Theory and the Initiation of Strategic Rivalries," in Thompson, *The Oxford Encyclopedia of Empirical International Relations Theory*, 225–244.

[15] William R. Thompson and David R. Dreyer, *Handbook of International Rivalries, 1494–2010* (Washington, DC: CQ Press, 2012). In addition to the "strategic rivalries" framework associated with Thompson and his collaborators that emphasizes decision-maker perceptions and the history of foreign relations between the contenders, other rivalry scholars adopt the dispute-density approach that relies on the number of militarized interstate disputes within a finite time period (although attempts have been made to bridge these different frameworks). On these other rivalry frameworks, see Paul F. Diehl and Gary Goertz, *War and Peace in International Rivalry* (Ann Arbor: University of Michigan Press, 2000); John Vasquez and Christopher S. Leskiw, "The Origins and War Proneness of Interstate Rivalries," *Annual Review of Political Science* 4.1 (2001): 295–316; Zeev Maoz and Ben D. Mor, *Bound by Struggle: The Strategic Evolution of Enduring International Rivalries* (Ann Arbor: University of Michigan Press, 2002); and Brandon Valeriano, *Becoming Rivals: The Process of Interstate Rivalry Development* (New York: Routledge, 2013).

the right to intervene in or manipulate the affairs of usually an adjacent state that resists said interventions and manipulations.

Given that some states have more than one rival to contend with, an important type of adversarial relationship is the *principal* rivalry. States that have only one rival are engaged in principal rivalries by default. States that have multiple rivals often rank order them according to which ones have greater significance. In such cases, the principal rival is the most important one. However, these categorizations can be either *symmetrical* or *asymmetrical*. Two states may accord the principal rival status to one another, or only one state may see it that way while the other state is actually more focused on some other conflict relationship.

One serious complication is that rivalries are not necessarily of one type or the other. They can be a complicated mix of various types that have been identified above. Our assertion, nonetheless, is that different types of rivalries behave differently,[16] and therefore we need to pay attention to typology when we are analyzing rivalries. Importantly, even asymmetries do not necessarily produce fixed effects, as they may give the differently ranked states in the dyad different incentives and motives related to conflict escalation and de-escalation. Exactly how these characteristics matter in general, and specifically in the case of the Sino-Indian rivalry, is addressed at length in the ensuing chapters.

Analytical Approach

Our research design is eclectic. We focus on a single rivalry case – the Sino-Indian rivalry. However, we rely on other cases to explore comparatively the various dimensions of this case that we think have not been given sufficient attention to date. Thus, one question to be addressed is whether there is more to the Sino-Indian rivalry than meets the eye. Our analysis of the origins and evolution of this rivalry demonstrates that despite the excessive focus on the spatial dimension of this rivalry their positional contest may be more consequential. Even though spatial issues are more likely to generate militarized conflict than positional issues, the latter with their emphasis on rank in a pecking order are far more difficult to resolve.[17]

---

[16] William R. Thompson, Kentaro Sakuwa, and Prashant Hosur Suhas, *Analyzing Strategic Rivalries in World Politics: Types of Rivalry, Regional Variation, and Escalation/De-escalation* (Singapore: Springer, 2022).

[17] William R. Thompson, "Status Conflict, Hierarchies, and Interpretation Dilemmas," in T. V. Paul, Deborah Welch Larson, and William C. Wohlforth (eds.), *Status in World Politics* (New York: Cambridge University Press, 2014), 219–245.

We rely on histories of foreign policy, theories of general wars, great power transitions, and processes thought to drive hostility escalation within rivalries as we analyze the Sino-Indian strategic rivalry and its inter-action with the Sino-American rivalry. This allows us to demonstrate that it is not always the rivalry between the two leading contenders for systemic leadership that is most critical to war/peace outcomes. In other words, we show that there is a pattern of regional rivalries playing critical roles in the movement toward systemic wars as opposed to a direct contest between a rising regional leader and a declining systemic leader.

Another question involves the role of asymmetries in rivalries as well as their interconnections with other (related) rivalries. Understanding this provides us insights into the likely future of the Sino-Indian rivalry. Asymmetries are associated with mixed effects and contain within them the possibilities for rivalry escalation as well de-escalation. Since asym-metries in particular domains – economic, nuclear, or naval – are nested within the larger politico-strategic context of rivalry, they produce differ-ent tendencies for conflict. Additionally, we also pay attention to factors that link the Sino-Indian rivalry with the belligerents' other rivalries, espe-cially the Sino-American and the Indo-Pakistani rivalries, given the Indo-American and Sino-Pakistani alignments. What are the factors in these interconnected rivalries that will escalate and de-escalate their hostilities? We probe this likelihood, subject to assumptions that are made as explicit as possible.

In undertaking this analysis, we make extensive use of published reports from the governments of the United States, India, and China (published in English). Additionally, we also rely on the existing scholarly litera-ture on the Sino-Indian dynamic in our assessment of the propensity for conflict in this dyad. Notably, we draw upon the Chinese literature on India (published in English) in the context of Sino-Indian and Sino-American rivalries. Of late, China's leading scholars of international relations are paying increased attention to India on matters related to war, peace, and international order (despite their asymmetries as shown subsequently). More specifically, we look at Chinese journals published by the institutions affiliated with the Chinese government. These jour-nals include *Contemporary International Relations*, published by the China Institutes of Contemporary International Relations (CICIR), and *China International Studies*, published by the China Institute of International Studies (CIIS). CICIR is a think tank that is closely associated with the Chinese Communist Party's (CCP) Foreign Affairs Office and China's Ministry of State Security (the ministry that oversees foreign intelligence), while CIIS is associated with China's Ministry of Foreign Affairs and the People's Liberation Army (PLA).[18]

Core Arguments and Chapter Outlines

There are different views on the Sino-Indian rivalry in the extant literature. Shirk argued that this is a "one-sided rivalry" because China does not think of India as a rival even though India thinks of China as a rival.[19] According to Garver, the Sino-Indian rivalry is not one-sided; it is asymmetric because China deliberately understates India as a rival due ultimately to the material power gap between them that favors China.[20] Finally, Westad asserted that "China's biggest foreign policy challenge in the future will be India" and that "it will be difficult for Beijing to avoid future rivalry with Asia's other rising power."[21]

What is noteworthy about these diverse views on the Sino-Indian rivalry is that these scholars do not engage with the theoretical literature on "rivalries" (though they use the term "rivalry" as it is a familiar term in the international relations discourse). In fact, most scholars of the Sino-Indian relationship do not employ the rivalries framework.[22] For example, focusing primarily on their border dispute in the Himalayas, Fravel argued that India is a "secondary" threat for China as Beijing has traditionally focused on (and continues to focus on) East Asia.[23] However, in the same volume, Zhang noted that the Sino-Indian contest is more than a mere border dispute. According to him, there is "pessimism about future prospects of this relationship" in China even though India is not considered "as important as the United States or Japan" because India affects "all the major arenas of Chinese foreign policy"

---

[18] David Shambaugh, "China's International Relations Think Tanks: Evolving Structure and Process," *The China Quarterly* 171 (2002): 579–590.

[19] Susan Shirk, "One-Sided Rivalry: China's Perceptions and Policies toward India," in Francine R. Frankel and Harry Harding (eds.), *The India-China Relationship: What the United States Needs to Know* (New York: Columbia University Press, 2004), 75–100.

[20] John Garver, "Asymmetrical Indian and Chinese Threat Perceptions," *Journal of Strategic Studies* 25.4 (2002): 109–134; and John W. Garver, *Protracted Contest: Sino-Indian Rivalry in the Twentieth Century* (Seattle: University of Washington Press, 2001).

[21] Odd Arne Westad, *Restless Empire: China and the World since 1750* (New York: Basic Books, 2015), 461–462.

[22] Notable exceptions are the chapters by T. V. Paul ("Explaining Conflict and Cooperation in the China–India Rivalry." 3–24) and Paul F. Diehl ("Whither Rivalry or Withered Rivalry?," 253–272) in T. V. Paul (ed.), *The China-India Rivalry in the Globalization Era* (Washington, DC: Georgetown University Press, 2018). However, these scholars take the dispute-density approach to rivalries as opposed to the "strategic rivalries" approach. Also see footnote 15.

[23] M. Taylor Fravel, "Stability in a Secondary Strategic Direction: China and the Border Dispute with India after 1962," in Kanti P. Bajpai, Selina Ho, and Manjari Chatterjee Miller (eds.), *Routledge Handbook of China-India Relations* (London: Routledge, 2020), 169–179.

related to major power relations, the periphery (neighbors), the developing world, and global governance.[24] In other words, there is a wide array of views in the extant literature on Sino-Indian strategic relations.

This book analyzes the Sino-Indian contest as a "strategic rivalry" given that most of the extant literature does not engage with this concept. The book is divided into five parts. Following this introduction in Part I, Chapter 2 provides an overview of the nature of the Sino-Indian antagonism as strategic rivalry, including the salience of the *spatial* and *positional* issues under contention. While the Sino-Indian territorial dispute in the Himalayas is hardly insignificant, it is their positional contest that is more central to their overall rivalry. More specifically, China and India have been engaged in positional rivalry for leadership not only in South Asia but in the larger Asian region (including Southeast Asia and the Indian Ocean). Furthermore, despite the widening asymmetry in their material capabilities in recent years, the Sino-Indian rivalry shows no signs of withering away. If anything, this contest seems to be intensifying, and although war is not preordained, the possibility of escalation cannot be discounted because of the multiple functional issues implicated in this rivalry (including Tibet, water, and space, among others). The entanglement of the Sino-Indian rivalry with other key players, especially the United States and Pakistan, further heightens the possibility of escalation.

Part II of this book builds on this overview of the Sino-Indian strategic rivalry to explain how positional and spatial concerns have influenced the course of their rivalry since the 1940s. Chapter 3 explains the early positional contest between China and India in the 1940s and the 1950s.[25] It explains the Indian and Chinese claims to Asian leadership as well as the roles that the two countries envisaged for the other in an Asia led by them. This Sino-Indian positional contest was most apparent in three venues: (i) in various Asian multilateral fora (such as the 1947 Asian Relations Conference and the 1955 Bandung Conference) and in India's attempts to mediate in conflicts involving China and other players; (ii) in the Himalayan states (Nepal, Bhutan, and Sikkim) and in Southeast Asia; and (iii) in Tibet. The Tibet issue was particularly fraught with strategic consequences. As China sought India's help to consolidate its own rule in Tibet, it gave India an

---

[24] Zhang Feng, "India in China's Strategic Thought," in Bajpai, Ho, and Miller, *Routledge Handbook of China-India Relations*, 139, 148. Also see, Srikanth Kondapalli, "Perception and Strategic Reality in India-China Relations," in Thomas Fingar (ed.), *The New Great Game: China and South and Central Asia in the Era of Reform* (Stanford: Stanford University Press, 2016), 93–115.

[25] In fact, the Sino-Indian strategic rivalry also began as a positional rivalry. See Manjeet S. Pardesi, "The Initiation of the Sino-Indian Rivalry," *Asian Security* 15.3 (2019): 253–284.

exalted but much-resented position in China's internal affairs (pertaining to Tibet). Matters related to Tibet also entangled the positional and spatial dimensions of the Sino-Indian rivalry because the territories in dispute between China and India had complex historical links with Tibet.

Chapter 4 builds on the Sino-Indian positional contest in the 1940s and 1950s and argues that the 1962 Sino-Indian War was not just a border war over disputed territory (or the outcome of the Sino-Indian spatial rivalry alone) as is generally argued because issues related to their positional rivalry were also at stake. Sino-Indian positional rivalry in the Himalayan states and in Burma was linked with the Tibetan issue, and Tibet itself was at the nexus of the Sino-Indian spatial and positional rivalries. Furthermore, the 1962 Sino-Indian War proceeded as wars between positional rivals tend to: with the near multilateralization of the war as India sought help from the United States (which was favorably considered). While China's unilateral ceasefire that was accepted by India precluded overt American participation, India's massive defeat also had positional consequences as it removed India as a contender for Asian leadership. Unlike the 1940s and 1950s, India became a marginal strategic player in Asia for the rest of the twentieth century. Although this did not result in Chinese leadership in Asia, China continued to remain important to the wider Asian strategic dynamic in the decades after 1962.

Consequently, India became more focused on South Asian affairs after 1962 (as opposed to pan-Asian affairs). However, Sino-Indian spatial considerations continued to maintain their salience as the war did not resolve their *spatial* rivalry though it reduced India's *position* in Asia. Chapter 5 in Part III of this book discusses four significant Sino-Indian militarized border disputes since 1962: the 1967 Nathu La Crisis, the 1986–87 Sumdorong Chu Crisis, the 2017 Doklam Crisis, and the 2020 Ladakh Crisis. The chapter notes that there are several common themes running across these disparate crises, especially the Chinese conviction of inherited colonial borders being subject to revision. The chapter argues that the frequency and intensity of the Sino-Indian crises have increased over the past decade (despite a temporary lull after 1986–87). Although the 2017 and 2020 crises (and others over the past decade) had their own logic, they occurred in the backdrop of India's gradual ascent during a period of closer US–India security alignment. Consequently, future border crises (that spiral into inadvertent wars) remain a distinct possibility, and the *spatial* issue continues to remain crucial to the Sino-Indian rivalry.

The book also attempts to provide insights into the Sino-Indian conflict dynamic in the coming years. India's slow and fitful (absolute) rise over the past three decades has happened in the context of relative decline vis-à-vis China because the latter has grown faster and more comprehensively.

Despite this asymmetry, newer functional areas have appeared in the ensuing Sino-Indian contest. Chapter 6 focuses on these newer domains – economics, nuclear, and naval – that are riddled with domain-specific asymmetries and domain-specific pathways to conflict escalation.

While there is no reason to believe that war is inevitable, the Sino-Indian relationship has entered a troubled phase because further asymmetry and the strategies to address these asymmetries are both conflict-prone. There are three specific pathways (which are not mutually exclusive) that cut across these different domains and point toward heightened conflict: any Chinese attempt to create a new status quo reflective of the power gap in its favor; any Indian endeavor to redress this power gap in order to be taken more seriously by China; and the United States' promotion of the rise of India. If China and India continue with their absolute rise in the years ahead, then trends point toward heightened *spatial* and *positional* strife in the Sino-Indian contest with consequences for the regional order in Asia given the growing American stake in their rivalry.

Part IV pursues the larger theme of interconnections between the Sino-Indian rivalry with the belligerents' other rivalries and explains its regional and systemic consequences. The entanglement of the Sino-Indian rivalry with the Indo-Pakistani rivalry is giving these distinct rivalries an increasingly "triadic" dynamic as a consequence of the deepening Sino-Pakistani alignment. This is the focus of Chapter 7. As Indo-Pakistani and Sino-Indian rivalries fuse, they are likely to raise the chances of conflict in the region. China's changing stance on the Kashmir issue, including the passage of the China–Pakistan Economic Corridor through territories claimed by India in its dispute with Pakistan, has implications for Indo-Pakistani *spatial* rivalry. Moreover, China is rapidly transforming Pakistan into its strategic surrogate in South Asia. Not only does the Sino-Pakistani alignment undercut India's *position* in South Asia but it also reduces India's standing in Asia at large by keeping it focused on South Asian affairs. In other words, this "triadic" rivalry is not without pan-Asian consequences.

Chapter 8 analyzes the larger Asian dimension of the Sino-Indian rivalry in the context of the budding Sino-American rivalry, which is fast emerging as the most consequential rivalry in the world with systemic repercussions. There are two noteworthy developments here. First, the rise of China, America's changing approach to the region, and India's gradual ascent are all transforming the strategic geography of Asia, as the traditional boundaries between South Asia, East Asia, and Southeast Asia begin to blur in addition to connecting the maritime dynamics in the Western Pacific and the Indian Ocean. As Asia's leading rising power, China has the potential to make a bid for regional hegemony in Asia. However, any such Chinese quest will intensify the Sino-Indian rivalry as this increasingly interconnected larger Asian region is the theater of their *positional* contest.

Second, regional hegemony in a consequential region (such as Asia) will provide the emerging regional hegemon (China) with the capabilities to challenge the United States for leadership at the systemic level. While the probability of conflict in this budding global-regional rivalry should not be minimized, the history of global wars over the past five centuries suggests that global wars tend to start not as global wars per se. Instead, they often begin as as regional wars in which the expanding lead land power scares an opposition coalition into being to oppose its expansion. In turn, the system's predominant maritime power usually leads this opposing coalition.[26] Whether or not India formally joins a US-led coalition to check China's rising power, India's growing alignment with the United States suggests that the Sino-Indian rivalry is in the process of fusing with the Sino-American rivalry. Put differently, a Sino-Indian regional war has some probability greater than zero of creating an opportunity or opportunities for escalation that drags in the United States with potentially systemic consequences.

Extrapolating from these findings, Chapter 9 in Part V, the final part of the volume, concludes that the China–India rivalry could be the key to global stability in the coming decades even though this may not be apparent at first. In Asia, the hotspots of Korea, Taiwan, the East China Sea, and the South China Sea tend to receive more attention, while the China–India militarized disputes are perceived as the backwaters of the regional theater.[27] However, a Sino-Indian confrontation – whether on land in the Himalayas or in maritime realm in the Indian Ocean – may very well be the trigger that leads to a systemic war involving the United States. Given that the Sino-Indian *spatial* contest has intensified in recent years, the probability of escalation in the Himalayas is a distinct possibility. In fact, the presence of the more consequential *positional* dimension of the Sino-Indian rivalry suggests that this rivalry would still be strong even if the *spatial* dimension were to disappear. For all these reasons, the Sino-Indian rivalry is not to be taken lightly.

---

[26] Thompson, *On Global War*; and William R. Thompson, "Introduction: How Might We Know That a Systemic Transition Is Underway? Clues for the Twenty-First Century," in Thompson, *Systemic Transitions*, 1–6.

[27] For a recent argument purporting this view, see Van Jackson, "America's Indo-Pacific Folly: Adding New Commitments in Asia Will Only Invite Disaster," *Foreign Affairs*, 12 March 2021, www.foreignaffairs.com/articles/asia/2021-03-12/americas-indo-pacific-folly. Similarly, contingencies involving India or the Indian Ocean are not listed in the five possible (East) Asian scenarios that might trigger a US–China conflict in Stacie L. Pettyjohn, "War with China: Five Scenarios," *Survival* 64.1 (2022): 57–66.

CHAPTER 2

The Sino-Indian Rivalry
Spatial and Positional Contestation

A number of books and articles have now been written about the rivalry between China and India.[1] The need for another work reflects dissatisfaction with some of the ways in which this rivalry has been analyzed. Rivalry analyses are hardly monolithic in focus or interpretation. We certainly do not insist that all analyses have gotten the case wrong. However, there are some views that we think deserve further discussion. More specifically, there are disagreements about when this rivalry began, what it is about, what its potential for escalation might be, and how significant it might be for the course of world politics. We think this case of rivalry began with the advent of Indian independence given that the earliest time point at which a rivalry between two states can commence is when both states are independent. There is not surprisingly a great deal of emphasis on disputes along the Tibetan border. These are not insignificant, but they may prove to be the least important part of the Sino-Indian rivalry: The positional contest between the two Asian giants seems more central to the rivalry overall. We think the rivalry has considerable potential for escalation – perhaps even more than the Sino-American rivalry does. If that is indeed the case, the Sino-Indian rivalry may hold one of the most critical keys to world peace and stability. It is not something that can be dismissed as a minor tempest in a frozen region.

But why stress that we are analyzing a rivalry? Surely, we all know what rivalry is. How does that help our cause to understanding the Sino-Indian relationship? Anyone who watches sports teams play at any level

---

[1] See, for instance, John W. Garver, *Protracted Conflict: Sino-Indian Rivalry in the Twentieth Century* (Seattle: University of Washington Press, 2001); Francine R. Frankel and Harry Harding (eds.), *The Indo-China Relationship: What the United States Needs to Know* (New York: Columbia University Press, 2004); C. Raja Mohan, *Samudra Manthan: Sino-Indian Rivalry in the Indo-Pacific* (Washington, DC: Carnegie Endowment for International Peace, 2012); Jeff M. Smith, *Cold Peace: Sino-Indian Rivalry in the Twenty-First Century* (Lanham, MD: Lexington Books, 2014); and T. V. Paul (ed.), *The China-India Rivalry in the Globalization Era* (Washington, DC: Georgetown University Press, 2018).

has some idea of which rival team is most hated and least trusted by their favorite team. Similar processes are at work in international politics. States compete with other states over all sorts of things. Decision-makers select which competitors are the most dangerous and give them special attention – sometimes to the point of fixation that leads to practically ignoring other competitors. Interstate rivalries are not very common. There have been only a few hundred of them in the past two centuries. But the real payoff of studying rivalries explicitly is that they dispropor-tionately account for conflict and war. Nonrivals simply do not go to war with other nonrivals all that much. Rivals do not always go to war either, but they are far more likely to do so. Moreover, they tend to be recidivists. They go to war repeatedly – the extreme example is the war record of India and Pakistan (1947, 1965, 1971, 1999). Thus, to understand conflict in world politics in general, we need to get a better handle on rivalry processes – why they begin, why they escalate, if they do, and why they end.[2] We also need to better understand specific rivalries. Not all rival-ries are equally significant. Some are more significant than others because they are linked to tinderboxes that might lead to world wars. We think that Sino-Indian rivalry is particularly dangerous – not so much because of what China and India can do to each other, although that is nothing to underestimate, but because it is becoming increasingly linked to the Sino-American rivalry, which in turn could be linked to renewed global warfare. We make no claim that war is imminent or even highly probable. Our point is merely that we should not dismiss the Sino-Indian rivalry as limited to South Asian quarrels over obscure Himalayan boundaries,

---

[2] The academic study of interstate rivalries has been underway for about three decades now. Rivalries, of course, have long been of interest to historians and political scientists. But it was really only after the end of the Cold War that analysts began taking seriously what the explicit study of rivalries entailed. See, among others, Paul F. Diehl and Gary Goertz, *War and Peace in International Rivalry* (Ann Arbor: University of Michigan Press, 2000); Zeev Maoz and Ben D. Mor, *Bound by Struggle: The Strategic Evolution of Enduring International Rivalries* (Ann Arbor: University of Michigan Press, 2002); Michael Colaresi, Karen Rasler, and William R. Thompson, *Strategic Rivalries in World Politics: Position, Space, and Conflict Escalation* (Cambridge: Cambridge University Press, 2007); Sumit Ganguly and William R. Thompson (eds.), *Asian Rivalries: Conflict, Escalation, and Limitations on Two-Level Games* (Stanford: Stanford University Press, 2011); William R. Thompson and David R. Dreyer, *Handbook of International Rivalries, 1494–2010* (Washington, DC: CQ Press, 2011); Karen Rasler, William R. Thompson, and Sumit Ganguly, *How Rivalries End* (Philadelphia: University of Pennsylvania Press, 2013); Tien-sze Fang, *Asymmetrical Threat Perceptions in India-China Relations* (New Delhi: Oxford University Press, 2013); Gary Goertz, Paul F. Diehl, and Alexandru Balas, *The Evolution of Peace in the International System* (New York: Oxford University Press, 2016); Imad Mansour and William R. Thompson (eds.), *Shocks and Rivalries in the Middle East and North Africa* (Washington, DC: Georgetown University Press, 2020); and William R. Thompson, Kentaro Sakuwa, and Prashant Hosur Suhas, *Analyzing Strategic Rivalries: Types and Dynamics* (Singapore: Springer, 2022).

accompanied by images of Chinese and Indian soldiers' fist-fighting in the snow at very high elevations from time to time.[3] There is more at stake than small groups fighting in the snow.

For instance, Sino-Indian relations cannot be reduced to another example of security dilemmas.[4] Such situations emerge when two states take steps to ensure their own security that inadvertently are perceived as threatening when in fact they were intended as defensive measures. This is not to argue that security dilemmas do not occur or that they are entirely absent from the history of Sino-Indian interactions. The point to be stressed, however, is that rivals have genuine reasons to be concerned about the behavior and intentions of their adversaries. Rivalries are relationships characterized by perceived threats emanating from competitors who are acknowledged as enemies.

Another peculiarity of the Sino-Indian rivalry is that observers have often termed it asymmetrical in a variety of ways, but the one that stands out most prominently is that the Indian side of the relationship freely acknowledges the existence of rivalry but the Chinese have often claimed that hostile perceptions are entirely one-sided.[5] Can rivalry be rivalry if only one side recognizes it? In this case, the answer is definitely yes. It is not unknown for decision-makers to officially deny the existence of rivalry. Indeed, a number of rivalries have begun without either side officially acknowledging the existence of an adversarial relationship. What matters is whether the parties in question take steps that demonstrate rivalry exists, regardless of public pronouncements. In the Sino-Indian case, the early Chinese official position reflected a perception that Indians were not yet sufficiently competitive to be taken seriously as a threat. It is possible that such expressions of superiority honestly reflected Chinese decision-makers' perceptions in the 1950s. It did not stop Sino-Indian competition in the 1950s. Nor was it a position maintained by Chinese officials in more recent years. Other types of asymmetries persist, but the acknowledgment of an ongoing rivalry is no longer one of them.

It would be rather difficult to argue that the Sino-Indian rivalry is not about disputes regarding who owns what territory. It most definitely is

---

[3] Rivalries can become trivial when they outlive their cancellation due date. Examples are the Cuba–US and Bolivia–Peru rivalries. The former is mired in domestic American politics and the latter is simply ignored by Peru.

[4] Contrast this position with Mohan, *Samudra Manthan*, 190–193, and Srinath Raghavan, "The Security Dilemma and India-China Relations," *Asian Security* 15.1 (2019): 60–72.

[5] See Susan Shirk, "One-Sided Rivalry: China's Perceptions and Policies toward India," in Francine R. Frankel and Harry Harding (eds.), *The India-China Relationship: What the United States Needs to Know* (New York: Columbia University Press, 2004), 75–100.

spatial rivalry.[6] But there is much more going on than boundary issues. The contest between India and China is very much a positional rivalry. Yes, it is about their respective statuses, but it is not about status in a vacuum. It is status within a regional structure that matters most. They are rivals for leadership in South Asia and an emerging super Asia. To a lesser extent, that has made them rivals in global politics as well – a dimension of their rivalry that is likely to expand in the near future.

All rivalries are subject to varying constraints on escalation. Asymmetrical military and economic power can give weaker adversaries pause. Why take on states that are stronger than one's own? States armed with nuclear weapons should be able to deter each other from attacking given the high and ostensibly unacceptable costs associated with nuclear exchanges. Yet asymmetry does not often suffice to head off escalation. On the contrary, a comparison of principal symmetrical and asymmetrical rivalries over the past two hundred years finds that principal asymmetrical rivalries are no less likely to go to war than principal symmetrical rivalries.[7] Moreover, asymmetries are not carved in stone. Rivals work hard to reduce power and positional asymmetries. Sometimes they succeed. Nor is it clear that the mutual possession of nuclear weapons will deter conventional warfare that somehow ultimately leads to the use of the maximal lethal weaponry in arsenals. Such usage has happened before.

Whatever else one might say about the Sino-Indian rivalry, it is not withering away.[8] Rivalries tend to blow hot and cold. At times, they seemed to have died out, only to spring forth with renewed vigor after a period of inactivity, not unlike volcanoes. But in retrospect, we can often tell that the impression that the grievances at stake had been forgotten was incorrect. Adversarial decision-makers may have been smiling at each other while they were hard at work preparing for the next round in their feud. Rivalries do not even have to engage frequently in militarized inter-state disputes (MIDs) to qualify as ongoing rivalries, but it is clear that the

[6] T. V. Paul suggests in "Explaining Conflict and Cooperation in the China-India Rivalry," in Paul, *The China-India Rivalry*, 5, that "most [scholars] treat the territorial dispute as the key source of the [Sino-Indian] conflict." Mahesh Shankar argues that "much of the scholarship on the China-India relationship agrees that the long-standing territorial dispute between the two countries constitutes one of the underlying pillars of their overarching 'rivalry.'" See his "Territory and the China-India Competition," in Paul, *The China-India Rivalry*, 27. We do not deny that it is one of the sources or "pillars," only that it is a minor pillar, not a major one nor necessarily key to understanding the rivalry.
[7] Thompson, Sakuwa, and Suhas, *Analyzing Strategic Rivalries*, 123–126.
[8] See Paul F. Diehl, "Whither Rivalry or Withered Rivalry?," in Paul, *The China-India Rivalry*, 253–272. We do concur, however, with his argument that power asymmetries should not rule out the possibility of a rivalry or that asymmetries are likely to influence how the rivalry plays out.

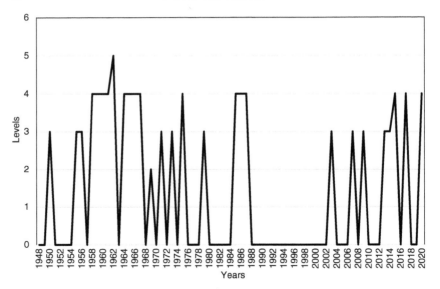

Figure 2.1   Sino-Indian MIDs, 1948–2020
Note: The MID data currently does not go beyond 2014. We have added post-2014
activity based on Will Green, "Conflict on the Sino-Indian Border: Background for
Congress." U.S.-China Economic and Security Review Commission Issue Brief, July 2,
2020. www.uscc.gov/research/conflict-sino-indian-border-background+forcongress#:
~text=Conflict%20on%20the%20Sino-indian%20Border%3A%20Background%20for+
Congress&form=ANNTH1&refig=6ccab101048e99e883ac5cad1b9e8.

Sino-Indian rivalry is still very much in play.[9] Figure 2.1 charts the ups and
downs of MIDs activity for this rivalry. The historical peak may have been
as long ago as 1962, yet the MIDs series shows consistent activity aside
from a respite period primarily in the 1990s. This rivalry is a "volcano" that
remains active at the use of force level (level 4 on the scale).

As for the rivalry's significance, we would certainly agree that rivalries
that have all but terminated, that are narrow in the scope of their issue
contention, or that involve opponents that are tightly constrained from
fighting are likely to be less significant than ones that could explode at
any time, that involve multiple points of contention, and that are not

---

[9] One of the arguments in rivalry analysis has been whether MIDs should be a primary criterion for
the existence of rivalry. The enduring rivalry school has insisted, at least early on, that MIDs should
be the best indicator of any ongoing rivalry. The strategic rivalry school has disagreed and argued
that rivalries can exist without any MIDs. What matters is not whether conflict is explicitly mani-
fested but whether decision-makers have singled out some state as a special adversary. As in the case
of India, there can be periods of relaxed tensions without a termination of the sense of rivalry.

tightly constrained. The question, however, is which end of the escalatory continuum does the Sino-Indian rivalry best approximate? We think its significance is higher than that of some others because the stakes associated with the rivalry are widening rather than narrowing. Fighting of some sort is more rather than less likely. Constraints matter but it is not clear that they will suffice in this case. The constraints themselves may actually work in the opposite direction to that in which they are thought to operate. What may seem irrational in a highly asymmetrical context can also be dangerous if it tempts the weaker side to preempt an expected attack. Moreover, the record on nuclear deterrence remains open-ended. It seemed to work in the Soviet–American case, and the Sino-Soviet rivalry did not escalate after the fighting on the Ussuri River. But a few more cases in the constrained column would make us all feel more comfortable about nuclear deterrence.

In the remainder of this chapter, we elaborate the spatial and positional natures of the Sino-Indian rivalry. We do not dismiss the reality of the territorial disputes. Yet we contend that the positional issues are more important to understanding what the rivalry is about. The question of nuclear deterrence will arise again but as a dimension of the positional rivalry.

Spatial Rivalry

The historical background to the main Sino-Indian territorial disputes would be almost humorous if it were not for people dying to defend the outcomes.[10] The two disputes – one in the west, Aksai Chin, and one in the east, North-East Frontier Agency (NEFA) – are both legacies of

---

[10] On the historical background of the Indo-Chinese territorial disputes, see R. A. Huttenback, "A Historical Note on the Sino-Indian Dispute over the Aksai Chin," *The China Quarterly* 18 (1964): 201–207; Alastair Lamb, *The McMahon Line: A Study in the Relationship between India, China, and Tibet, 1904 to 1914*, 2 vols (London: Routledge & Kegan Paul, 1966); Karunakar Gupta, "The McMahon Line 1911–1945: The British Legacy," *The China Quarterly* 47 (1971): 521–545; Alastair Lamb, *The Sino-Indian Border in Ladakh* (Columbia: University of South Carolina Press, 1973); Hsiao-ting Lin, *Tibet and Nationalist China's Frontier: Intrigues and Ethnopolitics, 1928–1949* (Vancouver: University of British Columbia Press, 2006); A. G. Noorani, *India-China Boundary Problems, 1846–1947: History and Diplomacy* (New Delhi: Oxford University Press, 2011); Nadeem Shafiq, "India versus China: A Review of the Aksai Chin Border Dispute," *Journal of Political Studies* 18.2 (2011): 207–223; Mohan Guruswamy, "A Rajah's Whims and Aksai Chin," *The Asian Age*, September 15, 2015, www.asianage.com/columnists/raja-s-whim-and-aksai-chin-189; Monika Chansoria, "India-China Unsettled Boundary and Territorial Dispute: Institutionalized Border Mechanisms since 39 Years, sans Resolution," Policy Brief, The Japan Institute of International Affairs, July 31, 2020, www.jiia-jie.jp/en/policybrief/pdf/PolcyBrief_Chansoira_2020731.pdf; and Mehul Singh Gill, "Aksai Chin: From Napoleon to Nehru," *Indian Defence Review*, January 4, 2022, www.indiandefencereview.com/spotlights/aksai-chin-from-napoleon-to-nehru/.

British colonialism that have led to similar problems elsewhere in the former British Empire. As regards the western dispute, the British defeat of the Sikh Confederacy in 1846 meant that Ladakh, an area adjacent to Kashmir, came under British control. At that time, Ladakh's eastern border was ill-defined. Traditionally, it did not seem to have mattered too much and the convention, again traditionally, was to act as if everyone understood exactly where the boundaries were. In this case, a mountain range with 22,000-foot peaks provided one clue. But a survey of Ladakh's territory in 1865, promulgated by Ladakh's maharaja, extended the boundary to include the Aksai Chin desert on the northeastern side of the mountains. It has been rumored that the surveyor was bribed, and the outcome was not appreciated by the Indian government because the extension made it more difficult to defend Ladakh from a military attack. A few years after the surveyor was fired by the Indian government, he was appointed the wazir, or governor, of Ladakh by a presumably grateful ruler. The extended boundary became known as the Johnson line, named after the surveyor.

In subsequent years, it became clear to the Indian government authorities that they would be better off if something like the Karakoram mountain range served as the boundary line. That would mean someone else would have to defend the desert on the other side of the mountains. The best candidate would be a China that could serve as a buffer between India and the Russian expansion into Central Asia and possibly beyond. A new line was drawn, the Macartney–MacDonald line, that essentially focused on the mountain range as the outer limit of Ladakh in British India. In the 1890s, the Macartney–MacDonald line was offered to China. The lack of a response from Peking was curiously viewed as an acceptance. Evidently, the Macartney–MacDonald line remained the quasiofficial boundary until 1941. Indian government intelligence then received a report that Soviet troops were showing up in Xinjiang, which was immediately north of the Aksai Chin desert. According to Guruswamy, the British Indian government's preference then reverted to the Johnson line. Nothing else during the Second World War caused them to move away from the extended boundary. Consequently, the newly independent Indian government in 1947 inherited the Johnson boundary for Ladakh. In 1954, China informed India that the Ladakh/Aksai Chin border had never been officially agreed upon and that the Macartney–MacDonald boundary was the only one ever proposed to China – implying as well that it was one that the Chinese could live with since they already had occupied Aksai Chin up to that boundary. By this point, they had used the territory that they occupied to build a road to move material from Xinjiang to Tibet. India learned of the road's existence only in 1957.

The eastern dispute's background is similar to the western one. The Manchu regime in China fell in 1911. Tibet's ruler, the Dalai Lama, made use of the opportunity to declare Tibetan independence. The new Chinese regime was not prepared to accept the idea of an independent Tibet. Britain wanted Tibet to serve as a buffer. A negotiating conference was convened in Simla, bringing together representatives from China, Tibet, and the Indian government. The British representative, who was also the Indian government's foreign secretary, proposed to copy what had recently happened in terms of Russia and China dividing Mongolia. China retained control of Inner Mongolia while Russia gained control of Outer Mongolia. The Tibetans were willing to accept a similar division since Lhasa would be located in Outer Tibet and therefore in the British sphere. Nevertheless, no decision was reached on creating an Inner/Outer Tibet.

The negotiations were protracted and moved back and forth between Tibet and India, depending on the severity of the weather in Tibet. A second point was brought up by the British representative who was seeking some clarification of the hazy boundary between Tibet and India. He proposed a line that pushed the boundary some sixty miles north of the then current boundary so that the Himalayas would become the dividing line between the two states. Acceptance of this McMahon line (named after the Indian government's foreign secretary, Henry McMahon) would entail India incorporating a number of lightly governed districts inhabited by indigenous tribes (later to be called the North-East Frontier Agency) and a more distinctive Tibetan area called the Tawang Tract. The Chinese representative signed off on this proposal, but his acceptance was repudiated by the Chinese government once they learned that it entailed a loss of territory. This meant that the McMahon line was negotiated only between the British Indian government and Tibet. Not only was Tibet's independent status to negotiate questionable, but it turned out that the British government in London had never approved the McMahon line idea. It had intended to tell McMahon that the line was not sanctioned but, upon learning that an agreement had already been reached, decided to accept it. The Chinese government did not know about the division of opinion within British ranks but stated that a British–Tibetan agreement that excluded Chinese acceptance was unacceptable.

That might have been the end of the McMahon line, but in 1935 a British explorer was imprisoned in Tibet and accused of entry into the country without permission. The explorer claimed he had entered through the Tawang Tract and had been granted entry by the chief Tibetan official presiding there. Obviously, the British had not taken over the Tawang Tract but bureaucrats in the Indian government saw this problem as an opportunity to revive the McMahon boundary and to occupy the Tawang Tract. Permission was not forthcoming from London for such an undertaking, but the Indian government's foreign secretary, Aubrey Metcalfe, acting on his own initiative, did instruct the Surveyor-General of India to show the McMahon line as the Indian–Tibetan boundary on official maps.[11] During the Second World War, the issue arose again in the context of the Chinese interest in having a road constructed through Tibet that could supply military forces in Szechuan province. The Indian government was reluctant to see this happen because it would or could eliminate Tibet's buffer utility. India insisted that a road would have to be agreed upon by Tibet, Britain, and China, thereby resurrecting the spirit of the 1913 Simla negotiations and, by inference, the McMahon line. At this point, the United States intervened and said that it would not approve treating Tibet as independent of China. The British government then communicated to the Indian government that all efforts should be made not to give any further grounds for irritating the Chinese. Continued prodding from the Indian government's foreign secretary, however, did get London's approval for a modified version of the McMahon line – one that excluded the Tawang Tract.

This story leads to the conclusion that the McMahon line and the incorporation of the NEFA territory was something of a fiction that must be attributed to the independent actions of the colonial Indian government. The McMahon line was never legitimized by Chinese acceptance. That it reappeared on Indian maps in 1938 was due to the sleight of hand of one of McMahon's bureaucratic successors and not any additional negotiation. Yet, once again, the newly independent Indian government of 1947 inherited a rather shaky title to a dubiously established boundary in the northeast of India. As it happens, the western and eastern disputes have been linked explicitly. In 1960, Zhou Enlai offered to trade Chinese acceptance of the NEFA outcome for Indian acceptance of the Aksai Chin outcome. Nehru declined to negotiate then. Deng Xiaoping also made a similar unofficial offer in 1980 that went nowhere. Giving away territory thought

---

[11] The 1971 article by Gupta, "The McMahon Line 1911–1945," provides a detailed account of the bureaucratic machinations of the 1930s' British Indian government to institutionalize the McMahon Line without approval from London.

to belong to one's own group is not something that can be contemplated casually or executed without major political costs.

To be clear, referring to one side's territorial claims as shaky does not imply that the other side's claims are on firmer ground. The Chinese claims – other than the one regarding actual military control of an area, which gives it some sort of possession claim – all rest on the status of Tibetan boundaries that are just as elusive as the Indian boundaries. In addition, of course, China's claim that Tibet is a province of China – which thereby allows China to inherit all Tibetan rights and privileges, including boundaries – is also specious. Its claim to speak for Tibet is based on military conquest and occupation after the Second World War.[12]

The historical background of these two territorial disputes is fascinating but it does not change the willingness of both sides to fight over their implications. And fight they did. Nehru ordered the Indian Army to push forward their bases in Ladakh. The Chinese warned against entering their territory and then attacked, pushing the Indian forces back in both the western and eastern sectors in 1962. After making their point quite successfully, Chinese forces moved back to the positions they had held before the war began. Schleicher offers a clear summary:

> India inherited her ill-defined northern border from the British Raj, and attempted to deal with them in the traditional British manner. The policies failed because India lacked Britain's resources and was confronted with a different kind of China.[13]

Some sixty years later, Chinese and Indian forces are still fighting in the western sector and China has escalated its once limited demands vis-à-vis the eastern sector. The fighting in the western sector went dormant for several decades and has subsequently escalated to hand-to-hand combat, so far without guns. Initially, the eastern sector claims of the Chinese appeared as something of a corollary to the western sector claims. Now, they are more independent in stridence and the claim is to the entire Indian state of Arunachal Pradesh, the successor to NEFA. Why have these disputes persisted even as they waxed and waned in intensity?

Part of this puzzle is clarified by Garver's analysis of the western sector development.[14] China began moving into Tibet in 1950. At that time, there

---

[12] Earlier attempts to conquer Tibet using military force had failed in the late eighteenth century and the early twentieth century.

[13] Charles P. Schleicher, "Review of India's China War by Neville Maxwell," *American Political Science Review* 66.2 (1972): 682.

[14] John W. Garver, *Protracted Contest: Sino-Indian Rivalry in the Twentieth Century* (Seattle: University of Washington Press, 2001), 80–91.

were four routes to move equipment and troops into Tibet. One was through India and was therefore not available. The other three were all utilized, but the superior route was through Xinjiang; the other two were afflicted by terrain obstacles, insurgency attacks, and climate problems. Building a road through Aksai Chin was not easy but proved less challenging than the other two routes. Thus, the early Chinese motivation seems clear-cut. Possession of Aksai Chin made the acquisition and control of Tibet much more feasible and probable. Time and technology, of course, have reduced the early motivation. Other ways of getting from China to Tibet have been improved and routinized. Integrating Tibet into the Chinese governance system is a different matter from mounting the initial military occupation.

But Garver also attributes the early Indian motivation to fight for Aksai Chin to Tibet. Nehru is depicted as realizing the strategic advantage of Aksai Chin for attacking/defending Tibet and, therefore, was motivated to improve the Indian position in that sector. That part of the explanation seems a bit far-fetched. While the Indian government and military did provide some assistance to the Tibetan resistance to Chinese occupation, Nehru's position seems more closely linked to the idea of never surrendering perceived Indian territory to a foreign power. If for no other reason, politicians do not tend to survive appeasing external rivals.[15] But in Nehru's case, his commitment to preserving the official boundaries of India seems quite genuine. That is one of the problems with territorial disputes. While it once might have seemed quite rational to trade one claim for another, the idea of surrendering national soil becomes akin to something like political suicide over time. The spatial boundaries of the state become interwoven with all sorts of symbolism and mythology. "Giving away" something so significant quickly becomes nonnegotiable – as shown by Nehru's early position and the position maintained by his successors.

Alternatively, Shankar argues that the early negotiations on Sino-Indian border problems can be explained as a function of the bargaining context.[16] Ironically, the more unfavorable the bargaining context from the perspective of the weaker party, the more likely it is that decision-makers will be intransigent. Compromise might draw attention to the weakness and encourage more challenges and get in the way of any attempts at deterrence. From this point of view, compromise on territorial issues requires a

---

[15] See Michael Colaresi, "When Doves Cry: International Rivalry, Unrecognized Cooperation, and Leadership Turnover," *American Journal of Political Science* 48.3 (2004): 555–570.

[16] Mahesh Shankar, *The Reputational Imperative: Nehru's India in Territorial Conflict* (Stanford: Stanford University Press, 2022).

favorable bargaining context in which concessions can be made that feed into a state's reputation for fairness and rationality.

These same processes apply, no doubt, to Chinese thinking on the Aksai Chin dispute. However, the eastern sector dispute seems more calculated in the sense that the Chinese claim has fluctuated in intensity according to its political utility. It has escalated in recent years because it is another rivalry club that can be used to remind India of its multiple vulnerabilities. A glance at a map confirms that northeast India is not well linked geographically to the rest of the country. Politically, long-standing insurgencies by local tribes have managed to defy the capabilities of the Indian counterinsurgency forces for quite some time. In this context, China seizing the area and holding (or "reclaiming") what it refers to as South Tibet would not seem to be a difficult military challenge should the occasion arise.

Both sides seem wedded to the correctness of their respective interpretations of where India's northern and China's southern border should lie. Yet for all the attention showered on these spatial contests, it is not clear that they are central to what animates the Sino-Indian rivalry. On this score, we have some company:

> Even if Beijing manages to tranquilize Tibet and resolves the boundary dispute with India, and even if New Delhi and Beijing successfully minimize the role of Pakistan in their bilateral relations, it is not clear that the Sino-Indian rivalry would ease. As a Chinese scholar put it, "Even if the territorial dispute were resolved, India and China would still retain a competitive relationship in the Asia-Pacific region, being as they are, two Asian giants aspiring [to] Great Power status." … As Nehru himself mused during the 1962 war with China, there was a larger competitive dimension to Sino-Indian relations:

> "It is a little naïve to think that the trouble with China was essentially due to a dispute over some territories. It had deeper reasons. Two of the largest countries in Asia confronted each other over a vast border. They differed in many ways. And the test was whether any one of them would have a more dominating position than the other on the border and in Asia itself."[17]

Another way of arriving at this conclusion can be via Scobell's Himalayan standoff discussion. Scobell creatively contrasts Himalayan and Mexican standoffs of film lore fame.[18] In a Mexican standoff, two or more gunfighters face each other and must quickly decide whether to draw and fire first, wait for the other fighter(s) to escalate, or retreat/run away in order

---

[17] Mohan, *Samudra Manthan*, 24.
[18] Andrew Scobell, "Himalayan Standoff: Strategic Culture and the China-India Rivalry," in Paul, *The China-India Rivalry*, 165–186.

to de-escalate. Given the uncertainties of the circumstances, the Mexican standoff tends to lead to someone escalating quickly in order to get the first shot. In the Himalayan standoff, China and India "have the luxury of being able to deliberate their next move without great urgency."[19] Of course, this kind of standoff works in this fashion only as long as both sides prefer non-escalation in the rivalry generally. If that facet of the rivalry should change on either or both sides, we are back to a Mexican standoff in the Himalayas.

We now turn to consideration of the positional dimension of rivalry in this case. If, as we contend, it is the more important dimension of the rivalry, what is it about? The problem with positional rivalries is that they have many facets, making boundary disputes an attractive focus if for nothing else than the simplicity of the competition and disagreements.

Positional Rivalry

The other main type of adversarial relationship is positional rivalry. While spatial rivalries focus on disputed territorial control, positional rivalries are about status and influence competitions. Yet it is not status and influence in the abstract. Very much in contrast to the idea of anarchic international systems, states operate in international environments centered around structured hierarchies. There is, of course, structured hierarchy in the international system as a whole. This is why we talk about superpowers, great powers, and global powers. Some states have the capability and willingness to roam the entire planet. Others are restricted to a single region. A few, selectively, can penetrate multiple regions. Yet most states operate in regional hierarchical structures that range from highly structured to very weakly structured hierarchies.

Regional hierarchies can be divided into five tiers.[20] Tier 1 encompasses significant external powers that play major roles in a region. There may be only one such state. The United States has played this role in several regions: East Asia, the Middle East and North Africa, and South America. There may also be more than one as exemplified by the on and off again role of the Soviet Union/Russia in the Middle East. But that is one of the most important features of this tier. States that qualify for tier 1 status can choose to increase their role(s) within the region or they can simply leave

---

[19] Scobell, "Himalayan Standoff," 166.

[20] The inspiration for the five tiers is Evelyn Goh, "Great Powers and Hierarchical Order in Southeast Asia: Analyzing Regional Security Strategies." *International Security* 32.3 (2008): 1113–1157. Goh has four tiers and gives them different names but the spirit is very much the same.

or be forced out of the region. Britain, for example, was once predominant in the Middle East, but as its relative power waned, so, too, did its visibility in the Middle Eastern region.

Tier 2 is occupied by the strongest state that is indigenous to the region. It is conceivable that there might be more than one "strongest" state if there are two or more states of roughly equal stature. If there is only one state that qualifies, the tier 2 state might also be a regional hegemon if its relative capabilities were considerably greater than the other states in the region. Yet a regional hegemon is unlikely as long as there are significant external powers operating in the region. In a nutshell, that is the crux of the problem in East Asia. The United States is the predominant external power; China is the leading indigenous regional power. Neither can improve its position or optimize its influence within the region without either removing or subordinating the other.

Tier 3 actors are major regional powers that have the capability to play region-wide roles but that do not compare favorably, capability-wise, to the tier 2 occupant(s). There can be considerable dynamism in movement to and from, as well as within, tiers 2 and 3. For example, Japan was once the regional hegemon of Asia until it was finally dethroned in 1945. It fell out of the hierarchy altogether when it was occupied by US forces, but it gradually worked itself back to a tier 3 position as an economic power. India also qualifies as tier 3 in a greater Asian region, even though it is the tier 2 power in South Asia. This is another Sino-Indian positional conflict. To lessen the probability of India becoming a tier 2 Asian power, China seeks to diminish or undermine its tier 2 South Asian position.

Tier 4 powers are states that can play some type of active regional role that falls short of qualifying as a major regional power. In greater Asia, South Korea and perhaps Indonesia come to mind. Whatever is left is consigned to a tier 5 of weak and failed states.

When all states know their "place" in the hierarchy and are more or less content with it, the hierarchy is both stable and efficacious. Without challengers, the hierarchy remains fairly fixed, doing what hierarchies are supposed to do. That is, they clarify the international/regional pecking order. Who should benefit the most and least is made crystal clear when a strong hierarchy exists. However, the hierarchy can be weak (the rungs of the status ladder are ambiguous and do not differentiate the relevant actors very well). It can also be contested as actors seek to move up the tier schedule and/or decline down the schedule. In the Middle East, Iran and Saudi Arabia aspire to tier 2 status. In greater Asia, India and China oppose each other in part because they have different conceptions of where

Table 2.1 *Spectrum of security alignment*

Weak	Moderate	Strong
Support for security policies and/or criticism of rivals; mixed arms acquisition	Joint training exercises; military assistance/some arms sales dependence	Formal military alliance; monopoly on arms purchases

Source: Modified from Darwen J. Lim and Zack Cooper, "Reassessing Hedging: The Logic of Alignment in East Asia," *Security Studies* 24.4 (2015): 696–727.

India fits in the hierarchy. China has long sought to convince India that it is a tier 4 or 5 actor. Whether Chinese decision-makers really believe that is entirely another matter. Indian decision-makers see their state as definitely tier 3, with some potential for moving up to tier 2. In general, though, as long as there is what Goh calls jostling among the tiers, instability in the hierarchy and region is more probable. And, of course, in Asia, we have plenty of jostling at the upper end of the scale, with China seeking to push the United States out of the region and, simultaneously, subordinate India and Japan, among others.

The second source of instability according to Goh is a tier 1 state seeking to withdraw from the region or suffering significant capability deterioration. The former is not in evidence but, arguably, the latter is in play. It is not so much that US power projection capabilities have decayed absolutely, but in the Asian region, its relative power position is declining and likely to decline further as local states expand their naval and space capabilities while US capabilities are not expanding in response.

Jostling states expand their capabilities and work on access to resources and support from other states in the region. Alignments normally revolve around tier 1 and 2 states and can range across the spectrum suggested in Table 2.1. In Asia, Australia, South Korea, and Japan are strongly aligned with the United States. The Philippines oscillates back and forth between a moderate and strong US alignment. India could be said to have moved tentatively into the moderate column vis-à-vis the United States. China has an apparent moderate link with Russia and a strong link to Pakistan. Many of the rest of the states in the region prefer avoiding strong alignments and may actually prefer the countervailing continuation of a combination of a Chinese economic powerhouse and American superior firepower.

While alignment issues tend to focus on contests between tier 1 and tier 2 states, the questions relating to taking sides percolate down the scale to contests between tier 3 and tier 2 states, but there is some interdependence with tier 1–2 competitions. For instance, states that side with the United States in the Asian region are likely to side with India in its competition with China over economic and political-military access/support.[21] Presumably, the converse is true as well, although path dependencies can interfere. Older Russian links to India, for instance, complicate its latest movement toward following the Chinese lead.

South Asian Positioning

One of the potential liabilities of focusing on rivalries is that we overlook bigger pictures. Obviously, rivalries do not exist in vacuums. The adversaries interact with other states and sometimes create more complicated rivalry structures in the process. One example is the India–Pakistan–China (IPC) triangle, which actually is pentagonal in shape because it often has involved the Soviet Union/Russia and the United States as well. Paul J. Smith has a useful take on this matter, which is almost constructed in rivalry terms.[22] With a few tweaks, we can put his interpretation of the IPC triangle to good use here.

Smith's basic point is that the "structure of 1947" has become subordinated to the "structure of 1962," as Pakistan's political-military significance has declined over time. The "structure of 1947" emerged as an Indo-Pakistani contest over who controls Kashmir. The "structure of 1962" followed the Sino-Indian war of the same year as a larger contest over boundaries and Tibet. Replace the term "structure" with "rivalry" or merely add the adjective "rivalry" to "structure" and we are on a similar page.

The United States seemed to favor India immediately after the Second World War but Cold War calculations swung US favoritism toward Pakistan as a state that was more likely to play a frontline role in anti-Soviet containment strategies. Consequently, the United States enhanced Pakistan's military capability until that military capability was used against India in the 1965 war. As the United States backed away from providing more support to Pakistan, Pakistan turned to China as an alternative supplier. But the Sino-American rapprochement in the early 1970s involved Pakistan and helped to reconnect Pakistan to US strategies in Central and South Asia. In the 1971 Indo-Pakistani war, the United States favored

---

[21] On this question, see Sinderpal Singh, "India-China Maritime Competition: Southeast Asia and the Dilemma of Regional States," in Rajesh Basrur, Anit Mukherjee, and T. V. Paul (eds.), *India-China Maritime Competition: The Security Dilemma at Sea* (London: Routledge, 2019), 137–160.

[22] Paul J. Smith, "The Tilting Triangle: Geopolitics of the China-India-Pakistan Relationship." *Comparative Strategy* 32.4 (2012): 313–330.

Pakistan over India, prompting the Soviet Union to promise its support to India if either China or the United States intervened in the war. By this point, the Soviet Union had already become an important source of aid to India, which had started when the United States began arming Pakistan.

In the late 1970s and early 1980s, the United States resumed providing military support to Pakistan after the Soviet Union entered Afghanistan to prop up a pro-Soviet regime. China did the same and took it one step farther by providing support to Pakistan for developing nuclear weapons. Once the Soviets left Afghanistan, the United States applied sanctions on Pakistan for its nuclear diffusion efforts, which made the Chinese connection all the more valuable to Pakistan. The late 1980s and early 1990s were characterized by a considerable reduction in Sino-Indian tensions. None of this show of friendly relations, however, slowed the nuclear developments in Pakistan and India. By the late 1990s, India was acknowledging that China was its primary enemy and that its nuclear program was designed to counter China, not Pakistan.

After 9/11 in 2001, the United States needed Pakistan once again, waiving the sanctions that had increased after the 1999 military coup. The US–Pakistan relationship was very awkward in the sense that the United States had reason to know that Pakistani intelligence had very close connections to al-Qaeda and the Taliban and that Pakistan was reluctant to get involved as a US ally. Among US decision-makers, some, no doubt, would have preferred a different ally as well but felt that there was little choice given the Afghan circumstances, while others preferred to ignore warnings about Pakistani involvement in Afghanistan.[23]

The rapid ascent of China in the twenty-first century and its increased presence in Southeast, South, and Central Asia, as well as in the Indian Ocean, have alarmed Indian decision-makers, making them somewhat more open to US ties without completely eliminating an engrained ambivalence or even mistrust based on past US policies in South Asia. Fortuitously, the US relationship with Pakistan has weakened considerably now that the United States has finally withdrawn from Afghanistan.

We are left with a crowded field of triangular rivalry relationships or structures in South Asia. The Indians cannot contemplate likely Pakistani moves without taking into consideration potential assistance from the Chinese, and vice versa. That is, Pakistan could choose to make problems should relations between India and China become very conflictual.

[23] See, for instance, Carlotta Gall, *The Wrong Enemy: America in Afghanistan, 2001–2014* (New York: Houghton Mifflin, 2014).

India could once count on Soviet assistance but now Russia and China act as if they are close to becoming full-fledged allies. Collaborating with the United States has some attractions but clear dangers as well, and also involves closer links to Australia and Japan. The only thing that is clear is that neither India nor China can view the likely strategies and maneuvers of its Asian adversary without also taking into consideration the possible moves of other pertinent actors in and near the South Asian region. The enormous complexity of the web of relevant actors accentuates the uncertainty associated with any international political activity.

Yet one of the ironies of the regional situation is that for decades the main South Asian challenger of Indian regional hegemony was Pakistan. Without Chinese support and a number of nuclear weapons, the Pakistani challenge would be even more muted than it has become. But its place has been taken by China through increased activity throughout South Asia, including several island states in the Indian Ocean. The Himalayas are zones of conflict once again. Belt and Road activity is extensive in the north and especially in Pakistan. Chinese naval and diplomatic visits have increased to the east and south of India. So, too, have Chinese investments in ports along the Indian Ocean littoral in Cambodia, Myanmar, Sri Lanka, Pakistan, and the Maldives. States such as Nepal and Bangladesh can exploit Chinese interest to undermine India's natural predominance in the region. For India, a feeling of being encircled by one's primary rival is rather difficult to avoid in what has been described as a competition for the "affection" of the region.[24] Add all this to the multidyadic complexities of South Asian rivalries and it leaves the construction of Indian foreign policy in an awkward place.

Nonetheless, the basic nature of the contest is straightforward. Garver considers this as one of the central taproots of the Sino-Indian rivalry.

> To guarantee its national security, [India] wants to keep China…out of the South Asian-Indian Ocean region or at least limit its presence there. Doing this, however, necessarily poses challenges to the security of the PRC. A South Asia organized and led by India would pose a far greater potential threat to China than a fragmented South Asia.[25]

---

[24] See, for example, Saneet Chakradeo, "How Does the India-China Rivalry Affect Secondary State Behaviour in South Asia?," *Brookings Institution Blog*, April 28, 2020, www.brookings.edu/blog/up-front/2020/04/28/sambandh-blog-how-does-the-india-china-rivalry-affect-secondary-state-behaviour-in-south-asia/; and Rajeswari Pillai Rajagopalan, "Sino-Indian Competition in South Asia: Another Round," *The Diplomat*, December 3, 2021, https://thediplomat.com/2021/12/sino-indian-competition-in-south-asia-another-round/.

[25] Garver, *Protracted Conflict*, 16.

Garver portrays this as a security dilemma. What one country does to preserve its security inadvertently lessens the security of another country. But that is the case only if the two states are interested in just preserving their security. India assumes that it deserves to be the leader of South Asia because it is much more powerful than the other states in the region and because it not only preserves its security but also enhances what it can achieve in foreign policy. China seeks to undermine Indian leadership in the region because a weaker India and a more fragmented South Asia serves its own foreign policy agenda. This contest is clearly a positional one. Either India is predominant in South Asia or it is not. India strongly prefers the former while China pursues the latter. Both sides cannot win; one (or both) side(s) of the rivalry has(have) to lose unless they find some way to compromise.[26]

Former Indian Foreign Secretary, Shyam Saran, has it right:

> There is little doubt in my mind that the most significant challenge to India comes from the rise of China. There is also no doubt in my mind that China will seek to narrow India's strategic space by penetrating India's own neighbourhood and this is what we see happening in each of our sub-continental neighbours. Unless India is able to confront this penetration and restore its primacy to its own periphery, it would be unable to play the larger game of countervailing Chinese power.[27]

Tibet

Independent India inherited from Britain the notion that Tibet served as a good buffer for keeping hostile armies away from the northern Indian border. For the British, the threat came from Russia. They preferred an independent Tibet and therefore discouraged Chinese efforts to subordinate Tibet. After 1947, India began with the notion that an independent Tibet was optimal but had to adjust their thinking when the Chinese occupied Tibet in the 1950s. Too weak to fight China, India acquiesced to Chinese control but urged that Tibet retain its autonomy as much as possible. China initially allowed for some autonomy but Tibetan

---

[26] In this respect, the Sino-Indian rivalry mirrors the Sino-American rivalry in East Asia. In both cases, the two adversaries cannot occupy the same leadership position at the same time. Something ultimately has to give, or the conflict will persist.

[27] Shyam Saran, "Is a China-Centric World Inevitable," India International Centre, July 20, 2017. Quoted in Bruce Vaughn (ed.), "China-India Great Power Competition in the Pacific Ocean Region: Issues for Congress," Congressional Research Service Report, April 20, 2018. https://sgp.fas.org/crs/row/R45194.pdf.

guerrilla warfare quickly led to severe repression and a quashing of the limited autonomy that had prevailed. Chinese decision-makers also came to believe that India was supporting the rebellion in Tibet in order to reestablish an independent buffer. One view of the 1962 war was that it was designed to punish the Indians for their efforts to eliminate Chinese control over Tibet. We think that interpretation is too narrow and will elaborate further in a subsequent chapter (see Chapter 4). But, while official Indian support for Tibetan liberation activities was limited prior to 1962, it only increased after the war. Tibetan exiles in India were given more support for their resistance projects. The Indian Army even created a special commando force that would specialize in Tibetan liberation operations should war with China resume.

The Tibetan grievance has persisted since the 1950s. China demands India muzzle the Tibetan exile community in India. India has done so to some extent but not to the maximum amount possible. As Garver puts it, both rivals have a card that they can threaten to play when appropriate. China has a Pakistan card in its capability to intervene in an Indo-Pakistani clash. India has a Tibetan card in its capability to invade Tibet and/or restimulate armed resistance to Chinese control. Whether these cards are real or simply imagined remains to be seen.

Water Wars

In the context of Tibet, there is some discussion of potential "water wars" between India and China.[28] The facts that pertain to water availability are clear.[29] Most of the major rivers in South and Southeast Asia have their origins in Tibet and melting water from glaciers in what is sometimes

[28] See, for instance, Brahma Chellaney, *Water: Asia's New Battleground* (Washington, DC: Georgetown University Press, 2011), who describes past battles being fought over land, present battles focusing on energy, and future battles centering on water and S. G. Padmanabhan, a retired army general, who is the author of *Next China-India War – World's First Water War – 2029* (New Delhi: Manas Publications, 2014).
[29] See Kenneth Pomeranz, "The Great Himalayan Watershed: Water Shortages, Mega-Projects and Environmental Politics in China, India, and Southeast Asia," *The Asia-Pacific Journal* 7.30 (2009): 2; Hungzhou Zhang, "Sino-Indian Water Disputes: The Coming Water Wars?," *WIREs Water* 3.3 (2016): 155–166, DOI: https://doi.org/10.1002/wat2.1123; Tao Shengli, Henry Zhang, Yuhao Feng et al., "Changes in China's Water Resource in the Early 21st Century," *Frontiers in Ecology and the Environment* 18.4 (2020): 188–193; Ameya Pratap Singh and Uri Tembey, "India-China Relations and the Geopolitics of Water," *The Interpreter*, July 23, 2020, www.lowinstitute.org/the-interpreter/india-china-relations-and-geopolitics-water; and Rajendra M. Abhyankar, "Assuring India's Water Security," in P. R. Kumaraswamy (ed.), *Facets of India's Security: Essays for C. Uday Bhaskar* (London: Routledge, 2022), 233–248.

called the Third Pole in view of the high concentration of glaciers in
Tibet. This means China controls the sources of most of the rivers in Asia.
The five that involve India are the Indus, Brahmaputra, Sutlej, Kosi, and
Ghaghara. Close to half of the water that flows out of the Tibetan glaciers
ends up in or flows through India.[30]

India and China already face water scarcity, which will only grow
worse in the future. Both have relied heavily on underground aquifers
that are disappearing. Both have extensive agricultural activities that
are heavily reliant on water and irrigation. Both India and China have
projects underway to move water from places where it is most abundant
to places where it is most scarce. But the Chinese projects have made
more progress and are of larger scale, moving water from the south to the
north and energy generated in the west to the east. Some of this diversion
involve rivers that serve China's southern neighbors. When China builds
dams, especially near its southern boundaries, fears escalate that the dams
will be used to monopolize river water for Chinese purposes. While the
potential for that happening is certainly real, the Chinese official response
usually is that neither its diversion projects nor its damming operations
are intended to alter the volume of river flow to the south, aside from
flood control efforts.

By and large, that seems to be the case to date. The question is whether
it will continue to be the case in the future. Water conflicts have not been
desecuritized elsewhere. Should we expect them to remain depoliticized in
the Sino-Indian rivalry context? The most likely answer is probably not.[31]
Yet it is surprising that this has not become a source of public contestation
between the two governments. There are various reasons why that might
be the case but the simplest one is that there is not much that the Indian
government can do to deter Chinese water diversion projects. As long as
no diversion is detected, perhaps it is best to remain officially silent, almost
as if voicing public concern might increase the probability of diversion

---

[30] As noted by Zhang, none of these rivers are exclusively Chinese and Indian rivers. The Indus and
Sutlej Rivers involve Pakistan, the Brahmaputra flows through or to Bhutan and Bangladesh,
and the Kosi and Ghaghara Rivers provide water to Nepal. See Zhang, "Sino-Indian Water
Disputes."

[31] An alternative answer is voiced in Selina Ho, Qian Neng, and Yan Yifei, "The Role of Ideas in the
China-India Water Dispute," *The Chinese Journal of International Politics* 12.2 (2019): 263–294. Ho,
Neng, and Yifei find in a survey analysis of selected experts on Chinese/South Asian water politics
that respondents were characterized by a desire to increase interstate collaboration. The problem
is that academic experts might not have the same mindset as governmental officials. In addition,
things might change in the future when water scarcity becomes even more acute than it already is
and/or if conflict between India and China becomes more intense.

schemes in the north.[32] At the same time, it also means that there are no negotiations ongoing about water sharing.[33]

Indo-Pacific Regional Positioning

South Asia and Tibet are not the only targets for gaining or defending influence.[34] Both India and China are heavily dependent on energy imports. Eighty to eighty-five percent of their energy is obtained through trade, and much of that trade happens via maritime routes in the Indian Ocean, which is bracketed by two choke points. In the west, about a third of all seaborne oil passes through the Strait of Hormuz. In the east, the Strait of Malacca must be transited to move commodities from the Indian Ocean to the South China Sea. One of the implications of these geographical bracketing is that China and India need friends from Indonesia and Malaysia in the east to East Africa in the west. They need dependable supplies of oil, gas, and food and predictable markets for their own exports. They need military bases and ports that can resupply and repair ships. Waterfront states on the Indian Ocean, therefore, are prime targets for Sino-Indian competition. Chinese and Indian embassies in the Indo-Pacific region (IOR) are in the process of being established or expanded.[35] Bases are being built in places such as Djibouti and the Andaman–Nicobar Islands. Ports are being expanded in places such as Pakistan, Sri Lanka, and Myanmar. Anti-piracy programs are underway at both ends of the Indian Ocean.

Ambitious projects range from the Chinese Belt and Road Initiative that seeks to generate a Sino-centric integration of Eurasia to Indian programs to develop its own version of specialized trade corridors to Iran, the United Arab Emirates, and Southeast Asia. These efforts are very concrete manifestations of influence-seeking, with the prime idea being to reduce strategic vulnerabilities – not by substituting the commodities needed but by smoothing the passage of the commodities already traded.[36] As in

---

[32] There were complaints in 2017 that hydrological data on the Brahmaputra River in the east was withheld after a Sino-Indian military clash in the western sector.

[33] Selina Ho argues that "countries with a history of managing the asymmetries in their relationships tend to have relatively stable relations," and Sino-Indian river basin interactions reflect this axiom. See her "Power Asymmetry and the China-India Water Dispute," in Paul, *The China-India Rivalry*. We wonder in this case, though, whether it is a generalization that has not yet been fully tested.

[34] South Asia and Tibet are hardly located outside of the IOR but we choose to treat these issue areas separately even if they do overlap geographically.

[35] India has opened twelve embassies in Africa while China has opened six in small Indian Ocean states.

[36] However, new, more reliable sources may be substituted for sources that have become dubious.

the case of other topics, access to resources such as petroleum or ports is difficult to share. Consequently, competitors tend to carve out separate arrangements to protect their continued access.

Naturally, far-flung markets and resource sources and the routes to and from them require military protection. In the IOR that means naval, air, and space forces that provide power projection over impressive distances. Are Chinese and Indian capabilities prepared to protect and contest sea lanes in the Indian Ocean? The answer is probably not at present. Both China and India have been slow to develop naval capabilities, in part because they both have been more attuned to building up military forces on land. China's initial development of sea power has been focused on coastal defenses and what it might take to reassert control over Taiwan. It also has the additional problem of challenging the United States, which had possessed the largest navy in the world until recently.[37] Yet challenging the United States in the South or East China Seas is one thing. Challenging the United States in the Pacific or perhaps the Atlantic is an entirely different matter. China may have improved its amphibious landing and submarine capabilities that are essential for a fight over Taiwan, but a genuine blue water navy is still a work in progress. Yet it appears to be a successful work in progress. By 2040, China is thought to be planning to add six ballistic missile submarines, ten nuclear attack submarines, four aircraft carriers, thirty-nine cruisers and destroyers, and thirty-eight frigates and corvettes to its already large fleet.[38] This rapid buildup could facilitate the development of a competitive naval position in the Indian Ocean if that ocean is given equal priority to the forces committed to China's first and second island chain priorities.[39]

---

[37] The issue here is whether one merely counts the number of ships that a navy claims are seaworthy. According to ship counts, the Chinese navy now surpasses the size of the US navy. But the problem with ship counts is that the procedure does not discriminate between an aircraft carrier and a frigate or submarine. Every ship gets the same count despite its firepower. To date, the Chinese navy favors small ships useful for coastal defense, some rudimentary and light carriers, and diesel submarines. The American navy favors heavy aircraft carriers and nuclear-driven submarines. If one weighted the ship count by tonnage or firepower, the American navy would look much more formidable than the Chinese navy, no matter how many small ships it possesses.

[38] It cannot be claimed that external observers know exactly how big the future Chinese navy is likely to become since there is no open discussion of approved plans. The numbers provided here are guesstimates generated by Ronald O'Rourke, "China Naval Modernization: Implications for US Navy Capabilities – Background and Issues for Congress," updated December 2, 2021, Congressional Research Service Report, https://sgp.fas.org/crs/row/RL33153.pdf. China is estimated to have about 460 ships by 2030.

[39] The first island chain refers to the first cluster of islands off the East Asian continent, which stretches from Sakhalin Island to Indonesia and encompasses Japan, Taiwan, and the South and East China Seas. The second island chain extends the line to be defended or controlled into the South Pacific

In contrast, India possesses a navy that is about a third the size of the current Chinese navy. By 2050, it proposes to expand its fleet by approximately 50 percent. Should this come to pass, and Chinese building plans proceed as anticipated, the Indian navy will still be about two-fifth's the size of the Chinese navy. It plans to build another aircraft carrier, twelve submarines of various types, and four frigates.[40] One Indian advantage is that it does not need to patrol the Pacific or the Atlantic; its naval capabilities can be concentrated in the Indian Ocean. Even so, the point is that it is clear that India is not attempting to catch up to the Chinese naval inventory. Rather, it hopes to expand its naval capability sufficiently to make a respectable contribution to the naval forces already on site due to US commitments and to the naval capabilities being expanded by Australia, Japan, and other states in the US orbit.

The commitment to aircraft carriers could turn out to be erroneous if they are proven to be sitting ducks for missile attacks and disappear very early in any sea battles.[41] But, so far, no one has developed an adequate substitute for floating bases with substantial air power capabilities – something considered vital to patrolling the vast Indian Ocean. Until someone does come up with an effective alternative, carriers cannot be dismissed as frivolous status symbols.

Nuclear Positioning

Narang has described the Sino-Indian nuclear deterrence situation as enviable.[42] What he implies is that both China and India have decided to maintain relatively small nuclear arsenals and both will achieve second strike capabilities. This means that nuclear deterrence is not likely to become a prominent issue. Conventional warfare cannot be ruled out but escalation to nuclear exchanges should be considered unlikely. The conclusion is understandable from a rational perspective. Why risk the high probability of nuclear devastation by introducing nuclear weapons

from Japan to New Guinea. For speculation on what a Chinese Indian Ocean fleet might look like, see Christopher Colley, "A Future Chinese Indian Ocean Fleet?," *War on the Rocks*, April 2, 2021, https://warontherocks.com/2021/04/q-future-chinese-indian-ocean-fleet/. At the same time, it cannot be assumed that China will be in a position to give equal priority to the Indian Ocean as it does to its home defense given apparent interests in the Arctic and the Atlantic.

[40] See Maj. Gen. C. P. Singh (retd.), "Indian Navy: The Guardians of the Indian Ocean," *Indian Defence Review*, January 6, 2022, www.indiandefencereview.com/spotlights/india-navy-the-guardians-of-the-indian-ocean/.

[41] To some degree, this is what happened to battle ships in the Second World War.

[42] See Vipin Narang, "Nuclear Deterrence in the China-India Dyad," in Paul, *The China-India Rivalry*.

in a future military clash, especially when Chinese and Indian armies are reluctant to escalate beyond fists and clubs in their border clashes?

But there are problems with this interpretation. One technical problem is that both sides have had persistent issues in developing the ability to maintain ballistic missiles on submarines, which could conceivably offer the optimal counterstrike capability. India has the additional problem of not wanting to rely on strategic bombers that would be too easy to detect and would require refueling to reach Chinese urban targets. There is also the question of how many expensive nuclear submarines are needed to fully exploit this approach to ensuring the survival of a counterstrike force.

The more general problem, however, is that nuclear forces in Asia function in what can be described as a daisy-chain process. The Soviet Union developed its nuclear forces in response to American planning and vice versa. China focused on the United States and the Soviet Union. India initially focused on Pakistan but switched its primary thrust to countering China. Pakistan has consistently focused on India. The structure of these orientations mean that stronger states worry less about weaker enemies because their efforts to cope with their own stronger enemies should cover the threats emanating from weaker rivals. Yet the weaker rivals must worry about keeping up with what the stronger states are doing to keep up with their own stronger enemies.

For instance, as noted, both India and China have appeared to be satisfied with relatively small numbers of nuclear warheads. In 2021, it was discovered that China appeared to be doubling its warhead arsenal and either redistributing the warheads among a number of missile sites or contemplating some type of mobile movement of warheads to confuse enemy planners. Presumably, this dramatic change on the part of the Chinese was not designed to cope with an Indian nuclear threat. Yet Indian planners must now take these changes into consideration. Does that mean India must also increase its warhead inventory? Does it mean it must find some way to accelerate and perhaps expand its ballistic submarine development? At this point in time, it is not clear what the Indian response might be. The bottom line, nonetheless, is that the potential for considerable instability lurks in the daisy chain of Asian strategic orientations. What might seem enviable in one year can quickly become something else in a subsequent year.

Space Positioning

Space, the proverbial last frontier, resembles in many respects the naval plans of India and China. Table 2.2 lists a number of highlights in their

Table 2.2 *A comparison of Sino-Indian space accomplishments*

	China	India
First orbital launch	1970	1980
Highest payload capacity	25,000 kg (2016)	10,000 kg (2017)
First flight of space shuttle program begun	2007	2016
Satellites in orbit, 2020	352	64
First successful human spaceflight	2003	planned 2023
First space laboratory	2016	proposed 2030
First lunar landing	2013	planned 2022
First space habitation module launch	2011	proposed 2030

Source: Based on data reported in Wikipedia, Comparison of Asian National Programs. www.bing.com/search?q+Wikipedia%2C+Comparison+of+Asian+National+Program& cvid=17a03216398a43f3bde0459071791c42&aqs+edge.69i57.2590,0,1&pglt=931.

respective space programs. The interest in developing space capabilities began early and preceded the dramatic improvements in economic development by several decades. Some of this interest is certainly military oriented, just as some of it is commercially oriented. Being able to utilize space to facilitate communication, monitor movements on Earth, and deny others the same privileges are important attributes of modern military forces. Pretty much the same can be said about economic development's relations to space capabilities. But the competition of India and China in space can hardly be called a race. China has a definitive head start and more resources to commit to its space program than India does. India may never close the gap but then it does not appear to be trying to catch up to China. It is simply trying very hard to be competitive with China and a crowded field of many other states involved with space programs that range from launching satellites to establishing bases on the Moon and Mars.

Economic Positioning

Navies, space launches, and interstate competition cost money. It has hardly gone unnoticed that the economic foundations of India and China are not the same. China has a much larger gross domestic product (GDP) than India does (Figure 2.2), and the gap is widening. There was a time when their economic sizes were similar. In 1987, their GDP figures were close to identical, with India very slightly in the lead. Since then, China has become the manufacturing center for the world. Massive amounts

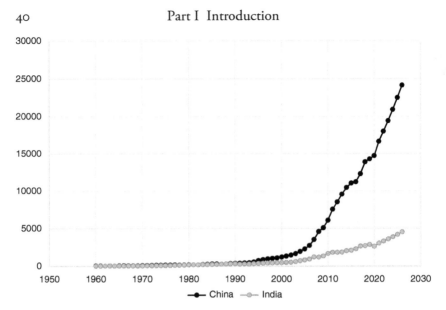

Figure 2.2   China and India GDP, 1960–2026
Source: Data taken from Statistics Times, "Comparing China and India by
Economy," May 16, 2021. The 1960–2020 data represents World Bank nominal
GDP estimates. The 2021–2026 data reflects International Monetary Fund estimates.
https://statistictimes.com/economy/china-vs-india-economy.php.

of multinational investment poured into the country, enabling China to
mobilize a good proportion of its then rural population into the industrial work force. In the process, China roughly doubled the size of its
nonagrarian work force. It is now in a position to move away from being
a middle-income economy by having developed the capability to inno-
vate new industries and, quite possibly, become the world's center for
technological innovation. Should this economic development attain the
targeted growth, China would be a genuine competitor for the global
system leader position.

India's economy, on the other hand, has also grown by opening up its
economy after 1991, albeit more reluctantly than in the China case and
nearly a decade and a half after China had initiated its own economic
reforms in 1979. The question is, how does a state with an economy
approximately one-fifth the size of its adversary expect to match its rival's
expenditures on strategic capabilities of power projection?

One Indian answer is found in a paper produced at the Pune
International Centre think tank. Authored by a former Indian ambassador

to China, Gautam Bambawale, the paper recognizes the economic asymmetry at the heart of the rivalry.[43] The paper counsels a short- and long-term approach to the competition. In the short term, India is too weak to take on China by itself. An allied coalition of states with overlapping grievances is the only recourse. In the long term, though, the paper argues that India can at least vastly improve its competitive economic position. It may not catch up to China by 2050 but it can alter the current 5 or 6 to 1 ratio in economic wealth to something like 2 to 1 or better.

However, what it must do to pull off this accelerated growth trajectory is formidable and frankly somewhat contradictory. Since the paper is written mainly by economists, the reform agenda for India begins with reducing the size of the Indian state and its micromanagement of business through excessive regulation.[44] Nor is the emphasis on the restoration of the rule of law surprising given the disciplinary background of the authors. They also add trade promotion, improvement of university quality, increased receptiveness to multinational corporations (MNCs) and the foreign direct investment (FDI) they bring with them, the protection of civil liberties, and the conversion of the military to a more technologically oriented organization. As a latecomer, India should have an advantage of avoiding errors made elsewhere. It should also be able to exploit China's declining number of workers and double India's labor force size. Moreover, India is a liberal democracy and therefore has an advantage over China in fostering innovation.

Should all these Indian reforms be accomplished, Indian growth rates could exceed China's growth rates considerably. If that could be sustained for several decades, India could converge toward China's GDP size, if not catch up completely. Yet India's economic growth rate would have to be double China's growth rate for many years for India to come closer to catching up with its rival. That kind of outcome is not wishful thinking if all or most of the reforms that are advocated are actually implemented. But it seems unlikely that all of the reforms could be executed successfully given the many path dependencies and bureaucratic and political resistance that would need to be overcome. The reforms are not impossible but

---

[43] See Gautam Bambawale, Vijay Kelkar, Raghurath Mashelkar et al., "Strategic Patience and Flexible Policies: How India Can Rise to the China Challenge," Pune International Centre, March 16, 2021, https://xkdr.org/paper/bambawaleeteal2021_strategicPatienceandFlexiblepolicies.pdf.

[44] A long-held axiom of most economists is that economic growth is a natural phenomenon. That is, if unfettered, economies tend to grow of their own volition. A principal culprit for "fettering" economies is governmental intervention. Therefore, to encourage growth one should remove the source of interference.

certainly improbable as a package. Nothing is said about how to reduce the large size of agrarian employment and turn it into industrial and service employment. Nor about how to construct a technological juggernaut to compete with China's, other than that liberal democracies provide a better environment for encouraging innovation than authoritarian regimes can. Should Indian reforms prove to be more limited, it would suggest that the short-term strategy of coalescing with other states is not something that can be abandoned in the long term. Allies will still be needed to cope with a stronger adversary. It might also be the case that a smaller bureaucracy could not be expected to protect or expand civil liberties, liberal democracy, international trade, universities, military technology, and MNC/FDI receptiveness in India.

There is no consensus on exactly where the Indian economy might end up in thirty to forty years. A Japan Center for Economic Research forecast has the United States, China, and India at 35, 32, and 25 trillion dollars, respectively, in 2060.[45] Along the way, the forecast indicated, China would pass the US economy around 2030 and the US economy would make a comeback to the first place in the 2050s. But that outcome depends on Sino-American conflict de-escalating, as opposed to persisting. Should the conflict persist, decoupling and protectionism are anticipated, with China passing the United States in the late 2020s and staying ahead until at least 2060. The Indian economy's fate in this case is not mentioned. Presumably, all states will experience less growth in such a world.

A Price Waterhouse Coopers forecast has India in the second place behind China but well ahead of the United States in 2050.[46] The Economist Intelligence Unit's 2050 forecast predicts China will be far ahead (105 trillion) of the United States (71 trillion), with Japan lagging behind the United States at 64 trillion.[47] On the one hand, all three of these forecasts suggest that India's GDP size vis-à-vis China will improve. The Japanese forecast suggests an Indian economy that is 78 percent the size of the Chinese economy – a forecast that is very close to the Price Waterhouse

---

[45] Sumio Suruyama and Kengo Tahara, "2060 Digital and Global Economy," Japan Center For Economic Research, January 2020, www.jcer.or.jp/jcer_download_log_php?f=eyJw63NOX21kjlo10D150Cw .ZmlsZu9wb3NoX21KjoioDMX0X0=&post.id=58298&file_post.id=58319.

[46] Price Waterhouse Coopers, "The Long View: How Will the Global Economic Order Change by 2050?' February 2017, www.pwc.com/gx/en/world-2050/assets/pwc-the-world-in-2050-full-report-feb-2017.pdf. This forecast has the 2050 GDP of China at 58.5 trillion, India at 44 trillion, and the United States at 34 trillion.

[47] The Economist Intelligence Unit, "Long-Term Macroeconomic Forecasts: Key Trends to 2050," London, 2015, https://espas.secure.europa.eu/orbis/sites/default/files/generated/document/ en/Long-termMacroeconomicForecasts_KeyTrends.pdf.

Coopers prediction of 75 percent. The older *Economist* forecast suggests an Indian catch-up to 60 percent of China's economic size. All three, therefore, forecast considerable improvement for India but something less than an overturning of the current economic asymmetry.

Economic forecasts that far ahead depend on strong assumptions. As the Japanese alternative forecasts illustrate, a lot could happen in the next forty years. Moreover, these forecasts focus on economic size, which is not the best indicator of future pecking orders. India's economic size will increase for sure. Population growth almost guarantees that. Its different demographic circumstances from the Chinese situation – India with an expanding youthful cohort and China with a graying population – almost guarantees as well that Indian GDP numbers will improve vis-à-vis China's numbers. Yet none of this tells us much about what kind of economic growth India is likely to experience. Will both China and India escape the middle-income trap and move their economies into technological innovation leadership? If only China does, the economic asymmetry will be all the more definitive. If China's economy moves far ahead of the US economy in both size and quality, even the short-term strategy of coalescing with kindred states to thwart Chinese bullying may not prevail.

How this works out, of course, remains to be seen. What seems most likely is that India's economy will not soon surpass China's in any significant fashion. India will continue to lag behind China and that restraint can only act as a drag on its ability to compete with China. But should Indian economic growth proceed at relatively high rates, it is more probable that Indian decision-makers will find the funds to subsidize their ambitious plans at sea, in space, and on land. Slow economic growth, in contrast, would suggest a probable dialing back on the ambitious plans and strategies. Covid has hit the Indian economy hard, but the post-Covid prospects appear to most likely approximate faster than slower growth in the near term.[48]

Economic asymmetry, consequently, seems unlikely to hold back India's participation in a rivalry with China. It will slow India's ability to play catch-up but seems unlikely to dent its enthusiasm for the geopolitical project, other factors being equal.

---

[48] See, for instance, Rumki Majundar, "India: Into the Light, but with Overcast Skies," *Deloitte Insights*, January 7, 2022, ww2.deloitte.com/us/en/insights/economy/asia-pacific/india-economic-outlook.html; India Brand Equity Foundation, "About India Economy Growth Rate & Statistics," October, 2021, www.ibef.org/economy/indian-economy-overview; Centre for Economics and Business Research, "World Economic League Table 2021," London, December 2020, https://cebr.com/wp-content/uploads/2020/12/welt-2021-final-23.12.pdf.

An Interim Conclusion

We are too early in the book to write any conclusions. As an interim conclusion, however, we can say that we do not view the Sino-Indian rivalry as a limited rivalry.[49] Perhaps it was once limited or managed, and we can argue about what limited it. But it is more than just spatial rivalry, characterized by a Himalayan standoff and power asymmetries. It is its positional nature that will make it difficult to limit or manage it in the future. The positionality facet is not new. It has been there all along, but India either chose not to push it too hard in the early years of the rivalry or backed off in more recent years as the rapid ascendance of China stunned most onlookers. China's position has not deteriorated but India's capabilities are now improving. An upswing in economic growth and naval–space capabilities along with the support of new, informal allies should be expected to encourage a stronger Indian stance. Yet as the Sino-Indian rivalry gets drawn into regional/global politics, its overall significance also increases. It becomes part of the puzzle over whether China becomes the Asian hegemon and whether the Third World War takes place within the potential context of a rising China/declining United States transition – or even whether a transition comes to pass.

---

[49] Paul has called it a limited rivalry thanks to the influence of three constraints: economic interdependence, Indian reluctance to escalate the fighting due to its relative weakness, and a Chinese reluctance to push India into alliance with the West. See his "Explaining Conflict and Cooperation in the China-India Rivalry," in Paul, *The China-India Rivalry*, 5–6. The influence of two of the three constraints may be expected to diminish in the future.

PART II

Spatial and Positional Considerations and Violence

CHAPTER 3

The Sino-Indian Rivalry
The Positional Dimension (1940s–1950s)

The Sino-Indian rivalry began as positional rivalry for leadership in post-war/postcolonial Asia along with their emergence as modern states in the late 1940s.[1] Positional rivals contend over relative influence and prestige within a system or a subsystem.[2] More specifically, positional rivalries are contests over relative pecking order – or rank in a hierarchy – in global or regional systems.[3] Although China's invasion and annexation of Tibet in 1950–51 after the proclamation of the People's Republic of China (the PRC) in 1949 did add a territorial/spatial dimension to their rivalry, positional concerns remained central to their rivalry (as shown in this chapter and Chapter 4 on the 1962 war). It is possible for positional issues to dominate rivalry dynamics or to be at least as important as territorial issues in contests involving both spatial and positional issues.[4]

Nationalist China had participated in the 1943 Cairo Conference (where the future of postwar Asia was discussed) as a great power, albeit a second-tier great power. A few years later, Communist China had received the backing of the Soviet Union to lead the Communist countries of Asia (and to promote Communism in Asia). In the meanwhile, postindependence India also harbored the ambition to lead Asia, partly informed by the important role that Indian troops had played during the Second World War, especially in Southeast Asia.[5] India's active diplomacy during the

[1] Manjeet S. Pardesi, "The Initiation of the Sino-Indian Rivalry," *Asian Security* 15.3 (2019): 253–284.
[2] Michael P. Colaresi, Karen Rasler, and William R. Thompson, *Strategic Rivalries in World Politics: Position, Space, and Conflict Escalation* (Cambridge: Cambridge University Press, 2007), 79–80.
[3] On this structural understanding of position as "relative rank" in a hierarchy, and how that differs from other social dimensions of status, see William R. Thompson, "Status Conflict, Hierarchies, and Interpretation Dilemmas," in T. V. Paul, Deborah Welch Larson, and William C. Wohlforth (eds.), *Status in World Politics* (New York: Cambridge University Press, 2014), 219–245.
[4] Colaresi, Rasler, and Thompson, *Strategic Rivalries in World Politics*, 80, 172.
[5] On India's contribution to the war effort in Southeast Asia, see Christopher Bayly and Tim Harper, *Forgotten Armies: The Fall of British Asia, 1941–1945* (Cambridge, MA: Harvard University Press, 2005); and Christopher Bayly and Tim Harper, *Forgotten Wars: Freedom and Revolution in Southeast Asia* (Cambridge, MA: Harvard University Press, 2007).

47

1950–53 Korean War and at the 1954 Geneva Conference on Indochina led the PRC to believe that India was trying to champion itself as "the third power" in Asia after the United States and the Soviet Union.[6] It was already clear to scholars in the early 1950s that "[b]ehind the day-to-day contacts and relations between India and China lies the *rivalry for leadership in Asia* which permeates their actions, though it is hardly ever visible to the naked eye."[7]

Despite its complexity, with the two interacting issues of position and territory under contention, the Sino-Indian rivalry began as an asymmetric rivalry (and continues to remain asymmetric as discussed in subsequent chapters).[8] Both India and China had (and continue to have) other rivals to worry about. When states have more than one rival, they rank order them depending upon capabilities, the imminence of the threat, and ego-relevancy.[9] By 1952, in the aftermath of the PRC's invasion of Tibet, India had begun to view China "as a potential security threat on a par with Pakistan,"[10] and China had become India's principal (or primary) rival by the late 1950s.[11] On the other hand, China viewed India as a "lesser" rival.[12] After 1949, the PRC's principal rival was the United States, followed by the Soviet Union in the 1960s (after the Sino-Soviet split that began in the late 1950s).

Although this asymmetry was partly rooted in the fact that India aspired to great power status while China was already recognized as one, it was also a function of Sino-Indian historical interactions. Modern China encountered modern India as an agent of British colonialism during China's "century of humiliation" (~1839–1949).[13] Indian troops of the British Raj

---

[6] Wang Hongwei (translated by Chen Guansheng and Li Leizhu), *A Critical Review of the Contemporary Sino-Indian Relations* (Beijing: China Tibetology Publishing House, 2011), 301.

[7] Werner Levi, *Modern China's Foreign Policy* (Minneapolis: The University of Minnesota Press, 1953), 353. *Emphasis added.*

[8] Manjeet S. Pardesi, "Explaining the Asymmetry in the Sino-Indian Strategic Rivalry," *Australian Journal of International Affairs* 75.3 (2021): 341–365.

[9] Manjeet S. Pardesi, "Image Theory and the Initiation of Strategic Rivalries," in William R. Thompson (ed.), *The Oxford Encyclopedia of Empirical International Relations Theory, Volume 2* (Oxford: Oxford University Press, 2018), 225–244.

[10] Steven A. Hoffmann, *India and the China Crisis* (Delhi: Oxford University Press, 1990), 24.

[11] On principal rivalries, see William R. Thompson, "Principal Rivalries," *Journal of Conflict Resolution* 39:2 (1995): 195–223.

[12] Andrew Scobell, "Himalayan Standoff: Strategic Culture and the China–India Rivalry," in T. V. Paul (ed.), *The China–India Rivalry in the Globalization Era* (Washington, DC: Georgetown University Press, 2018), 165–186; and John Garver, "Asymmetrical Indian and Chinese Threat Perceptions," *Journal of Strategic Studies* 25.4 (2002): 109–134.

[13] Zheng Wang, *Never Forget National Humiliation: Historical Memory in Chinese Politics and Foreign Relations* (New York: Columbia University Press, 2012); and Peter Hays Gries, *China's New Nationalism: Pride, Politics, and Diplomacy* (Berkeley: University of California Press, 2004), 43–53.

had participated in the Opium Wars and the suppression of the Boxer Rebellion. Ethnic Indians also worked as policemen in Britain's "treaty ports" in China (such as Shanghai and Hong Kong), and Indians constituted the "fourth largest foreign community" in China (after the Japanese, Russians, and the British) by the 1930s and were a visible symbol of China's subjugation at the hands of British imperialism.[14]

As China sought to prevent formal colonization during these decades, India also served as a prominent negative example of a country whose fate had to be avoided.[15] By contrast, China wanted to be wealthy and powerful like the Western powers and Japan. The PRC's disdain was also rooted in the fact India was viewed as a "successor" to British imperialism as independent India tried to assert its leadership in Asian strategic affairs.[16] Not only did India's "massive size" make it "a possible threat in the future" but the Chinese also "wondered whether the Indian state project was viable," because as a British creation, India was seen "more as an 'abstraction' than a country."[17] Not surprisingly, China saw British (and Anglo-American) power behind India's quest for leadership in Asia.

On the other hand, India initially viewed China as a fellow victim of colonialism. Notably, both the Communists and the Nationalists had sought help from India after the full-scale Japanese invasion of China in 1937.[18] The British Indian Army had not played any significant role in the Indian freedom movement. Consequently, the Indian political leadership was unable to fully appreciate the negative feelings that Britain's use of Indian troops of the Raj had generated in Asia and what that meant for independent India.[19] Furthermore, unlike the Chinese perception

---

[14] Claude Markovits, "Indian Communities in China, c. 1842–1949," in Robert Bickers and Christian Henriot (eds.), *New Frontiers: Imperialism's New Communities in East Asia, 1842–1953* (Manchester: Manchester University Press, 2000), 59.

[15] Rebecca E. Karl, *Staging the World: Chinese Nationalism at the Turn of the Twentieth Century* (Durham: Duke University Press, 2002), 159–163.

[16] Odd Arne Westad, *Restless Empire: China and the World since 1750* (New York: Basic, 2015), 342.

[17] Westad, *Restless Empire*, 432.

[18] In 1937, General Zhu De, the second most important Communist leader after Mao Zedong then, had written to the Indian leader (and future prime minister) Jawaharlal Nehru seeking India's assistance, which resulted in an Indian medical mission being sent to support the Eighth Route Army of the Communist Party of China. The Nationalist leader Chiang Kai-shek's visit to India is discussed later in this chapter.

[19] The British use of Indian troops to subjugate Asian countries such as Burma, Sri Lanka, Malaya, and Indonesia was raised at the 1947 Asian Relations Conference. An Indian representative explained it away by arguing that the Indians did not have any control over the British Indian Army and that independent India had withdrawn Indian troops from all Asian countries (unless they were present there with the consent of the host country). *Asian Relations, being Report of the Proceedings and Documentation of the First Asian Relations Conference, New Delhi, March–April 1947* (New Delhi: Asian Relations Organization, 1948), 73.

of Indian statehood, the Indian leadership believed that the end of the Chinese Civil War and the emergence of the PRC had led to the creation of a strong and centralized Chinese state for the first time in decades.[20]

In other words, Chinese and Indian mutual perceptions differed, and they accorded different priorities to the challenges posed by the other side. However, this did not preclude some degree of cooperation between them in their anti-colonial and anti-imperial endeavors. Pan-Asian ideas did have some appeal for the Chinese and Indian leaderships in the 1940s and 1950s.[21] However, it is "doubtful that a genuine spirit of Sino-Indian brotherhood ever truly existed."[22] By the late 1950s, the Indian prime minister Jawaharlal Nehru was describing the Chinese as "arrogant, devious, hypocritical and thoroughly unreliable,"[23] while the Chinese premier Zhou Enlai was describing Nehru as "very British" and an "heir to British colonial expansionism."[24]

Given this background, this chapter explains how the Sino-Indian positional rivalry unfolded in the late 1940s and through the 1950s. The chapter is divided into five sections. The first section elucidates the Indian and Chinese claims to Asian leadership and the role that each side envisaged for the other in their respective visions for an Asia led by them. The three subsequent sections focus on the positional contest between China and India from the late 1940s in three venues. First, the Sino-Indian positional rivalry was apparent in the various Asian multilateral fora, from the 1947 Asian Relations Conference (ARC) to the 1955 Bandung Conference. Additionally, India also sought to demonstrate its leadership through mediation in conflicts involving China and multiple other players in the 1950s.

Second, the two sides vigorously vied for influence in the Himalayan states (Nepal, Bhutan, and Sikkim) and in Southeast Asia. Third and finally, throughout this period, China needed India's help to consolidate

---

[20] See letter 37 dated December 31, 1950, in G. Parthasarathi (ed.), *Jawaharlal Nehru: Letters to Chief Ministers, 1947–1964, Volume 2, 1950–1952* (New Delhi: Jawaharlal Nehru Memorial Fund, 1986), 299–310.

[21] Brian Tsui, "Coming to Terms with the People's Republic of China: Jawaharlal Nehru in the Early 1950s," in Young-Chan Kim (ed.), *China-India Relations: Geo-political Competition, Economic Cooperation, Cultural Exchange and Business Ties* (Cham: Springer, 2020), 13–30.

[22] Bérénice Guyot-Réchard, *Shadow States: India, China, and the Himalayas, 1910–1962* (Cambridge: Cambridge University Press, 2017), 184.

[23] Manu Pubby, "Don't Believe in Hindi-Chini Bhai-Bhai, Nehru Told Envoy," *Indian Express*, January 22, 2010, https://indianexpress.com/article/news-archive/web/dont-believe-in-hindichini-bhaibhai-nehru-told-envoy/.

[24] Han Suyin, *Eldest Son: Zhou Enlai and the Making of Modern China, 1898–1976* (New York: Hill and Wang, 1994), 284.

its own rule in Tibet, thereby giving India an exalted but much-resented position in China's internal affairs (as they pertained to Tibet). The chapter concludes by noting that an understanding of the positional dimension of the Sino-Indian rivalry during these years is crucial for it was the entanglement of these positional issues with territorial concerns that precipitated the 1962 Sino-Indian War discussed in Chapter 4.

Leadership in Asia (1940s–1950s)

India and Asian Leadership

On the eve of India's independence, and in the context of the upcoming ARC, Nehru argued that "in the modern world it is inevitable for India to be the *centre* of things in Asia."[25] He had an expansive view of Asia that included not just "Southern Asia and South-Eastern Asia regions, in which of course India is included" but also the Indian Ocean, the Middle East, China, East Africa, Australia, and New Zealand.[26] Not only were these remarks made in English and published in one of India's leading journals but Nehru also articulated his views on India's strategic centrality before foreign/Asian leaders. While addressing the representatives of several Southeast Asian governments soon after Indian independence, he stated that India was the "*pivotal centre* of South, South-East and Western Asia," both in terms of trade and "in terms of defence."[27] Notably, he believed that the Second World War had made India's "dominant position ... [in Asia] obvious."[28]

For Nehru, India was one of the "four great powers of the world," the other three being America, the Soviet Union, and China.[29] That India was an emergent great power was also widely reported in the Western media.[30] While Nehru did want India to have good relations with all great powers, he was also a champion of decolonization. Consequently, a week before

---

[25] Jawaharlal Nehru, "Inter-Asian Relations," *India Quarterly* 2.4 (1946): 324. *Emphasis added.*

[26] Nehru, "Inter-Asian Relations," 323–324. Interestingly, this region is referred to as the "Indo-Pacific" today.

[27] "The Conquest of Air," November 23, 1948, in Jawaharlal Nehru, *Independence and After: A Collection of Speeches, 1946–1949* (New York: The John Day Company, 1950), 329. *Emphasis added.*

[28] "India and the Membership of the Security Council," October 30, 1946, *Selected Works of Jawaharlal Nehru, Series 2, Volume 1* (New Delhi: Jawaharlal Nehru Memorial Fund, 2014), 464. This series is hereafter referred to as *SWJN*.

[29] "Science in War and in Peace," October 19, 1946, *SWJN, Series 2, Volume 1*, 311.

[30] "India – A New Great Power," *The Economist*, October 23, 1948; "India: Anchor for Asia," *Time*, October 17, 1949; and "The Position of Nehru," *The New York Times*, August 29, 1950.

India's formal independence, he articulated a "Monroe Doctrine for Asia," because "foreign armies" had "no business to stay on the soil of an Asian country."[31] After all, the era of colonialism had not come to an end in Asia with the end of the Second World War and with India's independence.[32] In addition to the continuation of European colonial enclaves in India, the French went back to Indochina and the Dutch tried to reassert themselves in Indonesia. Furthermore, the British were still entangled in Malaya while postwar Japan was under American military occupation. Nehru saw India as a champion for Asian countries, especially on matters related to Western military presence.[33]

In this new era after the war, Nehru wanted to build the postwar, postcolonial order in Asia jointly with China – the other great power of Asia – given his "Asianism."[34] Since both the Chinese Nationalists and the Chinese Communists had sought India's help after the 1937 Japanese invasion of China, he believed that China also desired to work with India. Not only had China sought India's help in recent history but, as Nehru was aware, "China was more influenced by India" in the deep past because of the transmission of Buddhism "than India [had been] by China."[35] In other words, Nehru obviously gave precedence to India in the Sino-Indian relationship even as he hoped to work together with China in Asia.

However, tensions in Sino-Indian relations were apparent even in the late 1940s as explained in this chapter. The divergence between China and India was displayed most dramatically on the eve of the 1950–51 invasion and annexation of Tibet by the People's Liberation Army (PLA) when India even contemplated military intervention in Tibet.[36] While armed intervention was ruled out for several reasons,[37] it was also understood that

---

[31] "A Monroe Doctrine for Asia," August 9, 1947, *SWJN, Series 2, Volume 3*, 133–135.

[32] There was a tension in Nehru's policy on this matter as he had retained the services of many British officers in the Indian armed forces after independence, as explained subsequently.

[33] Birendra Prasad, *Indian Nationalism and Asia (1900–1947)* (Delhi: B. R. Publishing Corporation, 1979); and T. A. Keenleyside, "Nationalist Indian Ideas towards Asia: A Troublesome Legacy for Post-independence Indian Foreign Policy," *Pacific Affairs* 55.2 (1982): 210–230; and Carolien Stolte and Harald Fischer-Tiné, "Imagining Asia in India: Nationalism and Internationalism (ca. 1905–1940)," *Comparative Studies in Society and History* 54.1 (2012): 65–92.

[34] Francine R. Frankel, *When Nehru Looked East: Origins of India-US Suspicion and India-China Rivalry* (New York: Oxford University Press, 2020).

[35] Jawaharlal Nehru, *The Discovery of India*, centenary edition (Delhi: Oxford University Press, 1989 [1946]), 199.

[36] B. N. Mullik, *My Years with Nehru: The Chinese Betrayal* (New Delhi: Allied, 1971), 80–81.

[37] Independence and partition had divided the British Indian Army between India and Pakistan, and the two had immediately gone to war over Kashmir in 1947–48. Furthermore, Nehru had reduced the strength of the Indian army by 50,000 troops for financial reasons in 1950. See Pradeep P. Barua, *The State of War in South Asia* (Lincoln: University of Nebraska Press, 2005), 169.

the defense of Tibet against China could not be guaranteed with a solitary intervention north of the Himalayas. In fact, it would have required some form of military assistance from the United States, thereby destroying Nehru's Asianist vision.[38] Additionally, such a policy would have also put an end to his larger strategy of nonalignment between the superpowers during the Cold War.[39]

Nevertheless, the Chinese invasion of Tibet did change Nehru's perception of China. In early 1952, he noted the following in a conversation with his intelligence chief, B. N. Mullik:

> [Throughout history] China had always been a very aggressive country. ... China never believed in treating other countries on equal terms. ... [Contemporary China] would try to extend her influence and *leadership* over the rest of Asia. ... In this struggle for supremacy in Asia, the biggest obstacle in her way would be India. ... [A] continuous tussle had gone on between Indian and Chinese cultures for 2,000 years in Central Asia, Tibet, Burma and the whole of South-East Asia. ... [T]his war between the two cultures was not over and was still going on and would go on for a long time and no one could foretell what would be the final outcome. ... Many of the countries in South-East Asia ... were now independent and looked to India for *leadership*.[40]

Echoes of this view on the competition between India and China – especially in Southeast Asia – were also evident in Nehru's conversations with Zhou during his visit to China in October 1954 (discussed later in this chapter). Furthermore, according to his official biographer, Nehru had noted in mid-1954 that "Chinese expansionism had been evident during previous periods for about a thousand years, and a new period of such expansionism was perhaps imminent."[41]

In other words, Nehru was very conscious of India's positional rivalry with China for Asian leadership. He nevertheless believed that a modus vivendi had to be sought with Beijing, especially because India and China needed to work together in support of his Asianist vision in the postcolonial

---

[38] A. S. Bhasin, *Nehru, Tibet, and China* (Gurugram: Penguin, 2021), 69–109.

[39] On nonalignment and its complex links with Asianism, including the centrality of Nehruvian ideas for both, see Lorenz M. Lüthi, "Non-alignment, 1946–1965: Its Establishment and Struggle against Afro-Asianism," *Humanity* 7.2 (2016): 201–223. Also see Raju G. C. Thomas, "Nonalignment and Indian Security: Nehru's Rationale and Legacy," *Journal of Strategic Studies* 2.2 (1979): 153–171; and A. P. Rana, *The Imperatives of Nonalignment: A Conceptual Study of India's Foreign Policy Strategy in the Nehru Period* (Delhi: Macmillan, 1979).

[40] Mullik, *My Years with Nehru*, 178–179. *Emphasis added.*

[41] Sarvepalli Gopal, *Jawaharlal Nehru, A Biography: Volume Two, 1947–1956* (Delhi: Oxford University Press, 1979), 190.

world. Nehru's challenge was to accommodate the interests of both China and India, while giving precedence to India, without taking sides in the Cold War superpower rivalry (an endeavor in which he was clearly unsuccessful, as China and India went to war in 1962). However, in contrast with the Nehruvian approach, China was not interested in sharing Asian leadership with India.

China and Asian Leadership

Unlike India, China had not been formally colonized, and even the weak and quasi-occupied Nationalist China had participated in the Second World War as a recognized great power. Importantly, the Nationalist leader Chiang Kai-shek's 1942 visit to British India to seek the support of Nehru and Mahatma Gandhi for China's war efforts against Japan "marked China's first wartime gesture as a great power."[42] Furthermore, not only did Nationalist China obtain a permanent seat in the United Nations Security Council (UNSC) but Communist China had also displayed its great power credentials during the 1950–53 Korean War by fighting vigorously against the United States (even if at a great cost). Indeed, since the creation of the PRC in 1949, China has been recognized as a great power by the International Relations scholarship (even though there is some ambiguity regarding China's status before this date).[43]

On their part, Chinese elites of various ideological persuasions were determined to end all signs of China's "national humiliation" at the hands of Western imperial powers and Japan. Not only had China been subjected to imperial wars and indemnities during this period but it had also experienced partial occupation, territorial dismemberment, and extraterritoriality. Although scholars have recognized that modern China (the PRC) "is the legacy of two kinds of imperialism, one committed by China [in Tibet and elsewhere, and] one against it,"[44] Chinese nationalism emphasizes the latter while denying the former. Consequently, the PRC was determined

[42] Rana Mitter, *Forgotten Ally: China's World War II, 1937–1945* (Boston: Houghton Mifflin Harcourt, 2013), 249. Nationalist China had been unsuccessful in its debut as a great power in Asia for even as Nehru and Gandhi sympathized with Chiang (and China), they launched the Quit India movement against India's British rulers soon after Chiang's visit and were promptly incarcerated for the rest of the war.

[43] Jack S. Levy, *War in the Modern Great Power System, 1495–1975* (Lexington: University Press of Kentucky, 1983), 43.

[44] Andrew J. Nathan and Andrew Scobell, *China's Search for Security* (New York: Columbia University Press, 2012), 196. Also see Peter C. Perdue, "China and Other Colonial Empires," *The Journal of American-East Asian Relations* 16.1/2 (2009): 85–103.

to end all vestiges of its national humiliation so that it could (re)establish itself as a great power.

Imperial China's long history as a major power in historical East Asia – in the so-called Chinese tributary system – fueled the ambitions of its modern leaders.[45] Mao, who had been deeply influenced by China's past, had asked the Chinese leadership to "sum up" the thousands of years of this history from "Confucius to Sun Yat-sen" in order to "take over this precious legacy."[46] Not surprisingly, PRC foreign policy toward the countries in its "periphery" – those that were in the historical Sinosphere (Japan, Korea, and Vietnam) as well as those farther away in Southeast Asia and in the Himalayas – was tinged with "a 'traditional' look," which emphasized some form of Chinese primacy.[47] In fact, the PRC "clung to this role as *the leading Asian power* … with explicit approval, even encouragement of Moscow."[48]

The Chinese leadership was aware of India's historical role in Asia, both in deep history through the Buddhist impact and in modern history as a part of the British imperial system. When K. M. Panikkar, India's first ambassador to the PRC (and the last ambassador to Nationalist China), presented his credentials to Mao, he was informed that "there was an old belief" in China "that if a man lived a good life he would be reborn in India."[49] In fact, the Buddhist impact meant that historical India had "a unique place in the Chinese world order: a foreign kingdom that was culturally and spiritually revered as equal to the Chinese civilization."[50] And in more modern times, Sun Yat-sen, one of the greatest leaders of early twentieth-century China had argued that Britain had dominated the world "by relying on India" and that "the British Empire is nothing but a third-rate country … [w]ithout India."[51] China's leaders were

---

[45] This does not mean that the PRC wanted to create a modern tributary system. Instead, it implied that history itself conferred great power status upon China.

[46] "The Role of the Chinese Communist Party in the National War," October 1938, in *Selected Works of Mao-Tsetung, Volume II* (Oxford: Pergamom Press, 1975), 209.

[47] Michael H. Hunt, *The Genesis of Chinese Communist Foreign Policy* (New York: Columbia University Press, 1996), 221.

[48] Hunt, *The Genesis of Chinese Communist Foreign Policy*, 220. *Emphasis added.*

[49] K. M. Panikkar, *In Two Chinas: Memoirs of a Diplomat* (London: George Allen & Unwin, 1955), 80.

[50] Tansen Sen, *Buddhism, Diplomacy and Trade: The Realignment of Sino-Indian Relations, 600–1400* (Honolulu: University of Hawai'i Press, 2004), 8.

[51] "The Question of China's Survival (1917)," in Julie Lee Wei, Ramon Myers, and Donald Gillin (eds.) (translated by Julie Lee Wei, E-su Zen, and Linda Chao), *Prescriptions for Saving China: Selected Writings of Sun Yat-sen* (Stanford: Hoover Institution Press, 1994), 161–162. Although Sun may have exaggerated the importance of India for the British Empire, China was aware that Britain had projected its power into China and in Asia from its Indian base. See Matthew Mosca, *From Frontier to Foreign Policy: The Question of India and the Transformation of Geopolitics in Qing China* (Stanford: Stanford University Press, 2013).

also cognizant of India's role in Asia after 1947, including its ambitions to emerge as "the third power," noted earlier. Notably, a Chinese Ministry of Foreign Affairs document from 1956 identified India as a "great power of the world."[52]

Despite this recognition of India's power and potential by various Chinese governments in the twentieth century, China remained uninterested in sharing Asian leadership with India. Since China had encountered British imperial power through its Indian agents during the century of "national humiliation," it had a very negative view of India. Nationalist China's outreach to India in 1942 was largely due to wartime exigencies as other supply routes to China were in regions conquered by Japan. According to Sir Muhammad Zafarullah Khan, British India's first agent-general to Nationalist China (who was sent there in 1942 after Chiang's visit), Chiang (and his wife) aimed to create a "Chinese Raj" in India after the end of the British Raj. He was suspicious of China and wondered why "the claim of China to be ranked among the great nations [was] irresistible" to them while "the same claim on behalf of India [was] unacceptable."[53] Likewise, Panikkar also noted that China's attitude toward India was that of an "elder brother who was considerably older and well established in the world, prepared to give his advice to a younger brother ... it was understood that China as the recognized Great Power in the East after the war expected India to know her place."[54]

There were two important reasons behind such Chinese attitudes toward India that continued even after the creation of the PRC. First, "[d]uring Nehru's lifetime ... India was China's most serious rival for influence among the states of Asia," and relatedly, India was seen as "a creation of British colonialism."[55] Indeed, the PRC was unable to understand Indian independence, which was achieved via peaceful means under the leadership of Gandhi and Nehru. India's independence was an act of the British Parliament that had granted India the status of a Dominion under the British Commonwealth in 1947.[56] Independent India also

[52] Xiaoyuan Liu, "Friend or Foe: India as Perceived by Beijing's Foreign Policy Analysts in the 1950s," *China Review* 15.1 (2015): 126.
[53] Khan quoted in Laura Tyson Li, *Madame Chiang Kai-shek: China's Eternal First Lady* (New York: Atlantic Monthly Press, 2006), 179. Khan went on to become Pakistan's first foreign minister after the independence and partition of British India. His influence on Pakistan–China relations, if any, remains unknown.
[54] Panikkar, *In Two Chinas*, 26–27.
[55] Harold C. Hinton, *China's Turbulent Quest: An Analysis of China's Foreign Relations since 1949* (Bloomington: Indiana University Press, 1970), 244.
[56] India became a republic in 1950.

retained the services of 300 senior British military officers and instructors for several years.

Indeed, the positions of the commander-in-chief of the Indian Army, the commander-in-chief of the Indian Air Force, and the chief of the Indian Naval Staff were held by British officers until 1949, 1954, and 1958 respectively, while an Indian officer assumed the role of the chief of naval aviation only in April 1962.[57] In other words, China saw British power lurking behind "independent" India's expansive ambitions in Asia. In fact, even in 1973, Mao complained to the US national security advisor Henry Kissinger that India "did not win independence" because if "it did not attach itself to Britain" it sought to "attach itself" with the other super-powers, the Soviet Union and the United States.[58]

Second, as China sought to end all trappings of its "national humiliation," it also encountered India in Tibet. While it is widely believed that (Nationalist) China had ended all colonial-era unequal treaties by the end of the Second World War,[59] this was not true for Tibet. Although the historical status of Tibet is beyond the scope of this book,[60] Mao had come to see the "liberation of Tibet" to be as important as the "liberation of Taiwan" by the late 1940s according to Shi Zhe, his translator.[61] India had retained the services of Hugh Richardson, the British Indian representative to Lhasa, as the Indian representative there after independence.[62] Notably, Richardson was the only British citizen who was retained at an Indian mission abroad after independence.

Initially, India also continued with its British-era trade agencies in Gyantse, Yatung, and Gartok in Tibet while maintaining an Indian military escort in Gyantse. Furthermore, it operated Tibet's postal and telegraph services and maintained some guest houses along the trade routes.[63] In other words, China and India were aware of their mutual great power

[57] Stephen P. Cohen, *The Indian Army: Its Contribution to the Development of a Nation* (Delhi: Oxford University Press, 1990), 166; and Lorne J. Kavic, *India's Quest for Security: Defence Policies, 1947–1965* (Berkeley: University of California Press, 1967), 103, 122.

[58] "Memorandum of Conversation between Mao Zedong and Henry Kissinger," November 12, 1973, History and Public Policy Program Digital Archive, Gerald R. Ford Presidential Library, National Security Adviser Trip Briefing Books and Cables for President Ford, 1974–1976 (Box 19), https://digitalarchive.wilsoncenter.org/document/118069.

[59] Wesley R. Fishel, *The End of Extraterritoriality in China* (Berkeley: University of California Press, 1952).

[60] Michael van Walt van Praag, *The Status of Tibet: History, Rights, and Prospects in International Law* (Boulder: Westview, 1987); and Elliot Sperling, "Tibet and China: The Interpretation of History since 1950," *China Perspectives* 3 (2009): 25–37, https://doi.org/10.4000/chinaperspectives.4839.

[61] Shi Zhe (translated by Chen Jian), "With Mao and Stalin: The Reminiscences of a Chinese Interpreter," *Chinese Historians* 5.1 (1992): 41.

[62] Hugh Richardson, *Tibet and Its History* (Boulder: Shambala, 1984).

[63] Bhasin, *Nehru, Tibet, and China*, 32, 125.

ambitions in the late 1940s and early 1950s as they competed for Asian leadership. Although this did not preclude a certain degree of cooperation in Sino-Indian relations, the two sides viewed each other with suspicion (which also included Chinese suspicions related to Indian interference in China's "domestic affairs" in Tibet).

The Sino-Indian Positional Contest

Multilateral Fora

The Asian Relations Conference

There were at least four Asian conferences until the mid-1950s that had implications for the Sino-Indian positional rivalry for leadership: the 1947 ARC, the 1949 Conference on Indonesia, the 1949 Conference on Burma, and the 1955 Bandung Conference.[64] The first three of these conferences were held in New Delhi. The 1947 ARC is significant simply because it shows that the Sino-Indian contest began even before Indian independence and the creation of the PRC.[65] The ARC was the first postwar regional gathering of polities from across Asia. It was attended by twenty-eight "countries" (some not yet independent) and included observers from the United Nations (UN), the Arab League, and non-governmental organizations from Australia, Britain, and the United States.[66] Prominent Asian leaders such as Indonesia's Sutan Syahrir and Sri Lanka's S. W. R. D. Bandaranaike personally attended the conference, while Burma's Aung San and Vietnam's Ho Chi-Minh sent notes to associate themselves with it.[67]

While the ARC was organized to discuss social, cultural, and economic matters, it was rife with political implications. In his inaugural address, Nehru reiterated his thoughts on India as "the natural centre and focal point" in Asia for reasons related to history and geography.[68] Importantly, China was "displeased" that India had organized this event "without consulting" China,[69] the recognized Asian great power. Furthermore, India had sent separate invitations to the Nationalists and the Communists. While

---

[64] Amitav Acharya, *East of India, South of China: Sino-Indian Encounters in Southeast Asia* (New Delhi: Oxford University Press, 2017), https://doi.org/10.1093/acprof:oso/9780199461141.003.0003.

[65] The conference took place in March–April 1947.

[66] For the complete list, see *Asian Relations*, 263–264.

[67] Bimla Prasad, *The Origins of Indian Foreign Policy: The Indian National Congress and World Affairs, 1885–1947*, 2nd ed. (Calcutta: Bookland, 1962), 253.

[68] *Asian Relations*, 23.

[69] Yun-Yuan Yang, *Nehru and China, 1927–1949* (PhD Dissertation, University of Virginia, 1974), 170.

the Nationalist representatives attended the conference, they prevented the Communists from participating by refusing to issue passports for them.[70]

China was also unhappy because India had issued a separate invitation for the Tibetan delegation that entered India using Tibetan passports. "From the Tibetan point of view, attending an international conference as an equal with China was a major recognition of their de facto independent status."[71] The Chinese delegation complained to Nehru about this and was also angry because the map in the conference hall showed Tibet as a separate country. With Nehru's permission (who initially tried to ignore it), a Chinese delegate "made the correction by painting the Tibetan region and China in one color" on the map.[72] In spite of this change, the Tibetan delegation was otherwise treated on a par with the delegations from other countries and territories.

The Chinese delegation proposed to create a permanent organization – the Asian Relations Organization – and it was also agreed that the next session of the conference would be held in China.[73] However, for several reasons, including the Chinese Civil War and suspicions in other Asian countries about China's and India's ambitions meant that no permanent organization was created nor was its second session ever held (neither in China nor elsewhere). An early academic analysis of these events concluded that the "Chinese had no wish to be tied to an organization in which India was predominant. Their tactics at the conference were to keep India's status within bounds. No more did the Indians wish to surrender any power to the Chinese."[74]

The Conference on Indonesia

As the Chinese Civil War entered its final phase in early 1949, India organized the Conference on Indonesia to deal specifically with the issue of Indonesian independence. India had defied the Dutch air blockade over Indonesia from 1947 to 1949 while making several sorties to provide "supplies and military equipment" to the Indonesians fighting for their freedom against the Dutch.[75] Furthermore, it had stopped the Dutch from

---

[70] Xiaoyuan Liu, *The Sino-Indian Border Dispute and Sino-Indian Relations* (Lanham, MD: University Press of America, 1994), 83.
[71] Melvyn C. Goldstein, *A History of Modern Tibet, Volume 1: 1913–1951* (Berkeley: University of California Press, 1989), 563.
[72] Yang, *Nehru and China*, 174.
[73] *Asian Relations*, 245, 255.
[74] Werner Levi, *Free India in Asia* (Minneapolis: University of Minnesota Press, 1952), 38.
[75] Sudhir Devare, *India & Southeast Asia: Towards Security Convergence* (Singapore: Institute of Southeast Asian Studies, 2006), 71.

using the Indian air space from July 1947 onward.[76] Notably, Biju Patnaik, a prominent Indian politician, defied the Dutch air blockade and personally flew out the former prime minister Sutan Syahrir out of Indonesia.[77] Finally, in late 1948, India had also invited the Indonesian leadership "to set up a government-in-exile" in India if required.[78]

It was in this context that the Conference on Indonesia met in New Delhi. It was held in two parts – the first in January 1949 followed by a "confidential" second part in April 1949 – and was attended by nineteen countries.[79] The proceedings in India (in which Australia also played an important role) had a major impact on the UNSC and, along with Anglo-American pressure, ended the hostilities in Indonesia as Dutch–Indonesian negotiations began in April 1949.[80]

China had played a low-key role at this conference, having sent only observers. Nevertheless, *China Digest*, the English-language mouthpiece of the Chinese Communist Party (CCP), argued that the conference had served no useful purpose and wondered whether India was in the process of creating an "Asiatic Military Alliance" to curb the spread of Communism in Asia.[81] Notably, Nehru traveled to Singapore from India by air in June 1950 and then onward by sea aboard the *INS Delhi* to Jakarta accompanied by Indian naval vessels.[82] In Jakarta, he dismissed the possibility of a military alliance between India and Indonesia.[83] While the PRC's official reaction to Nehru's visit to Indonesia on an Indian naval vessel remains unknown, it is safe to assume that it heightened Chinese concerns about Indian intentions.

The Conference on Burma

A month after the first part of the Conference on Indonesia, India organized an "informal" Conference on Burma. Unlike the former, which was about Indonesian independence, the latter focused on Burma's internal affairs. The newly independent Burmese state was facing significant challenges posed by the Karen rebels. Nehru wanted the "Burmese government and the Karens to negotiate, thus freeing up the government to deal with the communist menace."[84] Therefore, unlike the far wider Asian

[76] Ton That Thien, *India and South East Asia, 1947–1960* (Genève: Librairie Droz, 1963), 91.
[77] Ton That, *India and South East Asia*, 92.
[78] "Minister Says India Will Aid Java Fight," *The New York Times*, December 14, 1948.
[79] Frankel, *When Nehru Looked East*, 104.
[80] Ton That, *India and South East Asia*, 98–102.
[81] "Asian Conference and Asia's Future," *China Digest*, February 8, 1949, 13.
[82] "To A. Soekarno," April 16, 1950, *SWJN, Series 2, Volume 14*, Part 2, 385.
[83] "Military Pact with Indonesia," June 16, 1950, *SWJN, Series 2, Volume 14*, Part 2, 393.
[84] Bayly and Harper, *Forgotten Wars*, Kindle Loc., 9036–9037.

participation in earlier conferences, India (and Britain) decided to assist Burma via the Commonwealth. "The Commonwealth leaders duly met in New Delhi, where they drew up a plan and issued a joint declaration stating their willingness to help negotiate a peace treaty in Burma."[85]

In March 1949 it became known that India had supplied Burma with arms, ammunition, and transport planes,[86] thus making Burma the first country to receive military assistance from independent India. New Delhi also wanted to help Burma with its debt obligations (of more than Rs. 500,000,000 by March 1946) incurred during the separation of Burma from British India in 1937. This debt was canceled by 1954.[87] India's defense planners were aware of the strategic significance of Burma. Not only had Japan attacked British India from Burma during the Second World War by entering it from the south but its northern frontiers with China were of concern too.[88]

Panikkar had specifically noted that the "defence of Burma" was in fact the "defence of India" itself.[89] He had even called for an Indo-British defense treaty for the defense of the Indian Ocean and the surrounding regions even as no such treaty existed after independence (although India retained the services of British officers as noted earlier).[90] Furthermore, just two months after the Conference on Burma, Nehru argued at the end of the Commonwealth Prime Ministers' Meeting in April 1949 that the "Commonwealth countries must be prepared to resist military and political aggression by the Soviet government,"[91] Given that the Communists were on the cusp of victory in China, and that the PLA had approached the borders of Burma by September 1949 as it followed thousands of Nationalist troops who fled to Burma, the PRC's suspicion of India having inherited Britain's imperial position in Asia was not simply ideological rhetoric (even as it was erroneous).

The Bandung Conference

The above three conferences were organized before the creation of the PRC. By contrast, the Bandung Conference was in some ways the PRC's debut in Asian affairs in the sense that not only did the PRC attend a gathering for the

---

[85] Bayly and Harper, *Forgotten Wars*, Kindle Loc., 9079–9081.
[86] Ton That, *India and South East Asia*, 170.
[87] Ton That, *India and South East Asia*, 172.
[88] Since Chinese troops had also played a role in fighting the Japanese along the Sino-Burmese frontier, and because Japan was hoping to enter China from the southwest through Burma, India understood that Chinese troops could also enter Burma from the north in the future.
[89] K. M. Panikkar, *The Future of Southeast Asia* (London: George Allen & Unwin, 1943), 45.
[90] K. M. Panikkar, *The Basis of an Indo-British Treaty* (New Delhi: Indian Council of World Affairs, 1946).
[91] Quoted in John Darwin, *The Empire Project: The Rise and Fall of the British World System, 1830–1970* (Cambridge: Cambridge University Press, 2009), 555.

first time without the Soviet Union but also because many Asian countries (especially those in Southeast Asia) did not have diplomatic links with China after 1949. (The PRC was not a member of the UN nor was it recognized by the United States at the time.) Though this conference was held in Indonesia, Acharya contended that "Nehru's consent was crucial to Indonesia's ability to get agreement to hold the conference."[92] After all, it was Nehru's determination that made the invitation and participation of the PRC possible. His position as the "key player" in Asia aided his goal of "introducing" the PRC "to the rest of Asia – something that would have taken the new Chinese regime enormous effort and concessions had it tried to do it without India's initiative."[93]

In the pursuit of his Asianist vision, Nehru was perturbed by America's Southeast Asia Treaty Organization (SEATO), which was established in September 1954.[94] China also wanted to push back against America's seeming military encirclement of China in Southeast Asia (after Korea and Taiwan).[95] Although China's and India's interests overlapped for the moment, their underlying motivations were different. Moreover, India's leadership in Asian multilateralism was useful for China, at least temporarily, as the PRC had not yet participated in any Asian conference and because both China and India wanted to prevent the expansion of SEATO's membership. Consequently, the PRC government consciously took "a specially cautious attitude towards India in order to avoid the impression of contending for *leadership* with it" at Bandung.[96]

At Bandung, Nehru "played an important part in bringing" the Chinese and the North Vietnamese leaders into talks with their Cambodian and Laotian counterparts.[97] He also convinced the North Vietnamese "to promise publicly" that "they would not intervene in the internal affairs" of their Indochinese neighbors.[98] In 1954, Nehru had asked Zhou to reassure Southeast Asia on their fears about Chinese expansionism.[99] Consequently, Zhou made it a point to reassure China's Southeast Asian neighbors at

---

[92] Acharya, *East of India, South of China*.

[93] Acharya, *East of India, South of China*.

[94] Frankel, *When Nehru Looked East*, 213; and Tanvi Madan, *Fateful Triangle: How China Shaped U.S.-India Relations during the Cold War* (Washington, DC: Brookings, 2020), 56–64.

[95] Ang Cheng Guan, *The Southeast Asia Treaty Organization* (London: Routledge, 2022).

[96] "Views and Suggestions of the Experts on the Asian-African Conference," April 5, 1955, History and Public Policy Program Digital Archive, PRC FMA 207-00004-10, 84–88. Obtained by Amitav Acharya and translated by Yang Shanhou, https://digitalarchive.wilsoncenter.org/document/112898. *Emphasis added.*

[97] Ton That, *India and South East Asia*, 202, 214.

[98] Lorenz M. Lüthi, *Cold Wars: Asia, the Middle East, Europe* (Cambridge: Cambridge University Press, 2020), 149.

[99] Ton That, *India and South East Asia*, 202.

Bandung.[100] The Thai, Cambodian, Indonesian, and Laotian representatives "were particularly impressed" by Zhou.[101] At Nehru's behest, Zhou also offered to enter into talks with the United States.[102] While China had its own reasons to appear conciliatory with Southeast Asia and the United States,[103] working with India was considered useful.

India's *position* in Asia was clearly on display at this conference for not only was Nehru bringing different Asian countries together but he was also mediating between Asia and the West. However, it was also apparent that Zhou had "emerged as a second key figure alongside Nehru" at Bandung.[104] After all, he had navigated the PRC's first formal interaction with Asian multilateralism with grace and sophistication and had allayed Southeast Asian fears (for now).

Nevertheless, the feeling of rivalry at Bandung between China and India was clear to contemporaries. This competition is best captured in the words of Nehru's official biographer: "If Chou [Zhou] appeared to many to be the star of Bandung, frequently timing his diplomatic operations so as to overshadow the Indian Prime Minister, Nehru regarded Chou's success as his own personal triumph."[105] This was in line with Nehruvian thinking that gave precedence to India even though both China and India were great powers. For the moment it seemed like the two countries were working together, with China following India's lead. In 1956, Zhou even informed the Indian ambassador in Beijing that "China will not do anything in South East Asian countries [Pakistan, Nepal, Burma, Thailand, Cambodia, and Laos] without informing or consulting India."[106]

Indian Mediation in Asian Conflicts

In addition to these conferences, India tried to assert its leadership and views in resolving Asian conflicts involving China, especially the 1950–53

[100] "Zhou Enlai's Speech at the Political Committee of the Afro-Asian Conference," April 23, 1955, History and Public Policy Digital Program Archive, PRC FMA 207-00006-04, 69–75. Translated by Jeffrey Wang, https://digitalarchive.wilsoncenter.org/document/114678.

[101] Ang Cheng Guan, *Southeast Asia's Cold War: An Interpretive History* (Honolulu: University of Hawai'i Press, 2018), 83.

[102] Lüthi, *Cold Wars*, 280.

[103] Chen Yifeng, "Bandung, China, and the Making of World Order in East Asia," in Luis Eslava, Michael Fakhri, and Vasuki Nesiah (eds.), *Bandung, Global History, and International Law* (Cambridge: Cambridge University Press, 2017), 177–195.

[104] Frankel, *When Nehru Looked East*, 222.

[105] Gopal, *Jawaharlal Nehru, Volume Two*, 241.

[106] Top Secret Telegram from the Indian Embassy in Beijing, September 28, 1956, in Avtar Singh Bhasin (ed.), *India–China Relations 1947–2000: A Documentary Study, Vol-V* (New Delhi: Geetika, 2018), 325. 5254–5255.

Korean War and the 1954 Geneva Conference on Indochina. During the Korean War, India took on the role of a diplomatic interlocutor between China and the United States in the absence of direct links between them. Both the United States and Britain corresponded more with India than with any other country (except for each other) during the war,[107] while "Mao cultivated the Indians by singling out Ambassador Panikkar for special treatment among the diplomatic corps in Beijing."[108] Furthermore, the informal "Arab-Asian bloc" at the UN that was "headed by India" also played an important role during the deliberations on the Korean War.[109]

India's ability to play this role was the result of its nonaligned credentials that gave Nehru the opportunity to pursue his Asianist agenda. During the war, Nehru even championed for the PRC (instead of the Republic of China on Taiwan) to be given the Chinese seat at the UN to lessen Chinese insecurity even though this irritated the United States for it would have been tantamount to rewarding Beijing's aggression. In fact, in August 1950, the United States had offered to unseat China as a permanent member of the UNSC and giving that seat to India instead.[110] India rejected the American offer as it would have destroyed Nehru's Asianist vision. Nevertheless, the fact that such an offer was made demonstrates that India was regarded highly in Asian affairs then although both China and the United States were at times unhappy with India's positions when they seemed to favor the other side.

India's most significant contribution during the Korean War had to do with the finding of a solution to the issue of the repatriation of prisoners of war (POWs), which paved the way for the Armistice Agreement of July 1953. It was the Indian idea of "nonforcible" repatriation that was to be carried out by "neutral" states acceptable to all parties that made this possible.[111] Thereafter, India's General K. S. Thimayya was appointed the chairman of the Neutral Nations Repatriation Commission, and Major

---

[107] Robert Barnes, "Between the Blocs: India, the United Nations, and Ending the Korean War," *The Journal of Korean Studies* 18.2 (2013): 263.

[108] William Stueck, *The Korean War: An International History* (Princeton: Princeton University Press, 1995), 52.

[109] Lüthi, *Cold Wars*, 273–275.

[110] It remains unclear how this offer was to be realized in practice. See Anton Harder, "Not at the Cost of China: New Evidence Regarding US Proposals to Nehru for Joining the United Nations Security Council," Cold War International History Project, Working Paper #76, Woodrow Wilson International Center for Scholars, March 2015, www.wilsoncenter.org/publication/not-the-cost-china-india-and-the-united-nations-security-council-1950.

[111] Charles Heimsath and Surjit Mansingh, *A Diplomatic History of Modern India* (Bombay: Allied, 1971), 71.

General S. P. P. Thorat led 6,000 Indian troops and administrative personnel in the Custodian Force that landed in South Korea to implement the exchange of POWs, 23,000 of whom did not wish to be repatriated (mostly to the PRC and North Korea).[112]

Later, it was "Indian mediation" through which China and the United States "eventually agreed to meet in informal ambassadorial talks in Geneva" in 1954 on Indochina "although Washington continued to refuse to recognize Beijing."[113] While India was not formally included in the 1954 Geneva Conference, it was Menon's "informal discussions at Geneva" that "helped to bring about an agreed formula" for armistice in Vietnam and influenced "discussions on the composition of the neutral nations commission."[114] Notably, all three Neutral Nations Supervisory Commissions for the three Indochinese states were headed by Indian chairmen.[115] By the end of 1954, India was being touted as "the official interpreter of the West to Communist China," just like India had until then "held the role of the interpreter of Red China to the West."[116]

Strategic Competition for Influence in Asian Countries

The Himalayan States – Nepal, Bhutan, and Sikkim

The Sino-Indian rivalry in the Himalayas centered on the Chinese challenge to the Indian quest for regional primacy. In continuation of the British Indian approach toward these states, independent India signed treaties with all three in 1949 and 1950 as New Delhi sought to shape and guide their foreign policies. Soon after the Chinese invasion of eastern Tibet in October 1950, Nehru informed the Indian Parliament that even as India "appreciate[d] the independence of Nepal," it "consider[ed] the Himalayan mountains [at northern edge of Nepal along the Tibet-Nepal frontier] as our [India's] border" from the perspective of defense and foreign affairs.[117] This statement was made though Nehru understood that "independence" was "fundamentally and basically" about "foreign

[112] Kim ChanWahn, "The Role of India in the Korean War," *International Area Studies Review* 13.2 (2010): 21–37.
[113] Lüthi, *Cold Wars*, 126.
[114] Frankel, *When Nehru Looked East*, 206, 211.
[115] D. R. SarDesai, *Indian Foreign Policy in Cambodia, Laos, and Vietnam, 1947–1964* (Berkeley: University of California Press, 1968).
[116] Robert Trumbull, "Nehru Said to Sway Peiping toward Moderate Policies," *The New York Times*, October 31, 1954.
[117] Nehru's statement reported in the Indian daily *The Hindu* on December 7, 1950, and quoted in Levi, *Free India in Asia*, 108.

relations," because that was "the test of independence" since "[a]ll else was local autonomy."[118]

Tibet had sought Nepal's help after the Chinese invasion in 1950, and Nepal had referred the request to India.[119] Nepal's relations with Tibet were governed by the 1856 Treaty of Thapathali, which was signed in the aftermath of the 1854–56 Nepalese invasion of Tibet. As per the treaty, Tibet had agreed to pay Nepal an annual tribute of Rs. 10,000. This agreement was negotiated "with the Chinese resident in Lhasa,"[120] and it was a massive setback for the Qing Empire because the treaty had put the Nepalese and Qing monarchs "on a level of equality" in Tibet.[121] A Nepalese agent was then stationed in Lhasa, who continued there even after the collapse of the Qing.

The PRC was concerned about the possibility of Nepalese military intervention in Tibet in 1950–51. In his conversation with the Soviet ambassador, the CCP secretary Liu Shaoqi noted that while the PLA was not worried about Tibet itself, Nepal was a different issue because it was "a country with a warlike [*voinstvennyi*] population of five million that serves in the Indian and other armies."[122] It was well known that the Nepalese (including the Gurkhas) were recruited into the Indian army (even after independence). In fact, China had reached out to India requesting New Delhi to "use their good offices and prevent Nepalese troops from entering on such an adventure."[123]

While Nepal had no such plans for military intervention, it was not keen to give up its interests in Tibet. Notably, Tibet continued to pay tribute to Nepal until 1952 – a year after the signing of the Seventeen Point Agreement between Tibet and China (which formalized Tibet's incorporation into the PRC).[124] Although the possibility of a Nepalese military challenge to China

---

[118] "Emergence of India in World Affairs," March 8, 1949, in Nehru, *Independence and After*, 237.
[119] Leo E. Rose, *Nepal: Strategy for Survival* (Berkeley: University of California Press, 1971), 188. Tibet had also reached out to India directly.
[120] Bertil Lintner, *China's India War: Collision Course on the Roof of the World* (New Delhi: Oxford University Press, 2018), 240.
[121] Joseph Fletcher, "The Heyday of the Ch'ing Order in Mongolia, Sinkiang, and Tibet," in John Fairbank (ed.), *The Cambridge History of China, Volume 10, Late Ch'ing, 1800–1911*, Part 1 (New York: Cambridge University Press, 1995), 406.
[122] "Memorandum of Conversation, Soviet Ambassador N. V. Roshchin with CC CCP Secretary Liu Shaoqi," May 6, 1951, History and Public Policy Program Digital Archive, AVP RF f. 0100, op. 44, por. 13, pap. 322, ll. 17–22. Translated by David Wolff, https://digitalarchive.wilsoncenter.org/document/118734.
[123] Top Secret Telegram from the Indian Embassy in Peking, August 22, 1950, in Bhasin, *India-China Relations, Vol-I*, 325.
[124] Rose, *Nepal*, 204.

had passed, the PRC was irked because it had to go via India to reach out to another country in Asia in order to settle what it regarded as a domestic Chinese issue. Since this was symbolic of India's centrality in Asian affairs, the PRC was keen to establish direct diplomatic links with Nepal. Formal links were established in 1955, and a year later China and Nepal signed a new treaty through which Nepal abrogated the 1856 treaty and withdrew its military escorts from Tibet and ended all old privileges.[125] However, China remained cautious for now as Nehru had told Zhou in 1954 that Nepal's "foreign policy must be coordinated with ours [India's]."[126]

Unlike Nepal, China was not able to establish formal diplomatic links with Bhutan and Sikkim in the 1950s.[127] Even though Bhutan did not have diplomatic links with the PRC, a Bhutanese agent remained in Lhasa (until the 1959 Lhasa Revolt) in line with Bhutan–Tibet relations that went back to the seventeenth century.[128] The PLA's entry into Tibet had perturbed Bhutan and Sikkim more than Nepal because of their closer ethnocultural links and the vague claims made by Chinese leaders over these countries. After the 1959 Lhasa Revolt against the Chinese government, the PLA annexed eight Bhutanese enclaves in Tibet that had been maintained by Bhutanese since the seventeenth century and made territorial claims upon Bhutanese territory.[129] These issues are discussed in Chapter 4.

Southeast Asia

India and China also vigorously competed for strategic influence in Southeast Asia, especially in Burma and Indochina. In the months after the Conference on Burma, Nehru had rejected Burma's 1950 request for a "defence pact" between India, Burma, Sri Lanka, and Pakistan because of his dislike for "military blocs" even as he noted that it was "true" that there was "a potential and perhaps even an even actual menace to Burma and to some other countries" from China.[130] In recognition of such a putative threat, "the Indian government in early May 1952 publicly warned the PRC that any 'aggression in Burma, Siam, [Thailand] or Malaya [Malaysia]

---

[125] Rose, *Nepal*, 210–211.
[126] "Minutes of the talks between Prime Minister Jawaharlal Nehru and Chinese Premier Chou En-lai on Situation in South East Asia," Peking, October 21, 1954, in Bhasin, *India-China Relations, Vol-II*, 1343.
[127] China still does not have formal links with Bhutan, and Sikkim was absorbed by India in 1975.
[128] Therry Mathou, "Bhutan-China Relations: Towards a New Step in Himalayan Politics," in Karma Ura and Sonam Kinga (eds.), *The Spider and the Piglet: Proceedings of the First International Seminar on Bhutan Studies* (Thimphu: The Centre for Bhutan Studies, 2004), 390.
[129] Leo E. Rose, *The Politics of Bhutan* (Ithaca: Cornell University Press, 1977), 80.
[130] "To Thakin Nu," January 7, 1950, *SWJN, Series 2, Volume 14*, Part 1, 505–506.

would be treated as warlike,' and promised military support" for these three states.[131] This was repeated in May 1954 when Nehru "guaranteed" military support to Burma "in case of communist aggression" and "even informed Beijing about the pledge," while considering "similar promises to Thailand, Cambodia, and Laos."[132]

During his October 1954 visit to China, Nehru spoke to Zhou about Southeast Asia in terms that sounded like the delineation of spheres of influence. He noted:

> [A]mong all these South East Asian countries there is influence of India and China both. Hence, for example, the name Indo-China. In islands like Indonesia influence of India is greater while on the mainland, the Chinese influence is greater. Culturally Cambodia is more Indian.[133]

India's interest in the Indochinese issue was evident in Geneva. Notably, the United States was even willing to support Indian leadership in Cambodia – to counter Chinese influence – and expressed its desire to channel its economic and military aid to Cambodia via India after the Bandung Conference.[134] However, given Nehru's Asianist vision and his opposition to SEATO, India refused.

India also signed air, naval, and army agreements with Indonesia in 1955, 1958, and 1960 respectively (after having initiated training for Indonesian military officers in India in 1951). These agreements "provided" for the "attachment" of officers with the respective service of the other country, while excluding "activities in the operational fields."[135] In the case of Malaya, India had given its "public approval" to the 1957 Malay–British mutual defense treaty (although New Delhi had vigorously opposed SEATO and other military pacts),[136] thereby further fueling Chinese suspicions of Indo-British collusion. Later, at the request of the Malayan government in 1959, India sent Major General Ibrahim Habibullah to Malaya as the deputy commanding officer of the Malayan army for a year.[137]

[131] Lorenz M. Lüthi, "India's Relations with China, 1945–74," in Amit R. Das Gupta and Lorenz M. Lüthi (eds.), *The Sino-Indian War of 1962: New Perspectives* (London: Routledge, 2017), 31.
[132] Lüthi, *Cold Wars*, 168.
[133] "Minutes of the Talks between Prime Minister Jawaharlal Nehru and Chinese Premier Chou En-lai on Situation in South East Asia," 1337. In his translation of the Chinese notes, Khan quotes Nehru's last sentence as follows: "In Indochina, Laos and Cambodia have been more influenced by India than has Vietnam." See Sulmaan Wasif Khan, "Cold War Co-operation: New Chinese Evidence on Jawaharlal Nehru's 1954 Visit to Beijing," *Cold War History* 11.2 (2011): 215.
[134] Frankel, *When Nehru Looked East*, 225.
[135] Ton That, *India and South East Asia*, 110–111.
[136] Ton That, *India and South East Asia*, 243.
[137] Veena Sikri, *India and Malaysia: Intertwined Strands* (New Delhi: Manohar, 2013), 388.

Not surprisingly, the PRC responded in its own way, especially after 1955, to diminish India's influence in Southeast Asia while promoting its own. While Cambodia initially looked to India for support after Bandung as its traditional rivals Thailand and South Vietnam turned toward the United States, India was unable to understand Cambodian concerns (and provided only rhetorical support). Meanwhile, China's economic aid to Cambodia in 1956 equaled India's total aid to all of Southeast Asia during 1950–57 (although this does not include the cancelation of the Indian debt owed by Burma).[138] After Bandung, China also supported Cambodia's neutrality as Beijing followed "a nonideological approach" in favor of the Cambodian monarchy instead of engaging Cambodia's Communists.[139] Consequently, Cambodia tilted toward China instead of India by the late 1950s.

After 1959, India's relations with Indonesia became lukewarm as Nehru was not interested in supporting a sequel to the Bandung Conference as relations between India and China began deteriorating. By contrast, Indonesia viewed China as "an anti-imperialist progressive power" while being "dismayed by India's persistence in clinging to the British-made frontiers and refusing to understand Peking's point."[140] Unlike China, India was unwilling to support Indonesia on the West Irian issue, and New Delhi also favored the creation of the Malaysian state in 1961 though Indonesia and China opposed it.[141] However, as explained in Chapter 4, the locus of the Sino-Indian rivalry in Southeast Asia had shifted to Burma in the aftermath of the 1959 Lhasa Revolt.

Tibet

Tibet is linked to both the positional and spatial dimensions of the Sino-Indian rivalry. Soon after India's independence, the Tibetan government sent a note to Nehru "regarding the return of Tibetan territories … such as:- Zayul and Walung, and in the direction of Pema Koe, Lonag, Men, Bhutan, Sikkim, Darjeeling and others on this side of river Ganges, and Lowo, Ladhak etc. up to the boundary of Yarkhim."[142] The status of some of these territories was linked with the 1913–14 Simla Agreement between

---

[138] Ton That, *India and Southeast Asia*, 301–305.
[139] Sophie Richardson, *China, Cambodia, and the Five Principles of Peaceful Coexistence* (New York: Columbia University Press, 2009), 27.
[140] L. P. Singh, "Dynamics of Indian-Indonesian Relations," *Asian Survey* 7.9 (1967): 657.
[141] Wang Gungwu, *China and the World since 1949: The Impact of Independence, Modernity and Revolution* (London: Macmillan, 1977), 81.
[142] Secret note of October 16, 1947, in Bhasin, *India-China Relations, Vol-I*, 47.

British India and Tibet (while the historical links between Bhutan and Sikkim, on the one hand, and Tibet, on the other, are separate matters altogether).[143] China had also participated in these talks, and one of the agreements at Simla had divided Tibet into two regions: an "outer" region under the government of the Dalai Lama where China had nominal authority but where British India was also allowed extraterritorial rights, including the stationing of a small contingent of troops, and an "inner" Tibet that was incorporated into China proper.[144]

Not surprisingly the Tibetan government also sent a letter to Mao after the proclamation of the PRC that explicitly stated that Tibet was an "Independent Country" and also sought "assurance that no Chinese troops would cross the Tibetan frontier from the Sino-Tibetan border," while requesting "negotiations" for "those Tibetan territories [in "inner" Tibet] annexed as part of Chinese territories some years back."[145] While Mao did not respond to this note, the PLA invaded eastern Tibet in October 1950,[146] and it incorporated Tibet into China in May 1951 after signing the Seventeen Point Agreement with the representatives of the Dalai Lama's government.[147]

Importantly, India was the only country that officially complained about China's military actions and exchanged notes with the PRC on this issue.[148] In the notes, India had explicitly referred to China's "invasion" of Tibet, whereas China had complained that India had been "affected by foreign influences hostile to China," perhaps in a reference to Britain. As noted earlier, India had earlier retained the services of Richardson in Tibet and in these notes had hoped that India's "rights" that had "grown out of usage and agreements" will be maintained. But Nehru was surprised because while India had expected "a demand" from China for the "withdrawal of

---

[143] See Guyot-Réchard, *Shadow States*; and Kyle J. Gardner, *The Frontier Complex: Geopolitics and the Making of the India-China Border, 1846–1962* (Cambridge: Cambridge University Press, 2021).

[144] For the full analysis of the three different agreements that were signed in Simla, see Goldstein, *A History of Modern Tibet, Volume 1*, 192–197.

[145] For the full text of this letter dated November 2, 1949, see Goldstein, *A History of Modern Tibet, Volume 1*, 624.

[146] Chen Jian, "The Chinese Communist 'Liberation' of Tibet, 1949–51," in Jeremy Brown and Paul G. Pickowicz (eds.), *Dilemmas of Victory: The Early Years of the People's Republic of China* (Cambridge, MA: Harvard University Press, 2007), 130–159.

[147] Tsering Shakya, "The Genesis of the 17 Point Agreement: An Analysis of the Sino-Tibetan Agreement of 1951," in Per Kvaerne (ed.), *Tibetan Studies: Proceedings of the Papers Presented at the 6th Seminar of the International Association for Tibetan Studies* (Oslo: The Institute of Comparative Research in Human Culture, 1994), 754–793.

[148] For the full-text of these notes of late 1950, including the Chinese response, see *Tibet, 1950–1967* (Hong Kong: Union Research Institute, 1968), 10–18.

these agents" and the "military escort," the "fact that they have not done so has some significance."[149]

While Mao was silent on this issue in his correspondence with Nehru, he privately expressed anger because not only was India interfering in China's "internal affairs" but it also sought to "maintain its governmental delegation, commercial organs, post and telecommunication facilities, and troops stationed in Tibet."[150] In fact, the PLA had even seized arms and ammunition in Tibet in 1950–51 that had been supplied by India between 1947 and 1949.[151]

China did not complain to India about these issues because it needed India's help to consolidate its own rule in Tibet. Trade and physical infrastructure connected Tibet with India (as opposed to China) for reasons related to history and geography. The first two motor roads connecting China and Tibet – the Sichuan/Sikang–Tibet and the Qinghai–Tibet Highways – were inaugurated only in 1954.[152] In fact, Zhang Jingwu, Mao's representative to Tibet after the 1950 invasion went to Yadong/Yatung through the "quicker" route via India instead of going directly (overland) to Lhasa and then to Yadong as that route would have taken "months."[153]

Furthermore, there was the issue of feeding the 8,000 PLA troops who were now stationed in Lhasa (a city of some 30,000 inhabitants). Notably, China shipped food to Tibet in the early 1950s via Calcutta with the approval of the Indian government.[154] As for Tibet's foreign trade, 80 percent of Tibet's exports went to India in the late 1940s (with most of the remaining exports going to China).[155] Consequently, Mao was aware that it was imperative to "establish trade relations with India" to ensure Tibet's complete integration with China.[156]

Therefore, Mao consciously adopted a strategy "to reduce Nehru's fear."[157] The difficulties that the PLA was facing in Tibet – related to food

---

[149] "Note by the Prime Minister setting the Policy regarding China and Tibet, 18 November 1950," in Bhasin, *India-China Relations, Vol-I*, 458.

[150] "Cable from the Chinese Foreign Ministry, 'Report on Negotiations Regarding the Tibet Issue between China and India'," November 24, 1950, History and Public Policy Program Digital Archive, PRC FMA 105-00011-02, 42–44. Obtained by Dai Chaowu and translated by 7Brands, https://digitalarchive.wilsoncenter.org/document/114749.

[151] Melvyn C. Goldstein, *A History of Modern Tibet, Volume 2, 1951–1955* (Berkeley: University of California Press, 2007), 24.

[152] *Tibet, 1950–1967*, 54–55.

[153] Goldstein, *A History of Modern Tibet, Volume 2*, 109.

[154] Goldstein, *A History of Modern Tibet, Volume 2*, 244–264.

[155] Goldstein, *A History of Modern Tibet, Volume 1*, 571.

[156] "On the Policies for Our Work in Tibet," April 6, 1952, in *Selected Works of Mao Tse-tung, Volume 5* (Oxford: Pergamom Press, 1977), 74.

[157] Michael M. Sheng, "Mao, Tibet, and the Korean War," *Journal of Cold War Studies* 8.3 (2006): 27.

and physical infrastructure – led Nehru to believe that Chinese military presence in Tibet would remain small, thereby minimizing any military pressure on India. The fact that Mao was implicitly willing to accommodate Indian interests in Tibet was reassuring. India's chief goal in Tibet was the maintenance of Tibetan autonomy – with limited Chinese military presence – while maintaining some degree of India's political and economic influence there.

On the eve of his departure to China as the Indian ambassador, Panikkar had highlighted the strategic importance of Tibet for India by noting the following:

> [T]he essential point about the Himalayas ... is not their width of 150 miles, but the [Tibetan] plateau behind it, which in itself is an elevation of about 15,000 feet and is guarded on all four sides by high mountains. ... No centre of dynamic power can be created anywhere near the ranges. ... *It is essentially a defense in depth* in the largest sense. ... [This] will give to the Indian peninsula sufficient area for the development of her defence potential free from interference.[158]

In other words, India's ability to develop its defense resources to project its power in the rest of Asia – with India at its center as noted earlier – required the absence of a "dynamic power" in Tibet. For Nehru and Panikkar, this did not require the independence of Tibet if both Chinese and Indian interests were accommodated there. However, while India's ability to function as the center of Asia depended on Tibet's autonomy, China felt that Tibet had to be "liberated" from foreign influences for the era of Chinese "national humiliation" to end. Therefore, in addition to their *spatial rivalry*, Tibet also had implications for their *positional rivalry*.

Nevertheless, for the moment it seemed like India and China could work together even as Nehru and Mao were suspicious of the intentions of the other. The 1951 Seventeen Point Agreement had given Tibet considerable autonomy. Although the PLA's strength in Tibet increased to 20,000 troops, "the Dalai Lama's government was permitted to maintain important symbols from its de facto independence period – its own army, its own flag, and its own currency – as well as to continue to collect its own taxes."[159] Furthermore, trade between Tibet and India (as well as the Himalayan states) "was left in the hands of the Tibetans," for several reasons including the fact that "the PLA did not control the Tibetan borders,

---

[158] K. M. Panikkar, "The Himalayas and Indian Defence," *India Quarterly* 55.3/4 (1999 [1947]) 73–90. This article was originally published in the same journal in 1947.
[159] Goldstein, *A History of Modern Tibet, Volume 2*, 541.

and Beijing did not maintain custom services along the borders."[160] No other region of the PRC had been incorporated through such an agreement nor its "local" government allowed such autonomy.

Therefore, when the issue of the removal of India's British-era extraterritorial rights came up in the following years, India agreed. In April 1954, India signed a trade agreement with China – the Agreement on Trade and Intercourse between Tibet Region of China and India – that implicitly recognized Tibet as a part of the PRC and removed its military escorts.[161] This ended India's extraterritorial privileges in Tibet. While this was not a border agreement, Nehru believed that India's frontier had been "finalized not only by implication in this Agreement but the specific passes mentioned" were "direct recognitions" of India's frontiers with China.[162] The agreement was to remain in force for eight years and included the provisions for extension.

For Nehru, the political significance of this agreement was further raised because of the inclusion of Panchsheel or the Five Principles of Peaceful Coexistence into its preamble. These five principles – territorial integrity and sovereignty, nonaggression, noninterference in internal affairs, equality, and peaceful coexistence – were also seen as China's and India's response to America's SEATO.[163] In fact, Zhou had told Nehru that he wanted to "extend those principles to every country in Asia."[164] In the following years, Nepal, Cambodia, Laos, Burma, and others accepted Panchsheel. In other words, the 1954 Tibetan agreement had implications for the border territories and for larger Asian affairs as China and India jostled for influence.

Conclusion

The Sino-Indian positional rivalry for Asian leadership played out in three theaters: Asian multilateral fora, in the Himalayas and Southeast Asia, and in Tibet. While analytically distinct, they were interlinked. Developments related to Tibet had direct implications for the Himalayan states where India sought priority and tried to position itself as a go-between for China's

---

[160] Xiaoyuan Liu, *To the End of Revolution: The Chinese Communist Party and Tibet, 1949–1959* (New York: Columbia University Press, 2020), 323.
[161] The Agreement on Trade and Intercourse between Tibet Region of China and India, April 1954, in Bhasin, *India–China Relations, Vol-II*, 1097–1101.
[162] "Trade and Frontier with China," July 1, 1954, *SWJN*, Series 2, Volume 26, 482.
[163] Madan, *Fateful Triangle*, 61; and Frankel, *When Nehru Looked East*, 139.
[164] Quoted in Sulmaan Wasif Khan, *Muslim, Trader, Nomad, Spy: China's Cold War and the People of the Tibetan Borderlands* (Chapel Hill: University of North Carolina Press, 2015), 119.

relations with these states. While India and China seemed to be working together in Southeast Asia when it came to Bandung and Panchsheel, India wanted China to follow the Indian lead, an attitude that China (temporarily) encouraged.

In turn, Panchsheel was also included in the preamble to the 1954 Sino-Indian agreement on Tibetan trade and was extended by China to Nepal in the Himalayas. While India sought Tibetan autonomy and a modicum of Indian influence there, China viewed it as Indian interference in its domestic affairs even though it relied upon Tibetan–Indian trade to consolidate its own position there. China could end its national humiliation only if the regions lost to the imperial powers (including Tibet) were reintegrated with the Chinese state, whereas India could develop its power potential with relative ease and project it across Asia if Chinese military presence in Tibet – on India's northern frontiers – was limited.

Finally, the Sino-Indian territorial dispute was also linked to the Tibetan issue as the territories under contention had complex historical links with Tibet. These positional and spatial issues became entangled after the 1959 Lhasa Revolt, which led China and India down the path to war in 1962 as explained in Chapter 4. However, this prior history of the Sino-Indian positional contest is important simply because the "crucial and original insight" of the rivalry scholarship is that "war emerges from an underlying *relationship* between states," and therefore it is "theoretically" important "to study relations between [rival] states over time."[165] In other words, these positional issues along with China's perception of Anglo-American power lurking behind India mattered in the run-up to 1962 as "political leaders and adversarial states do not ignore their past interactions."[166]

---

[165] Sara McLaughlin Mitchell and John A. Vasquez, "What Do We Know about War?," in Sara McLaughlin Mitchell and John A. Vasquez (eds.), *What Do We Know about War?*, 3rd ed. (Lanham, MD: Rowman & Littlefield, 2021), 332. *Emphasis original.*

[166] Jack S. Levy and William R. Thompson, *Causes of War* (Malden: Wiley-Blackwell, 2010), 58.

CHAPTER 4

Positional Issues and the 1962 Sino-Indian War

On 19–20 October 1962, the Chinese People's Liberation Army (PLA) launched simultaneous attacks on Indian positions along both the eastern and the western sectors of the disputed Sino-Indian frontiers. A few weeks later, the PLA began a second offensive wave on 15–16 November 1962, which has been described as "the most significant show of force since the PLA had moved across the Yalu River into Korea in October 1950."[1] Indian forces were decisively defeated – twice – in these devastating blows within a month as the PLA reached the Chinese-claimed territories in both the sectors: "the upper Indus Valley, the strategic Kongka Pass, and the area down to Pangong Lake" in the west, and Tawang, Walong, Subansiri, and Siang in the east.[2]

As India's ill-prepared and underequipped forces quickly fell in the face of the massive Chinese onslaught, Beijing announced a unilateral ceasefire on November 21, 1962 (effective from November 22), while noting that the PLA would withdraw to positions twenty kilometers behind the line of actual control (as it existed on November 7, 1959) beginning on December 1, 1962.[3] The war altered the Sino-Indian territorial distribution in China's favor. Although China reestablished the prewar Sino-Indian frontier known as the McMahon Line in the eastern sector, the PLA "was clearly able to occupy whatever areas it wanted" in the western sector given its victory.[4]

---

[1] Paul M. McGarr, *The Cold War in South Asia: Britain, the United States and the Indian Subcontinent, 1945–1965* (Cambridge: Cambridge University Press, 2013), 167.

[2] Bertil Lintner, *China's India War: Collision Course on the Roof of the World* (New Delhi: Oxford University Press, 2018), xxv.

[3] "Statement given by the Chinese Government, 21 November 1962," in *Notes, Memoranda and Letters Exchanged between the Governments of India and China, October 1962–January 1963, White Paper No. VIII* (Delhi: Ministry of External Affairs, 1963), 19. The notes exchanged between China and India in the run-up to 1962 were published by the Indian government, and these volumes are hereafter referred to as *White Paper*.

[4] M. Taylor Fravel, *Strong Borders, Secure Nation: Cooperation and Conflict in China's Territorial Disputes* (Princeton: Princeton University Press, 2008), 197.

Even though China "did not withdraw" to the "*status quo ante bellum* control line in the Western sector," the "loss of territory for India was small,"[5] as large parts of this region had been under Chinese control since 1951.[6] The PLA had used this western route through Aksai Chin to consolidate Chinese rule over all of Tibet after the invasion of eastern Tibet in October 1950.[7]

According to Chinese sources, 4,885 Indian soldiers had been killed compared to only 722 Chinese soldiers.[8] As per Indian estimates, India suffered 2,616 "casualties" (war dead and seriously wounded), while the PLA was believed to have suffered "at least 1,000 casualties."[9] Furthermore, 3,968 Indian soldiers were captured by the Chinese whereas India captured no Chinese soldiers, "a rarity in the history of warfare."[10] Lüthi has recently described the first wave of the PLA attacks as "a pre-emptive strike against what the PRC [the People's Republic of China] perceived – wrongly – to be an impending Indian assault across the McMahon Line," while the second wave constituted "a punitive attack designed to destroy India's military infrastructure south of the disputed border."[11] While India was pursuing its so-called "Forward Policy" along the Sino-Indian frontier to consolidate its position in the no-man's-land between Indian and Chinese positions in Aksai Chin (and to politically dominate the PLA posts where it could), it had no war plans vis-à-vis China even though it expected localized military skirmishes at several points along the Sino-Indian frontier.[12]

Why did Sino-Indian hostilities escalate to war in 1962? Existing explanations in the academic literature tend to emphasize their territorial

---

[5] Steven A. Hoffmann, "Anticipation, Disaster, and Victory: India 1962–71," *Asian Survey* 12.11 (1972): 963.

[6] China "retain[ed] control to its 1960 claim-line" in this sector according to India. Srinath Raghavan, *War and Peace in Modern India: A Strategic History of the Nehru Years* (Ranikhet: Permanent Black, 2010), 308.

[7] Sulmaan Wasif Khan, *Muslim, Trader, Nomad, Spy: China's Cold War and the People of the Tibetan Borderlands* (Chapel Hill: University of North Carolina Press, 2015), 17.

[8] Fravel, *Strong Borders, Secure Nation*, 174.

[9] P. B. Sinha and A. A. Athale, *History of the Conflict with China, 1962* (New Delhi: History Division, Ministry of Defence, 1992), 378. This restricted report of the Indian government was leaked and is now available online: www.bharat-rakshak.com/ARMY/history/1962war/266-official-history.html.

[10] Larry M. Wortzel, "Concentrating Forces and Audacious Action: PLA Lessons from the Sino-Indian War," in Laurie Burkitt, Andrew Scobell, and Larry M. Wortzel (eds.), *The Lessons of History: The Chinese People's Liberation Army at 75* (Carlisle, PA: Strategic Studies Institute, U.S. Army War College, 2003), 343.

[11] Lorenz M. Lüthi, *Cold Wars: Asia, the Middle East, Europe* (Cambridge: Cambridge University Press, 2020), 172.

[12] Steven A. Hoffmann, *India and the China Crisis* (Delhi: Oxford University Press, 1990), 92–114.

dispute as the primary cause of war. Almost five decades ago, Maxwell blamed Indian belligerence, especially the Forward Policy, for the war.[13] More recently, Lintner challenged Maxwell's claims and argued that "Chinese preparations for the war obviously began long before October 1962 – and the November 1961 meeting where Nehru had outlined his Forward Policy."[14] Fravel referred to this war as a "border war" as it was a contest over disputed territory in his opinion.[15] Miller argued that it was China and India's collective trauma due to colonial victimhood that made them intransigent in their border negotiations that eventually culminated in the war.[16] For Shankar, it was reputational considerations associated with resolve, weakness, generosity, and the perception of being a bully that prevented China and India from successfully negotiating their territorial dispute.[17]

The territorial dimension is clearly central to most explanations of the Sino-Indian War. As such, the focus in scholarship has been on the decision-making process in China and India – with an emphasis on domestic politics and/or misperceptions – to explain the causes of this war.[18] It is well established in the literature that "domestic pressure to defend the borders drove India's assertive policies" while "internal developments in the PRC triggered China's decision to go to war."[19] India's assertive policy was the result of domestic pressure on the government of Jawaharlal Nehru from the Indian Parliament (and public opinion) as the Sino-Indian border dispute came to the fore (in the late 1950s, and especially after the Dalai Lama's escape to India). It was also an outcome of civil–military relations in India.[20] Likewise, Chinese assertiveness toward

---

[13] Neville Maxwell, *India's China War* (London: Jonathan Cape, 1970). This Maxwellian argument was also repeated in Xuecheng Liu, *The Sino-Indian Border Dispute and Sino-Indian Relations* (Lanham, MD: University Press of America, 1994), 17–46.

[14] Lintner, *China's India War*, xiii.

[15] Fravel, *Strong Borders, Secure Nation*, 174–197.

[16] Manjari Chatterjee Miller, *Wronged by Empire: Post-Imperial Ideology in India and China* (Stanford: Stanford University Press, 2013), 55–81.

[17] Mahesh Shankar, *The Reputational Imperative: Nehru's India in Territorial Conflict* (Stanford: Stanford University Press, 2022), 89–162.

[18] On the historiography of the war, see Lorenz M. Lüthi and Amit R. Das Gupta, "Introduction," in Amit R. Das Gupta and Lorenz M. Lüthi (eds.), *The Sino-Indian War of 1962: New Perspectives* (London: Routledge, 2017), 12–17.

[19] Lüthi, *Cold Wars*, 171.

[20] Hoffmann's study remains the most detailed account of the Indian decision-making process where he emphasizes its "normal" practices since they are also "found in governments elsewhere." Hoffmann, *India and the China Crisis*, 265. Also see, Nancy Jetly, *India China Relations, 1947–1977: A Study of Parliament's Role in the Making of Foreign Policy* (New Delhi: Radiant, 1979), 1–199; and Raghavan, *War and Peace in Modern India*, 227–310.

India was also rooted in the revolutionary fervor of Chinese domestic politics after the disastrous Great Leap Forward as Mao Zedong sought to reassert his leadership in China (and in the Communist world by challenging the Soviet Union).[21]

As for misperceptions, Vertzberger claimed that even though "Nehru was no fool," he "overestimated India's deterrent power, which contributed to a concept of threat that did not take a war into account and was insensitive to the other side's concept of threat."[22] On Chinese decision-making, Garver argued that "China's decision for war was based, to some degree, on misperceptions rather than on actual assessment of the situation."[23] Garver's account is noteworthy mainly because it goes beyond the issue of a territorial dispute. For Garver, not only was China concerned with Indian aggression along the frontier due to India's Forward Policy but Beijing also (erroneously) believed that India was seeking to undermine Chinese control in Tibet (by attempting to restore Tibet's pre-1950–51 status as a buffer between China and India).

With the partial exception of Garver, who focused on Sino-Indian *positional* issues related to Tibet in the analysis of the 1962 war, other scholars conceive the underlying cause as *spatial* rivalry over territory, although none employ the framework of "strategic rivalry" to explain this war. Furthermore, though Garver discussed the Tibetan factor specifically, he did not connect it to the larger Sino-Indian positional rivalry in Asia. Consequently, building on Garver's work and developing on Whiting's insight that "the political significance of the war far transcended the actual border issue,"[24] we argue that the 1962 Sino-Indian War was not only an outcome of *spatial rivalry* over disputed territory but also a result of the Sino-Indian *positional rivalry* for leadership in Asia (including Tibet). Notably, the outcome of the war also transformed their positional rivalry, as explained in this chapter (in addition to altering their territorial status quo).

[21] Roderick MacFarquhar, *The Origins of the Cultural Revolution, Volume 3: The Coming of the Cataclysm, 1961–1966* (New York: Columbia University Press, 1997), 297–323; and Niu Jun, "1962: The Eve of the Left Turn in China's Foreign Policy," Cold War International History Project, Working Paper No. 48, Woodrow Wilson International Center for Scholars, October 2005, www.wilsoncenter.org/publication/1962-the-eve-the-left-turn-chinas-foreign-policy.

[22] Yaacov Y. I. Vertzberger, *Misperceptions in Foreign Policymaking: The Sino-Indian Conflict, 1959–1962* (Boulder: Westview, 1984), 288, 297.

[23] John W. Garver, "China's Decision for War with India in 1962," in Alastair Iain Johnston and Robert S. Ross (eds.), *New Directions in the Study of China's Foreign Policy* (Stanford: Stanford University Press, 2006), 87.

[24] Allen S. Whiting, *The Chinese Calculus of Deterrence: India and Indochina* (Ann Arbor: University of Michigan Press, 1975), xii.

Recent scholarship has emphasized that the 1959 Lhasa Revolt, which the Chinese leadership blamed on India, was "*the* turning point" in Sino-Indian relations as it brought about "a fundamental change" in Chinese attitudes toward India.[25] As the PLA sought to bring Tibet under the control of the PRC again, China also looked at the Himalayan states and Burma (given their shared borders with India and Tibet). China was concerned about India's strategic interests in these South and Southeast Asian states. In late 1959, Nehru had publicly committed India to defending the Himalayan states, while also asserting that a Sino-Indian war would be "a struggle for life and death" that would "shake Asia and shake the world."[26]

Not surprisingly, the PLA had come to believe that, among other goals that India had in its border conflict with China, it also wanted to create "a Himalayan Union" and noted that India had "publicly declared" itself as the "guardian" of these countries.[27] China was also aware of Indian security guarantees for Burma, which were issued in 1952 and 1954 as noted in Chapter 3. Consequently, as explained here, China's military-diplomatic efforts after 1959 focused on transforming Nepal and Burma into buffer states between China and India. Indeed, Nepal and Burma remained neutral during the Sino-Indian war.

In mid-1959, Nehru had also publicly dismissed Panchsheel during his visit to Nepal because of the deteriorating Sino-Indian relationship.[28] Not only was Panchsheel included in the preamble to the 1954 Sino-Indian agreement on Tibetan trade but China also regarded these five principles as crucial to the settlement of its territorial disputes.[29] In addition to dismissing these principles, India also rejected the PRC's request – thrice between December 1961 and May 1962 – to extend the 1954 agreement.[30]

---

[25] Dai Chaowu, "From 'Hindi-Chini Bhai-Bhai' to 'International Class Struggle' against Nehru: China's India Policy and the Frontier Dispute, 1950–62," in Das Gupta and Lüthi, *The Sino-Indian War of 1962*, 75. *Emphasis added.*

[26] Quoted in Paul Grimes, "Nehru Promises to Defend Nepal; Wins House Vote," *The New York Times*, November 28, 1959.

[27] "Report from the PLA General Staff Department, 'Behind India's Second Anti-China Wave'," October 29, 1959, History and Public Policy Program Digital Archive, PRC FMA 105-00944-07, 84–90, translated by 7Brands, https://digitalarchive.wilsoncenter.org/document/114758.

[28] Leo E. Rose, *Nepal: Strategy for Survival* (Berkeley: University of California Press, 1971), 221.

[29] Eric Hyer, *The Pragmatic Dragon: China's Grand Strategy and Boundary Settlements* (Vancouver: UBC Press, 2015), 67.

[30] "Premier Chou En-Lai's [Zhou Enlai's] Letter to the Leaders of Asian and African Countries on the Sino-Indian Boundary Question (November 15, 1962)," November 15, 1962, History and Public Policy Program Digital Archive, Peking: Foreign Languages Press, 1973, https://digitalarchive.wilsoncenter.org/document/175946.

Consequently, the agreement on Tibetan trade lapsed in June 1962. In the mid-1950s, China and India had approached Panchsheel as the Asian response to America's Southeast Asian Treaty Organization (SEATO), as noted in Chapter 3. Not surprisingly, the PLA now believed that India was giving up on Panchsheel for reasons that included "flatter[ing] the US for aid" by becoming assertive against China.[31] It also believed that America wanted to promote India at the expense of China in Asia.[32]

In other words, not only was Sino-Indian spatial rivalry (border dispute) linked with the status of Tibet as noted by Garver but issues related to Tibet also had implications for Sino-Indian positional rivalry in the Himalayas, in Burma, and in Asia through issue linkage. Issue linkage implies that developments in one issue under contention will have implications on other issues under contention and that these links may be direct or indirect. "Implicit issue linkages do not mean that they are understated or secret, but rather, they must send a clear signal to the recipient in order to be effective."[33] The rivalry scholarship has shown that it is possible to miss "the forest for the trees" when multiple issues are involved in conflict-ridden dyads.[34] Therefore, this chapter demonstrates how *spatial* and *positional* issues were connected in the run-up to 1962. These links between *spatial* and *positional* issues were both implicit and explicit.

The remainder of this chapter is divided into four sections. The first section highlights the salience of positional issues and shows that China and India in fact understood the 1962 war as a *positional* war. The next section explains China's efforts in the Himalayas and in Burma to neutralize Indian influence as Beijing attempted to pacify Tibet and its frontiers. Tibet – with its spatial and positional dimensions – is the focus of the subsequent section. As India gave refuge to the Dalai Lama after 1959 and imposed an economic embargo on Tibet, Beijing believed not only that India had explicitly linked Tibet and the border (spatial) issue but that the positional issue of Asian leadership was also at stake since India wanted a sphere of influence in Asia (which included Tibet). The 1962 Sino-Indian War culminated out of these positional concerns that had

---

[31] "Report from the PLA General Staff Department."

[32] Xiaoyuan Liu, "Friend or Foe: India as Perceived by Beijing's Foreign Policy Analysts in the 1950s," *China Review* 15.1 (2015): 128. Also see, Tanvi Madan, *Fateful Triangle: How China Shaped U.S.-India Relations during the Cold War* (Washington, DC: Brookings, 2020), 85–148.

[33] Krista E. Wiegand, *Enduring Territorial Disputes: Strategies of Bargaining, Coercive Diplomacy, & Settlement* (Athens: The University of Georgia Press, 2011), 59.

[34] Susan G. Sample, "Arms Races," in Sara McLaughlin Mitchell and John A. Vasquez (eds.), *What Do We Know about War?*, 3rd ed. (Lanham, MD: Rowman & Littlefield, 2021), 71.

become intertwined with spatial issues (with Tibet serving as a complex and crucial link between them).

The chapter concludes by noting that the 1962 war also proceeded as wars between positional rivals tend to: with the near multilateralization of the war as India sought help from the United States and other Western powers (especially Britain) who had in fact started supporting India during the short war itself, and even considered expanding the scope of their participation.[35] While a much-larger conflagration was avoided because of China's unilateral ceasefire that India accepted, the war eliminated India's status as a major Asian power because of its massive defeat. The 1962 Sino-Indian War removed India as a contender for Asian leadership for the rest of the twentieth century even though it did not result in Chinese leadership in Asia.

Before proceeding, a brief note must be made of China's deep-rooted bitterness toward India. During his talks with the Soviet leader Nikita Khrushchev in 1959 (after the Dalai Lama's escape to India), the PRC foreign minister Chen Yi "hinted to him openly that the Chinese belligerence towards India was dictated by the desire to take revenge for the century of humiliation at the hands of European great powers."[36] During these talks, the Chinese premier Zhou Enlai also told Khrushchev that the "Hindus" (Indians) had "conducted large-scale anti-Chinese propaganda for 40 years until this provocation."[37]

It is unclear what Zhou meant by "40 years," although he may have been referring to the continuities between the approaches of British India and independent India toward Tibet (as it had then been forty-five years since the 1914 Simla Agreement). Earlier in 1958, a PLA general had even told the Indian general J. F. R. Jacob that "China would never forget that Indian troops took part in the sacking and looting of the summer Palace [in Beijing] during the 2nd Opium War [in 1860]," while also making

---

[35] Wars fought over positional issues are more likely to become multilateral through the war-joining efforts of others that have a stake in the said positional issues compared to wars fought only over disputed territory. Michael P. Colaresi, Karen Rasler, and William R. Thompson, *Strategic Rivalries in World Politics: Position, Space, and Conflict Escalation* (Cambridge: Cambridge University Press, 2007), 169.

[36] Vladislav M. Zubok, "The Mao-Khrushchev Conversations, 31 July–3 August 1958 and 2 October 1959," *Cold War International History Project Bulletin* Issue 12/13 (2001): 248.

[37] "Discussion between N. S. Khrushchev and Mao Zedong," October 2, 1959, History and Public Policy Program Digital Archive, Archive of the President of the Russian Federation (APRF), f. 52, op. 1, d. 499, II. 1–33, copy in Volkogonov Collection, Manuscript Division, Library of Congress, Washington, DC, translated by Vladislav M. Zubok, http://digitalarchive.wilsoncenter.org/document/112088.

"other contentious remarks."[38] Although there is no direct evidence that these historical factors played into the Chinese decision to attack India in 1962, both Chen and Zhou were included in the meetings led by Mao where this decision was taken.[39]

The Salience of Positional Issues, 1959–1962

It is possible for rivalries involving both spatial and positional issues to be largely about position.[40] Until at least as late as 1959 – after the clashes at Longju (in August 1959) and Kongka (in October 1959) – Nehru believed that the disputed territories between China and India were not worth fighting over. While addressing the Indian Parliament, he observed that although India and China were facing each other angrily on an armed border, the two countries were going to be neighbors "for hundreds and hundreds of years" as neither was going to "walk out of Asia." Consequently, he urged his fellow parliamentarians to look at the issue from this larger perspective instead of the "petty, quibbling point of view of a little area being here or there."[41] Notably, Nehru had made this point after the full extent of the Sino-Indian territorial dispute had become clear to him (in the notes exchanged between Zhou and him in September 1959).[42]

Similarly, in October 1959, Mao had told Khrushchev that the "border conflict with India" was "only a marginal border issue" and that "the McMahon line with India will be maintained, and the border conflict with India will end."[43] A few weeks later he told the Soviet ambassador that the border dispute with India was "an argument over inconsequential pieces of territory."[44] In fact, even as late as January 10, 1962, the Indian defense

---

[38] Lt. Gen. J. F. R. Jacob, *An Odyssey in War and Peace: An Autobiography* (New Delhi: Roli, 2011), 45. While the name of the Chinese general is not mentioned here, he was very likely Marshal Ye Jianying, a founder of the PLA, who had visited India in 1958.

[39] Garver, "China's Decision for War with India in 1962," 121.

[40] Colaresi, Rasler, and Thompson, *Strategic Rivalries in World Politics*, 80, 172.

[41] "In the Rajya Sabha: India-China Relations," December 9, 1959, *Selected Works of Jawaharlal Nehru, Series 2, Volume 55 (1–31 December 1959)* (New Delhi: Jawaharlal Nehru Memorial Fund, 2014), 305. This series is hereafter referred to as *SWJN*.

[42] For the full text of Zhou's note and Nehru's reply to him, see *White Paper, September–November 1959*, 27–46.

[43] "Discussion between N. S. Khrushchev and Mao Zedong."

[44] "From the Journal of Ambassador S. F. Antonov, Summary of a Conversation with the Chairman of the CC CPC Mao Zedong," October 14, 1959, History and Public Policy Program Digital Archive, SCCD, Fond 5, Opis 49, Delo 235, Listy 89–96, translated by Mark H. Doctoroff, https://digitalarchive.wilsoncenter.org/document/114788.

minister Krishna Menon declared that the Sino-Indian "border dispute was not of such magnitude as could precipitate a war."[45]

The above statements are not meant to imply that the Sino-Indian spatial rivalry did not matter in the run-up to the war as it most certainly did (and is well attested in the scholarship, as noted above). Instead, the argument is that spatial issues may have precipitated the war even as the larger issue of position related to Asian leadership was at stake. More specifically, we argue that it was the process of rivalry itself, especially its positional dimension, that caused the war in 1962. Since rivalry is a process (as opposed to an event) past interactions matter. Furthermore, issue linkage – or the interaction of spatial and positional issues – only increases the propensity of conflict as it did in the Sino-Indian dyad after the late 1950s.

For China, "the crux of the border issue was the Tibetan question."[46] But Tibet itself was connected with larger Asian issues in the Sino-Indian relationship. According to the historian Wang Gungwu, "[o]f greater long-term interest was whether the Sino-Indian troubles of 1959–62 affected China's image as a potential leader of the colonial and anti-imperialist countries in Asia and Africa."[47] In his explanation of Nehru's motives for "insisting" upon a military confrontation with China, Wang Hongwei, one of the leading Chinese scholars of Sino-Indian relations, had argued that as the world's "third power" Nehru's India was hoping for an Asian order with "India as its center," before adding the following:

> He [Nehru] still hoped that China would join in the Asian community centering on India and the whole Asia speak [*sic*] with one voice. Without China's participation and support, he knew, India would not become "a country with power and grandeur" and be on an equal footing with the USA and Soviet Union.[48]

Similarly, the Chinese leader Liu Shaoqi, the chairman of the PRC (who had participated in the meetings with Mao where the final decision to attack India was taken), had argued that "one chief purpose of their [China's] military campaign had been to demolish India's 'arrogance' and 'illusions of grandeur'" and that China "'had taught India a lesson and, if necessary …

---

[45] Quoted in D. R. Mankekar, *The Guilty Men of 1962* (Bombay: Tulsi Shah Enterprises, 1968), 126.

[46] Xiaoyuan Liu, *To the End of Revolution: The Chinese Communist Party and Tibet, 1949–1959* (New York: Columbia University Press, 2020), 410.

[47] Wang Gungwu, *China and the World since 1949: The Impact of Independence, Modernity and Revolution* (London: Macmillan, 1977), 74.

[48] Wang Hongwei (translated by Chen Guansheng and Li Peizhu), *A Critical Review of Contemporary Sino-Indian Relations* (Beijing: China Tibetology Publishing House, 2011), 309–310.

would teach her a lesson again and again'."[49] This vision of Asia with India at its "centre" that China viewed as India's inheritance of British imperialism was "naturally repugnant" to Beijing according to Wolters because it was believed that China had been the traditional dominant power in Southeast Asia prior to "the intruding European imperialists."[50]

It is noteworthy that just days after the first wave of the Chinese attacks the *New York Times* noted that the Sino-Indian War was a Chinese "challenge" to India "for political leadership in Asia."[51] On the eve of the war, Nehru understood that the PRC government believed that India was "encouraging" the "rebellion" in Tibet despite India's recognition of China's "special position" in Tibet.[52] During the war itself, India perceived the Chinese invasion to be akin to eighteenth- and nineteenth-century-style "imperialism," which marked "a turning point" in "the history of India and Asia and possibly even of the world."[53] At the same Nehru believed that India had become China's "enemy No. 1" because the Chinese came to view the Indians as "the stooges of America, ... [because America was China's] chief *bete noire*, their chief enemy."[54] In the immediate aftermath of China's unilateral ceasefire, Nehru argued that the war was motivated not only by China's desire "to expand ... territories" but also by its intention that India had to be "humiliated and defeated ... into mental surrender" so that China could "become much stronger in Asia."[55]

China also officially justified the war after the start of the first wave of PLA assaults by noting that India perceived itself to be at the "centre of Asia" and was seeking a "sphere of influence" in Asia that included "China's Tibet."[56] In fact, the *Renmin Ribao* editorial specifically included

[49] Liu's conversations with Sri Lanka's Felix Bandaranaike as narrated to Nehru's official biographer in 1981 by the Sri Lankan leader. Sarvepalli Gopal, *Jawaharlal Nehru: A Biography, Volume Three: 1956–1964* (London: Jonathan Cape, 1984), 230.

[50] O. W. Wolters (edited by Craig J. Reynolds), *Early Southeast Asia: Selected Essays* (Ithaca: Cornell University Press, 2008), 74.

[51] Robert Trumbull, "Behind India-China Dispute: Leadership of Asia," *The New York Times*, October 28, 1962.

[52] Press Conference in Colombo, October 15, 1962, in *Prime Minister on Chinese Aggression* (New Delhi: Ministry of External Affairs, n.d.), 8.

[53] In the Lower House of the Indian Parliament, November 8, 1962, in *Prime Minister on Chinese Aggression*, 40, 45.

[54] In the Upper House of the Indian Parliament, November 9, 1962, in *Prime Minister on Chinese Aggression*, 54–55.

[55] Nehru's letter dated December 22, 1962, in G Parthasarathi (ed.), *Jawaharlal Nehru: Letters to Chief Ministers, 1947–1964, Volume 5: 1958–1964* (New Delhi: Oxford University Press, 1989), 547–551.

[56] "More on Nehru's Philosophy in the Light of the Sino-Indian Boundary Question," by the Editorial Department of "Renmin Ribao," October 27, 1962, in *The Sino-Indian Boundary Question*, enlarged edition (Peking: Foreign Languages Press, 1962), 96–98.

an excerpt from one of Nehru's books, *The Discovery of India* (which was first published in 1946 in English followed by a Chinese translation in the PRC in 1956), in which he had expressed his pan-Asian ambitions with India at its "centre," to justify the Chinese position.[57] The editorial also cited the Canadian political scientist Michael Brecher's biography of Nehru (published in London in 1959) in which Nehru was quoted as saying that he "was perhaps more an Englishman than an Indian" in his likes and dislikes.[58] It was also noted that American imperialism was taking over "British imperialism's monopoly position in India."[59]

The *Renmin Ribao* editorial then went on to discuss the resolution of China's border disputes with Burma and Nepal and even stated that Nehru had "mounted a series of attacks on China on much broader terms than the boundary question; he also tried in the most despicable and sinister way to sow dissension between China and other countries."[60] It was also noted that India was the "the only country in Asia" with a "protectorate" (perhaps in a reference to the Himalayan states).[61] In other words, positional concerns were deeply implicated in this "border dispute," and both China and India perceived the war in such terms.

The Himalayan States and Burma

Many scholars have argued that China resolved its border disputes with Burma and Nepal after 1959 in order to put pressure on India to resolve its border dispute with China.[62] While some also note other Chinese considerations in resolving these disputes, including those related to Tibet and the United States, they ignore *positional* concerns regarding India. In the case of Nepal, Nehru had publicly committed India to defend Nepal in the event of military aggression in 1959, as noted earlier. In fact, it was

---

[57] Nehru's thinking on India's "centrality" in Asia was discussed in Chapter 3. The specific quote in the editorial includes the following extract (on page 96): "Though not directly a Pacific state, India will inevitably exercise an important influence there. India will also develop as the centre of economic and political activity in the Indian Ocean area, in southeast Asia and right up to the Middle East." Also see Jawaharlal Nehru, *The Discovery of India*, centenary edition (Delhi: Oxford University Press, 1989 [1946]), 536. Nehru's book was translated into Chinese by Qi Wen.

[58] "More on Nehru's Philosophy in the Light of the Sino-Indian Boundary Question," 97. Also see Michael Brecher, *Nehru: A Political Biography* (London: Oxford University Press, 1959), 50.

[59] "More on Nehru's Philosophy in the Light of the Sino-Indian Boundary Question," 112.

[60] "More on Nehru's Philosophy in the Light of the Sino-Indian Boundary Question," 103.

[61] "More on Nehru's Philosophy in the Light of the Sino-Indian Boundary Question," 97.

[62] Wang, *China and the World since 1949*, 73; Fravel, *Strong Border, Secure Nation*, 88, 92; Hyer, *The Pragmatic Dragon*, 67–105; and Bérénice Guyot-Réchard, *Shadow States: India, China and the Himalayas, 1910–1962* (Cambridge: Cambridge University Press, 2017), 218.

made public in 1959 that India and Nepal "shall consult with each other *and devise effective countermeasures*" if either side was threatened "by a foreign aggressor."[63] The strategic significance of this understanding implied Nepal's potential involvement in a Sino-Indian war.

This was not just a theoretical possibility given the 1950 treaty between India and Nepal and the close links between their armies (discussed in Chapter 3). Of equal salience was the fact that the passage via the Kuti Pass (in Tibet) into Nepal is "second only" to the Chumbi Valley (also in Tibet but sandwiched between Sikkim and Bhutan) as an invasion route between the Tibetan plateau and the Indian subcontinent.[64] A small contingent of Indian military personnel had been deployed in Nepal "in the northern border posts on the access routes between Nepal and Tibet" from 1952 to 1958, while a few were "retained as advisors at staff Headquarters" after 1958.[65] Furthermore, the Indian Army had already completed the Tribhuvan Highway connecting Kathmandu with Raxaul on the Indian border by 1956.[66]

In the aftermath of the 1959 Lhasa Rebellion, many Tibetans (especially those from the historic Kham region) followed the Dalai Lama into India and Nepal. More specifically, members of the so-called Chushi Gangdrug Army (CDA) leading the Tibetan resistance against the PRC (as discussed in the next section) had set up a base in Mustang in Nepal in liaison with the American Central Intelligence Agency (CIA) and with the knowledge of the Nepalese government.[67] India was complicit in these activities. Reports on armed Tibetans in Mustang being "aided by Indians" was "forwarded to military commanders in Xinjiang and Tibet by Chinese intelligence."[68] As explained subsequently, New Delhi was also working with the "revitalized" CDA in India.[69]

The fact that Mustang lay south of the Xinjiang–Tibet Highway that passed via the disputed Aksai Chin region made the situation more complex (as the PLA also had to worry about Mustang and its Indian and

[63] Rose, *Nepal*, 186. Text from the Indo-Nepalese treaty with *emphasis added* by Rose.

[64] John W. Garver, *Protracted Contest: Sino-Indian Rivalry in the Twentieth Century* (Seattle: University of Washington Press, 2001), 147.

[65] Rose, *Nepal*, 197, 218.

[66] Mahnaz Z. Ispahani, *Roads and Rivals: The Political Uses of Access in the Borderlands of Asia* (Ithaca: Cornell University Press, 1989), 177.

[67] John Kenneth Knaus, *Orphans of the Cold War: America and the Tibetan Struggle for Survival* (New York: PublicAffairs, 1999), 236–254.

[68] Khan, *Muslim, Trader, Nomad, Spy*, 80–81.

[69] Carole McGranahan, "Tibet's Cold War: The CIA and the Chushi Gangdrug Resistance, 1956–1974," *Journal of Cold War Studies* 8.3 (2006): 123.

American connections when it came to guarding this highway).[70] In fact, this connected the territorial dispute between China and India with other concerns, including the Sino-Indian *positional* rivalry in Nepal. Therefore, when Chinese and Nepalese troops briefly clashed in June 1960 in Mustang as the PLA pursued the Tibetans, Zhou issued a prompt apology to Nepal, and China also paid a small financial compensation for the incident.[71]

China had already resolved its border dispute with Nepal prior to this incident, in March 1960, on terms that were favorable to Nepal.[72] Nepal also allowed the PLA to conduct a secret military operation against Tibetan rebels inside Nepalese territory sometime in 1960, even as "Indian intelligence assets within Nepal" became aware of it.[73] Nepal's dependence on India had generated domestic resentment, and Kathmandu was trying to "transform" Nepal's "special relationship with India into a triangle involving China."[74] China and India were already competing in Nepal through their economic aid programs by this time.[75] Later, during the signing of a border treaty in October 1961, China and Nepal also concluded an agreement on the Tibet–Nepal Highway – via the Kuti Pass – that led Nehru to complain about it in the Indian Parliament as it clearly had implications for Indian security.[76]

China had also suggested "a non-aggression treaty" with Nepal but Kathmandu seemed "unwilling to go that far."[77] Nevertheless, two weeks before the PLA began its first wave of attacks on India, Chen Yi assured Nepal that "should any foreign power dare to attack Nepal, the Chinese government and people ... will forever stand by Nepal."[78] As a result, China had effectively diminished India's attempts at strategic primacy in Nepal as Kathmandu remained militarily neutral during the Sino-Indian War (although Nepal did impose a partial economic embargo on Tibet, as explained subsequently).

While New Delhi did not have any war plans with China via Nepal, India's public guarantees to Nepal and statements that noted that any

---

[70] Tsering Shakya, *The Dragon in the Land of Snows* (New York: Penguin, 1999), 326–328.
[71] Rose, *Nepal*, 228–231; and Fravel, *Strong Borders, Secure Nation*, 93.
[72] Fravel, *Strong Borders, Secure Nation*, 91.
[73] Garver, *Protracted Contest*, 148.
[74] Rose, *Nepal*, 217.
[75] Rose, *Nepal*, 214, 226; and Hyer, *The Pragmatic Dragon*, 90–91.
[76] Garver, *Protracted Contest*, 146–147.
[77] Hyer, *The Pragmatic Dragon*, 87.
[78] Document 310, Chen Yi's speech at a Nepalese Embassy reception to mark the first anniversary of the signing of the Boundary Treaty, October 6, 1962 (Extracts), in R. K. Jain (ed.), *China South Asian Relations 1947–1980, Vol. 2* (Brighton: The Harvester Press, 1981), 366–367.

Sino-Indian war would have a large impact on Asia meant that China's interests in Nepal were larger than the China–Nepal border dispute. By extension, China's interest in resolving its border dispute with Nepal was not simply about pressuring India to resolve the Sino-Indian territorial dispute. Although the specifics regarding Burma were different compared to Nepal, the underlying logic was similar.

Notably, China had resolved its border dispute with Burma in January 1960, two months prior to its border agreement with Nepal. China was reassured by the fact that Burma had not made any public statement in the aftermath of the 1959 Lhasa Revolt. Sino-Burmese border negotiations – which included discussions on the so-called McMahon Line since it extended eastward from the Sino-Indian frontier and partially marked the Sino-Burmese frontier – had dragged on since the mid-1950s but took off after 1959. The final agreement was concluded merely "after five days of intense negotiations" in early 1960.[79] Not surprisingly, India interpreted China's settlement of its dispute with Burma as a strategy of isolating India. As China began its overtures related to territorial settlement with Burma in late 1959, the Indian ambassador in Rangoon observed that it was "obvious that China has been deliberately trying to isolate us from our friends" and that China's assurance to Burma on the territorial dispute "was obviously a step in this direction."[80]

China's concerns regarding the presence of several thousand Nationalist troops there since 1949 as well as India's interest in the stability of the Burmese government in the face of the challenges posed by the Karen rebels were discussed in Chapter 3. However, many Nationalists were also collaborating with the Karens against the Burmese government.[81] Furthermore, the CIA had also collaborated with the Nationalists in Burma to harass the PRC in the 1950s.[82] According to Stuart-Fox, an alliance between Burma and the Western powers "could have posed a danger [to China], not least to the Chinese position in Tibet."[83]

Consequently, India's security guarantees given to Burma in 1952 and 1954 – which were conveyed to the PRC as noted in Chapter 3 – were

[79] Hyer, *The Pragmatic Dragon*, 67.
[80] Extracts from the letter of Lalji Mehrotra, Ambassador of India, Rangoon, to Shri M. J. Desai, Commonwealth Secretary, Ministry of External Affairs, New Delhi, October 21, 1959, in Avtar Singh Bhasin (ed.), *India–China Relations 1947–2000: A Documentary Study, Vol-V* (New Delhi: Geetika, 2018), 5274.
[81] Werner Levi, *Modern China's Foreign Policy* (Minneapolis: The University of Minnesota Press, 1953), 348.
[82] John Prados, *Safe for Democracy: The Secret Wars of the CIA* (Chicago: Ivan R. Dee, 2006), 134–138.
[83] Martin Stuart-Fox, *A Short History of China and Southeast Asia: Tribute, Trade, and Influence* (Crows Nest: Allen & Unwin, 2003), 160.

not inconsequential in the Chinese approach toward Burma after 1959, especially since the PRC was also concerned about potential collaboration between the United States and India. Therefore, though China resolved its territorial dispute with Burma (which included the acceptance of the McMahon Line without actually naming it as such), Beijing "retained control" over "three villages" to ensure that it held sway over "the southernmost pass connecting the Salween and Irrawaddy valleys" that is "strategically important for troop movement in the area because they provide[d] access to eastern Tibet and India's northeastern region, an area disputed by China and India."[84]

Furthermore, unlike Nepal, Beijing was successful in signing a nonaggression treaty with Burma that was jointly concluded with the border agreement. Given its prior opposition to SEATO, China had effectively neutralized Burma, which had historically "served as a corridor for the movement of goods and armies between East Asia and South Asia," including in the Second World War.[85] The PRC and Burma also conducted joint military operations against the Nationalist troops in Burma in late 1960 and early 1961 "and forced those troops not killed or captured into Laos."[86] These developments had completely diminished the impact of all Indian warnings related to Burma that were conveyed to the PRC in the 1950s. The PRC had reduced India's position in Burma, and Rangoon remained neutral during the 1962 Sino-Indian War.

Unlike Nepal and Burma, the PRC was less successful when it came to the small states of Bhutan and Sikkim in the Himalayas where Indian predominance continued. India had successfully intervened as Bhutan and China tried to open direct diplomatic channels in 1959.[87] Many Bhutanese were linked to Tibet through marital ties and had followed the PLA's crackdown there with horror. "For instance, Prime Minister Jigme Dorji's father-in-law, the Tsarong Shape, was arrested and subjected to such indignities by the Chinese that he committed suicide."[88] In addition to ousting the Bhutanese representative from Lhasa and annexing the eight Bhutanese enclaves in Tibet after 1959 (as noted in Chapter 3), China also sealed its borders with Bhutan via the Chumbi Valley into Sikkim and India.[89] Bhutan had heretofore been connected northward with Tibet and

[84] Hyer, *The Pragmatic Dragon*, 78–79.
[85] Garver, *Protracted Contest*, 243.
[86] Fravel, *Strong Borders, Secure Nation*, 90.
[87] Garver, *Protracted Contest*, 177.
[88] Leo E. Rose, *The Politics of Bhutan* (Ithaca: Cornell University Press, 1977), 77.
[89] Hyer, *The Pragmatic Dragon*, 99.

had no direct roads connecting it with India. Consequently, India began constructing a road linking Bhutan with India in 1960.[90]

The Indian Army also began training the small Bhutanese Army in 1961.[91] As the Bhutan–China border dispute came to the fore after 1959, Bhutan asked India to discuss its boundary dispute with China in the absence of direct diplomatic links with Beijing.[92] During the China–India border talks in 1961, the Indian ambassador complained that China had "not recognized India's right to represent Bhutan and Sikkim," while his Chinese counterpart replied saying, "[I] don't know what this refers to."[93] China was clearly not willing to recognize India's special position in Bhutan and Sikkim.

While these two small Himalayan states did not participate in the 1962 Sino-Indian War, "another main PLA force ... stood at the head of the Chumbi valley" after the second wave of the PLA's onslaught against India in November 1962.[94] Given that Tawang (to the east of Bhutan, in India's northeast) was already under Chinese occupation then, a strike through the Chumbi Valley (on Bhutan's west) would have isolated Bhutan from India. In fact, a strike through the Chumbi Valley would have led the PLA into the Siliguri Corridor – a sliver of Indian territory between the Himalayan states and Bangladesh that is about twenty-four kilometers wide at its narrowest point – that connects the Indian mainland with northeast India. Fearful that a Chinese strike could sever northeastern India altogether, New Delhi had sent troops into Sikkim (to the immediate west of the Chumbi Valley) in early November 1962.[95] However, China's unilateral ceasefire and India's acceptance of it meant that Bhutan and Sikkim did not witness military hostilities. In other words, *positional* issues related to the Sino-Indian rivalry in Bhutan, Sikkim, Nepal, and Burma were clearly a part of China's and India's strategic calculus in 1962.

Finally, it should be noted that Pakistan–China border negotiations had begun in 1961 and that they were in their final phase during the 1962 Sino-Indian War.[96] Though these negotiations became public only in May

[90] Ispahani, *Roads and Rivals*, 179.
[91] Rose, *The Politics of Bhutan*, 78.
[92] Rose, *The Politics of Bhutan*, 80.
[93] "Memorandum of Conversation between Director Zhang Wenji and Indian Ambassador Parthasarathy (1)," July 17, 1961, History and Public Policy Digital Archive, PRC FMA 105-01056-03, 51–59, obtained by Sulmaan Khan and translated by Anna Beth Keim, https://digitalarchive.wilsoncenter.org/document/121625.
[94] Whiting, *The Chinese Calculus of Deterrence*, 147.
[95] Lintner, *China's India War*, 163.
[96] Amit R. Das Gupta, "Pakistan and 1962," in Das Gupta and Lüthi, *The Sino-Indian War of 1962*, 124–140.

1962, India was already aware of these talks. China and Pakistan were discussing their frontiers that connected Pakistan's Gilgit–Baltistan region with China's Xinjiang. However, India claimed ownership over Gilgit–Baltistan as a part of Kashmir in its rivalry with Pakistan.[97]

This issue had come up during the 1961 Sino-Indian border talks when the Indian representative told his Chinese counterpart that it was "impossible" for India to not consider China's discussion of "the Kashmir issue" with Pakistan as "hostile."[98] In fact, at Bandung in 1955, Zhou had made a speech in which he had openly stated that the Pakistani prime minister Muhammad Ali Bogra had informed him that "Pakistan did not join the Manila Pact [SEATO] for the purpose of opposing China" and that Pakistan did not suspect China "of having aggressive intentions."[99] Given the budding Sino-Pakistani entente, India was worried about the possibility "of a two-front war" involving Pakistan and China during the 1962 Sino-Indian War and maintained "substantially more than one-half of its force on the front facing Pakistani troops" at the time of the Chinese attacks "in late October 1962."[100] While concerns related to Pakistan, the Himalayan states, and Burma were hardly secondary in 1962, it was the Tibetan issue that was at the front and center of this dispute.

Tibet: At the Nexus of Spatial and Positional Issues

The Tibetans had been perturbed by the 1954 Sino-Indian agreement on Tibetan trade since no Tibetans had been included in these negotiations that had implications for Tibet's future.[101] Therefore, Gyalo Thondup, the Dalai Lama's brother who had been living in India since the PLA's invasion of eastern Tibet, created a grouping in May 1954 along with other Tibetan exiles (which was informally called Jenkhentsisum) "to develop

[97] On Kashmir and the India–Pakistan rivalry, see Sumit Ganguly, *Conflict Unending: India-Pakistan Tensions since 1947* (New York: Columbia University Press, 2002); and T. V. Paul (ed.), *The India-Pakistan Conflict: An Enduring Rivalry* (Cambridge: Cambridge University Press, 2005).
[98] "Memorandum of Conversation between Director Zhang Wenji and Indian Ambassador Parthasarathy (1)."
[99] "Zhou Enlai's Speech at the Political Committee of the Afro-Asian Conference," April 23, 1955, History and Public Policy Program Digital Archive, PRC FMA 207-00006-04, 69–75, translated by Jeffrey Wang, https://digitalarchive.wilsoncenter.org/document/114678.
[100] Charles H. Heimsath and Surjit Mansingh, *A Diplomatic History of Modern India* (Calcutta: Allied, 1971), 171.
[101] Nehru had informed the Dalai Lama in January 1954 that these negotiations were underway. Avtar Singh Bhasin, *Nehru, Tibet, and China* (Gurugram: Penguin, 2021), 141. However, it remains unclear if many Tibetans were aware of it.

a strategy for organizing opposition to the Chinese from Indian soil."[102] Nehru had also encouraged the Indian intelligence to help the Tibetan exiles to a limited degree because the maintenance of "Tibetan autonomy" required "India's strength," while ruling out any military assistance.[103] Consequently, the Tibetan exiles in India turned toward the American CIA for military help.

In the meanwhile, the PRC began implementing Communist "reforms," including land reforms, in "inner" Tibet after 1956, and these resulted in several small-scale insurgencies and localized revolts against the PRC. From Beijing's point of view, the autonomy that was given to Tibet – where no Communist reforms were to be implemented for the time being – was meant for the Dalai Lama's Tibet ("outer" Tibet) as opposed to all the ethnic Tibetan regions of the PRC. However, since Buddhist monasteries were the largest landowners in Tibet, the PRC's land reforms were perceived by the Tibetans as an attack on their very identity itself.

The PRC responded militarily to this unrest, including through the aerial bombing of prominent monasteries where large numbers of Tibetans had taken refuge.[104] By 1958, the Tibetan grassroots' armed resistance against the PRC had become more organized throughout Tibet ("inner" and "outer") with the creation of the CDA. The CDA was a "pan-Tibetan" organization even though it was "dominated" by the Khampas and included "several Nationalist Chinese soldiers."[105]

The Dalai Lama's government provided only lukewarm support for the CDA even though some personnel from the small Tibetan army (which had continued after 1951) joined the CDA.[106] Notably, the Kalimpong-/India-based Gyalo was the liaison between the CDA and the CIA.[107] Moreover, "a new secret arrangement was created in India with the Dalai Lama's knowledge and approval, in which anti-Chinese resistance organizations in India [including Gyalo's Jenkhentsisum] would work together with the Tibetan government."[108] The CDA also carried out relatively

[102] Melvyn C. Goldstein, *A History of Modern Tibet, Volume 2, 1951–1955* (Berkeley: University of California Press, 2007), 471.
[103] B. N. Mullik, *My Years with Nehru: The Chinese Betrayal* (New Delhi: Allied, 1971), 184.
[104] Shakya, *The Dragon in the Land of Snows*, 140–141.
[105] McGranahan, "Tibet's Cold War," 109.
[106] McGranahan, "Tibet's Cold War," 118.
[107] McGranahan, "Tibet's Cold War," 117.
[108] Melvyn C. Goldstein, *A History of Modern Tibet, Volume 4, 1957–1959* (Berkeley: University of California Press, 2019), 64.

large raids and ambushes against the PLA in 1958, including those along the "checkpoints on the Sichuan-Tibet and Qinghai-Tibet roads."[109] According to the Chinese government, there had been "twelve armed conflicts" between the PLA and the Tibetan rebels throughout 1958 and in the first two months of 1959.[110]

While India was not involved in organizing or supporting armed Tibetan resistance against the PRC, New Delhi was not unaware of the activities of these groups (although India's knowledge of its scale remains unclear). During his talks with Zhou in 1956–57, Nehru had acknowledged that he had heard that "Kalimpong has a nest of spies and the spies are probably more than the population."[111] Zhou had visited India twice in late 1956 and early 1957 when the Dalai Lama was there to celebrate the 2,500th birth anniversary of the Buddha. Mao was worried that the Dalai Lama would visit Kalimpong and "meet spies from different countries" there and that "he may not come back" to Tibet and even "declare 'Tibetan independence' in India."[112] In turn, Nehru had invited Zhou to India – twice, in quick succession – to allay any Chinese fears.

During his trips to India, "Zhou made it clear that he expected the Government of India to prevent any disturbances or demands for independence by Tibetans at Kalimpong or elsewhere. Nehru replied that there was no reason why there should be any trouble *if* an assurance were given that Tibet would have full internal autonomy."[113] Although the Dalai Lama did return to Tibet/China in April 1957, he did so after spending a month in Kalimpong. However, he had not declared Tibetan independence in India. The PRC was not necessarily reassured by his return because Zhou had come to "link the notion of greater Tibetan autonomous region with that of [Tibetan] independence" by 1957.[114] Notably, the Dalai Lama had returned from India asking for Communist "reforms" to be halted in "inner" as well as "outer" Tibet. In other words, he was seeking autonomy for "greater Tibet." China was also irked because India had become crucial in resolving what the Chinese perceived to be a domestic issue related to Tibet.

[109] Fravel, *Strong Borders, Secure Nation*, 77.
[110] Liu, *To the End of Revolution*, 356.
[111] "Talks with Chou En-lai," December 31, 1956–January 1, 1957, *SWJN Series 2, Volume 36*, 598.
[112] Mao Zedong, "Speech at the Second Plenum of the Eighth Central Committee," dated November 15, 1956, in John K. Leung and Michael Y. M. Kau (eds.), *The Writings of Mao Zedong, 1949–1976, Volume II – January 1956–December 1957* (Armonk, NY: M. E. Sharpe, 1992): 170.
[113] Gopal, *Jawaharlal Nehru, Volume Three*, 36. *Emphasis added.*
[114] Quoted in Liu, *To the End of Revolution*, 313.

In July 1958, China specifically asked India to "repress the subversive and disruptive activities against China's Tibetan region carried out in Kalimpong" by Tibetan exiles and foreign spies.[115] The PRC had its own spies in Kalimpong, and Beijing was consequently aware of the presence of Nationalist/Taiwanese, American, and of course Indian spies in that city.[116] China had even asked India to expel the Dalai Lama's brother from India.[117] While India did not expel Gyalo (or any Tibetan exiles already in the country), it tried to assure China by asking the state government of Bengal to keep a watchful eye on the Tibetans living in Kalimpong.[118]

It was in this larger context that three further developments precipitated the 1962 Sino-Indian War. These developments demonstrate how the positional and spatial dimensions of the Sino-Indian rivalry became entangled through issue linkage over the Tibetan issue. First, the events in Tibet culminated in the March 1959 Lhasa Revolt, "the single largest revolt against the CCP,"[119] which led to the Dalai Lama's dramatic escape into exile to India. On April 21, 1959, he declared the creation of a Tibetan government-in-exile in India.[120] While India officially received him as an honored and a revered spiritual leader (as opposed to a political exile) and did not recognize such a government, the Tibetan issue had become internationalized. In the meanwhile, China also scrapped the 1951 Seventeen Point Agreement and Tibet lost all autonomy. Tibet's small army was disbanded, and the PLA undertook a massive military operation to stabilize Tibet and sealed its borders with India (and the Himalayan states).

Given the scale of this event and the connections between the Tibetans in Tibet and India, China blamed India for the Lhasa Revolt,[121] although India was not involved in it.[122] In fact, Zhou believed that India was the

---

[115]   *White Paper, 1954–59*, 60–62.
[116]   Tansen Sen, "The Chinese Intrigue in Kalimpong: Intelligence Gathering and the 'Spies' in a Contact Zone," in Tansen Sen and Brian Tsui (eds.), *Beyond Pan-Asianism: Connecting China and India, 1840s–1960s* (New Delhi: Oxford University Press, 2021), 410–459.
[117]   Hoffmann, *India and the China Crisis*, 37.
[118]   Gopal, *Jawaharlal Nehru, Volume Three*, 81.
[119]   Fravel, *Strong Borders, Secure Nation*, 71.
[120]   Stephanie Roemer, *The Tibetan Government-in-Exile: Politics at Large* (London: Routledge, 2008), 64.
[121]   "The Revolution in Tibet and Nehru's Philosophy," published by the editorial department of *Renmin Ribao* (May 6, 1959) in *Peking Review*, May 12, 1959, 6–15. According to Garver, this article was published on Mao's orders and was vetted by him before publication. See Garver, "China's Decision for War with India in 1962," 93–94.
[122]   Shakya, *The Dragon in the Land of Snows*, 197–220.

"frontline state" that had led this rebellion from Kalimpong and that Britain and the United States were working behind the scenes.[123] The "entire PLA establishment, except for one branch (the navy) and one military region (Inner Mongolia), joined the rebellion suppression in Tibet."[124] The PLA had "neutralized" 87,000 Tibetan rebels by October 1960,[125] and its stabilization efforts lasted "well into 1961."[126] The PRC believed that the Tibetans could not have organized such a rebellion themselves.

In the meanwhile, the CDA battalions entered India from April 1959 onward – as they fled from the PLA – and established links with the Indian government and the CIA. One group was sent to Rajasthan for training by the Indian intelligence,[127] while another group was being trained in Uttarakhand (then in Uttar Pradesh).[128] Although India's official support for the Tibetan rebels had now begun – after the Dalai Lama's escape, in collusion with the CIA – India's goal remained Tibetan autonomy. This was clearly distinct from the goals of the CIA (related to distracting the PLA from the East Asian hotspots in Korea, Taiwan, and Indochina) or from those of the Tibetans themselves who were fighting for their independence.[129]

Second, when seen from Beijing's point of view, just as the PLA was bringing the situation in Tibet under control, India had launched its Forward Policy in November 1961 in Aksai Chin. China felt that India was taking advantage of China's temporary weakness given the unrest in Tibet. (China had also lost forty-five million people by 1961 because of the Great Leap Forward, "the greatest man-made catastrophe in human history."[130]) The Aksai Chin region had become particularly sensitive for New Delhi after September 1957 with the announcement of the Xinjiang–Tibet Highway. The Indians claimed that a stretch of this road – 112 miles – traversed through Indian territory in Aksai Chin.[131] While the Indians had

---

[123] Chen Jian, "The Tibetan Rebellion of 1959 and China's Changing Relations with India and the Soviet Union," *Journal of Cold War Studies* 8.3 (2006): 85.

[124] Liu, *To the End of Revolution*, 383.

[125] Jianglin Li, *Tibet in Agony, Lhasa 1959* (Cambridge, MA: Harvard University Press, 2016), Kindle Loc. 6087.

[126] Khan, *Muslim, Trader, Nomad, Spy*, 36.

[127] Carole McGranahan, *Arrested Histories: Tibet, the CIA, and Memories of a Forgotten War* (Durham: Duke University Press, 2010), 139.

[128] Bhasin, *Nehru, Tibet, and China*, 64.

[129] Kenneth Conboy and James Morrison, *The CIA's Secret War in Tibet* (Lawrence: University Press of Kansas, 2002); and Knaus, *Orphans of the Cold War*.

[130] Odd Arne Westad, *Restless Empire: China and the World since 1750* (New York: Basic, 2015), 336.

[131] Ispahani, *Roads and Rivals*, 168.

cartographic claims in this region, they did not have physical presence on the ground (but China had been using this route since 1951).[132]

As the PRC tried to bring the situation in Tibet under control after 1959 and "moved PLA outposts" into the disputed territory with India "to provide *defense in depth* for the Aksai Chin road,"[133] New Delhi worried that China was expanding into Indian territory. India believed that there was a discrepancy of some 2,500 square miles in Aksai Chin between the Chinese maps of 1956 and 1960 as China was pushing deeper into India.[134] For India, the Forward Policy was a "response to what was perceived to be a similar effort by the Chinese."[135] Not surprisingly, China not only viewed India's Forward Policy in this region as creeping territorial aggression but was also concerned about the security of the Xinjiang–Tibet Highway/Aksai Chin Road, and by extension of Tibet itself.

This road "crossed a flat plateau and was serviceable in the winter," unlike the other two highways from China into Tibet that traversed "more hazardous terrain and climatic conditions."[136] Therefore, it was "essential to Chinese control of *western* Tibet and very important to its control over *all* of Tibet."[137] In the far western regions of Tibet, this highway was also far from the main zones of the activities of the Tibetan rebels. In fact, in 1958, the CDA had specifically targeted the PLA along the other two highways connecting Tibet with China.[138] Furthermore, the CDA battalions had set up operations in Mustang in Nepal after 1959 near this western route where they were being supported by the CIA as well as the Indians, as noted earlier. In other words, the issues at stake amounted to more than a mere territorial dispute.

Third and finally, India's economic embargo on Tibet after the Dalai Lama's escape "was of great strategic significance."[139] In April 1959, India had stopped exporting grain to Tibet.[140] This exacerbated the situation in Tibet given the famines caused in China because of the disastrous Great Leap Forward as Tibet depended on the subcontinent for its grain.[141]

---

[132] This route was transformed into an all-weather motor road in 1957.
[133] Whiting, *The Chinese Calculus of Deterrence*, 11.
[134] Raghavan, *War and Peace in Modern India*, 266.
[135] Hoffmann, "Anticipation, Disaster, and Victory," 966.
[136] Ispahani, *Roads and Rivals*, 170.
[137] Garver, *Protracted Contest*, 83. *Emphasis original.*
[138] Goldstein, *A History of Modern Tibet, Volume 4*, 493. Also see footnote 109.
[139] Chaowu Dai, "China's Strategy for Sino-Indian Boundary Disputes, 1950–1962," *Asian Perspective* 43.3 (2019): 443.
[140] Note given by the Ministry of Foreign Affairs, Peking, to the Embassy of India in China, June 2, 1962, *White Paper No. VI*, 203–205.
[141] Khan, *Muslim, Trader, Nomad, Spy*, 88–105.

China also accused India of restricting "daily necessities" such as "cooking oil, beans, sugar, tea, kerosene, fuel, farm implements, utensils, as well as important materials for construction, telecommunications, motor, and other transport."[142] India replied by noting that obstructions had been created because of Chinese "monetary" manipulations and that it was restricting "non-traditional goods" such as diesel, oil, petroleum products, motor parts etc." as these were not a part of the "traditional commerce with Tibet." Furthermore, India itself was in short supply of these goods at a time when "there was a sudden increase in import of these goods into Tibet for an obviously aggressive purpose."[143]

Under the autonomy given to Tibet before the escape of the Dalai Lama, it was allowed to have its own currency (as noted in Chapter 3). Furthermore, given its economic orientation, the Indian rupee was also in wide circulation in the Tibetan economy, albeit unofficially. However, the lapse of Tibetan autonomy after 1959 meant that the Tibetan currency was scrapped, and China clamped down on the Indian rupee as well. This currency issue led to a huge uproar in the Indian Parliament, which was viewed as interference in China's internal affairs by Beijing.[144] In any case, the total trade between India and Tibet had declined by 80 percent between October 1959 and December 1960,[145] and China believed that the decline in this trade was "solely of the Indian Government's making."[146]

Furthermore, Bhutan also imposed a total ban on trade with Tibet in 1960, while Nepal imposed a partial embargo limited to strategic goods (iron, cement, petrol, kerosene, and coal) in December 1961.[147] The trade embargo was particularly hard on Bhutan since Bhutanese rice surplus meant for Tibet did not have a market in India. Furthermore, the road connecting Bhutan and India became operational only in 1963.[148]

---

[142] *White Paper No. VI*, 203–205.

[143] *White Paper No. VI*, 216–218.

[144] On this August 29, 1959, uproar in the Indian Parliament on the status of the rupee in Tibet, see *Indian Parliament on the Issue of Tibet: Rajya Sabha Debates, 1952–2005* (New Delhi: Tibetan Parliamentary and Policy Research Centre, 2006), 42–43.

[145] *Indian Parliament on the Issue of Tibet*, 136.

[146] *White Paper No. VI*, 205.

[147] The Bhutanese and Nepalese decisions had their own logic that was not limited to Indian pressure. See Therry Mathou, "Bhutan-China Relations: Towards a New Step in Himalayan Politics," in Karma Ura and Sonam Kinga (eds.), *The Spider and the Piglet: Proceedings of the First International Seminar on Bhutan Studies* (Thimphu: The Centre for Bhutan Studies, 2004), 394; and Rose, *Nepal*, 242.

[148] Rose, *The Politics of Bhutan*, 79.

However, China was discussing food transportation with Nepal in 1961 only to discover that India was putting pressure on Nepal to terminate its trade with Tibet. In the absence of the Tibet–Nepal Highway (which became operational in 1967), food from Nepal had to be sent to Tibet via India.[149] As a result, the Chinese government had come to believe by 1961 that not only were the Indians linking trade and the boundary dispute but they were also trying to weaken China in Tibet and to undermine its relations with Nepal and Bhutan.[150] The famine in Tibet was exacerbated because of Sino-Indian tensions.

It was in this context that the issue of the extension of the 1954 agreement between India and China on Tibetan trade that had Panchsheel in its preamble came up in December 1961. When China enquired about the extension, India declined after arguing that the 1954 agreement was not just about trade but was also meant "to promote peace and rapid economic and cultural development in the two countries" and in "South East Asia." Furthermore, while India was trying to create a "zone of Asia free from cold-war conflicts," China was creating problems for Indian traders in Tibet followed by "aggressive military activity" on Indian territory.[151] Consequently, this agreement lapsed in June 1962, around the time when their territorial dispute became more intractable because of the Indian military post in Dhola near the Thagla Ridge in the eastern sector. For China, India's aggression against it was no longer limited to Aksai Chin but was now spreading all along their disputed frontier.[152]

China had by now concluded that it was India that had made the connection between Tibet, the boundary dispute, trade, and Asian issues (including Panchsheel). India's Forward Policy, which was threatening the Xinjiang–Tibet Highway, and the presence of the Dalai Lama's Tibetan government-in-exile in India meant that New Delhi wanted nothing short of Tibet as a buffer state between India and China. In this quest, India was actively undermining China in the Himalayan states. But India's ambitions of Asian leadership went beyond the Himalayas and included Burma and Southeast Asia too. All these grievances were promptly included in the Justification for the 1962 Sino-Indian war, as noted earlier. On its part, India also interpreted Chinese activities in Tibet,

---

[149] Rose, *Nepal*, 242.
[150] Khan, *Muslim, Trader, Nomad, Spy*, 106.
[151] *White Paper No. VI*, 189–190.
[152] Hoffmann, *India and the China Crisis*, 110.

the Himalayas, and in Burma as their attempts to undermine India's position, while the 1962 invasion itself was seen as a part of China's strategy to diminish India's position in Asia. In other words, positional concerns were at the core of the 1962 Sino-Indian War, and it was the Tibet issue that connected their spatial rivalry over territory with their positional rivalry for leadership in Asia.

The War and Its Aftermath

As China launched simultaneous offensives in the eastern and western sectors in October 1962, the Indian military – underequipped, lacking winter clothing and even adequate food supplies – crumbled. On the other hand, PLA military presence in Tibet over the previous years (which included battle-hardened veterans of the 1950–53 Korean War) and the Chinese leadership's careful operational planning meant that Chinese troops faced no organized opposition. For example, the PRC government had carefully assessed that "Indian military forces [along the frontier] were about one-sixth of China's,"[153] whereas India perceived the Chinese attacks in "quantity and quality ... like a thunder-bolt,"[154] and it "did not know" whether the Chinese troop strength was "six, seven, or eight times the number of troops" that India had.[155] The result was absolute panic on the Indian side. Indian forces were pushed behind the Chinese-claimed boundary in Aksai Chin while the Indian military and civilian administration abandoned their positions in Tawang (and elsewhere in the eastern sector).[156]

As this first wave of Chinese attacks ended, the PLA had captured many senior Indian army officers, including Brigadier John Dalvi, who has left an account of his observations.[157] While China's physical control over Tibet was never in doubt during the war, the PLA did note that the Tibetans were tending to the Indian prisoners of war in Tibet/China.[158] Meanwhile, south of the McMahon Line, the PLA behaved very professionally as the

---

[153] Garver, "China's Decision for War with India in 1962," 118.
[154] Nehru's statement made on November 4, 1962, in New Delhi, in *Prime Minister on Chinese Aggression*, 30.
[155] In the Lower House of the Indian Parliament, November 8, 1962, in *Prime Minister on Chinese Aggression*, 46.
[156] Guyot-Réchard, *Shadow States*, 233.
[157] Brig. J. P. Dalvi, *Himalayan Blunder: The Curtain-Raiser to the Sino-Indian War of 1962* (Dehradun: Natraj, 1969).
[158] Lintner, *China's India War*, 79.

locals were not harmed even as Indian civilian and military infrastructure was destroyed.[159] Although China's second wave was even more devastating for the Indian forces, the PLA entered only those areas of the eastern sector that were populated by "Tibetan-speaking people or people speaking languages and dialects related to Tibetan."[160] Nevertheless, the fear of another Chinese attack was so great that the Indian military and civilian administration had also abandoned Tezpur in Assam (beyond the Chinese-claimed territory).

Therefore, in spite of India's opposition to military blocs (including SEATO), Nehru turned toward the United States for help and wrote to President John F. Kennedy.[161] The United States was aware of the China–India positional rivalry, and as senator in May 1959, Kennedy had noted that no "struggle in the world" deserved "more of our [American] time and attention than that which grips the attention of all Asia … that is the struggle between India and China for leadership of the East, for the respect of all Asia, for the opportunity to demonstrate whose way of life is better."[162]

Consequently, the United States publicly condemned the Chinese aggression, and American support for India took multiple forms. After the first wave of the Chinese attacks, the United States used its Boeing 707 planes in Europe to supply basic infantry equipment to India, while America's C-130 aircraft transported these to Indian soldiers on the frontier.[163] The Americans also prodded the British to support India, while New Delhi had also reached out to London. Britain began contemplating a joint Commonwealth response along with Australia and New Zealand.[164] American pressure on Pakistan also ensured that a second front was not opened against India at this time.[165] An American aircraft carrier, the USS *Kitty Hawk*, was also en route to southern India as a symbol of American support.[166]

[159] Guyot-Réchard, *Shadow States*, 233.
[160] Lintner, *China's India War*, xiv.
[161] Bruce Riedel, *JFK's Forgotten Crisis: Tibet, the CIA, and the Sino-Indian War* (Washington, DC: Brookings, 2015).
[162] Remarks of Senator John F. Kennedy, Conference on India and the United States, Washington, DC., May 4, 1959, John F. Kennedy Presidential Library and Museum, www.jfklibrary.org/archives/other-resources/john-f-kennedy-speeches/india-and-the-us-conference-washington-dc-19590504.
[163] Conboy and Morrison, *The CIA's Secret War in Tibet*, 172.
[164] Paul McGarr, "The United States, Britain, and the Sino-Indian Border War," in Das Gupta and Lüthi, *The Sino-Indian War of 1962*, 105–123.
[165] Das Gupta, "Pakistan and 1962," 124–140.
[166] Riedel, *JFK's Forgotten Crisis*, Kindle Loc. 2228.

The United States and India also created the Special Frontier Force (SFF, also known as Establishment 22) during the Sino-Indian War.[167] This was a special commando force of ethnic Tibetans trained in guerilla tactics and high-altitude operations. This force was placed under the leadership of the Indian intelligence and remained "a secret not only from the general Indian public but also from the bulk of the Indian military."[168] While the official aim behind the creation of this force remains unknown, the SFF was expected to be dropped behind the PLA lines while the regular Indian army directly engaged them on the frontline. In addition to the SFF, India also created a paramilitary organization during the war that included ethnic Tibetans. The Indo-Tibetan Border Police Force (ITBF) was set up under the auspices of India's Ministry of Home Affairs to help guard India's Tibetan frontiers.[169]

In the face of China's second offensive, Nehru, who feared for the very "survival" of India, wrote to Kennedy requesting nothing short of America's defensive intervention in an air war with China.[170] Nehru worried that China was on the verge of "taking over the whole of Eastern India [east of the Chumbi Valley/Siliguri Corridor]" and that the states of "U.P. [Uttar Pradesh], Punjab, and Himachal Pradesh" were also under threat. Therefore, he requested Kennedy for twelve squadrons of American supersonic fighters and two squadrons of B-47-type bombers. Notably, he added that India hoped that the "U.S. planes manned by U.S. personnel" would participate "in air battles with the Chinese air force over Indian areas." The bombers were to help "neutralise their [Chinese] bases and airfields by striking from the air," and India was eager to send its pilots and technicians for training to the United States. For Nehru this was not simply a bilateral Sino-Indian war, for he told Kennedy that this was also a "fight" for the "survival of freedom and independence in this sub-continent as well as the rest of Asia."

Before the United States could respond to this request made on November 19, China announced its unilateral ceasefire, and the possibility of wider escalation soon passed. However, it was not lost on the

---

[167] The SFF was set up between October 26, 1962, and November 24, 1962. The former date is noted in Conboy and Morrison, *The CIA's Secret War in Tibet*, 284, while the latter is mentioned in McGranahan, *Arrested Histories*, 139.
[168] Conboy and Morrison, *The CIA's Secret War in Tibet*, 184.
[169] The ITBF was established on October 24, 1962. See McGranahan, *Arrested Histories*, 139.
[170] For the full text of this letter dated November 19, 1962, see Nehru Correspondence, November 1962: 11–19, John F. Kennedy Presidential Library and Museum, www.jfklibrary.org/asset-viewer/archives/JFKNSF/111/JFKNSF-111-016.

United States (and the Soviet Union) that China had attacked India while the Cuban Missile Crisis was ongoing. In fact, Sino-Soviet relations had been tensed since the late 1950s, in part for reasons related to India. "Soviet-proclaimed neutrality in the Sino-Indian conflict in 1959 was one of the most serious blows to the Sino-Soviet alliance."[171] Given that the Soviets expected some support from the PRC during the Cuban Missile Crisis while trying to prevent India from tilting decisively toward the United States, Soviet intervention was also highly unlikely at this time.[172]

While a larger conflict involving the superpowers was avoided, India's Asian neighbors also perceived the 1962 war as a positional contest. The Malayan premier Tunku Abdul Rehman who was in India in late October 1962 at the start of this war noted that China did "not want a rival in this part of the world"; instead, China wanted the "whole of Asia" to "look to her."[173] After returning to Southeast Asia on November 1, he added that Malaya would give "all-out support" to India if a formal declaration of war was made.[174] While Malaya's support was overt and exceptional, the "reactions" of the Southeast Asian countries "to the Sino-Indian dispute left no doubt that India would fail to arouse confidence in her leadership after the debacle of 1962."[175]

Although the pro-Western Southeast Asian states of Thailand, the Philippines, and South Vietnam did extend their sympathies to India, other countries, especially Burma, remained neutral. The only Southeast Asian state that explicitly sided with China was Communist North Vietnam. It is noteworthy that unlike Indian diplomacy in the 1940s and 1950s, post-1962 India did not organize or lead any Asian conferences nor did New Delhi seek to mediate between China and the West in its aftermath. Furthermore, unlike India's military assistance to Indonesia and Malaya in the 1950s as noted in Chapter 3, New Delhi did not even respond to the 1965 Singaporean request – which was made on the day that Singapore became independent – for a military team,

---

[171] Sergey Radchenko, *Two Suns in the Heavens: The Sino-Soviet Struggle for Supremacy, 1962–1967* (Stanford: Stanford University Press, 2009), 27.

[172] Andreas Hilger, "The Soviet Union and the Sino-Indian Border War, 1962," in Das Gupta and Lüthi, *The Sino-Indian War of 1962*, 142–158.

[173] Quoted in Vishal Singh, "The Reactions of South-East Asian Countries," *International Studies* 5.1–2 (1963): 80.

[174] Quoted in Singh, "The Reactions of South-East Asian Countries," 81.

[175] D. R. SarDesai, *Indian Foreign Policy in Cambodia, Laos, and Vietnam, 1947–1964* (Berkeley: University of California Press, 1968).

including a military advisor, to help train the newly independent city-state's army.[176]

On the other hand, 1962 was "expensive" but "necessary" for China's "rise" as an Asian "great power."[177] By exposing India's dependence on the United States, China had demonstrated that India was not an "independent" strategic player in Asia. Furthermore, an India that could not look after its own security was hardly capable of exercising leadership in Asia. Not surprisingly, India became more focused on subcontinental – South Asian – affairs in its aftermath. In fact, its military modernization after 1962 enabled New Delhi to dismember its subcontinental rival, Pakistan, during the 1971 Bangladesh War. After 1962, India began seeking regional dominance in South Asia.[178]

Until the 1962 Sino-Indian War, there was a tendency in the scholarly and policymaking communities to see Asia in "pan-Asian" terms instead of the now more familiar subregions of South Asia, Southeast Asia, and (North)East Asia.[179] While there were also other reasons behind this division of Asia into the smaller subregions in the 1960s, especially those related to the Cold War,[180] the diminishing of India's status and power in 1962 contributed to it even though it did not transform China into Asia's "leader." In fact, the failure of the Great Leap Forward and the Cultural Revolution, the PRC's attempts to export its own revolutionary ideology to Southeast Asia, and the creation of the Association of Southeast Asian Nations (ASEAN) in the 1960s meant that the region remained wary of China.

Nevertheless, China had become far more important to Asian strategic affairs than India, a trend that continued into the 1970s (and beyond) with the US–China rapprochement and China's economic reforms.[181] It was only in the last decade of the twentieth century that China's economic rise

---

[176] See Chak Mun, "Singapore-India Strategic Relations – Singapore's Perspective," in Anit Mukherjee (ed.), *The Merlion and the Ashoka: Singapore-India Strategic Ties* (Singapore: World Scientific, 2016), 48–49.

[177] John W. Garver, *China's Quest: The History of the Foreign Relations of the People's Republic of China* (New York: Oxford University Press, 2016), 181.

[178] Hoffmann, "Anticipation, Disaster, and Victory."

[179] Michael Brecher, "International Relations and Asian Studies: The Subordinate State System of Southern Asia," *World Politics* 15.2 (1963): 213–235; A. W. Stargardt, "The Emergence of the Asian System of Powers," *Modern Asian Studies* 23.3 (1989): 561–595; and Pekka Korhonen, "Monopolizing Asia: The Politics of a Metaphor," *The Pacific Review* 10.3 (1997): 347–365.

[180] Martin W. Lewis and Kären Wigen, *The Myth of Continents: A Critique of Metageography* (Berkeley: University of California Press, 1997).

[181] Evelyn Goh, *Constructing the U.S. Rapprochement with China, 1961–1974: From "Red Menace" to "Tacit Ally"* (New York: Cambridge University Press, 2005).

and dependence on the Indian Ocean sealines for energy security began to make the pan-Asian dimension important again. India's own economic reforms and "Look East" policy did add some momentum toward this larger Asia. However, it was not until the early twenty-first century when the United States started taking an interest in India's slow ascent – in the context of the budding US–China rivalry – that India began to be factored into pan-Asian strategic affairs again.[182] The region is increasingly referred to as the Indo-Pacific today.[183] In other words, not only was the positional dimension an important cause of the 1962 Sino-Indian War but the outcome of that war also had positional consequences.

[182] On the eve of becoming President George W. Bush's national security advisor, Condoleezza Rice had noted that "India is an element in China's calculation, and it should be in America's, too. India is not a great power yet, but it has the potential to emerge as one." See Condoleezza Rice, "Promoting the National Interest," *Foreign Affairs* 79.1 (2000): 56.

[183] Manjeet S. Pardesi, "The Indo-Pacific: A 'New' Region or the Return of History?," *Australian Journal of International Affairs* 74.2 (2020): 124–146.

PART III

The Evolution of the Rivalry

CHAPTER 5

Crises in Sino-Indian Relations

In a recent book on the future of the Sino-Indian rivalry Paul Diehl argues that the likelihood of severe crises in the rivalry are, in all likelihood, a matter of the past.[1] This book, in all fairness, was published prior to the Galwan Valley crisis of the summer of 2020. However, the crisis that engulfed Sino-Indian relations in 2020 clearly underscored that a violent clash along the Sino-Indian border is not a matter that can be effectively ruled out. On the contrary, the Galwan Valley incident, despite the existence of a range of confidence-building measures, indicated that the strategic rivalry has far from withered. And, contrary to Diehl's assertion that "[t]he Line of Actual Control (LAC) over time has become the established border around which both sides have converged in terms of expectations and behavior,"[2] the crisis highlighted that the territorial dispute remains a critical element of the ongoing rivalry.

Furthermore, it is far from clear that, contrary to his views and those of a number of other contributors to this volume, the Sino-Indian rivalry, for all practical purposes, has genuinely ended. Indeed, as this chapter will demonstrate, despite a long hiatus in crises after a major flare-up in 1967, the underlying causes of this rivalry, which include the territorial dispute as well as differing perceptions of each other's roles in Asia, have remained robust even though both sides have made efforts from the early 1980s to stabilize if not resolve the border dispute.[3]

Apart from the disastrous Sino-Indian border war of October 1962, several crises have punctuated Sino-Indian relations. Do these crises, both before and after the momentous 1962 war, have any common features? The first shared characteristic stems from the People's Republic of China's

---

[1] Paul F. Diehl, "Whither Rivalry or Withered Rivalry?," in T. V. Paul (ed.), *The China-India Rivalry in the Globalization Era* (Washington, DC: Georgetown University Press, 2018), 253–272.

[2] Diehl, "Whither Rivalry or Withered Rivalry?," 255.

[3] Sumit Ganguly, "The Sino-Indian Border Talks: A View from New Delhi," *Asian Survey* 29.12 (1989): 1123–1135.

(PRC) conviction that the inherited colonial border was subject to revision. While India had seen the colonial border as largely inviolate, the PRC, from the outset, had seen it as colonial imposition and thereby subject to contestation.[4] Indeed, it considered substantial tracts of land abutting the border as "lost territories" that had to be reclaimed from India, the principal successor state to the British Indian Empire.[5] Second, despite having several rounds of border talks between India and the PRC starting in 1981, the PRC has not abandoned these claims and has, in fact, expanded them over time.[6] To that end, from the late 1950s it has been prepared to periodically probe India's willingness and ability to defend its Himalayan frontiers.[7] Third, these recurrent attempts to test India's resolve have been linked to domestic developments within the PRC, changes in regional politics, and shifts in India's foreign relations. The most recent challenges that it has mounted against India can be attributed to two important factors: India's fitful economic growth since the early 1990s and its increased security cooperation with the United States since the beginning of the twenty-first century.[8] The two developments, in concert, have led the PRC to conclude that India constitutes a strategic rival despite the significant asymmetries in their capabilities.[9]

The Onset of the Crises

The first border crisis had erupted before the 1962 war, which comprised two border skirmishes along the contested border at Kongka Pass and at Longju in 1959. These were armed clashes between units of the Indian Army and police forces and the People's Liberation Army (PLA). The first had occurred in August 1959 in the eastern sector where, according to the PLA, Indian forces had set up posts across the McMahon Line, the

[4] For a discussion and assessment of the competing claims see Steven A. Hoffmann, *India and the China Crisis* (Delhi: Oxford University Press, 1990); Also see Bérenice Guyot-Réchard, *Shadow States: India, China and the Himalayas, 1910–1962* (Cambridge: Cambridge University Press, 2017).
[5] Allen S. Whiting, *The Chinese Calculus of Deterrence: India and Indochina* (Ann Arbor: University of Michigan Press, 1975).
[6] Ganguly, "The Sino-Indian Border Talks," 1123–1135.
[7] Jeff M. Smith, *Cold Peace: China-India Rivalry in the Twentieth Century* (Lanham, MD: Lexington Books, 2015).
[8] Šumit Ganguly and M. Chris Mason (eds.), *The Future of US-India Security Cooperation* (Manchester, Manchester University Press, 2021).
[9] For an assessment of their respective military capabilities see Oriana Skylar Mastro and Arzan Tarapore, "Asymmetric but Uneven: The China-India Conventional Military Balance," in Kanti Bajpai, Selina Ho, and Manjari Chatterjee Miller (eds.), *Routledge Handbook of China-India Relations* (London: Routledge, 2020), 240–251.

inherited British colonial border that the PRC contested.[10] The second episode took place on October 21 when the PLA ambushed an Indian police patrol in the Kongka Pass area of Ladakh in the western sector. This incident was clearly the more serious of the two as it led to the deaths of five Indians and the capture of several others.[11]

Both these skirmishes played an important role in leading Indian decision-makers, especially Prime Minister Jawaharlal Nehru, to conclude that the PRC was indeed intransigent and that the entire border needed to be delimited before any meaningful boundary negotiations could proceed. However, this did not happen, even though representatives of the two sides did meet in 1960, leading to the drafting and release of the Official's Report, which summarized their respective claims to the border areas.

Negotiations, however, ceased at this point and India went on to adopt the so-called "Forward Policy," which involved sending in small "penny packets" of lightly armed troops into areas that the PRC had claimed to assert India's control over them. In the words of a senior Indian military officer who had been involved in the implementation of the policy, it had neither teeth nor tail: It had lacked both firepower and logistics.[12] In effect, it had amounted to a flawed policy of compellence: Resolve was not combined with appropriate military capabilities.[13]

The border war has been discussed at length in Chapter 4. The military debacle along the Himalayan border undermined India's standing in global affairs. The Non-Aligned Movement, to the dismay of India's leadership, did little or nothing to come to India's aid. Worse still, in a moment of desperation India was forced to turn to the United States and the United Kingdom for much-needed military assistance. Such assistance, though forthcoming, was limited, especially from the United States owing to American concerns about the misgivings of its ally, Pakistan.[14]

In the wake of the war, as is well known, India had embarked upon a significant military modernization program. It involved building a

---

[10] The Chinese claim was not unfounded. In September 1959, India withdrew from its post at Tamadem, east of Longju. "India Withdraws from Post on NEFA Border," *The Times of India*, September 29, 1959.

[11] Mahesh Shankar, *The Reputational Imperative: Nehru's India in Territorial Conflict* (Palo Alto: Stanford University Press, 2022), 115.

[12] Sumit Ganguly, personal interview, New Delhi, June 1988.

[13] For a discussion of the concept of compellence, see Thomas Schelling, *Arms and Influence* (New Haven: Yale University Press, 2008).

[14] For a discussion of the roles of the United States and the United Kingdom, see Paul McGarr, "The United States, Britain and the Sino-Indian Border War," in Amit R. Das Gupta and Lorenz M. Lüthi (eds.), *The Sino-Indian War of 1962* (London: Routledge, 2019).

million-man army with ten new mountain divisions trained and equipped for high-altitude warfare, a forty-five-squadron air force with supersonic aircraft, and a modest program of naval modernization.[15] In the meanwhile, in 1965 India had fended off a Pakistani military attack in Kashmir. Though the war had ended in a stalemate India's forces had acquitted themselves creditably and had even captured the strategic Haji Pir Pass in the disputed state of Jammu and Kashmir. It should also be highlighted that India had stood up to an ultimatum that the PRC had issued in the middle of the war.[16] Consequently, when the next crisis in Sino-Indian relations ensued in 1967, India's forces had, in considerable part, recovered, in terms of both morale and capabilities, from the debacle of the 1962 war.

It is important to underscore that despite the disastrous defeat the PLA had inflicted on the Indian Army in the 1962 war, the border dispute remained unresolved. More to the point, despite the territory that the PRC had captured in the war it remained unreconciled to the territorial status quo. Instead, it reiterated its claim to a further 90,000 square miles in the northeast in what would eventually become the Indian state of Arunachal Pradesh.[17] Consequently, skirmishes and crises along the disputed border were to prove all but inevitable.

The Nathu La Crisis

The first crisis in Sino-Indian relations following the 1962 war took place in 1967 near Nathu La and Cho La, two high-altitude passes in Sikkim. This crisis, in all likelihood, stemmed from political developments within Sikkim, which, at the time, was an independent Himalayan kingdom but closely aligned with and dependent on India, especially on economic and military matters. In fact, for all practical purposes, it was deemed to be an Indian protectorate. Among other matters the Indian Army provided the guards to the ruler of Sikkim, the Chogyal. These were composed of two companies' worth of the Gorkha Regiment.[18] (Sikkim was formally incorporated into India in May 1975.) More specifically, the PRC leadership may have feared that the Chogyal, who had been on a state visit to India

---

[15] Raju G. C. Thomas, *The Defence of India: A Budgetary Perspective of Strategy and Politics* (Delhi: Macmillan, 1978).

[16] Russell Brines, *The Indo-Pakistani Conflict* (New York: Pall Mall, 1968).

[17] It had initially asserted this claim as early as the deadlocked border talks of 1960.

[18] Personal correspondence with a senior Indian military official with long experience on the Sino-Indian frontier, November 2021.

in September 1967, was inclined toward forging a closer relationship with New Delhi. According to an informed Indian source, the PRC probably used this incident to send a warning to both Gangtok and New Delhi.[19]

In early September 1967 tensions started building up along the border following heated verbal exchanges between the local PLA commissar and the Indian commander, Brigadier M. M. S. Bakshi. In the wake of these verbal duels apparently some Indian soldiers roughed up the commissar on September 11. Shortly thereafter, when the Indian forces continued with a fence-laying operation that they had begun earlier, the PLA started an assault using medium machine guns and followed up with both mortar and artillery fire, causing as many as forty casualties. The Indian units, much better armed and prepared than in 1962, responded with considerable vigor using their artillery, blowing up a substantial number of PLA bunkers and exacting a significant human toll. The fighting continued for several days despite an Indian overture for a ceasefire. After a brief hiatus in the fighting, PLA units sought to overrun an Indian position at Cho La, the highest pass on the Sikkim–Tibet border. At this point the Indian Army had reinforced its defensive positions with elite troops. Consequently, when the PLA attacked, they responded with verve, fending off the onslaught.[20]

In this case, in marked contrast to 1962, there was little difference of opinion between local commanders and the higher echelons of the military and civilian leadership. In fact, according to an informed account of the crisis, Prime Minister Indira Gandhi granted permission for the use of heavy artillery in the conflict as the chief of staff of the Indian Army, General S. H. F. J. Manekshaw, was out of the country and local commanders lacked the authority to respond with an artillery barrage.[21]

The immediate precipitant of the clash at Nathu La Pass was an Indian decision in August 1967 to place barbed wire fencing to create a barrier between Indian and Chinese forces to reduce tensions. The local PLA commander, however, construed this effort as an attempt to seize Chinese territory. This led to verbal assaults and shoving matches between the military

[19] A former, retired, senior Indian Foreign Service officer with considerable experience with and knowledge of the PRC suggests an alternative explanation. He attributes the Chinese intransigence to domestic developments related to the upheavals of the Cultural Revolution and the need to demonstrate that it was not weak. Sumit Ganguly, personal correspondence with a retired senior Indian Foreign Service official, December 2021.
[20] Arjun Subramaniam, *A Military History of India since 1972* (Lawrence: University of Kansas Press, 2021), 128.
[21] For details of this incident, see Probal Dasgupta, *Watershed 1967: India's Forgotten Victory over China* (New Delhi: Juggernaut, 2020).

personnel of the two sides. Later, in September, Indian forces sought to install a new stretch of fencing. The Chinese protested and then opened fire with machine guns and artillery.[22] They also threatened to use air power but in the end did not resort to such action.[23] The Indians, who held the high ground, retaliated with artillery fire, which led to the destruction of several PLA fortifications. The Indian forces demonstrated considerable resolve in repelling the attack as they feared that their PLA counterparts were keen on dislodging them from the commanding heights that they held in the Chumbi Valley.[24] In early September the tensions started to taper off with the government of India proposing a ceasefire and a meeting of local military commanders.[25] By mid-September, the conflict, for all practical purposes, had drawn to a close.[26] One scholar of Chinese security policy has argued that the vigorous Chinese response to the Indian moves can be attributed to the insecurities that the upheaval of the Cultural Revolution had generated in the minds of the Chinese political elite.[27]

The robust and unyielding Indian response is also worth noting for two reasons. First, the region is deemed to be extremely sensitive as it provides the best route for invasion from Tibet to the narrow neck of land in the state of West Bengal, which links the Indian mainland with the states of the northeast. Second, following the debacle of the 1962 border war, Indian military capabilities along the border had been significantly bolstered and the morale of the Indian troops altogether improved.[28] Nevertheless, press reports from the time indicate that local commanders felt that they did not have adequate freedom of action in dealing with Chinese provocations.[29]

The Sumdorong Chu Crisis of 1986

After a long hiatus, a major crisis erupted in 1986 at Sumdorong Chu in the Tawang District of the North-East Frontier Agency (NEFA), which

[22] James S. Keat, "India, China Troops Swap Border Fire," *The Baltimore Sun*, September 12, 1967.
[23] Bernard Nossiter, "China, India Troops Renew Border Clash," *The Boston Globe*, September 14, 1967.
[24] "Chinese Troops Start an Intense Duel with Indian Troops on Sikkim Border," *The Times of India*, September 12, 1967.
[25] "Cease Fire and Start Talks: New Delhi Note," *The Times of India*, September 12, 1967.
[26] "All Quiet on the Nathu La front," *The Times of India*, September 15, 1967.
[27] M. Taylor Fravel, *Strong Borders, Secure Nation: Cooperation and Conflict in China's Territorial Dispute* (Princeton: Princeton University Press, 2008).
[28] J. D. Singh, "Nathu La Border I: The Chinese Threat," *The Times of India*, October 14, 1967.
[29] J. D. Singh, "Nathu La Border II: Enemy Intentions," *The Times of India*, October 16, 1967.

would be converted into the state of Arunachal Pradesh in February 1987.[30] The long-term origins of this crisis stem from the decision of the Indian Subsidiary Intelligence Bureau (SIB) to set up an observation post at Wangdung on the Indian side of the Line of Actual Control, the de facto border, in the summer of 1984. Subsequently, the new commander of the Fourth Corps, Lieutenant-General J. M. Singh, upon assuming office realized that the existing Indian defenses were inadequate for the purposes of defending the area. The more immediate precipitants of the crisis can be traced to a PLA incursion in the area in June 1986, which resulted in the seizure of a seasonal Indian observer post near the Thag La ridge. This incursion had taken place after India had been bolstering its security presence in the area primarily to defend the border monastery town of Tawang.

When Lieutenant-General N. S. Narahari took command of the Fourth Corps, his colleague Major-General J. M. Singh, the commander of the Fifth Mountain Division, cautioned that Indian forces would need to be bolstered in the event the PLA challenged existing deployments in the area. While Narahari agreed with Singh's assessment, he did not receive appropriate authorization to proceed from Eastern Command headquarters in Calcutta.[31]

At any event, apparently irked with the SIB post the PLA boosted its patrolling in the area in May–June 1986. Seeking to avoid provoking the PLA the SIB chose not to revive its previous Wangdung post in 1986. However, some local herdsmen alerted the SIB of growing Chinese patrols around Lungro La, a pass that provided access to the Sumdorong Chu Valley from the Indian side. In June 1986, to the dismay of the Indian Army the SIB reported that the PLA was in the midst of building a large camp at Wangdung. This led the local Indian commander to promptly occupy Lungro La with a protective patrol. Furthermore, he gave his men leeway to use small arms if the PLA units approached the pass.[32]

---

[30] It is necessary to highlight that Arunachal Pradesh, the former North-East Frontier Agency (NEFA), had been brought under formal Indian control in 1951 thanks to the efforts of an entrepreneurial Indian Frontier Administrative Service officer, Robert Khathing. The governor of the northeastern state of Assam, Daulat Ram, had tasked Khathing to ensure effective administrative control of this area. For details see Claudi Arpi, "Major Bob Khathing, the Indian Hero Who Secured Tawang," *The Daily Guardian*, February 20, 2021. Sumit Ganguly is grateful to Major-General Dipankar Banerjee, formerly of the Indian Army, for alerting him to Khathing's critical role.

[31] Subramaniam, *A Military History of India since 1972*, 131.

[32] Details of these military activities have been derived from Subramaniam, *A Military History of India since 1972*, 130–133.

From the PRC's standpoint India's actions represented a challenge to the status quo in a sensitive area. Furthermore, the Indian military moves in the area were part of its wider efforts to strengthen its military presence in the area.[33] Subsequently, General Krishnaswami Sundarji, the successor to General A.S. Vaidya, launched "Operation Falcon," which involved airlifting a brigade of Indian troops to Zemithang, south of the McMahon Line, in October 1986. Furthermore, he oversaw the construction of a helipad on a hill overlooking the Sumdorong Chu Valley, arranged to have heavy artillery placed in position, and sent in long-range patrols into neighboring areas.[34]

This led to a stern warning from the Chinese leader Deng Xiaoping, reminding India of dire consequences. The Indian Army, despite some political disquiet on the part of Prime Minister Rajiv Gandhi, nevertheless went ahead with beefing up its capabilities in the area.[35] In fact, at General Sundarji's initiative, the Indian Army launched "Exercise Chequerboard." The purpose of this exercise was to simulate India's battle preparedness vis-à-vis the McMahon Line.

Apart from the PRC's assertiveness along the troubled frontier, other developments in the region had also contributed to India's willingness to flex its muscles. In July 1986, in a speech in Vladivostok, Soviet president Mikhail Gorbachev had adopted a distinctly neutral stand on Sino-Indian relations. This change in the Soviet stance, given the existence of the twenty-year Indo-Soviet treaty of "peace, friendship and cooperation" of 1971, had rattled decision-makers in New Delhi.[36] Closer to home, in July 1987 the PRC had signed a defense pact with Pakistan in which it had promised to safeguard Pakistan's territorial integrity.[37]

Finally, it is impossible to discount the role of the chief of staff of the Indian Army, General Sundarji. Known as a flamboyant military officer, who was keen on modernizing the Indian Army, he was also inclined to be risk-prone.[38] Indeed, under his watch, in late 1986 and early 1987, he

---

[33] Fravel, *Strong Borders, Secure Nation*, 200–201.

[34] Bertil Lintner, *China's India War: Collison Course on the Roof of the World* (New Delhi: Oxford University Press, 2018), 264.

[35] Manoj Joshi, "Operation Falcon: When Gen Sundarji Took the Chinese by Surprise," *The Quint*, March 14, 2017, www.thequint.com/voices/opinion/operation-falcon-sundarji-took-china-by-surprise.

[36] Among other matters, Article 9 of the treaty had an implicit security guarantee to India. On this matter see Robert Donaldson, *Soviet Policy toward India: Ideology and Strategy* (Cambridge, MA: Harvard University Press, 1974).

[37] Manjeet S. Pardesi, "Managing the 1986–87 Sino-Indian Sumdorong Chu Crisis," *The India Review* 18.5 (2019): 534–551.

[38] Sekhar Gupta, "General Krishnaswami Sundarji, 'Soldier of the Mind,' Who Rewrote India's Military Doctrine," *The Print*, February 8, 2018, https://theprint.in/opinion/general-krishnaswamy-sundarji-soldier-mind-rewrote-indias-military-doctrine/34227/.

had organized the largest peacetime military exercise near India's western border with Pakistan, drawing on as many as half a million Indian military personnel. The sheer size, scope, and location of the exercise had provoked Pakistani fears of an impending invasion and had culminated in a crisis, which had been brought to a close through timely US and Soviet intercession.[39]

Tensions along the disputed border flared once again in 1987, which, it is widely believed, stemmed from India's decision in February 1987 to change the status of the North-East Frontier Agency to that of a new state, renamed as Arunachal Pradesh. Observers also argued that the PRC may have felt more emboldened to adopt a tougher stance toward India than before because of the loosening of Indo-Soviet ties and an improvement in Sino-Soviet relations. Furthermore, earlier in the decade the chief of staff of the Indian Army, General Krishna Rao, had persuaded Prime Minister Indira Gandhi of the need to reestablish India's military presence in Arunachal Pradesh. Prime Minister Gandhi had authorized this program, "Operation Falcon," which was expected to take most of a decade.[40]

The final precipitant of these tensions might have also been General Sundarji's decision to pursue a major military exercise, "Chequerboard," in the early months of 1987.[41] This effort involved the restart of long-planned but never implemented road-building activities as well as the bolstering of military capabilities near Hathung La.[42] Among other matters, the PRC accused India's of "nibbling" at Chinese territory. Furthermore, official spokesmen in Beijing claimed that India had conducted large-scale military exercises near the disputed border and had committed airspace violations.[43] These tensions continued until the visit of the Indian minister for external affairs, Narayan Dutt Tiwari, to Beijing in June 1987, which subsequently paved the way for Rajiv Gandhi's maiden visit to the PRC in December 1988.

Gandhi's visit set in motion a series of high-level discussions designed to bring an end to the border dispute. However, despite multiple bilateral meetings, including upgrades in the levels of the participating officials, the

[39] Kanti Bajpai, Pervaiz Iqbal Cheema, P. R. Chari, Stephen P. Cohen, and Sumit Ganguly, *Brasstacks and Beyond: Perception and the Management of Crisis in South Asia* (New Delhi: Manohar, 1995).

[40] Pardesi, "Managing the 1986–1987 Sino-Indian Sumdorong Chu Crisis," 534–551.

[41] Ravi Rikhye, "China's Border Build-Up," *The Times of India*, April 16, 1987.

[42] Manoj Joshi, "Operation Falcon: When General Sundarji Took the Chinese by Surprise" Observer Research Foundation, July 3, 2017, www.orfonline.org/research/operation-falcon-when-general-sundarji-took-the-chinese-by-surprise/.

[43] Daniel Southerland, "China Accuses India of Violating Border: New Delhi Rejects Charge of Nibbling," *The Washington Post*, April 23, 1987.

two parties are no closer to a settlement of the dispute. Even confidence-building measures, most notably those implemented in 1993 and 1996, have proven to be of little significance, as the PRC has conducted several "limited probes" along the disputed border, with one of them culminating in the Galwan Valley crisis of 2020.[44]

According to a detailed analysis of the Sumdorong Chu crisis, two factors were critical in contributing to its resolution. The first involved the military capabilities of both sides along the border. More specifically, the crisis can be attributed to the Indian belief that Chinese revisionist behavior was limited in scope and that the Indian military had the requisite capabilities to fend off any PLA attempts at incursion. The second was the shifting position of the Soviet Union in its relations with India. Under Gorbachev the Soviet Union had started to move away from its traditional ironclad commitment to guaranteeing India's security.[45]

Since then, there have been some minor incursions, including one that was singularly ill-timed, in that it took place during Xi Jinping's visit to India in September 2014. The intrusion that took place near Chumar in the region of Ladakh had involved over a thousand PLA troops. Indian analysts had concluded that Xi, despite protestations to the contrary, had allowed this incursion to take place. Modi, obviously discomfited by this episode, made his unhappiness known to his visitor, stating that "[a] little toothache can paralyze the entire body."[46]

The Doklam Crisis

The next crisis erupted near Doklam, a Bhutan–India–PRC trijunction area, in mid-June 2017. The immediate precipitant of the crisis was Bhutan's objection to Chinese road-building activity in a disputed stretch near this trijunction. More specifically, according to reliable Indian press reports, the key precipitant of the crisis was the move of a PLA platoon that razed stone bunkers of the Royal Bhutan Army (RBA) on the night of June 8. In slightly over a week, a PLA road construction crew entered Doklam

---

[44] On the concept of a "limited probe," see Alexander George and Richard Smoke, *Deterrence in American Foreign Policy* (New York: Columbia University Press, 1975).

[45] Pardesi, "Managing the 1986–1987 Sino-Indian Sumdorong Chu Crisis," 535.

[46] TNN, "Chinese Incursion in Ladakh: A Little Toothache Can Paralyze Entire Body, Modi Tells Xi Jinping," *The Times of India*, September 20, 2014. For a formulation that suggests that the PLA may have acted on its own contrary to Xi's wishes, see: Gordon G. Chang, "The Real Threat from China's Military: Going Rogue," *The National Interest*, September 26, 2014, https://nationalinterest.org/feature/the-real-threat-chinas-military-going-rogue-11356

with road rollers, bulldozers, and excavators. The Chinese troops faced resistance from units of the RBA and apparently some clashes ensued. At this point, it is believed, Bhutan sought India's military assistance.[47] Later in the same month, the PRC accused India of halting construction in what it deemed to be its "sovereign territory" based upon an 1890 "Convention between Great Britain and China Concerning Sikkim and Tibet."[48] Indian officials, however, dismissed these claims suggesting that the PRC 's reading of the convention documents was questionable, especially since it had not specified a boundary that both Britain and China had accepted. After independence the two states had failed to delineate and demarcate the boundary.[49]

The region in question is a plateau of about 100 square kilometers. According to reliable Indian sources, the issue arose when on June 16, 2017, PLA troops entered the area with road-building equipment to extend a road southward toward a Bhutanese Army camp near the Jampheri Ridge. It is not entirely clear whether or not Bhutan, which relies on India to protect its foreign and security policy interests, sought India's military assistance to fend off the Chinese encroachments. Regardless of the Bhutan actions (or the lack thereof) India did move troops into the disputed area from a nearby garrison to stop the Chinese construction efforts.[50] India's security interests pretty much dictated that the PRC not construct a road in this area, as it is perilously close to the narrow strip of land, popularly referred to as the "chicken's neck," that connects the Indian mainland with its states of the northeast.[51]

The initial response from the PRC for India's decision to deploy these troops was quite intransigent. In early July, a senior Chinese foreign policy official in Beijing stated in an interview that the onus was on India to withdraw its forces "unconditionally" to resolve what he deemed to be a "grave" situation.[52] The situation remained tense even in early August owing to tough statements from the Chinese Defense Ministry. Furthermore, a Chinese newspaper reported that the PLA had recently concluded artillery exercises using live ammunition in Tibet near the disputed area and that

[47] Ananth Krishnan and Raj Chengappa, "India-China Standoff: All You Need to Know about Doklam Dispute," *India Today*, July 17, 2017.
[48] HT Correspondent, "Blow by Blow: A Timeline of India, China Face-Off over Doklam," *Hindustan Times*, August 28, 2017; also see Simon Denyer and Annie Gowen, "India, China Agree to Pull Back Troops to Resolve Tense Border Dispute," *The Washington Post*, August 28, 2017.
[49] Krishnan and Chengappa, "India-China Standoff."
[50] Denyer and Gowen, "India, China Agree to Pull Back Troops to Resolve Tense Border Dispute."
[51] Josy Joseph, "What Is the Doklam Issue All About?," *The Hindu*, January 27, 2018.
[52] Rajat Pandit, "India Asks China to Retreat from Doklam," *The Times of India*, July 6, 2017.

these exercises had included simulated long-distance attacks on armored units and missile launchers.[53]

The standoff lasted seventy-three days, with both sides agreeing to disengage their troops from the contested area in late August. Three factors, it appears, may have contributed to the drawdown of forces from this eyeball-to-eyeball confrontation. First, some analysts argued, despite India's seemingly bold initial stance it came to the realization that it did not have the economic and military wherewithal to sustain a long standoff. Some informed Indian analysts, however, dispute this claim and assert that "better sense prevailed on both sides."[54] Second, others argued, the PRC was also averse to escalate this issue and thereby make it a major strategic concern with India.[55] Third and finally, the PLA may have temporarily wound up its operations because of an approaching BRICS (Brazil, Russia, India, China, and South Africa) summit in Xiamen. However, as subsequent events would clearly demonstrate, this retreat was simply tactical as PLA forces would return in force within a month or so.[56]

Despite this initial withdrawal of Chinese troops from the disputed areas, press reports that surfaced later in the year suggested that as many as 1,600 PLA troops had returned to the vicinity and had even constructed prefabricated huts in the area. Additionally, they had apparently constructed two helipads and upgraded nearby roads.[57] The building of these shelters suggested that the PLA was planning on maintaining a presence in the region through the winter.[58]

Ironically, even though China's actions had precipitated this crisis, New Delhi sought to smoothen relations with the PRC. This attempt to paper over their differences took place at an informal summit in the Chinese city of Wuhan in late April 2018.[59] This effort, however, proved far from

---

[53] Chris Buckley and Ellen Barry, "China Tells India That It Won't Back Down in Border Dispute," *The New York Times*, August 4, 2017.

[54] Sumit Ganguly, personal correspondence with a retired senior Indian general with considerable experience with and knowledge of the Sino-Indian frontier.

[55] Jeffrey Gettleman and Javier C. Hernández, "China and India Ease Tensions in Border Dispute Both Declare Victory," *The New York Times*, August 29, 2017.

[56] Sandeep Unnithan, "Month after Doklam Withdrawal, More Chinese Troops on Plateau than Before," *India Today*, October 9, 2017.

[57] Rajat Pandit, "In First Winter Stay, 1,800 Chinese Troops Camping at Doklam," *The Times of India*, December 11, 2017.

[58] HT Correspondent, ""1,600 Chinese Troops Still Hold Position Near Doklam Faceoff Site," *The Hindustan Times*, December 12, 2017.

[59] Saibal Dasgupta, "PM Modi, Xi Jinping Meet on April 27–28, to 'Reset' Ties after Doklam Standoff," *The Times of India*, April 23, 2017.

productive, and indeed earlier signs that the PRC had not abandoned its claims came to the fore later in the year. A reliable Indian security affairs journalist reported that around 1,600 to 1,800 PLA troops had established a permanent presence in the Doklam area. This was evident from the construction of two helipads, upgraded roads, the presence of a number of prefabricated huts, and adequate stores to cope with the harsh winter that prevailed in the area.[60]

The Galwan Crisis

The most recent crisis to punctuate Sino-Indian relations took place in the Galwan Valley in Ladakh, starting in June 2020. As early as January 2020, Indian newspapers had reported that PLA units were carrying out significant military exercises in Tibet in areas bordering India. Toward mid-April the PLA, using the same forces, occupied a number of positions that are disputed near the Galwan River Valley, the northern bank of the Pangong Tso Lake, Hot Springs, Gogra, the Depsang plains, and the Charding Nala area of Demchok. On May 5, Chinese forces entered the Galwan Valley and the Gogra–Hot Springs area but apparently the Indian Army still did not realize the full extent of the threat.[61]

Over the remainder of the month, according to one report, the Chinese military seized about forty square miles of territory, including the Galwan River Valley whose ridges overlook the vital Darbuk–Shyok–Daulat Beg Oldi road that leads to Aksai Chin and the Karakoram Pass. In the wake of this development India protested and talks started between local military personnel to defuse the crisis. Consequently the PLA agreed to vacate some of the positions that it had occupied. However, when Indian forces sought to verify these claims they encountered several hundred Chinese soldiers and a clash ensued. In hand-to-hand combat at least twenty Indian soldiers and an unspecified number of PLA troops were killed.[62] No weaponry was deployed in this skirmish as both sides are expected to patrol these disputed areas without carrying side arms or other weaponry. Instead, the violence that ensued involved the use of fence posts and clubs

---

[60] Pandit, "In First Winter Stay, 1,800 Chinese Troops Camping at Doklam."

[61] Manoj Joshi, "Eastern Ladakh, the Longer Perspective," *ORF Occasional Paper*, Number 319, June 2021.

[62] Ajai Shukla, "How China and India Came to Lethal Blows," *The New York Times*, June 19, 2020; also see Niharika Mandhana, Rajesh Roy, and Chun Han Wong, "The Deadly India-China Clash: Spiked Face-to-Face for Four Hours in the Dark, Some Falling off Cliffs, Indian Officials Said," *The Wall Street Journal*, June 17, 2020, www.wsj.com/articles/spiked-clubs-and-fists-at-14-000-feet-the-deadly-india-china-clash-11592418242

wrapped with barbed wire.[63] As several sources have reported this was the first loss of life on the Sino-Indian border since a clash that had taken place in 1975.[64]

It was really not until late June that Indian authorities acted with any alacrity to bolster their capabilities in the area. Belatedly recognizing the severity of the threat, the Indian Army moved a substantial number of troops from other parts of the country into Ladakh. Furthermore, the Indian Air Force stationed fighter aircraft in forward locations in Punjab and Haryana. It also dispatched the newly acquired Apache helicopters to Leh.[65]

Despite these moves on India's part the PLA apparently continued with its efforts to strengthen its presence in these disputed areas. In late June, for example, evidence emerged through satellite imagery that the PLA had constructed new structures on a terrace overlooking the Galwan Valley. The construction included camouflaged tents or covered structures against the base of a cliff. This was a short distance away from a potential new camp under construction with walls or barricades. On the Indian side, however, the same imagery revealed that the army had constructed defensive barriers.[66]

What factors precipitated the Galwan crisis? There is no clear-cut answer to this question. However, it can be argued on the basis of inference and attribution that it probably stemmed from four possible sources. First, the PRC leadership under Xi Jinping had looked upon the growing security partnership between India and the United States with increasing alacrity and hostility.[67] India, reliant solely on its own military capabilities, is not in a sound position to cope with a threat from the PRC. However, a more robust and secure strategic partnership with the United States can potentially enable India to balance more effectively against its rival. Second,

[63] Russell Goldman, "India-China Border Dispute: A Conflict Explained," *The New York Times*, June 17, 2020.

[64] Michael Safi and Hannah Ellis-Petersen, "India Says 20 Soldiers Killed on Disputed Himalayan Border with China; First Loss of Life in Area in At Least 45 Years Comes amid Renewed Dispute," *The Guardian*, June 16, 2020; also see Joanna Slater and Gerry Shih, "India and China Trade Barbs after 'Gang War' High in the Himalayas," *The Washington Post*, June 17, 2020.

[65] Man Aman Singh Chhina, "Army Rushes More Troops to Ladakh after Galwan Clash," *The Indian Express*, June 20, 2020.

[66] Lily Kuo, "Satellite Images Show Chinese Construction Near Site of Border Clash; Images of Potential New Camp in Disputed Territory Raise Fears of Further Conflict," *The Guardian*, June 25, 2020.

[67] Tom O'Connor, "China Warns of 'Cold War' after US-India Talks, Pakistan Protests Terror Accusations," *Newsweek*, October 28, 2020, www.newsweek.com/china-cold-war-us-india-talks-pakistan-protests-terror-accusations-1543078.

the PRC was also dismayed with India's abrogation of Article 370 of the Indian Constitution in August 2019, which fundamentally altered the status of the disputed state of Jammu and Kashmir.[68] The termination of the state's special status also meant that it was now more closely integrated into India, thereby undermining both Pakistani and Chinese claims to any part of the state.[69] (Some Indian analysts, however, argue quite forcefully, and not without some merit, that it is the PRC that had changed the status quo in Kashmir as early as 1963 when it had concluded an agreement with Pakistan that had led the latter to cede disputed territory in the state to the PRC.)[70] Third, the PRC was also agitated with India's construction of a border road that linked the Indian Air Force base at Daulat Beg Oldi with Darbuk–Shyok in the Galwan Valley. The construction of this road near the Line of Actual Control conferred some strategic advantage to India in this sensitive region.[71] A fourth and final explanation, however, suggests a more aggressive intent on the part of the PRC. This interpretation holds that the Galwan episode is simply a continuation of previous probes that the PRC had undertaken, including those at Depsang in 2013, Chumar in 2014, and Doklam in 2017. All of these episodes, it can be argued, represent an ongoing attempt on the part of the PRC to test India's capabilities and resolve along the Himalayan border. In this context it may be worth recalling that an Indian scholar-diplomat, Sisir Gupta, decades ago had sounded the tocsin about the possibility of the PRC pursuing this strategy.[72]

Conclusion

In the wake of the Galwan crisis, it is reasonable to surmise that the Modi government is most unlikely to return to its past efforts of setting aside the border dispute and focusing on promoting economic ties with the PRC in the hope that economic interdependence might smooth the rough edges

[68] Sumit Ganguly, "Modi Crosses the Rubicon in Kashmir," *Foreign Affairs*, August 8, 2019, www .foreignaffairs.com/articles/india/2019-08-08/modi-crosses-rubicon-kashmir.

[69] Associated Press, "China Objects to Ladakh Status, Indian Border Activities," September 29, 2020, https://news.yahoo.com/china-objects-ladakh-status-indian-095814241.html?fr=yhssrp_catchall.

[70] For a discussion see Andrew Small, *The China-Pakistan Axis: Asia's New Geopolitics* (New York: Oxford University Press, 2015).

[71] Sanjeev Miglani and Fayaz Bukhari, "New Indian Roads, Airstrips, Sparked Standoff with China, Observers Say," *NTD*, May 25, 2020, https://ntdca.com/new-indian-roads-airstrips-sparked-border-standoff-with-china-india-observers-say/.

[72] Sisir Gupta, "The Indian Dilemma," in Alastair Buchan (ed.), *A World of Nuclear Powers?* (Englewood Cliffs: Prentice Hall, 1966).

of the rivalry.[73] The PRC, in turn, is equally unlikely to abandon its claims along the border and beyond. Instead, there is evidence that it intends to maintain continued pressure along the disputed frontiers. It is reasonable to make this inference because, among other matters, it has continued to build up its military capabilities and infrastructure along the disputed areas. More to the point, evidence has emerged that it has constructed a village in an area inside what India deems to be a part of the state of Arunachal Pradesh.[74]

All these developments portend that the rivalry will play out in continuing crises along the disputed border, as the PRC with improved infrastructure and greater military capabilities will continue to prod and probe Indian capabilities and resolve. As these attempts continue, further clashes are all but inevitable. The question then that must be addressed is, how to prevent future incidents from escalating into a wider war as the existing range of confidence-building measures have been found to be clearly wanting?

In the midst of the Vietnam war, in the wake of a major North Vietnam attack on an American military base in Pleiku, McGeorge Bundy, the National Security Adviser told a reporter that "Pleikus are like streetcars" – there was always another one coming.[75] The same, it appears, may be said for crises along the Sino-Indian border. The key issue then is whether or not any future crisis can be contained or if it may spiral into a wider, inadvertent war. Consequently, despite the view of some scholars that the Sino-Indian rivalry may be losing its potency, the eruption of significant crises, especially the one in the Galwan Valley, demonstrates that it remains quite robust.

---

[73] For a useful discussion see Vijay Gokhale, *The Road from Galwan: The Future of India-China Relations* (Washington, DC: Carnegie Endowment for International Peace, 2021).

[74] Office of the Secretary of Defense, *Annual Report to Congress, Military and Security Developments Involving the PRC* (Washington, DC: United States Department of Defense, November 2021).

[75] McGeorge Bundy, as quoted in Andrew Preston, *The War Council: McGeorge Bundy, the NSC and Vietnam* (Cambridge, MA: Harvard University Press, 2006).

CHAPTER 6

Asymmetries and Rivalry
Economic, Nuclear, and Naval

China and India are asymmetric rivals because even though India's elites view China as India's "principal rival,"[1] ranked above Pakistan, China's elites regard India as a "lesser rival," ranked below the United States and Japan. However, this asymmetry in ranks has been exacerbated by the material power asymmetry between China and India that is of relatively recent vintage (as discussed in Chapter 2). In other words, the current asymmetries between China and India are rooted in both cognitive and material factors.[2] However, the Sino-Indian relationship is not representative of what Womack has referred to as "asymmetric normalcy."[3] Under conditions of asymmetric normalcy, there is an exchange of "autonomy for deference" between the higher- and lower-ranking states.[4] In the Sino-Indian dyad, neither is India willing to defer to China's interests given its higher rank (whether in Pakistan or in the Indian Ocean, for example) nor is China willing to respect India's autonomy (whether bilaterally in Kashmir or regionally in [South] Asia, for example).

The Sino-Indian asymmetric relationship is not characterized by this so-called "normalcy" because they are engaged in a strategic rivalry. Unlike normal dyadic relationships, in strategic rivalry "current competitions are connected to past competitions" between the rivals, and there is also an "expectation that they will be remembered in the future."[5] It is therefore

---

[1] William R. Thompson, "Principal Rivalries," *Journal of Conflict Resolution* 39.2 (1995): 195–223.

[2] For a useful overview of the emerging literature on asymmetries in International Relations, see Paul Musgrave, "Asymmetry, Hierarchy, and the Ecclesiastes Trap," *International Studies Review* 21.2 (2019): 284–300.

[3] Brantly Womack, *Asymmetry and International Relationships* (New York: Cambridge University Press, 2016), 105.

[4] Womack, *Asymmetry and International Relationships*, 105.

[5] These psychological findings are valid "even when scaled up to the level of nations." See Benjamin A. Converse and David A. Reinhard, "On Rivalry and Goal Pursuit: Shared Competitive History, Legacy Concerns, and Strategy Selection," *Journal of Personality and Social Psychology* 110.2 (2016): 193, 207.

possible for the higher-ranking power to engage in "coerced deference," with such coercion being material or cognitive (or both),[6] and simultaneously for the lower-ranked actor to perceive a greater threat than actually warranted due to the dismissiveness of the higher-ranked actor toward its concerns.[7] Consequently, the existence of a strategic rivalry "increase[s] motivation and effort compared to mere competition" and "can also promote reckless behavior and thoughtless mistakes."[8]

In other words, the asymmetries in the Sino-Indian rivalry are prone to instability and conflict. While there is a feeling among China's elites that "China has become more powerful than in the past, ... they have problems in agreeing to how powerful China is compared to other great powers, such as Russia, Japan, India, or Europe," although there is agreement that the United States continues to remain more powerful than China.[9] On the one hand, scholars such as Yan are dismissive of India as a "subregional power" (as opposed a full-fledged regional power – let alone a great power – because India is not the "dominant state" in its South Asian home region unlike its early modern predecessor, the Mughal Empire).[10] Yan is of the opinion that the Sino-Indian "strength disparity" is approaching "that between a superpower and the world's largest developing country."[11]

On the other hand, scholars such as Li believe that "India's rise is accelerating," even though its emergence "as a great power will not be smooth" due to its myriad challenges.[12] Furthermore, the United States no longer views "India as an unimportant country" but treats it as "a world power" instead.[13] More importantly, this allows India, "a rising regional power," to "reverse its relatively weaker position in the asymmetric relationship

[6] Joey T. Cheng and Jessica L. Tracy, "Toward a Unified Science of Hierarchy: Dominance and Prestige Are Two Fundamental Pathways to Human Social Rank," in Joey T. Cheng, Jessica L. Tracy, and Cameron Anderson (eds.), *The Psychology of Social Status* (New York: Springer, 2014), 4.

[7] Leanne ten Brinke and Dacher Keltner, "Theories of Power: Perceived Strategies for Gaining and Maintaining Power," *Journal of Personality and Social Psychology* 122.1 (2022): 53–72; and Marc A. Fournier, D. S. Moskowitz, and David C. Zuroff, "Social Rank Strategies in Hierarchical Relationships," *Journal of Personality and Social Psychology* 83.2 (2002): 425–433.

[8] Converse and Reinhard, "On Rivalry and Goal Pursuit," 207–208.

[9] Zhimin Chen, "China's Power from a Chinese Perspective (II): Back to the Center Stage," in Jae Ho Chung (ed.), *Assessing China's Power* (New York: Palgrave, 2015), 281.

[10] Yan Xuetong, *Leadership and the Rise of Great Powers* (Princeton: Princeton University Press, 2019), 60.

[11] Yan Xuetong (trans. Alexander A. Bowe), *Inertia of History: China and the World by 2023* (Newcastle upon Tyne: Cambridge Scholars Publishing, 2019), 115.

[12] Li Li, "The New Trend of India's Rising as a Great Power," *Contemporary International Relations* 28.2 (2018): 43, 48.

[13] Ye Zicheng (trans. Steven I. Levine and Guoli Liu), *Inside China's Grand Strategy: The Perspective from the People's Republic* (Lexington: The University Press of Kentucky, 2011), 57.

with China."[14] Consequently, Zheng has cautioned that even as "China is chasing after the US and India is chasing after China" it will be "no minor mistake" to "forget about those who are after us by setting our eyes only on those ahead."[15]

On their part, leading Indian scholars are also aware of the growing asymmetry in the material capabilities between China and India.[16] However, India is not reconciled with its "lesser" status vis-à-vis China. While it is true that India's material power has declined relative to China over the past three decades, this recent past was also characterized by India's slow and halting economic and military rise (in absolute terms) even if significant challenges remain.[17] Consequently, India's approach toward China does not stem from a defeatist attitude though there is recognition of the challenges and the vast and growing gap.

Indeed, Womack has argued that as a rising power India has a "future-oriented" approach toward China (unlike Japan or the United States, which are "basically trying to reverse or slow" their relative decline vis-à-vis China).[18] Not surprisingly, on the eve of becoming India's current foreign minister, S. Jaishankar categorically asserted the following in a conversation with Professor Wang Gungwu in Singapore: "A country like India would not be able to deal with China, except on a basis of *equality* [*emphasis added*]."[19] After becoming India's foreign minister, Jaishankar urged that India and China "should strive to occupy a greater

[14] Wu Lin, "India's Perception of and Response to China-US Competition," *China International Studies* 85.6 (2020): 130, 133.

[15] Zheng Yongnian, "On China-India Border Standoff," *China-US Focus*, July 24, 2017, www .chinausfocus.com/peace-security/on-china-india-border-standoff.

[16] C. Raja Mohan, "Mind the Power Gap," *Indian Express*, August 2, 2017, https://indianexpress .com/article/opinion/columns/india-china-standoff-mind-the-power-gap-4777926/; and Swaran Singh, "China and India: Coping with Growing Asymmetry," *The Asan Forum*, December 19, 2014, https://theasanforum.org/china-and-india-coping-with-growing-asymmetry/. Also see, Kanti P. Bajpai, *India versus China: Why They Are Not Friends* (New Delhi: Juggernaut, 2021).

[17] There is a vast literature on India's rise and concomitant challenges. Some of the more notable works include Baldev Raj Nayar and T. V. Paul, *India in the World Order: Searching for Major Power Status* (Cambridge: Cambridge University Press, 2002); Stephen P. Cohen, *India: Emerging Power* (Washington, DC: Brookings, 2002); Ashley J. Tellis, Travis Tanner, and Jessica Keough (eds.), *Strategic Asia 2011–12: Asia Responds to Its Rising Powers, China and India* (Washington, DC: National Bureau of Asian Research, 2011); Teresita C. Schaffer and Howard B. Schaffer, *India at the Global High Table: The Quest for Regional Primacy and Strategic Autonomy* (Washington, DC: Brookings, 2016); and Sumit Ganguly and William R. Thompson, *Ascending India and Its State Capacity: Extraction, Violence, and Legitimacy* (New Haven: Yale University Press, 2011).

[18] Brantly Womack, "Mapping the Multinodal Terrain of the Indo-Pacific," *Settimana News*, February 28, 2018, www.settimananews.it/italia-europa-mondo/mapping-multinodal-terrain-indo-pacific/.

[19] S. Jaishankar and Wang Gungwu, "Asia in the New World Order," HT–MintAsia Leadership Summit, May 2, 2018, Singapore (quote at 14m 20s), www.channelnewsasia.com/watch/asia-new-world-order-1545236.

mind space of the other,"[20] thereby implying that India also wishes to redress their perceptual asymmetry (as he wants China to take India more seriously).

Given the peculiar nature of Sino-Indian asymmetries, and the fact of their rivalry, this relationship is rife with "uncertainty and risks" as China cannot impose its preferred vision of bilateral relations or regional/Asian order upon India despite being the more powerful actor because their asymmetry is not "lopsided" enough to make China "hegemon[ic]."[21] Under such conditions, there are at least three major pathways to conflict. First, if material power continues to shift in China's favor, then China may wish to create new political realities reflective of that power gap, including through the use of force.[22] Second, any "shift toward equality" may give either side the incentive to use force because material power equality makes rivals more conflict-prone.[23] China's cognitive disdain for India makes any shift toward material power equality more dangerous as China does not think of India as an equal or a peer.[24] Third, even if the power asymmetry between them continues (or widens), India, as the weaker power, may be tempted to undertake strategies for China to take it more seriously (as India wishes to occupy "greater mind space" in China, according to Jaishankar). This may precipitate an inadvertent crisis if India were to cross any unknown Chinese red lines.[25] India's turn toward the United States in the context of the widening gap with China has not gone unnoticed in Beijing, as mentioned above.

---

[20] S. Jaishankar, *The India Way: Strategies for an Uncertain World* (Noida: HarperCollins, 2020), 137.

[21] Xiaoyu Pu, "Ambivalent Accommodation: Status Signaling of a Rising India and China's Response," *International Affairs* 93.1 (2017): 155–156.

[22] It is widely acknowledged in International Relations scholarship, especially in the realist tradition, that any increase in power is likely to create new interests and opportunities. For the classic statement of this thesis, see Robert Gilpin, *War and Change in World Politics* (Cambridge: Cambridge University Press, 1981). A notable recent view of how rising powers may exploit such power shifts is presented in Joshua Shifrinson, *Rising Titans, Falling Giants: How Great Powers Exploit Power Shifts* (Ithaca: Cornell University Press, 2018).

[23] Daniel S. Geller, "Power Differential and War in Rival Dyads," *International Studies Quarterly* 37.2 (1993): 173–193.

[24] Relatedly, scholars have noted that one of the chief challenges in the Sino-Japanese rivalry stems from the fact that they "have little experience of dealing with each other as equals." See Barry Buzan and Evelyn Goh, *Rethinking Sino-Japanese Alienation: History Problems and Historical Opportunities* (Oxford: Oxford University Press, 2020), 231.

[25] There are several strategies available to the economically and militarily weaker power in asymmetric relationships that make such dyads more conflict prone. Such strategies range from low-intensity warfare to alignments with the rival's other rivals. See T. V. Paul, *Asymmetric Conflicts: War Initiation by Weaker Powers* (New York: Cambridge University Press, 1994). The weaker party in such relationships may also seek to "increase the volume" on issues that matter. See Charles F. Doran, "Living with Asymmetry," *Mershon International Studies Review* 38.2 (1994): 262.

We are in no way predicting war nor implying that war is inevitable. Instead, we are arguing that not only is the Sino-Indian asymmetry not stable but the Sino-Indian relationship has also entered a troubled phase because further asymmetry and the strategies to redress this asymmetry are both conflict-prone. It is therefore not surprising that the Sino-Indian *spatial* rivalry has come to the fore again in recent years (as discussed in Chapters 2 and 5). At the same time, their *positional* rivalry also continues. Unlike Nehru's India that thought of itself at the "center" of Asia in the 1940s and 1950s (as discussed in Chapters 3 and 4), it is President Xi Jinping's China that hopes to move "closer to the center stage" today as China strives to realize its "dream" of "national rejuvenation."[26] For Yan, East Asia is becoming the "center of the world," in a transformation driven by China's "rise" at its "core."[27] According to Wang Jisi, another influential scholar, contemporary China is "far more than it [China] ever was in antiquity, truly 'a state in the middle,' a 'central country'."[28] Unlike Yan, Wang is of the opinion that China must "reevaluate the 'East Asian' framework," because "the world's political and economic gravity has shifted to the Asian mainland and the regions where the Indian and Pacific Oceans merge, but not exactly to East Asia itself."[29]

In turn, India's leading analysts also believe that China seeks to create "a China-centric hierarchic order" in this wider Asian region, a vision that they reject.[30] On his part, Jaishankar has already expressed India's desire to create a "multipolar world" with "its foundation in multipolar Asia."[31] India clearly aspires to be one of the poles in the emerging world order on a par with China, especially in Asia. While India has not formally articulated a clear strategy beyond this broad vision,[32] scholars have long noted that it seeks some form of leadership, especially in South Asia and

---

[26] Xi Jinping, "Speech Delivered at the 19th National Congress of the Communist Party of China," October 18, 2017, www.xinhuanet.com/english/download/Xi_Jinping%27s_report_at_19th_CPC_National_Congress.pdf.

[27] Yan, *Inertia of History*, 40, 67.

[28] Wang Jisi, "China in the Middle," *The American Interest*, February 2, 2015, www.the-american-interest.com/2015/02/02/china-in-the-middle/.

[29] Wang, "China in the Middle."

[30] Shivshankar Menon, *India and Asian Geopolitics: The Past, Present* (Washington, DC: Brookings, 2021), 335.

[31] "Multipolar World Should Include Multipolar Asia: Jaishankar," *The Hindu*, September 19, 2020, www.thehindu.com/news/national/multipolar-world-should-include-multipolar-asia-jaishankar/article32644407.ece.

[32] Former Indian prime ministers Indira Gandhi and Inder Kumar Gujral had also enunciated their visions of Indian primacy in South Asia and the Indian Ocean (respectively referred to as the Indira Doctrine and the Gujral Doctrine).

in the Indian Ocean, and aspires to great power status in the wider Asian region.[33] Notably, China's 2013 *Science of Military Strategy* specifically mentioned that ever since independence India has continued to see itself at "the heart of Asia" and is pursuing a strategy that includes "dominating" South Asia and "controlling" the Indian Ocean. Furthermore, with itself at "the center" of that region (South Asia and the Indian Ocean), India is "advancing" into East Asia, as it strives to emerge as "a first-rate power in the world."[34]

In other words, the Sino-Indian *positional* rivalry also continues (in addition to their *spatial* rivalry) despite their simultaneous albeit asymmetric rise. There are three functional areas – economics, nuclear, and naval – where Sino-Indian asymmetries, and strategies to redress these asymmetries, may intensify their rivalry with some probability of conflict. While these three functional areas have their own logics with implications for competitive dynamics and conflict as discussed in the following three sections, there are three potential pathways across these functional areas that may exacerbate Sino-Indian tensions, as mentioned earlier: any attempt by China to exploit the power gap with India in its favor, strategies pursued by India to be taken more seriously by China, and the United States' promotion of the rise of India.[35]

Each of these pathways has a finite nonzero potential for conflict on its own. What makes the Sino-Indian rivalry worrisome is that more than one of these pathways are likely to be simultaneously operational.

---

[33] Devin T. Hagerty, "India's Regional Security Doctrine," *Asian Survey* 31.4 (1991): 351–363; and Manjeet S. Pardesi, "Is India a Great Power? Understanding Great Power Status in Contemporary International Relations," *Asian Security* 11.1 (2015): 1–30.

[34] *Science of Military Strategy (2013)*, 80–81. The full text of this document, which was prepared by China's Academy of Military Sciences, was translated into English and published under the auspices of Project Everest and the China Aerospace Studies Institute on February 8, 2021, www.airuniversity.af.edu/CASI/Display/Article/2485204/plas-science-of-military-strategy-2013/.

[35] There is now a vast literature on the American support for the rise of India over the past two decades. Some of the more notable works include Evan A. Feigenbaum, "India's Rise, America's Interest: The Fate of the U.S.-Indian Partnership," *Foreign Affairs* 89.2 (2010): 76–91; T. V. Paul and Mahesh Shankar, "Status Accommodation through Institutional Means: India's Rise and the Global Order," in T. V. Paul, Deborah Welch Larson, and William C. Wohlforth (eds.), *Status in World Politics* (New York: Cambridge University Press, 2014), 165–191; Ashley J. Tellis and C. Raja Mohan, *The Strategic Rationale for Deeper U.S.-Indian Economic Ties: American and Indian Perspectives* (Washington, DC: Carnegie Endowment for International Peace, 2015); Aseema Sinha, "Partial Accommodation without Conflict: India as a Rising Link Power," in T. V. Paul (ed.), *Accommodating Rising Powers: Past, Present, and Future* (Cambridge: Cambridge University Press, 2016), 222–245; Robert D. Blackwill and Ashley J. Tellis, "The India Dividend: New Delhi Remains Washington's Best Hope in Asia," *Foreign Affairs* 98.5 (2019): 173–183; and Sumit Ganguly and M. Chris Mason, *An Unnatural Partnership? The Future of U.S.-India Strategic Cooperation* (Carlisle, PA: Strategic Studies Institute, 2019).

Furthermore, as explained in the subsequent sections, America's support for India's ascent will not only augment India's economic and military capabilities but also have implications for India's relative *position* vis-à-vis China. Given the implications for the *spatial* and *positional* dimensions of the Sino-Indian rivalry, developments in these three functional domains point toward a difficult period in Sino-Indian relations in the years ahead.

Economic Asymmetries

The Sino-Indian cross-border trade was almost "nonexistent" after 1962.[36] Although meaningful bilateral trade resumed in 1978, and the two sides offered the reciprocal most-favored nation status to each other in 1984,[37] bilateral trade significantly took off only after 2001 when China joined the World Trade Organization (WTO) and India "abolished its licensing on consumer goods."[38] Since then, China has emerged as India's largest trading partner along with the United States (though there is some degree of fluctuation between the United States and China for the rank of India's top trading partner).[39] By contrast, India is not among China's top ten trading partners. Ranking at number twelve in 2019,[40] India's lower rank as a trade partner notwithstanding, bilateral Sino-Indian trade has boomed and crossed $125 billion in 2021 while it was barely $3.6 billion in 2001.[41]

What do international relations theories tell us about the prospects for peace because of the growing commercial interdependence between China and India? Enhanced trade (and bilateral investment, which is discussed subsequently) in the Sino-Indian dyad is taking place within an emerging geopolitical context with three main characteristics: the

---

[36] William Norris, "Economic Statecraft as a Tool of Peacemaking? China's Relationships with India and Russia," in Steven E. Lobell and Norrin M. Ripsman (eds.), *The Political Economy of Regional Peacemaking* (Ann Arbor: University of Michigan Press, 2016), 182.

[37] Deepa M. Ollapally, "China and India: Economic Ties and Strategic Rivalry," *Orbis* 58.3 (2014): 344.

[38] Hu Shisheng, "Competitive Cooperation in Trade: A Chinese Perspective," in Kanti P. Bajpai, Jing Huang, and Kishore Mahbubani (eds.), *China-India Relations: Cooperation and Conflict* (London: Routledge, 2015). 67.

[39] "China Regains Slot as India's Top Trade Partner despite Tensions," *BBC News*, February 23, 2021, www.bbc.com/news/business-56164154.

[40] Trade and Economic Relations, Embassy of India (Beijing, China), updated July 9, 2021, www.eoibeijing.gov.in/eoibejing_pages/Mjg.

[41] Ananth Krishnan, "India's Trade with China Crosses $125 billion, Imports near $100 billion," *The Hindu*, January15, 2022, www.thehindu.com/business/Economy/indias-trade-with-china-crosses-125-billion-imports-near-100-billion/article38272914.ece; and Jingdong Yuan, "Sino-Indian Economic Ties since 1988: Progress, Problems, and Prospects for Future Development," *Journal of Current Chinese Affairs* 45.3 (2016): 40.

growing gap between the size of the Chinese and Indian economies, China's growing commercial links with India's South Asian neighbors, and China's rise through the technological ladder to compete with the United States for the status of the *lead economy* (as the system's largest and most innovative economy) while India languishes relatively.[42] Asymmetries along each of these three dimensions – along with the asymmetric nature of the Sino-Indian bilateral commercial relationship – are discussed in this section. These asymmetries are likely to accentuate the Sino-Indian *positional* rivalry, and their prognosis for their *spatial* rivalry is also unsettling.

Growing GDP Gap

As discussed in Chapter 2, even though GDP figures of China and India were identical until 1987, China's GDP of $14.7 trillion in 2020 was nearly six times India's GDP of $2.6 trillion.[43] In theory, a loss in economic capability is a potential shock that can de-escalate rivalries, either because the larger power perceives diminished threat from the smaller power or because the smaller power rethinks the goals that it can accomplish (or both).[44] However, as mentioned earlier, India's relative decline vis-à-vis China has come in the context of India's slow but absolute rise in the international system, and therefore, India's rivalry with China continues. At the same time, there is a general perception among international relations scholars that China has become more assertive recently, at least as far as its territorial disputes are concerned.[45] Indeed, as shown in Chapters 2 and 5, the militarized border disputes between China and India have been on the

---

[42] On the concept of *lead economy*, see Rafael Reuveny and William R. Thompson, *Growth, Trade, and Systemic Leadership* (Ann Arbor: University of Michigan Press, 2004), 33–57. On the US–China technological competition for the status of the *lead economy*, see William R. Thompson, *American Global Pre-eminence: The Development and Erosion of Systemic Leadership* (New York: Oxford University Press, 2022).

[43] World Development Indicators, The World Bank, https://databank.worldbank.org/source/world-development-indicators.

[44] William R. Thompson, "Economic Incentives, Rivalry Deescalation, and Regional Transformation," in Lobell and Ripsman, *The Political Economy of Regional Peacemaking*, 96–117.

[45] For the argument that Chinese assertive behavior is "a deliberate long-term strategy," see Oriana Skylar Mastro, "Why Chinese Assertiveness Is Here to Stay," *The Washington Quarterly* 37.4 (2015): 151–170. Also see Rush Doshi, *The Long Game: China's Grand Strategy to Displace American Order* (New York: Oxford University Press, 2021). By contrast, China has become more assertive only in the context of maritime territorial disputes according to Johnston. He is of the opinion that China has not become more assertive in general. Unfortunately, he did not analyze the Sino-Indian relationship (including the territorial dispute). Alastair Iain Johnston, "How New and Assertive Is China's New Assertiveness?," *International Security* 37.4 (2013): 7–48.

rise in terms of frequency and intensity since 2003 despite a temporary lull after 1987, their growing commercial relationship notwithstanding.

China has recently adopted a new military strategy of "active defense" that favors offensive actions, at least operationally, even when launched for defensive purposes. As long as the Sino-Indian border dispute remains unresolved, it will, along with contingencies in Taiwan and the South China Sea, "occupy the bulk of strategic planning and be the central focus of China's military strategy."[46] China is now believed to have the "capacity to deploy and sustain military forces against India" relatively quickly, as well as undertake "short and swift operations" in the disputed regions.[47] Until recently, Indian security planners had envisaged fighting a defensive war against China in any future conflict on Indian territory. While this strategy might have worked if their military capabilities were relatively equal, their growing economic asymmetry is also reflected in their widening military power now. Although China and India had relatively equal defense expenditures in 1989, China now outspends India by a factor of four.[48] Furthermore, this asymmetry is not just quantitative but also extends to the quality of their weapons.[49]

Given their growing conventional military asymmetry, India is upgrading its conventional military strategy from defense to deterrence.[50] In particular, the Indian military is developing limited offensive capabilities vis-à-vis China with the aim of imposing higher costs on China, including by taking military hostilities into Chinese territory (at the local level) in order to prevent any loss of territory to China and/or to annex small chunks of strategically salient points that may be used as bargaining chips in future political negotiations.[51] While not exactly

---

[46] M. Taylor Fravel, *Active Defense: China's Military Strategy since 1949* (Princeton: Princeton University Press, 2019), 276.

[47] Rajeswari Pillai Rajagopalan, "An Indian Perspective on China's Military Modernization," in Bates Gill (ed.), *Meeting China's Military Challenge: Collective Responses of U.S. Allies and Security Partners* (Washington, DC: National Bureau of Asian Research, NBR Special Report #96, 2022), 39, 42, www.nbr .org/publication/meeting-chinas-military-challenge-collective-responses-of-u-s-allies-and-partners/.

[48] China spent $11.25 billion in 1989 when India spent $10.6 billion. However, China's defense expenditure in 2020 stood at $252.3 billion compared to India's $72.9 billion. See SIPRI Military Expenditure Database, Stockholm International Peace Research Institute, www.sipri.org/databases/milex.

[49] Oriana Skylar Mastro and Arzan Tarapore, "Asymmetric but Uneven: The China-India Conventional Military Balance," in Kanti P. Bajpai, Selina Ho, and Manjari Chatterjee Miller (eds.), *Routledge Handbook of China-India Relations* (London: Routledge, 2020), 240–251.

[50] Yogesh Joshi and Anit Mukherjee, "Offensive Defense: India's Strategic Response to the Rise of China," in Bajpai, Ho, and Miller, *Routledge Handbook of China-India Relations*, 227–239.

[51] Manjeet S. Pardesi, "India's Conventional Military Strategy," in Sumit Ganguly, Nicolas Blarel, and Manjeet S. Pardesi (eds.), *The Oxford Handbook of India's National Security* (New Delhi: Oxford University Press, 2018), 114–131.

analogous, it is noteworthy that during the 2017 Doklam Crisis, the Indian military crossed the international boundary and entered a disputed region between Bhutan and China.[52] And during the 2020 Galwan Valley Crisis, India responded to China's creation of a new territorial status quo around the Pangong Tso by occupying some features to the south of that lake (which were claimed by India but where India had no physical presence).[53]

The Chinese military has taken note of India's changing military strategy. Analogous to Indian fears of a more powerful China exploiting the power shift with India, Chinese analysts fear that India has adopted "dissuasive deterrence" against China, because although India's overall posture is "defensive," it is using "offense as a defense to actively seek local superiority," while using its "unremitting nibbling away [of territory?] in peacetime to create conditions for switching from defense to offense in wartime."[54] In other words, as the economic asymmetry between China and India widens, both sides seem to be adopting more risky military strategies that emphasize limited offensive moves, at least at the operational level, thereby raising the stakes in their *spatial* rivalry.

Regional Trade (and Connectivity)

In 2013, China became the world's largest trading nation in goods, "ending the post-war dominance of the US."[55] It is now the largest trading partner of over 120 countries and regions, including the United States, the European Union, and Japan, while being in near parity with the United States as India's largest trade partner.[56] In South Asia, the total trade of Afghanistan, Pakistan, Bangladesh, and the Maldives with China exceeds their total trade with India, while China is rapidly catching up with India in Sri Lanka (see Table 6.1). Although the total trade of

---

[52] Sumit Ganguly and Andrew Scobell, "The Himalayan Impasse: Sino-Indian Rivalry in the Wake of Doklam," *The Washington Quarterly* 41.3 (2018): 177–190.

[53] Shivshankar Menon, "Some Consequences of the India-China Crisis of 2020," in Leah Bitounis and Niamh King (eds.), *Domestic and International (Dis)Order: A Strategic Response* (Washington, DC: The Aspen Institute, 2020), 77, www.aspeninstitute.org/wp-content/uploads/2020/10/Foreign-Policy-2021-ePub_FINAL.pdf.

[54] *Science of Military Strategy (2013)*, 81.

[55] Phillip Inman, "China Overtakes US in World Trade," *The Guardian*, February 11, 2013, www.theguardian.com/business/2013/feb/11/china-worlds-largest-trading-nation.

[56] Jun Wang, *A Preliminary Study of the New Normal of China's Economy* (Singapore: Springer, 2021), 173.

Table 6.1 *China–South Asia trade relations*

	India (imports)	India (exports)	India (total)	China (imports)	China (exports)	China (total)
Afghanistan	453,695	410,135	863,830	1,192,426	31,001	1,223,427
Pakistan	1,008,553	66,306	1,074,859	12,406,397	2,036,877	14,443,274
Bangladesh	5,882,080	517,890	6,399,970	10,349,332	715,214	11,064,546
Nepal	6,519,702	420,179	6,939,881	1,267,431	22,332	1,289,763
Bhutan	781,471	497,716	1,279,187	24,845	46.08	24,891
Sri Lanka	4,494,065	789,586	5,283,651	4,189,426	430,444	4,619,870
Maldives	286,674	2,816	289,490	488,344	270.76	488,615
China	17,970,064	74,924,285	92,894,349	-	-	-

Source: World Integrated Trade Solution, The World Bank, https://wits.worldbank.org/. All figures are in US$ thousand. The data is for the year 2019 except for Bangladesh (2015), Nepal (2017), Bhutan (2012), Sri Lanka (2017), and the Maldives (2018).

Nepal and Bhutan with India exceeds their total trade with China, they are minor trading powers. Even then, Nepal–China commercial ties are rapidly expanding, as explained later in the chapter. China's emergence as the principal trading partner of all South Asian nations (including India but excluding Bhutan, at least for now) has implications for the Sino-Indian *positional* rivalry.

Unlike India, which has traditionally sought some form of leadership in South Asia, "China is not seeking dominant status in South Asia."[57] China has two primary goals in South Asia. First, it seeks to prevent India from dominating South Asia – a region that Beijing considers its "back yard," while East Asia remains its "front yard" – because it wants to transform South Asia into a "strategic buffer zone" as Beijing focuses on East Asia.[58] Indeed, Yan has even argued that China should use its "ability to get involved in South Asian affairs so as to give India a warning" to prevent New Delhi from getting "involved in East Asian affairs."[59] Second, South Asia's importance for China has increased because "that region is located at the intersection of" the overland and maritime components of China's Belt and Road Initiative (BRI).[60] In other words, even though India and South Asia may be located in the "secondary strategic direction" for China

[57] Yan, *Inertia of History*, 122.
[58] Yan, *Inertia of History*, 163.
[59] Yan, *Inertia of History*, 178–179.
[60] Lin Minwang, "China, India, and Asian Connectivity: China's View," in Bajpai, Ho, and Miller, *Routledge Handbook of China-India Relations*, 304.

while Beijing prioritizes East Asia over other regions,[61] South Asia's importance for China has increased in recent years.

While India perceives China's growing profile in South Asia as Beijing's
strategy to "encircle" India,[62] China's growing strategic role in South
Asia is in fact undermining India's self-proclaimed *position* of regional
leadership, especially through the Sino-Pakistani relationship (discussed
in Chapter 7). Elsewhere, China's growing trade and connectivity links
with landlocked Nepal mean that Kathmandu has begun to reduce its
dependence on India. According to a 2018 agreement between China and
Nepal, Kathmandu will be allowed to use the Chinese seaports of Tianjin,
Shenzhen, Lianyungang, and Zhanjiang for overseas trade (instead of
Nepal's traditional dependence upon Kolkata and other Indian ports), in
addition to the use of other cities such as Lanzhou, Lhasa, and Shigatse for
trade with third countries.[63]

These new corridors of connectivity will allow Nepal to circumvent
any Indian politico-economic coercion of Nepal (such as the "unofficial
blockade" of 2015).[64] While South Asian states (including Nepal) may be
"hedging" their bets between India and China, as opposed to engaging
in balance-of-power politics,[65] the net effect of such policies has been to
diminish India's *position* in South Asia as China emerges as a potential
choice on a par with India despite their official "India-first" policies in
the region.[66] In fact, it may even be possible for China to trump India's
regional *position* – even without dominating South Asia – if China's commercial and connectivity initiatives are followed by an enhanced security
footprint in the region.[67]

Given the Sino-Indian economic disparities in South Asia, New Delhi
has turned toward the United States (and Japan) to jointly reach out to
its South Asian neighbors. According to Jaishankar, this helps "reassure

---

[61] M. Taylor Fravel, "Stability in a Secondary Strategic Direction: China and the Border Dispute with
India after 1962," in Bajpai, Ho, and Miller, *Routledge Handbook of China-India Relations*, 169–179.

[62] Francine R. Frankel, "The Breakout of the China-India Strategic Rivalry in Asia and the Indian
Ocean," *Journal of International Affairs* 64.2 (2011): 1–17.

[63] Lin, "China, India, and Asian Connectivity," 305. Plans are underway to connect Nepal and Tibet
with high-speed rail links.

[64] T. V. Paul, "When Balance of Power Meets Globalization: China, India, and the Small States of
South Asia," *Politics* 39.1 (2019): 53; and Constantino Xavier, "Across the Himalayas: China in India's
Neighborhood," in Bajpai, Ho, and Miller, *Routledge Handbook of China-India Relations*, 426.

[65] Darren J. Lim and Rohan Mukherjee, "Hedging in South Asia: Balancing Economic and Security
Interests amid Sino-Indian Competition," *International Relations of the Asia-Pacific* 19.3 (2019):
493–522.

[66] Xavier, "Across the Himalayas," 426.

[67] Jabin T. Jacob, "China, India, and Asian Connectivity: India's View," in Bajpai, Ho, and Miller,
Routledge Handbook of China-India Relations, 319.

India's smaller neighbors, which may have been less welcoming of India alone."[68] While partnering with the United States (and Japan) may help India partially offset China's growing regional profile, this is in fact an admission of its diminishing regional *position* (as India now feels the need to work with its bigger partners in South Asia itself). In the meanwhile, the United States remains committed to enhancing India's "leadership," especially in South Asia (and the Indian Ocean, as discussed subsequently).[69] America's growing involvement in South Asia – and its promotion of India in the vanguard in the region – will mean that China will face new hurdles in transforming that region into a "strategic buffer zone" and to fend off "far-off [American] pressure."[70] In other words, trade and connectivity asymmetries are raising the stakes in the Sino-Indian *positional* rivalry in South Asia.

Technological Gap

China is not only the world's largest center of economic production and exchange – because of its status as the world's largest trading power in goods – but it is also rapidly emerging as a major innovation economy, especially in the *leading* global sectors.[71] Indeed, China has long sought to "catch-up and surpass" the United States as the leading technological power.[72] The leading technologies of any given era of world politics tend to be dual-use as they confer economic and military-strategic advantages. While the United States has maintained the position of the *lead economy*, dominating the *leading sectors* since at least the middle of the twentieth century, Xi has stated that China is aiming "for the frontiers of science and

---

[68] Indrani Bagchi, "India Wary as Japan, US Seek Quadrilateral with Australia," *The Times of India*, October 28, 2017, https://timesofindia.indiatimes.com/india/india-wary-as-japan-us-seek-quadrilateral-with-australia/articleshow/61281250.cms.

[69] Under President Donald Trump, the United States was committed to ensuring that "India remains preeminent in South Asia." The current administration of President Joe Biden is also supportive of India's "regional leadership." See "U.S. Strategic Framework for the Indo-Pacific," The White House, January 5, 2021, 3, https://trumpwhitehouse.archives.gov/wp-content/uploads/2021/01/IPS-Final-Declass.pdf; and "Indo-Pacific Strategy of the United States," The White House, February 2022, 16, www.whitehouse.gov/wp-content/uploads/2022/02/U.S.-Indo-Pacific-Strategy.pdf.

[70] Yan, *Inertia of History*, 163.

[71] George Modelski and William Thompson, *Leading Sectors and World Powers* (Columbia: University of South Carolina Press, 1996); and Espen Moe, "Mancur Olson and Structural Economic Change: Vested Interests and the Industrial Rise and Fall of the Great Powers," *Review of International Political Economy* 16.2 (2009): 202–220.

[72] Julian Baird Gewirtz, "China's Long March to Technological Supremacy," *Foreign Affairs*, August 27, 2019, www.foreignaffairs.com/articles/china/2019-08-27/chinas-long-march-technological-supremacy.

technology" while coordinating "the development of the real economy with technological innovation" and noting that "technology is the core combat [military] capability."[73]

Indeed, China is now second only to the United States in terms of performance in research and development (and with a significant lead over India).[74] While it is difficult to a priori identify the leading technologies of any era, renewable energy, the new industrial revolution (heralded by artificial intelligence, robotics, and 3D printing), biomedical engineering, space, and cyberspace technologies are among the most-likely candidates for the coming era.[75] Not only is China at the forefront of many of these emerging technologies, but its advances in areas such as space and cyberspace are also beginning to challenge America's dominance of the global commons.[76] While this does not mean that China has displaced the United States as the leading scientific superpower, the Pentagon has noted that China is "producing capabilities that have the potential to reduce core U.S. military technological advantages."[77]

Unlike China, India has "not accorded due importance to innovation as an instrument of policy."[78] While China aims to be the leading technological power in the world, India's goals are more modest and are related to sustainable development and to ensuring that its development is not hampered by international technology-denial regimes.[79] Although India does aspire to be among the leading technological powers in the world, it is perhaps better characterized as a "fast follower" (at least when it comes to niche technologies) as opposed to being at the forefront of global

[73] Xi Jinping, "Speech Delivered at the 19th National Congress of the Communist Party of China."

[74] The leading countries in 2019 as measured by research and development performance (in terms of the share of global expenditure) were the United States (27 percent), China (22 percent), Japan (7 percent), Germany (6 percent), and South Korea (4 percent) followed by France, India, and the United Kingdom with about 2–3 percent each of the global total. See *The State of U.S. Science & Engineering 2022*, Science and Engineering Indicators, National Science Board, January 2022, https://ncses.nsf.gov/pubs/nsb20221/u-s-and-global-research-and-development.

[75] James Manyika, Michael Chui, Jacques Bughin et al., "Disruptive Technologies: Advances That Will Transform Life, Business, and the Global Economy," McKinsey Global Institute, May 2013, www.mckinsey.com/business-functions/mckinsey-digital/our-insights/disruptive-technologies.

[76] Kevin Pollpeter, "Controlling the Information Domain: Space, Cyber, and Electronic Warfare," in Ashley Tellis and Travis Tanner (eds.), *Strategic Asia 2012–13: China's Military Challenge* (Washington, DC: National Bureau of Asian Research, 2012).

[77] Annual Report to the Congress, Military and Security Developments Involving the People's Republic of China 2016, Department of Defense, 2016, i, https://dod.defense.gov/Portals/1/Documents/pubs/2016%20China%20Military%20Power%20Report.pdf.

[78] "Science, Technology, and Innovation Policy 2013," Ministry of Science and Technology, New Delhi, 2, http://dst.gov.in/sites/default/files/STI%20Policy%202013-English.pdf.

[79] "Science, Technology, and Innovation Policy 2020 (Draft)," Ministry of Science and Technology, New Delhi, www.psa.gov.in/psa-prod/psa_custom_files/STIP_Doc_1.4_Dec2020.pdf.

innovation.[80] India lags behind China in four of the five industries that are currently seen as high-tech – aerospace, communications, computers and office machinery, and scientific instruments – while being at relative par with China in pharmaceuticals and chemicals.[81] In most of the emerging technologies, China's lead over India is considerable, although there are select areas such as wind turbine manufacturing (for renewable energy) where India performs relatively well.[82]

Ultimately, these differences reflect China's and India's different strategic ambitions. While Xi's China hopes to be at the "center" of Asia and the even the world, India is simply aiming to be one great power among many in a multipolar Asia. Clearly, their different technological capabilities mean that they are playing for different *positions* in the international system. While China is engaged in a rivalry with the United States at the global/systemic level, the Sino-Indian rivalry is playing out at the regional level in Asia. China's considerable technological (commercial and military) lead means that not only is it rapidly linking the economies of India's South Asian neighbors with its own but it has also emerged as a major weapons supplier. Pakistan, Bangladesh, and Myanmar have been the recipients of almost two-thirds of China's weapons sales since 2010.[83]

In the meanwhile, India is turning to its overseas partners given its technological gap with China. Indeed, former prime minister Manmohan Singh had identified three countries – the United States, Japan, and Germany – as "transformational" since they have the "technological and innovation heft [that] India needs in spades."[84] In turn, the United States is also keen to augment India's technological development, including in the defense-industrial sector.[85] In other words, the Sino-Indian technological

---

[80] Andrew B. Kennedy, "Powerhouses or Pretenders? Debating China's and India's Emergence as Technological Powers," *The Pacific Review* 28.2 (2015): 281–302.

[81] Kalim Siddiqui, "A Comparative Political Economy of China and India: A Critical Review," in Young-Chan Kim (ed.), *China-India Relations: Geo-political Competition, Economic Cooperation, Cultural Exchange and Business Ties* (Cham: Springer, 2020), 54; and Hu, "Competitive Cooperation in Trade," 80.

[82] Samantha Gross, "The Global Energy Trade's New Center of Gravity," in Tarun Chhabra, Rush Doshi, Ryan Haas, and Emilie Kimball (eds.), *Global China: Assessing China's Growing Role in the World* (Washington, DC: Brookings, 2021), 321.

[83] China Power Team, "How Dominant Is China in the Global Arms Trade?," China Power, April 26, 2018 (updated May 27, 2021), https://chinapower.csis.org/china-global-arms-trade/.

[84] Indrani Bagchi, "India Should Bond with Japan and Stop Looking over Its Shoulder at China," *The Economic Times*, May 27, 2013, https://economictimes.indiatimes.com/opinion/et-commentary/india-should-bond-with-japan-and-stop-looking-over-its-shoulder-at-china/articleshow/20281787.cms?from=mdr.

[85] "India Gets a High-Tech Boost as US Elevates India to Most-Important Allies List," *The Economic Times*, July 31, 2018, https://economictimes.indiatimes.com/news/politics-and-nation/india-gets-a-high-tech-boost-as-us-elevates-india-to-most-important-ally-list/articleshow/65209391.cms.

gap is fostering another set of linkages between the Sino-Indian rivalry on the one hand and the Sino-American, Sino-Japanese, and Indo-Pakistani rivalries on the other. These technological linkages – with implications for their *positional* rivalry – are likely to make their relations more complex. For now, Chinese analysts have taken note of such developments, while pointing out that whether India benefits from this technological assistance will ultimately depend upon its ability to absorb these technologies through its domestic economic reforms.[86]

Commercial Pacification?

Economic interdependence is believed to dampen security competition between states through numerous pathways, including by creating mutual dependency and by raising the costs for conflict and war.[87] Will the growing trade relationship between China and India help ameliorate the potential for conflict generated in their relationship due to the three pathways discussed earlier? It should be noted that the empirical evidence between economic interdependence and peace is ambiguous,[88] and scholars continue to debate the outbreak of the First World War in this light.[89] Not surprisingly, it has been noted that for every study that supports the liberal hypothesis there are others that reject it or argue that there is no significant relationship between economic interdependence and peace.[90]

Given this ambiguity, scholars have looked at the role of intermediate variables in this relationship. For example, nationalism and the legacies of history have played some role in preventing spillover from economic

---

[86] Wu, "India's Perception of and Response to China-US Competition," 148, 153.

[87] There is a vast literature on the peace-producing effects of commerce. Some of the more notable works include Richard Rosecrance, *The Rise of the Trading State* (New York: Basic, 1986); Edward Mansfield and Brian Pollins (eds.), *Economic Interdependence and International Conflict* (Ann Arbor: University of Michigan Press, 2003); Robert Keohane and Joseph Nye, *Power and Interdependence*, 4th ed. (Boston: Longman, 2012); Michael Doyle, *Ways of War and Peace* (New York: Norton, 1997); Erik Gartzke, Quan Li, and Charles Boehmer, "Investing in Peace: Economic Interdependence and International Conflict," *International Organization* 55.2 (2001): 391–438; and John Ravenhill, "Economic Interdependence, Globalization, and Peaceful Change," in T. V. Paul, Deborah Welch Larson, Harold A. Trinkunas, Anders Wivel, and Ralf Emmers (eds.), *The Oxford Handbook of Peaceful Change in International Relations* (New York: Oxford University Press, 2021), https://doi.org/10.1093/oxfordhb/9780190097356.013.9.

[88] Katherine Barbieri, *The Liberal Illusion* (Ann Arbor: University of Michigan Press, 2002); and Patrick Lieberman, *Does Conquest Pay* (Princeton: Princeton University Press, 1998).

[89] Norman Angell, *The Great Illusion*, 2nd ed. (New York: Putnam's, 1933); and Patrick McDonald and Kevin Sweeney, "The Achilles' Heel of Liberal IR Theory," *World Politics* 59.3 (2007): 370–403.

[90] Karen Rasler and William R. Thompson, "Assessing Inducements and Suppressors of Interstate Conflict Escalation," Paper presented at the Annual Meeting of the International Studies Association, San Diego, March 22–25, 2006.

intercourse onto security in the Sino-Japanese relationship.[91] Similarly, the deepening of the US–China rivalry means that the world's two largest economies are "decoupling" to some degree (even though the overall trade volume is likely to remain high).[92] Scholars such as Copeland have argued that it is not merely high levels of economic interdependence but policymakers' perceptions and expectations of future trade that matter.[93]

In the Sino-Indian case, the growing trade interdependence between them is asymmetric, both in terms of volume and value-added (reflecting their technology gap). While Sino-Indian trade amounted to $125.6 billion in 2021, India imported $97.5 billion worth of goods, and its trade deficit with China stood at $69.5 billion.[94] In fact, its trade deficit with China has steadily increased for more than a decade now.[95] Furthermore, with the notable exception of the pharmaceuticals and chemicals sector as mentioned earlier, India mainly exports raw materials to China (or products that "are not India's strengths") while importing manufactured goods (that "are [in fact] China's strengths").[96] Furthermore, while bilateral investment between the two countries is growing,[97] it remains relatively small. China's cumulative investment in India (until September 2019) amounted to $5.08 billion, while India's cumulative investment in China was merely $0.92 billion.[98]

What are policymakers' future expectations of the Sino-Indian commercial relationship? On the Indian side, there are concerns related to growing annual trade deficit and lack of access to the Chinese market in areas where India has strengths, such as information technology–related services. (However, even there, the lack of Chinese language skills means that these Indian services remain oriented toward the Anglo-American world.) Furthermore, India is also wary of Chinese investment in critical

---

[91] Michael Yahuda, "The Limits of Economic Interdependence: Sino-Japanese Relations," in Alastair Iain Johnston and Robert Ross (eds.), *New Directions in the Study of China's Foreign Policy* (Stanford: Stanford University Press, 2006), 162–185.

[92] Edward Luce, "The New Era of US-China Decoupling," *Financial Times*, December 21, 2018, www.ft.com/content/019b1856-03c0-11e9-99df-6183d3002ee1.

[93] Dale Copeland, *Economic Interdependence and War* (Princeton: Princeton University Press, 2015).

[94] Krishnan, "India's Trade with China Crosses $125 billion."

[95] Yuan, "Sino-Indian Economic Ties since 1988."

[96] Hu, "Competitive Cooperation in Trade," 68.

[97] Ananth Krishnan, "Following the Money: China Inc's Growing Stake in India-China Relations," Impact Series, Brookings India, March 2020, www.brookings.edu/research/following-the-money-china-incs-growing-stake-in-india-china-relations/.

[98] Trade and Economic Relations, Embassy of India (Beijing, China), updated July 9, 2021, www.eoibeijing.gov.in/eoibejing_pages/Mjg.

sectors such as energy and telecommunications (including 5G) and has sought to limit the entry of some Chinese companies into India.[99] While unrealistic, there were even calls for an economic boycott of China in the aftermath of the June 2020 Ladakh Crisis (although India did ban close to 200 Chinese apps).[100] In fact, Jaishankar has openly stated that "border tensions cannot continue with cooperation in other areas."[101] However, it remains unclear to what degree India can "decouple" from China.[102]

On their part, Chinese scholars have noted that China may be able to import the raw materials obtained from India "from other countries" at "good rates" (because they are not India's strengths).[103] However, India is an attractive destination for some Chinese companies, especially in the context of the decoupling of the US and Chinese economies, although this economic potential has remained unfulfilled thus far.[104] Nevertheless, as China reorients its economy "from an investment- and export-driven model" to one predicated on domestic consumption, the Chinese economy is likely to become "less reliant on international ties."[105] Not surprisingly, it has been argued that commercial interdependence can only "reinforce" peace as opposed to cause it in the first place in the Sino-Indian relationship.[106] As such, evidence points to the "primacy of politics" in the Sino-Indian economic relationship, or the reversal of the causal arrow running from economic interdependence to peace.[107] Commerce cannot guarantee the pacification of the pathways to conflict in this dyad that are emerging out of their economic asymmetries.

---

[99] Tanvi Madan, "Managing China: Competitive Engagement, with Indian Characteristics," in Chhabra, Doshi, Haas, and Kimball, *Global China*, 120–131.

[100] Sherisse Pham, "India Bans More Chinese Apps as Tensions Remain High," *CNN*, November 25, 2020, https://edition.cnn.com/2020/11/25/tech/india-bans-chinese-apps-hnk-intl/index.html.

[101] "India-China Ties 'At Crossroads': Foreign Minister S. Jaishankar," *NDTV*, May 20, 2021, www .ndtv.com/india-news/india-china-ties-at-crossroads-foreign-minister-s-jaishankar-2446060.

[102] Shivshankar Menon, "Economic Decoupling to Self-Strengthening: How India Can Rise to China Challenge," *The Times of India*, October 16, 2021, https://timesofindia.indiatimes.com/blogs/voices/economic-decoupling-to-self-strengthening-how-india-can-rise-to-china-challenge/.

[103] Hu, "Competitive Cooperation in Trade," 71.

[104] Paul Caussat, "Facing Political Issues and Protecting National Sovereignty: The Sino-Indian Economic Relation since 1947," in Kim, *China-India Relations*, 88.

[105] William J. Norris, "Geostrategic Implications of China's Twin Economic Challenges," Discussion Paper, Council on Foreign Relations, June 2017, 1, www.cfr.org/report/geostrategic-implications-chinas-twin-economic-challenges.

[106] Norris, *"Economic Statecraft as a Tool of Peacemaking?,"* 183.

[107] Omar Keshk, Brian Pollins, and Rafael Reuveny, "Trade Still Follow the Flag: The Primacy of Politics in a Simultaneous Model of Interdependence and Armed Conflict," *Journal of Politics* 66.4 (2004): 1155–1179.

Nuclear Asymmetries

The Sino-Indian nuclear relationship is asymmetric as well. While China conducted its first nuclear test in 1964 to meet its American challenge (and its Soviet challenge to a lesser degree), India conducted its first nuclear test in 1974 – partially driven by the presence of Chinese nuclear weapons – but did not weaponize its nuclear program until the late 1980s.[108] India openly went nuclear in 1998 and justified its tests based on a perceived Chinese threat and the Sino-Pakistani strategic linkage.[109] Not only were China and India motivated by different sets of rivalries in their nuclear pursuits, but China had also conducted fifteen nuclear tests before India's solitary "peaceful" explosion of 1974.

In fact, China has conducted a total of forty-five nuclear tests compared to India's six. It is also far more technologically capable than India in the nuclear realm. It had already acquired the capabilities to develop fission weapons, boosted fission weapons, and thermonuclear weapons (with yield in the megatons) before India's 1974 test, and eventually developed neutron bombs. On the other hand, India is believed to have the capabilities to develop fission and boosted fission weapons (with yield in the kilotons range), while the success of India's thermonuclear weapons remains doubtful. Quantitative and qualitative differences also favor China over India when it comes to nuclear warheads and delivery systems (as shown in Table 6.2).

Not surprisingly, this has led at least one scholar to argue that "India is almost a nuclear afterthought" for China.[110] However, there is an element of exaggeration in this assessment because others have noted that there is "consistent concern – albeit expressed in a tempered fashion – in Beijing about New Delhi's nuclear weapons program and [its] strategic

[108] On the Chinese nuclear program, see John Wilson Lewis and Xue Litai, *China Builds the Bomb* (Stanford: Stanford University Press, 1988); and Nicola Horsburgh, *China and the Global Nuclear Order: From Estrangement to Active Engagement* (Oxford: Oxford University Press, 2015). On the Indian nuclear program, see George Perkovich, *India's Nuclear Bomb: The Impact on Global Proliferation* (Berkeley: University of California Press, 1999); and Ashley J. Tellis, *India's Emerging Nuclear Posture: Between Recessed Deterrent and Ready Arsenal* (Santa Monica: RAND, 2000).

[109] Manjeet S. Pardesi, "China's Nuclear Forces and Their Significance to India," *The Nonproliferation Review* 21.3–4 (2014): 337–354; Sumit Ganguly, "India's Pathway to Pokhran II: The Prospect and Sources of New Delhi's Nuclear Weapons Program," *International Security* 23.4 (1999): 148–177; and T. V. Paul, "Chinese-Pakistani Nuclear/Missile Ties and Balance of Power Politics," *The Nonproliferation Review* 10.2 (2003): 21–29.

[110] Vipin Narang, "Nuclear Deterrence in the China-India Dyad," in T. V. Paul (ed.), *The China-India Rivalry in the Globalization Era* (Washington, DC: Georgetown University Press, 2018), 187.

Table 6.2 *Sino-Indian nuclear balance*

	China	India
Nuclear warheads	350	150
Land-based ballistic missiles/ range	DF-4 (5,500 km) DF-5A (12,000 km) DF-5B (13,000 km) DF-15 (600 km) DF-17 (1,800+ km) DF-21A/E (2,100+ km) DF-26 (4,000 km) DF-31 (7,200 km) DF-31A (11,200 km) DF-41 (12,000 km)	Prithvi-II (350 km) Agni-I (700 km) Agni-II (2,000+ km) Agni-III (3,200+ km) Agni-IV (3,500+ km) Agni-V (5,200+ km)
Sea-based ballistic missiles/ range	JL-2 (7,000+ km) JL-3 (9,000+ km)	Dhanush (400 km) K-15 (700 km) K-4 (3,500 km)
Aircraft/range	H-6K (3,100+ km)	Mirage 2000H (1,850 km) Jaguar IS (1,600 km)
Total number of launchers	372	134

Source: Hans M. Kristensen and Matt Korda, "Chinese Nuclear Weapons, 2021," *Bulletin of the Atomic Scientists* 77.6 (2021): 318–336; and Hans M. Kristensen and Matt Korda, "Indian Nuclear Forces, 2020," *Bulletin of the Atomic Scientists*, 76.4 (2020): 217–225.

implications."[111] Notably, Chinese contingency planning and wargaming through the 1980s and the 1990s – even before India's 1998 nuclear tests – "involved the possible use of nuclear weapons, both of the battlefield tactical variety and possibly a Chinese surgical strike against Indian nuclear facilities."[112] In the aftermath of India's May 1998 nuclear tests, a senior Chinese foreign ministry official noted that "China would consider resuming nuclear tests" (even while expressing commitment to the

[111] Li Hong, "Shoring Up the Nuclear Proliferation Regime: The View from China," in Lora Saalman (ed.), *The China-India Nuclear Crossroads* (Washington, DC: Carnegie Endowment for International Peace, 2012), Kindle Loc. 2273.
[112] David Shambaugh, "The Insecurity of Security: The PLA's Evolving Doctrine and Threat Perceptions towards 2000," *Journal of Northeast Asian Studies* 13 (1994): 21. While China toyed with the idea of tactical nuclear weapons in the 1980s, it is not believed to be pursuing this option anymore.

Comprehensive Test Ban Treaty signed in 1996) because Beijing now had reasons to rethink India.[113]

While China is certainly interested in extricating itself (at least in terms of perceptions) from the China–India–Pakistan nuclear equation and/or any nuclear equivalence with India,[114] it does pay attention to nuclear developments related to India.[115] In fact, the "the nuclear issue has emerged as a late but significant issue" between the two countries.[116] However, the asymmetries between them in the nuclear domain are not necessarily conducive to strategic stability as they are engaged in a "nuclear rivalry."[117] This is not to imply that a high-tempo nuclear competition is underway between them but simply that the Sino-Indian nuclear asymmetries add to the instability for at least three different reasons.

First, China is qualitatively and quantitatively upgrading its nuclear forces as it is seeking an "assured retaliation" capability vis-à-vis the United States.[118] The United States' lead over China is considerable. In quantitative terms – measured by the number of nuclear warheads – the United States has an advantage of 15:1 over China compared to China's 3:1 advantage over India (although qualitative differences in these dyads make the quantitative disparity between China and India starker than that between the United States and China).[119] While China already possesses "rudimentary retaliatory capabilities" against the United States,[120] and "assured retaliation" against India,[121] the Sino-American nuclear competition is

---

[113] "China Would Consider Resuming Tests If the Nuclear Arms Tension [*sic*]," *South China Morning Post*, June 2, 1998, 11, accessed via ProQuest.

[114] Lora Saalman, "China's Detachment from the South Asian Nuclear Triangle," SIPRI Commentary, September 8, 2020, www.sipri.org/commentary/blog/2020/chinas-detachment-south-asian-nuclear-triangle.

[115] Lora Saalman, "Divergence, Similarity, and Symmetry in Sino-Indian Threat Perceptions," *Journal of International Affairs* 64.2 (2011): 169–194.

[116] Tien-Sze Fang, "Asymmetrical Threat Perceptions in India–China Relations," (New Delhi: Oxford University Press, 2013)

[117] Rajesh Basrur, "India and China: A Managed Nuclear Rivalry," *The Washington Quarterly* 42.3 (2019): 151–170.

[118] Fiona S. Cunningham and M. Taylor Fravel, "Assuring Assured Retaliation: China's Nuclear Posture and U.S.-China Strategic Stability," *International Security* 40.2 (2015): 7–50.

[119] The United States is believed to have 5,550 nuclear warheads compared to China's 350 and India's 150. See Hans M. Kristensen and Matt Korda, "United States Nuclear Weapons, 2021," *Bulletin of the Atomic Scientists* 77.1 (2021): 43–63; Hans M. Kristensen and Matt Korda, "Chinese Nuclear Weapons, 2021," *Bulletin of the Atomic Scientists* 77.6 (2021): 318–336; and Hans M. Kristensen and Matt Korda, "Indian Nuclear Forces, 2020," *Bulletin of the Atomic Scientists* 76.4 (2020): 217–225.

[120] Nicola Leveringhaus, "Beyond 'hangovers': The New Parameters of Post-Cold War Nuclear Strategy," in Russell W. Glenn (ed.), *New Directions in Strategic Thinking 2.0* (Canberra: ANU Press, 2018), 84.

[121] Narang, "Nuclear Deterrence in the China-India Dyad," 188.

intensifying.[122] As China addresses its much larger gap with the United States than India has with China in the nuclear realm – driven partly by China's much larger economic and technological capabilities than India's – it will generate new difficulties for India. Since India "does not yet possess the technical means that could undergird a regime of stable nuclear deterrence with China,"[123] New Delhi will find it challenging to keep up with China's growing capabilities.

Relatedly, India is pursuing "nuclear and nonnuclear counterforce capabilities" against Pakistan.[124] Although Clary and Narang believe that India continues to pursue countervalue strategy toward China,[125] others contend that any "movement of Indian nuclear doctrine toward limited warfighting – even if designed primarily to address Pakistan's nuclear challenge – could push China in the same direction."[126] In any case, it should be noted that China's nuclear targeting strategy does not make a distinction between counterforce and countervalue.[127] Furthermore, as China modernizes its nuclear forces to seek assured retaliation against the United States, it is likely to develop some degree of counterforce capabilities against India given their asymmetry. After all, Chinese contingency planning has involved targeting Indian nuclear sites since the 1980s, as noted above.

Second, the above developments take on added significance in the context of the continuities between Indian and Chinese conventional and nuclear strategies, including the (perceived) dilution of their no-first-use (NFU) pledges (or the commitment to not be the first to initiate a nuclear strike). China's 2013 military strategy has already noted that India's concept of deterrence increasingly combines nuclear as well as conventional deterrence.[128] Furthermore, advanced conventional weapons (such as high-yield long-range precision-guided weapons) are also blurring the

---

[122] Caitlin Talmadge, "The U.S.-China Nuclear Relationship: Why Competition Is Likely to Intensify?," in Chhabra, Doshi, Haas, and Kimball, *Global China*, 86–91.

[123] Gaurav Kampani, "China-India Nuclear Rivalry in the 'Second Nuclear Age'," *IFS Insights* 3, November 2014, 24, http://hdl.handle.net/11250/226454.

[124] Christopher Clary and Vipin Narang, "India's Counterforce Temptations: Strategic Dilemmas, Doctrine, and Capabilities," *International Security* 43.3 (2018/2019): 38.

[125] Clary and Narang, "India's Counterforce Temptations," 8. Counterforce strategy implies targeting the opponent's military-strategic assets, while countervalue implies threatening civilian targets, especially cities.

[126] Eric Heginbotham, Michael S. Chase, Jacob L. Heim et al., *China's Evolving Nuclear Deterrent: Major Drivers and Issues for the United States* (Santa Monica: RAND, 2017), 79.

[127] Jeffrey Lewis, "China's Nuclear Modernization: Surprise, Restraint, and Uncertainty," in Ashley J. Tellis, Abraham M. Denmark, and Travis Tanner (eds.), *Strategic Asia 2013–14: Asia in the Second Nuclear Age* (Washington, DC: National Bureau of Asian Research, 2013), 80.

[128] *Science of Military Strategy (2013)*, 80.

distinction between conventional and nuclear conflicts.[129] For example, will India perceive a Chinese conventional first strike on its nuclear-capable (but nonnuclear armed) Su-30MKI fighters deployed in the Indian northeast as a nuclear or a nonnuclear attack?[130] While the limited range of India's ballistic missiles and its smaller nuclear arsenal make such plat-forms important to India's nuclear strategy, China's conventional strat-egy of "active defense" increasingly emphasizes "strategic bombardment" campaigns using the Chinese air force against India's military targets in a conventional war.[131] It seems like neither China nor India believe the other side's NFU pledges to be ironclad anymore.[132]

Third, advances in missile defense systems are adding yet another layer of complexity because this ostensibly defensive system complicates the strategic calculus of nuclear deterrence. To the extent that missile defenses incentivize the rivals to develop systems that can overcome such defenses – anti-satellite (ASAT) weapons, hypersonic weapons, multiple independently targetable reentry vehicles (MIRVs), and nuclear-tipped cruise missiles – India's quest for assured retaliation against China will be a constantly moving target since China is developing these technologies with the United States in mind. Given India's smaller nuclear arsenal, India's missile defense plans do factor in China's ballistic missiles, at least for damage limitation if not for guaranteed security.[133] Therefore, they are unlikely to be ignored by China with its relatively modest nuclear force.

While China is not unduly worried about India's missile defenses per se, it is wary of US–India missile defense cooperation.[134] There are mul-tiple reasons behind Chinese concerns. First, cooperation with the United States has the potential to enhance India's technological capabilities, and therefore its relative capabilities vis-à-vis China. American support may also tilt the strategic balance in South Asia in India's favor at the expense of Pakistan. Furthermore, US–India missile defense partnership will also

---

[129] Christopher P. Twomey, "Asia's Complex Strategic Environment: Nuclear Multipolarity and Other Dangers," *Asia Policy* 11 (2011), 63.

[130] Lora Saalman, "Introduction," in Saalman, *The China-India Nuclear Crossroads*, Kindle Loc. 165.

[131] You Ji, *China's Military Transformation: Politics and War Preparation* (Cambridge: Polity, 2016), 152.

[132] Basrur, "India and China," 163; Pan Zhenqiang, "Thinking beyond Nuclear Doctrine and Strategy: The View from China," in Saalman, *The China-India Nuclear Crossroads*, Kindle Loc. 561; and Srikanth Kondapalli, "Revisiting No First Use and Minimum Deterrence: The View from India," in Saalman, *The China-India Nuclear Crossroads*, Kindle Loc. 1012.

[133] Rajeswari Pillai Rajagopalan, "Linking Strategic Stability and Ballistic Missile Defense: The View from India," in Saalman, *The China-India Nuclear Crossroads*, Kindle Loc. 1145.

[134] Ashley J. Tellis, "The Evolution of U.S.-Indian Ties: Missile Defense in an Emerging Strategic Relationship," *International Security* 30.4 (2006): 113–151.

undermine South Asia as a "strategic buffer zone" as desired by China (and discussed earlier in the chapter). Finally, if connected with the American missile defense network in East Asia, US–India missile defense cooperation has the potential to enhance India's strategic profile in the wider Asian region.[135] In other words, US–India missile defense cooperation has implications for the Sino-Indian *positional* rivalry.

China is already concerned that the 2008 US–India civil nuclear deal is helping India "expand its nuclear arsenal."[136] Not surprisingly, it responded with a similar deal for Pakistan irrespective of its commitment to the Nuclear Suppliers Group (NSG).[137] It has also not gone unnoticed in China that the US–India agreement enabled India's membership of certain global nuclear regimes – such as the Missile Technology Control Regime and the Wassenaar Agreement – that China has not been allowed to join thus far.[138]

Consequently, the Sino-Indian nuclear asymmetries are not only increasing the potential for inadvertent escalation in that dyad but also raising the *positional* stakes in their rivalry. In fact, nuclear stability in the Sino-Indian dyad is now an intrinsic part of the US–China–India–Pakistan chain (and its multiple linkages). China is not willing to engage with India in a nuclear dialogue given India's status as a nuclear weapons state outside of the Nuclear Nonproliferation Treaty. Furthermore, Beijing wants to "prolong the status quo of [formal] Asian nuclear asymmetry" with India,[139] thus ensuring that mutual nuclear suspicions between China and India will endure while heightening India's quest for parity with China.

Naval Asymmetries

Naval rivalry is a relatively new addition to the Sino-Indian strategic dynamic. Not only did the naval dimension play no role during the 1962 Sino-Indian War but there were also physical limits to their naval interactions throughout the Cold War since both navies were essentially coastal

---

[135] Toby Dalton and Tong Zhao, "At a Crossroads: China-India Nuclear Relations after the Border Clash," Working Paper, Carnegie Endowment for International Peace, August 2020, 11, https://carnegieendowment.org/2020/08/19/at-crossroads-china-india-nuclear-relations-after-border-clash-pub-82489.

[136] Fang, "Asymmetrical Threat Perceptions in India–China Relations."

[137] Ashley J. Tellis, "The China-Pakistan Nuclear 'Deal': Separating Fact from Fiction," Policy Outlook, Carnegie Endowment for International Peace, July 16, 2010, https://carnegieendowment.org/2010/07/16/china-pakistan-nuclear-deal-separating-fact-from-fiction.

[138] Shen Dingli, "A Chinese Perspective on India-U.S. Strategic Partnership and Its Implications for China," in Rajiv Narayanan and Qiu Yonghui (eds.), *India and China Building Strategic Trust* (New Delhi: United Service Institution of India, 2020), Kindle Loc. 4588.

[139] Li, "Shoring Up the Nuclear Proliferation Regime," Kindle Loc. 2258.

fleets. China was largely preoccupied with contingencies in the Taiwan Strait and had only limited ability to project power (with no power projection capabilities to the west of the Strait of Malacca into the Indian Ocean). Likewise, India did not pay much attention to its naval forces until the 1970s. While India began to upgrade its military facilities on the Andaman and Nicobar Islands at the western entrance of the Strait of Malacca in the 1970s–80s, its naval development and modernization was slow and fitful.

However, the naval issue has risen in importance relatively quickly over the past two decades. China's naval transformation is driven by its quest to protect its commerce (since China is now the world's largest trading power) and the need to secure stable supplies of energy resources imported primarily from the Middle East and Africa. More than 80 percent of China's energy imports traverse through the Strait of Malacca, which has created a "Malacca dilemma" for its strategic planners. Nevertheless, it has developed the ability to project power into the Strait of Malacca, at least partially due to the transformation of its maritime disputes in the South China (including through the creation of militarized artificial islands).[140] This has led at least one notable analyst to argue that trends are pointing toward "China's now-permanent presence in the Indian Ocean."[141]

Garver, a long-time China-watcher, has even asserted that China's emergence "as a naval power in the Indian Ocean" is an event "as transformative of India-China relations as China's occupation of Tibet in 1951."[142] Not only does China reject "the idea of the Indian Ocean being India's Ocean" but Chinese analysts also believe that India cannot protect the Indian Ocean sealines "by itself."[143] While India sees itself as a "net security provider" in the Indian Ocean,[144] and also has interests in the Western Pacific (to the east of the Strait of Malacca),[145] its naval capabilities remain limited to the Indian Ocean, at least for now, despite wider ambitions.[146]

[140] You Ji, "The Indian Ocean: A Grand Sino-Indian Game of 'Go'," in David Brewster (ed.), *India and China at Sea: Competition for Naval Dominance in the Indian Ocean*, Oxford Scholarship Online, May 2018, https://doi.org/10.1093/oso/9780199479337.003.0006.

[141] Rory Medcalf, "India and China: Terms of Engagement in the Western Indo-Pacific," in Brewster, *India and China at Sea*, https://doi.org/10.1093/oso/9780199479337.003.0014.

[142] John W. Garver, "Calculus of a Chinese Decision for Local War with India," in Jagannath P. Panda (ed.), *India and China in Asia: Between Equilibrium and Equations* (London: Routledge, 2019), 92.

[143] You, *China's Military Transformation*, 187.

[144] Anit Mukherjee, "India as a Net Security Provider: Concepts and Impediments," Policy Brief, S. Rajaratnam School of International Studies, Singapore, August 2014, www.rsis.edu.sg/wp-content/uploads/2014/09/PB_140903_India-Net-Security.pdf.

[145] Abhijit Singh, "India's Naval Interests in the Pacific," in Brewster, *India and China at Sea*, https://doi.org/10.1093/oso/9780199479337.003.0011.

[146] Rahul Roy-Chaudhury and Kate Sullivan de Estrada, "India, the Indo-Pacific, and the Quad," *Survival* 60.3 (2018): 181–194.

Furthermore, although India is likely to work with the United States and other powers in the Indian Ocean given its inability to cover that vast body of water by itself, it remains wary of China's growing naval presence.

However, China's 2013 military strategy specifically called for "establishing" China in the "two oceans region" that encompasses the Pacific and the Indian Oceans, especially "the western Pacific Ocean and the northern Indian Ocean."[147] Given China's physical distance from the Indian Ocean, its leading scholars are now thinking in complementary terms between the land and sea connections and have proposed the establishment of "continental bridges" from China into the Indian Ocean.[148] Although they are aware that any such bridges in the form of energy pipelines connecting China with the Indian Ocean via Pakistan or Myanmar "cannot replace" China's dependence on the Strait of Malacca and the long maritime routes, they can nevertheless play an ameliorative role in preventing "other countries from blackmailing China on the pretext of the security of the seaway."[149]

In other words, the importance of South Asia and the Indian Ocean is increasing for China (although East Asia remains more important). Garver has even argued that "unless China can secure its interests" in South Asia and the Indian Ocean, "China will remain a regional East Asian power and fall short of its aspiration of becoming a global power."[150] On their part, some Chinese scholars believe that its rise is transforming the region's "artificial divides" (into South Asia, East Asia, and so on) since that fragmented strategic geography was ultimately reflective of America's Cold War priorities.[151] In fact, the drive toward this larger Asian strategic region is a function of both China's policies, including the BRI (as noted earlier), and the United States' Indo-Pacific strategy.[152] (Nevertheless, China's overland pipelines from Russia and Central Asia do have the ability to decrease its "Malacca Dilemma" to some degree. They will also add to Asia's changing strategic geography.)

[147] *Science of Military Strategy (2013)*, 18–19 and 309–310.
[148] Wang, "China in the Middle."
[149] Hailin Ye, "The Strategic Landscape of South Asia and Indian Ocean Region," in Rong Wang and Cuiping Zhu (eds.), *Annual Report on the Development of International Relations in the Indian Ocean Region (2014)* (Heidelberg: Springer, 2015), 38.
[150] Garver, "Calculus of a Chinese Decision for Local War with India," 93.
[151] Cuiping Zhu, "Changes of the International Environment in the Indian Ocean Region and the Strategic Choices for China," in Cuiping Zhu (ed.), *Annual Report on the Development of the Indian Ocean Region (2019)* (Singapore: Springer, 2021), 6.
[152] Indo-Pacific Strategy Report, Department of Defense, June 1, 2019, https://media.defense.gov/2019/Jul/01/2002152311/-1/-1/1/DEPARTMENT-OF-DEFENSE-INDO-PACIFIC-STRATEGY-REPORT-2019.PDF. Additionally, Japan's foray into the Indian Ocean, India's Look/Act East strategy, and Australia's Indo-Pacific thrust are also adding to this momentum.

Table 6.3 *Sino-Indian naval balance*

	India	China
Navy (personnel)	69,050 (+ 55,000 Reserve)	260,000
Naval aviation	7,000	26,000
Marines	1,200	35,000
Submarines (SSBN)	1	6
Submarines (tactical)	15 (including 1 SSN)	53 (including 6 SSNs)
Aircraft carriers	1	2
Destroyers	10	31
Frigates	17	46
Principal amphibious ships	1	6
Landing ships	8	49
Naval aviation (combat capable aircraft)	73	426

Source: The Military Balance 2021 (by the International Institute for Strategic Studies) (London: Routledge, 2021), 249–265.

However, like the other dimensions of the Sino-Indian rivalry, their naval rivalry is also asymmetric (and will be largely limited to South Asia and the Indian Ocean for now, the occasional Indian foray into the Western Pacific notwithstanding). For example, for the period 2014–18, China launched naval vessels "with a total tonnage greater than the tonnages of the entire French, German, Indian, Italian, South Korean, Spanish, or Taiwanese navies."[153] Additionally, the Indian navy has inducted "bluewater assets at a lower rate" compared to the Chinese navy in recent years.[154] Furthermore, China's Southern Theater Fleet that looks after its interests in the South China Sea and the Indian Ocean (and is one of its three fleets along with its Eastern and Northern Fleets) is also larger than the entire Indian navy (see Table 6.3).[155]

Given its implications for both the *spatial* and *positional* dimensions of their rivalry, the Sino-Indian naval asymmetry is conflict-prone for at least

[153] Nick Childs and Tom Waldwyn, "China's Naval Shipbuilding: Delivering on Its Ambition in a Big Way," Military Balance Blog, May 1, 2018, www.iiss.org/blogs/military-balance/2018/05/china-naval-shipbuilding.

[154] Koh Swee Lean Collin, "China-India Rivalry at Sea: Capability, Trends, and Challenges," *Asian Security* 15.1 (2019): 8.

[155] China's Southern Theater Fleet includes six SSBNs, fifteen tactical submarines (including two SSNs), one aircraft carrier, ten destroyers, fourteen frigates, four principal amphibious vessels, and an estimated twenty-one landing ships.

four reasons. First, both China and India are connecting their *spatial* rivalry over disputed land borders with their incipient naval competition. For example, during the 2017 Doklam Crisis, China sent a small naval detachment into the Indian Ocean, and it is now believed that it is likely to "increase its presence in the Indian Ocean, partly for supporting PLA infantry along the Sino-Indian border, and partly for preparation of any maritime conflicts in the Indian Ocean as a result of land-border confrontation."[156]

On their part, Indian strategists are also debating whether to escalate any Sino-Indian border conflict in the Himalayas by raising the stakes in the Indian Ocean by making China's commerce and energy supplies vulnerable (given China's long supply routes in the Indian Ocean).[157] Potential escalation in the Indian Ocean is a very risky prospect since coercion by either side will likely result in countercoercion by the other in addition to raising the overall stakes. Moreover, India cannot implement a distant blockade of China given its naval inferiority. Even the United States' ability to do so "in circumstances other than a global war" is doubtful.[158]

Second, China is worried that the US Indo-Pacific construct promotes India "from the periphery of the Asia-Pacific region to the core of the Indo-Pacific region."[159] The United States' promotion of the rise of India clearly has implications for the Sino-Indian *positional* rivalry. Chinese scholars have noted that India has been "showing greater acceptance" of working along with the United States (and Japan) in South Asia and the Indian Ocean to offset China's growing role in those regions.[160] At the same time, China is also concerned that the Quad grouping of the United States, Japan, Australia, and India enhances India's profile in the wider Asian region. As such, China perceives the US–India relationship and the Quad not just in terms of power balances but also in the context of the Sino-Indian *positional* rivalry because India's linkages with the United States (and others) enhance India's standing in Asia.

However, it has also been observed that even though the Quad may be "a quasi-alliance" in the making,[161] "China only needs to hold India to neutralize the Quad" as it represents an "uneasy 3+1 rather than a monolithic

---

156 You, "The Indian Ocean."
157 Shashank Joshi, "Can India Blockade China?," *The Diplomat*, August 12, 2013, https://thediplomat .com/2013/08/can-india-blockade-china/.
158 Gabriel B. Collins and William S. Murray, "No Oil for the Lamps of China?," *Naval War College Review* 61.2 (2008): 92.
159 Li, "The New Trend of India's Rising as a Great Power," 45.
160 Wu, "India's Perception of and Response to China-US Competition," 138.
161 Zhang Jie, "The Quadrilateral Security Dialogue and Reconstruction of Asia-Pacific Order," *China International Studies* 74.1 (2019): 67.

quartet" because India has no formal alliances (unlike Japan and Australia, which are formally allied with the United States),[162] and because India eschews formal alliances.[163] China has already started preparing for two "1.5 war scenarios" with India in the context of a US/Japan–China war in maritime East Asia: the first scenario envisages India exploiting such a war by initiating hostilities on land in the Himalayas, while the second scenario sees India taking advantage of China's maritime vulnerabilities in the Indian Ocean.[164] India is motivated by its quest to improve its relative position in these scenarios, both bilaterally with China and regionally in Asia.

Third, increasing encounters at sea will create more opportunities for conflict, including through miscalculations or accidents, given that China and India are in the early stages of their transformation from continental to maritime powers, and therefore have relatively limited experience of oceanic encounters. For example, as India contemplated military intervention in the Maldives in 2017, largely driven by China's growing influence in that country, China deployed its largest force into the Indian Ocean since the Ming naval expeditions of the early fifteenth century "to dissuade New Delhi," although it remains unclear whether India "backed down" due to the Chinese pressure (or because of other developments).[165]

A few years before that, in 2011, a Chinese frigate had confronted an Indian amphibious assault vessel in the South China Sea after the Indian vessel completed a port call in Vietnam. China claimed that the Indian vessel was "entering Chinese waters," while Indian officials argued that they were forty-five nautical miles off Vietnam's coast and within Vietnam's economic zone.[166] China is concerned about India's joint offshore oil and gas exploration with Vietnam in the South China Sea in a region disputed between Vietnam and China, because Japan's southward thrust and India's approach eastward "might intersect in the South China Sea."[167]

Meanwhile, India remains concerned about Chinese submarines and potential military bases in the Indian Ocean.[168] China's first overseas base

[162] Feng Zhang, "China's Curious Nonchalance towards the Indo-Pacific," *Survival* 61.3 (2019): 200–201.
[163] Ian Hall, *Modi and the Reinvention of Indian Foreign Policy* (Bristol: Bristol University Press, 2019); and Rajesh Rajagopalan, "Evasive Balancing: India's Unviable Indo-Pacific Strategy," *International Affairs* 96.1 (2020): 75–93.
[164] You, "The Indian Ocean."
[165] Garver, "Calculus of a Chinese Decision for Local War with India," 97.
[166] Ben Bland and Girija Shivakumar, "China Confronts Indian Navy Vessel," *Financial Times*, September 1, 2011, www.ft.com/content/883003ec-d3f6-11e0-b7eb-00144feab49a.
[167] *Science of Military Strategy (2013)*, 89.
[168] Nilanthi Samaranayake, "Securing the Maritime Silk Road in South Asia and the Indian Ocean," *Asia Policy* 14.2 (2019): 21–26.

was established in 2017 in the western Indian Ocean in Djibouti (in the context of anti-piracy operations in the Horn of Africa region). There have been unconfirmed reports in recent years that China has been seeking additional bases across the Indian Ocean (from Myanmar and Bangladesh to Sri Lanka and the Maldives). According to a leading Chinese scholar of India, China "has many ways to hurt India. … China could send an aircraft carrier to the Gwadar port in Pakistan. China had turned down the Pakistan[i] offer to have [the Chinese] military stationed in that country. If India forces China to do that, of course we [China] can put a navy at your [India's] doorstep."[169]

Finally, the naval domain also has implications for the Sino-Indian nuclear rivalry. Given its much smaller nuclear arsenal, many in the Indian strategic community are of the opinion that India can have a credible deterrent only by developing nuclear-armed nuclear-powered submarines (or SSBNs, since they are least susceptible to a first strike as they are stealthy and difficult to locate). While India has one operational SSBN at the moment, the INS *Arihant*, it is probably "a training vessel and technology demonstrator,"[170] and it has faced several technical issues since being commissioned in 2016. In any case, the range of India's submarine-launched ballistic missiles (SLBMs) – the K-15 and K-4 missiles (see Table 6.2) – means that Indian SSBNs will not be able to hit targets along China's eastern coast (where China's major technological, industrial, and population centers are located) from the Bay of Bengal.[171] Consequently, they will need to be deployed in the waters of maritime East Asia (at least until India can build SLBMs with a range greater than 5,000 kilometers).[172] In turn, this will make them vulnerable to detection by China and put them within the striking range of the Chinese submarine base on Hainan Island.[173]

---

[169] Fudan University's Shen Dingli quoted in Ellen Barry, "U.S. Proposes a Naval Coalition," *The New York Times*, March 3, 2016, www.nytimes.com/2016/03/03/world/asia/us-proposes-india-naval-coalition-balance-china-expansion.html.

[170] Kristensen and Korda, "Indian Nuclear Forces, 2020," 222.

[171] Nuclear submarines also raise additional issues related to the delegation of nuclear authority due to challenges associated with communications during crises. In other words, they have implications for command-and-control structures and nuclear decision-making (including the civil–military balance related to such decisions).

[172] Fiona Cunningham and Rory Medcalf, "The Dangers of Denial: Nuclear Weapons in China-India Relations," Lowy Institute for International Policy, October 2011, www.lowyinstitute.org/sites/default/files/pubfiles/Cunningham_and_Medcalf%2C_The_dangers_of_denial_web_1.pdf.

[173] This will also raise the sensitive issue of India's nuclear-armed nuclear submarines traversing through Southeast Asian waters (even if they pass into maritime East Asia via the maritime passageway to the south of Australia).

Although China does not need SSBNs to credibly deter India given its older and more advanced land-based capabilities, the Indian Ocean (along with the South Pacific) is emerging as a new site for Chinese SSBNs as they leave the shallow waters of maritime East Asia to avoid detection by the United States.[174] If deployed in the Indian Ocean, they will make India more vulnerable while also raising the possibility of detection given India's relatively advanced capabilities with respect to maritime domain awareness (especially in the larger context of US–India cooperation). (Furthermore, while China's technological capabilities should not be underestimated, it should be noted that it has faced considerable challenges in developing SLBMs over the decades.)

The consequence of the above-mentioned four pathways in the naval domain means that Holmes and Yoshihara's prognosis of "neither rivalry nor naval war" between China and India is now doubtful.[175] Though war is not preordained, naval rivalry already exists between China and India, and it also contains some potential for escalation. Finally, it should be noted that even though China's naval power is expanding rapidly the developments in the Indian Ocean are not pointing toward Chinese naval hegemony. "China has a surface fleet without organic airpower and nuclear-powered submarines that remain relatively noisy."[176] Furthermore, as China seeks to overcome these shortcomings through technological capabilities and/or military bases, other powers, especially the United States, will also respond in addition to India. The Indian Ocean is a multipolar naval region, with the United States, China, and India being the main players in addition to other important players such as Japan, France, and Australia.[177] However, this emergent multipolarity will also foster more connections and more points of friction between China and India.

---

[174] You, *China's Military Transformation*, 188. The path that Chinese nuclear submarines use to travel from maritime East Asia into the Indian Ocean will also raise political sensitivities in Southeast Asia and Australia.

[175] James R. Holmes and Toshi Yoshihara, "Redlines for Sino-Indian Naval Rivalry," in John Garofano and Andrew J. Dew (eds.), *Deep Currents and Rising Tides: The Indian Ocean and International Security* (Washington, DC: Georgetown University Press, 2013), 185–209 (205).

[176] Paul Dibb, "The Return of Geography," in Glenn, *New Directions in Strategic Thinking 2.0*, 98.

[177] Japan and France have military bases in Djibouti, and France and the United Kingdom also have island territories across the Indian Ocean. The United States remains the strongest naval power in the Indian Ocean with a major base in Diego Garcia, a British Indian Ocean Territory. See Andrew S. Erickson, Walter C. Ladwig III, and Justin D. Mikolay, "Diego Garcia and the United States' Emerging Indian Ocean Strategy," *Asian Security* 6.3 (2010): 214–237; David Brewster, "The Red Flag Follows Trade: China's Future as an Indian Ocean Power," in Ashley J. Tellis, Alison Szalwinski, and Michael Wills (eds.), *Strategic Asia 2019: China's Expanding Strategic Ambitions* (Washington, DC: National Bureau of Asian Research, 2019), 174–209; and Frédéric Grare and Jean-Loup Samaan, *The Indian Ocean as a New Political and Security Region* (Cham: Springer, 2022).

Conclusion

Material and cognitive asymmetries in the Sino-Indian dyad – whether economic, nuclear, or naval – are pushing these rivals toward more intensified competition with some probability for conflict. The fact that asymmetric rivalries are conflict-prone should not be surprising. Not only was the Soviet economy only half as big as the American economy through much of the Cold War,[178] the material power disparity between the United States and China during the first round of their rivalry (1949–71) was that between a superpower and the world's largest developing country (to paraphrase Yan on the contemporary disparity between China and India mentioned earlier). Furthermore, the United States thought of the Soviet Union (and not China) as its principal rival then, though China perceived the United States as its principal rival in the 1950s.[179] The US–China asymmetries in the 1950s did not prevent their direct clash during the Korean War, nor did they help avoid two major militarized crises in the Taiwan Strait during that decade.

Not surprisingly, despite Sino-Indian asymmetries today, scholars have also noted that India is hardly a "pushover."[180] In fact, India's status as the "weaker and less threatening of the two Asian powers" is partially the reason behind the United States' embrace of India in the first place.[181] Consequently, there are three common pathways across their multiple asymmetries with some potential for escalation: China's potential exploitation of the power shift in its favor, India's pursuit of strategies in order to be taken more seriously by China, and the United States' promotion of the rise of India. All three pathways have implications for the *spatial* and/or the *positional* dimension of the Sino-Indian rivalry (in addition to domain-specific pathways toward heightened conflict). If India and China continue with their absolute rise in the years ahead, then the Sino-Indian rivalry may turn out to be one of the most consequential rivalries in Asia – one with global implications given the American stake in their rivalry.

[178] Marc Trachtenberg, "Assessing Soviet Economic Performance during the Cold War: A Failure of Intelligence," *Texas National Security Review* 1.2 (2018): 76–101.
[179] Robert Jervis, "The Impact of the Korean War on the Cold War," *Journal of Conflict Resolution* 24.4 (1980): 563–592; and Warren I. Cohen, *America's Response to China: A History of Sino-American Relations*, 5th ed. (New York: Columbia University Press, 2010).
[180] T. V. Paul, "The Rise of China and the Emerging Order in the Indo-Pacific Region," in Huiyun Feng and Kai He (eds.), *China's Challenges and International Order Transition: Beyond Thucydides's Trap* (Ann Arbor: University of Michigan Press, 2020), 73.
[181] Frankel, "The Breakout of the China-India Strategic Rivalry in Asia and the Indian Ocean," 14.

PART IV

Interconnected Rivalries and Systemic Considerations

CHAPTER 7

The Emergence of a Triadic Rivalry

Two major rivalries exist in South Asia. The first is the India–Pakistan rivalry, which started almost immediately after the British colonial withdrawal from the subcontinent and the partition of the British Indian Empire. Within months of the British departure the two nascent states of India and Pakistan became quickly embroiled in a significant *territorial* dispute. Pakistan claimed the state of Jammu and Kashmir, a princely state, that abutted both India and Pakistan on the grounds that it was a predominantly Muslim state with which it shared a border.[1] Its claim to Kashmir was strictly irredentist.[2] Simultaneously, India sought to hold on to this Muslim-majority state to demonstrate that Muslims could thrive under the aegis of a predominantly Hindu but constitutionally secular polity.[3] In effect, the basis of this rivalry from the outset was, and remains, *spatial.*

The Sino-Indian rivalry, on the other hand, as argued in Chapter 3, has had both *spatial* and *positional* dimensions from the outset. The *spatial* dimensions stemmed from different understandings of the alignment of their Himalayan borders.[4] The *positional* element of the rivalry can be traced to their competing visions about leadership in a postcolonial Asia. The latter dimension would manifest itself quite early. At the 1955

[1] Over 500 such princely states had existed under the aegis of the British Indian Empire. They were nominally independent as long as they recognized the paramount status of the British Crown. At the time of the British colonial withdrawal from the subcontinent the rulers of the princely states were given the option of joining either India or Pakistan based on their demographic features and their geographic location. For a discussion of the princely states at the time of independence, see Ian Copland, *The Princes of India in the Endgame of Empire, 1917–1947* (Cambridge: Cambridge University Press, 1997).

[2] Myron Weiner, "The Macedonian Syndrome: An Historical Model of International Relations and Political Development," *World Politics* 23.4 (1971): 665–683.

[3] Robert L. Hardgrave, Jr. "The Challenge of Ethnic Conflict: India – The Dilemmas of Diversity," *Journal of Democracy* 4.4 (1993): 54–68.

[4] Stephen P. Westcott, *Armed Coexistence: The Dynamics of the Intractable Sino-Indian Border Dispute* (Singapore: Palgrave Macmillan, 2022).

Bandung Summit in 1955, both Prime Minister Jawaharlal Nehru and Premier Zhou En-Lai had vied for a leadership role in Asia for their respective states.

The Sino-Pakistani strategic nexus must be seen in the context of a triadic rivalry in South Asia.[5] Triadic rivalries appear to have some particular characteristics. Some scholars have referred to them as "complex rivalries" as they are not simple, dyadic, rivalries. Among the important features of complex rivalries, a key factor is the impact of one state's actions on the other two actors or the actions of two actors on the third party. Furthermore, complex rivals are more likely to fight in dyadic and triadic wars.[6] This description certainly dovetails with the empirical features of the Sino-Pakistani-Indian triad.

Other discussions of strategic triangles also yield relevant propositions about triadic rivalries. In this analysis a triangle may emerge where there is symmetric amity between two players and enmity between these two and the third. This triangular relationship aptly describes the Sino-Pakistani-Indian triad. However, in the case of this triad, one of the inferences, namely that the ostracized party might seek amity with one or both of the other players, is simply not borne out.[7]

The following section will trace the emergence of this triangular rivalry. As the Sino-Indian *positional* and *spatial* rivalry came to the fore in the early 1960s, especially after the Sino-Indian border war of 1962, it became entangled with the Indo-Pakistani rivalry. The latter rivalry had ensued almost immediately after their emergence as independent states in 1947.[8] With the deepening of the Sino-Indian rivalry the People's Republic of China (PRC) saw an opportunity to place India at a greater strategic disadvantage through the cultivation of a security partnership with Pakistan. This opportunity arose in the first place because the Indo-Pakistani rivalry had an important *spatial* dimension involving the Kashmir dispute. This feature of their rivalry was hardly lost on the PRC. Consequently, it has

[5] On triadic rivalries see William R. Thompson, "Trends in the Analysis of Interstate Rivalries," in Robert Scott and Stephen Kosslyn (eds.), *Emerging Trends in the Social and Behavioral Sciences* (New York: John Wiley and Sons, 2015); also see Joshua Goldstein, Jon C. Pevehouse, Deborah J. Gerner, and Shibley Telhami, "Reciprocity, Triangularity, and Cooperation in the Middle East, 1979–97," *Journal of Conflict Resolution* 45.5 (2001): 594–620.

[6] Brandon Valeriano and Matthew Powers, "Complex Interstate Rivals," *Foreign Policy Analysis* 12 (2016): 552–570.

[7] Lowell Dittmer, "The Strategic Triangle: An Elementary Game-Theoretical Analysis," *World Politics* 33.4 (1981): 485–575.

[8] On the India–Pakistan rivalry see Sumit Ganguly, *Deadly Impasse: Indo-Pakistani Relations at the Dawn of a New Century* (Cambridge: Cambridge University Press, 2016); also see T. V. Paul (ed.), *The India-Pakistani Conflict: An Enduring Rivalry* (Cambridge: Cambridge University Press, 2005).

exploited this dimension of the Indo-Pakistani rivalry through the waxing and waning of its stance toward the Kashmir dispute.

Furthermore, this chapter will also show that through its alignment with Pakistan, the PRC turned it into a strategic surrogate in South Asia. The substantial support of the PRC along multiple dimensions has enabled Pakistan to balance against India despite stark asymmetries on a number of dimensions: diplomatic, economic, and military.[9] Through its informal alliance with Pakistan, the PRC has been able to pursue its *positional* goals in South Asia vis-à-vis India. Keeping India focused on Pakistan helps tie it down to the subcontinent.

This chapter will trace the origins of the Sino-Pakistani strategic nexus. It will examine the growth of significant Chinese arms transfers, including support for Pakistan's nuclear weapons and ballistic missile programs, the building of the Karakoram Highway through disputed territory, the implications of India's termination of the special status of the state of Jammu and Kashmir in 2019, the development of the China–Pakistan Economic Corridor (CPEC), and finally the PRC's efforts to protect Pakistan from India's efforts to censure it for its involvement with terror. The central argument here is that the China–Pakistan entente has long had significant implications for the Sino-Indian *spatial/territorial* rivalry as well as their *positional* rivalry. Furthermore, there is every reason to believe that they are likely to be more intertwined in the foreseeable future.[10]

The Formation of the Sino-Pakistani Nexus

In the early 1960s the PRC started to forge a strategic partnership with Pakistan. Pakistan's courtship of the United States had resulted in the US–Pakistan security pact of 1954. Its subsequent involvement in the Southeast Asia Treaty Organization (SEATO) and the Central Treaty Organization (CENTO) had caused some misgivings in Beijing. Islamabad had, however, sought to paper over these differences to avoid provoking the PRC.

---

[9] "India vs. Pakistan: A Tale of Two Economies," *The Times of India*, November 27, 2020, https://timesofindia.indiatimes.com/business/india-business/india-vs-pakistan-a-tale-of-two-economies/articleshow/79450051.cms; also see www.statista.com/chart/17172/estimated-military-strength-of-india-pakistan/.

[10] It is worth noting the Pakistan is also important to the PRC for reasons that have little to do with India. The PRC has an interest in Pakistan because of the latter's influence within the Muslim world. Furthermore, it also seeks Pakistan's silence on the status of the Muslim Uighur minority in Xinjiang province. See Michael Kugelman, "Imran Khan's Silence on Uighurs Undercuts His Defense of Muslims Worldwide," *Foreign Policy*, January 29, 2021, https://foreignpolicy.com/2021/01/29/imran-khan-uighurs-muslims-china/.

In turn, the principal reason that the PRC did not react adversely to Pakistan's membership in these US-sponsored pacts was because it correctly surmised that Pakistan's participation in them stemmed from its hostility toward India rather than any firm commitment to anti-Communism. Chou En-Lai had stated at the Bandung Conference in Indonesia in 1955 that his Pakistani counterpart, Mohammed Ali, had informed him that "although Pakistan was a party to a military treaty, Pakistan was not against China. Pakistan had no fear China would commit aggression against her. As a result, we achieved a mutual understanding although we are against military treaties."[11]

Furthermore, when Prime Minister Suhrawardy and Zhou En-Lai exchanged state visits in 1956 they emphasized that despite their different political systems and divergent views on various international conflicts Pakistan and the PRC shared common interests and should affirm their friendly ties.[12] It is worth noting that the two countries managed to maintain this cordial relationship even though Pakistan had shifted its position on the PRC's UN membership following its mutual defense treaty with the United States in 1954.

China's forbearance proved to be useful. Pakistan, fixated on the Kashmir dispute with India and confronting an unsettled border with Afghanistan, decided to open negotiations with the PRC to tackle some differences between Chinese and Pakistani maps regarding small areas along the frontier between the Pakistani-controlled section of Kashmir and the Chinese province of Xinjiang. Accordingly, in 1959 Islamabad approached Beijing about opening border negotiations. Beijing, which was in the middle of fraught border negotiations with New Delhi, did not respond favorably until January 1961, by which time the negotiations had reached an impasse.

Despite the risk of alienating the United States, Pakistan proved more inclined to reach out to the PRC owing to other external developments. The new Kennedy administration seemed far less interested in sustaining the alliances forged during the Eisenhower administration, dismissing them as "pactitis." Furthermore, President Kennedy was an advocate of increased economic assistance to India to enable it to serve as an alternative to China's claim to leadership in Asia.[13]

---

[11] William J. Barnds, "China's Relations with Pakistan: Durability amidst Discontinuity," *The China Quarterly* 63 (1975): 463–489.

[12] Barnds, "China's Relations with Pakistan," 469.

[13] Anwar H. Syed, *China and Pakistan: Diplomacy of an Entente Cordiale* (Amherst: University of Massachusetts Press, 1974), 81.

At any event, the PRC reached out to Islamabad shortly after the debacle of the Sino-Indian border war because it had a keen interest in obtaining land access from Tibet to Xinjiang through a disputed region of the northern reaches of the disputed state of Jammu and Kashmir, which was under Pakistani control.

Sino-Pakistani border negotiations started in May 1962 and concluded on December 26, 1962. In the meanwhile, the Sino-Indian border war had taken place and the PRC had seized what India deemed to be at least 14,000 square miles of its territory in this conflict.[14] India, quite predictably, reacted sharply to this border agreement between the PRC and Pakistan as, according to its estimation, Pakistan had ceded as much as 2,500 square miles of disputed territory to the PRC in this agreement. Pakistan, of course, denied such a concession, arguing that it had, in fact, gained as much as 750 square miles previously under Chinese control.[15]

Following the conclusion of these border negotiations, Sino-Pakistani relations gathered considerable momentum. Not only had the two parties settled their minor border differences, they now also had other grounds for cooperation. India's humiliation at the hands of the People's Liberation Army (PLA) in the 1962 border war, in all likelihood, had convinced some in Pakistan that resorting to war against India on the Kashmir issue might enable it to achieve its irredentist objectives. Furthermore, they may have also concluded that military assistance from both the United States and the Soviet Union in the wake of the 1962 war would make India less willing to hold a plebiscite to determine the future of the disputed state. The PRC, in turn, had little reason to be concerned about building ties with Pakistan as it was now contemptuous about Indian pretentions to power.[16] Not only had the Indian Army suffered an abject humiliation at the hands of the PLA but India's hopes and aspirations to serve as a leader of the decolonizing world had been significantly damaged as well.[17] In effect, the PRC had clearly bested India on both the *spatial* and *positional* elements of the rivalry. Yet the intensified hostility toward India led the PRC to deepen its incipient strategic partnership with Pakistan. Accordingly, ties between the two states grew, including the conclusion of the Air Transportation Agreement in August 1963. Later that year, in October, Pakistan signaled

[14] Robert Farley, "How China Defeated India in a Terrifying 1962 War," *The National Interest*, February 11, 2020, https://nationalinterest.org/blog/buzz/how-china-defeated-india-terrifying-1962-war-122406.
[15] Barnds, "China's Relations with Pakistan," 471.
[16] Klaus H. Pringsheim, "China's Role in the Indo-Pakistani Conflict," *The China Quarterly* 24 (1965), 170–175.
[17] Selig S. Harrison, "Trouble India and Her Neighbors," *Foreign Affairs* 43.2 (1965), 312–330.

its growing warmth for the PRC when it departed from its prior stance and voted to admit China into the United Nations.[18]

A Deepening Partnership

Given the formation of this nexus in the early 1960s it is hardly surprising that the PRC played an important, if restricted, role when the second Indo-Pakistani war took place in September 1965.[19] China's actions during this war, though limited, were clearly designed to keep India off balance and to bolster its position in the region. The PRC not only supported Pakistan following the outbreak of war but also presented India with an ultimatum. Specifically, it demanded that India "dismantle the 56 aggressive military works she had built within Chinese territory on the China-Sikkim border and withdraw the intruding Indian troops."[20] In the event, India ignored the Chinese warning and the PLA did not undertake any hostile actions along the disputed Himalayan border. The PRC's unwillingness to follow through on its threat may have stemmed from prevailing domestic and external considerations. Mao Zedong was in the process of planning the onset of the Cultural Revolution and so may have been preoccupied with internal matters.[21] Furthermore, with the Sino-Soviet split out in the open it is possible that he may have been loath to antagonize the Soviet Union.[22]

However, in the wake of the war, the Sino-Pakistani strategic nexus continued to expand. China's courtship of Pakistan in the late 1960s can reasonably be attributed to the dramatic deterioration in Sino-Soviet relations as exemplified in the Ussuri River clashes of 1969.[23] Furthermore, having gone through a phase of considerable domestic upheaval owing to the Cultural Revolution,[24] bereft of allies and faced with an ongoing hostile relationship with India, it made sense for the PRC to reach out to Pakistan. The worsening of the Sino-Soviet rivalry, it is entirely reasonable to surmise, made the PRC even more inclined to strengthen its ties with

[18] Pringsheim, "China's Role in the Indo-Pakistani Conflict," 172.
[19] Russell Brines, *The Indo-Pakistani Conflict* (New York: Pall Mall, 1968).
[20] As quoted in Norman D. Palmer, "China's Relations with India and Pakistan," *Current History* 61.361 (1971), 151.
[21] Frank Dikötter, *The Cultural Revolution: A People's History, 1962–1976* (Pittsburgh; Bloomsbury, 2017).
[22] The classic statement on the origins of the Sino-Soviet split remains; Donald S. Zagoria, *The Sino-Soviet Conflict, 1956–1961* (Princeton: Princeton University Press, 1962).
[23] Harrison E. Salisbury, *The Coming War between China and Russia* (London: Martin Secker and Warburg, 1969).
[24] For a detailed account of the origins and ravages of the Cultural Revolution, see Roderick MacFarquhar, *The Origins of the Cultural Revolution, Volume 3: The Coming of the Cataclysm: 1961–1966* (New York: Columbia University Press, 1997).

Pakistan. In this context, it is worth recalling that the Soviets because of their rivalry with the PRC had also floated the prospect of a collective security system in Asia. This proposal, which did not find much support, was clearly directed toward isolating the PRC.[25]

To that end, in 1969, the PRC revived the historic "silk route" between Sinkiang and Gilgit, which had been closed for the past twenty years. Barely a year and a half later it forged an even more significant road link, the Friendship (Karakoram) Highway.[26] Subsequently, the PRC has made significant further investments in ensuring that this road remains operational despite periodic landslides. The highway is of considerable strategic significance because in the event of another India–Pakistan conflict the PLA could launch a strategic feint through this highway, especially as it has been upgraded. Such a tactical move could thereby threaten the Indian region of Ladakh.[27]

Both these road projects had a direct bearing on the two rivalries.[28] They effectively merged the *spatial* dimensions of the rivalries as the roads were built through disputed areas of the state of Jammu and Kashmir. India's concerns about Pakistan–PRC collaboration were heightened because both states were increasingly undermining India's legal claim to various disputed parts of Kashmir through these extensive road-building activities. In the eyes of New Delhi, the Sino-Indian and Indo-Pakistani rivalries were now increasingly and inextricably intertwined.

The collusive relationship between the PRC and Pakistan deepened in 1970. When Richard Nixon wanted to reach out to the PRC as part of his strategy to exploit Sino-Soviet discord he and his national security adviser, Henry Kissinger, turned to Pakistan because of its extensive ties with the PRC. Islamabad, keen on repairing its ties with Washington, DC, which had been strained as a consequence of the American arms embargo during the 1965 war, was only too happy to oblige. In a brief visit to Pakistan in August 1969, President Nixon not only blessed Pakistan's ties with the PRC but asked the military dictator, President Yahya Khan, to sound the PRC out about a possible policy overture.[29]

---

[25] Arnold L. Horelick, "The Soviet Union's Asian Collective Security Proposal: A Club in Search of Members," *Pacific Affairs* 47.3 (1974): 269–285.

[26] Palmer, "China's Relations with India and Pakistan,"152.

[27] Brigadier Anil Gupta, "Karakoram Highway: A Security Challenge for India," *Indian Defence Review*, October 2, 2015, www.indiandefencereview.com/news/karakoram-highway-a-security-challenge-for-india/.

[28] For a general discussion on the significance of roads amidst rivalries, see Mahnaz Z. Ispahani, *Roads and Rivals: The Political Uses of Access in the Borderlands of Asia* (Ithaca: Cornell University Press, 1989).

[29] G. W. Choudhury, "China's Policy toward South Asia," *Asian Perspective* 14.2 (1990): 131–132; also see Mohammad Habib Sidky, "Chinese World Strategy and South Asia: The China Factor in Indo-Pakistani Relations," *Asian Survey* 16.10 (1976): 965–980.

Following Pakistan's first free and fair election in December 1970, a domestic political crisis ensued with the emergence of Bengali subnationalism in East Pakistan. As negotiations for power-sharing reached a deadlock, the Pakistani Army embarked on a brutal military crackdown in East Pakistan. Despite the crisis in East Pakistan, the PRC remained keen on maintaining good ties with Pakistan. Apart from the common rivalry with India, it saw few prospects for the emergence of a Communist alternative in East Pakistan. Even though evidence of widespread repression in East Pakistan and the flight of millions of refugees into India emerged, the PRC released the most anodyne statements about the developments. More to the point, it expressed support for the territorial integrity of Pakistan.[30]

In the event, when India militarily intervened in East Pakistan, the PRC, while still supportive of Pakistan, did not attempt to open a second front along the Himalayas. Two factors constrained the PRC. First, in August 1971 India had signed a treaty of "peace, friendship and cooperation" with the Soviet Union. A key article in this treaty, for all practical purposes, granted India a tacit security guarantee.[31] Under its aegis the Soviets felt compelled to use their veto in the United Nations Security Council when the United States introduced resolutions that India deemed to be hostile toward its position.[32] Second, since the Indian Army had waited until December to act, the Himalayan passes were snow-bound, making any incursion in that region all but impractical. Despite the PRC's inability (or unwillingness) to act militarily on behalf of its ally during this existential crisis, for Pakistani decision-makers the diplomatic support that it had offered was still deemed to be crucial. Consequently, the Sino-Pakistani nexus remained robust throughout the 1970s.

Bolstering the Partnership: The Security Dimension

Even prior to the Indian nuclear test of May 1974, as early as 1972 Pakistan had already decided to embark on a nuclear weapons program. Prime Minister Zulfiquar Ali Bhutto, who had succeeded President Yahya Khan in the wake of the break-up of Pakistan in 1971, had concluded that only the option of acquiring nuclear weapons could guarantee his country's

---

[30] Palmer, "China's Relations with India and Pakistan," 153.

[31] Robert H. Donaldson, *Soviet Policy toward India: Ideology and Strategy* (Cambridge, MA: Harvard University Press, 1974).

[32] In effect, three rivalries intersected during this crisis: The India–Pakistan rivalry, the Sino-Indian rivalry, and the Sino-Soviet rivalry. On this subject see Paul J. Smith, "The Tilting Triangle: Geopolitics of the China-India-Pakistan Relationship," *Comparative Strategy* 32.4 (2013): 313–330.

security. Not surprisingly, shortly after making this decision Bhutto reached out to the PRC for assistance. In 1974, he received assurances of Chinese assistance.[33] The PRC proved to be forthcoming principally because of its enduring rivalry with India.[34] Building up Pakistan's military and especially nuclear capabilities would induce India to focus on Pakistan's capabilities and divert its attention from the Himalayan border. The Chinese decision to provide nuclear assistance to Pakistan helped entwine the two rivalries even further. India, already locked into *territorial* and *positional* rivalry with Pakistan, could hardly afford to ignore the PRC's willingness to strengthen Pakistan's conventional capabilities and to assist it in acquiring nuclear weapons.[35]

In the event, the PRC, throughout the 1970s and especially in 1980, became a major supplier of nuclear weapons technology to Pakistan. It also went on to provide substantial assistance to Pakistan's missile development program.[36] A complete accounting is unnecessary at this juncture but suffice to say that it made three key contributions in the nuclear realm. First, it provided Pakistan with assistance for constructing a fifty-to-seventy-watt plutonium-production reactor at Khusab. Once operational, this facility would provide Pakistan with an unsafeguarded source of plutonium-laden spent fuel. Second, Chinese companies were involved in the construction of an unsafeguarded reprocessing center in Chasma. Finally, in 1996, a Chinese company supplied Pakistan's Kahuta Research Laboratory with 5,000 custom-made ring magnets for use in high-speed centrifuges.[37] These devices are crucial in uranium enrichment and helped Pakistan acquire weapons-grade uranium.

The PRC also played a crucial role in the development of Pakistan's ballistic missile program. Several of Pakistan's short- and medium-range missiles were based on Chinese designs and technology, including the Chinese M-9 and M-11 missiles. Subsequently, the PRC may have also assisted

---

[33] Henrik Stålhane Hiim, *China and International Nuclear Weapons Proliferation: Strategic Assistance* (London: Routledge, 2019), 51; also see the detailed discussion in Andrew Small, *The China-Pakistan Nexus: Asia's New Geopolitics* (New York: Oxford University Press, 2015).

[34] T. V. Paul, "The Causes and Consequences of China-Pakistani Nuclear/Missile Collaboration," in Lowell Dittmer (ed.), *South Asia Nuclear Security Dilemma: India, Pakistan and China* (London: Routledge, 2015).

[35] For multiple perspectives on the rivalry, see T. V. Paul, *The India-Pakistan Conflict: An Enduring Rivalry* (Cambridge: Cambridge University Press, 2005).

[36] For a discussion see T. V. Paul, "Chinese-Pakistani Nuclear/Missile Ties and Balance of Power Politics," *The Nonproliferation Review* 10.2 (2003): 21–29.

[37] Evan S. Medeiros, *Reluctant Restraint: The Evolution of China's Nonproliferation Policies and Practices, 1980–2004* (Stanford: Stanford University Press, 2007), 65–66.

Pakistan to develop the Babur cruise missile, which could have a nuclear role.[38] China's support for Pakistan's acquisition of both nuclear and ballistic missile capabilities has given Pakistan a significant military edge against India. On its own, it would have been significantly constrained from acquiring these capabilities.

Apart from the crucial nuclear and ballistic missile transfers, the PRC has considerably strengthened Pakistan's conventional military capabilities. As early as 1974, shortly after the first Indian nuclear test, the PRC provided Pakistan 60 MiG-19 fighter jets, 150 tanks, and various other forms of weaponry as part of a $300 million economic and military aid agreement.[39] More recently, bilateral military ties have significantly deepened and broadened. For example, between 2000 and 2010, the PRC exported $3.195 billion worth of weaponry to Pakistan. More specifically, during that decade the two states jointly developed a fighter aircraft for the Pakistan Air Force known as the JF-17 or "Thunder." The first batch of these fighters were manufactured in the PRC in 2009 and then flown to Pakistan, where they were reassembled. The JF-17 is designed to eventually replace other combat aircraft in Pakistan's inventory. One of the attractions of this aircraft is that it is equipped with beyond-visual-range air-to-air missiles – a feature that the United States was unwilling to supply when it sold Pakistan a contingent of F-16s during the Afghan war years. Aside from this combat aircraft the PRC also signed an agreement in December 2008 to provide four KJ-2000/ZDK03 airborne early warning aircraft. Furthermore, in August 2011, for the very first time the PRC offered to sell Pakistan thirty-six of its most advanced frontline fighter jets, the Chengdu J-10 Vigorous Dragon.[40]

These arms transfers kept apace in the past decade. In 2009, for example, Chinese weapons sales to Pakistan amounted to as much as $758 million and since 2009, until 2020, to about $584 million annually. In July 2015, in a significant arms deal, the PRC agreed to provide Pakistan with eight stealth attack submarines. Four of these are expected to be delivered in 2023 and the remaining four will be built at the Karachi dockyards by 2028.[41]

More recently, as Sino-Indian relations have significantly deteriorated, the PRC seems even more willing to keep providing Pakistan with military

---

[38] Hiim, *China and International Nuclear Weapons Proliferation*, 61.
[39] Claude Rakisits, "Pakistan-China Bilateral Relations 2001–2011: A Deepening but Cautious Partnership," *Security Challenges* 8.3 (2012): 86.
[40] Rakisits, "Pakistan-China Bilateral Relations 2001–2011," 93–94.
[41] Shantanu Roy-Chaudhury, "Analysing China's Arms Sales to South Asia," *India Foundation Journal* (July–August 2020): 43.

equipment that can help counter growing Indian military capabilities. In January 2022, Indian news sources reported that the PRC had agreed to provide Pakistan with the DF-17 mobile, solid-fueled medium-range ballistic missile with hypersonic features. Owing to its hypersonic dimensions it can evade India's extant air defense capabilities, including the newly acquired Russian S-400 missile battery.[42]

There is a striking leitmotif that runs through the PRC's conventional and nuclear transfers to Pakistan. They cannot be primarily attributed to commercial motivations. Instead, they not only are designed to bolster Pakistan's security but have been carefully tailored to keep India preoccupied with Pakistan. These deals have granted Pakistan sufficient military capabilities and options to ensure that India is forced to divert a significant segment of its own military resources to the Indo-Pakistani border. Furthermore, Pakistan's earlier nuclear and ballistic missile transfers enabled it to have a viable nuclear deterrent against India, thereby ensuring that India's nuclear arsenal would have to contend with two nuclear-armed adversaries.[43]

Bolstering the Partnership: The Economic Dimension

The PRC has not only been a major weapons supplier to Pakistan. It has also, especially in the recent past, stepped up its economic partnership. Few bilateral initiatives are more important than the CPEC, which is part of the PRC's more ambitious Belt and Road Initiative. In April 2015, President Xi Jinping announced a $46 billion project (subsequently expanded to $62 billion in April 2017) designed to dramatically boost Pakistan's infrastructure through the construction of a series of highways, ports, and pipelines. The purpose of this vast project is twofold. At one level it is simply the continuation of a long-standing bilateral economic relationship harking back to the 1950s. The difference, however, is that the Sino-Pakistani nexus has strengthened considerably over the past several decades even as the PRC's rivalry with India has waxed and waned. In this context, it is telling that a Chinese expert stated:

> We would like to help Pakistan stand on its own two feet. We want to change the mindset. Pakistan talks about catching up with India militarily, we want to see it *balancing India* (emphasis added) more comprehensively – economically, socially, culturally.[44]

[42] Shishir Gupta, "China Supplies Mounted Howitzers to Pak to Maintain Arms Parity with India," *The Hindustan Times*, January 27, 2022.
[43] Mohan Malik, "The China Factor in the India-Pakistan Conflict," *Parameters* 33.1 (2003): 35–50.
[44] As quoted in Small, *The China-Pakistan Axis*, 191.

In part the PRC's decision to buttress Pakistan economically also stems from the realization that its "all weather ally" is beset with structural economic problems.[45] Some of these problems, such as low foreign exchange reserves, have been fluctuating issues. Others, however, including low exports, high levels of inflation, and an ongoing fiscal deficit, have been endemic for some time.[46]

At another level, the goal, of course, is to connect Pakistan's coast with the PRC's northwestern Xinjiang region.[47] The PRC's interest in linking these two areas stems from an interest in partially alleviating the "Malacca Dilemma" – the potential chokepoint that it faces in the Malacca Straits in the event of a conflict with India or, worse still, with the United States. This concern from Beijing's standpoint is hardly chimerical: As much as 60 percent of its seaborne trade passes through the Malacca Straits.[48] With the CPEC deal the PRC obtained the rights to operate the port of Gwadar in Baluchistan for forty years. This will enable it to ship some of the petroleum that it obtains from the Persian Gulf to the port and then pump it through pipelines into western China. The port, though currently being developed as a commercial venture, holds the potential to serve as a possible facility for the People's Liberation Army navy. This prospect is of no minor concern to India.[49] Since this facility is on the Arabian Sea Indian naval planners, quite understandably, fret over its strategic significance.[50]

The CPEC, according to another analysis, is probably also quite invaluable to the PRC because it could promote the economic development of its northwest. Among other matters, the PRC hopes that economic development of its restive Xinjiang province can assuage the existence of separatist sentiments. Another advantage is that the successful development of the proposed economic corridor could provide the region access to the sea.[51]

There may be a fourth motivation for the CPEC project. Though unstated, it may have been the growing rapprochement between India

[45] Small, *The China-Pakistan Axis*, 190–191.
[46] Shahroo Malik, "Pakistan's Economic Woes: The Way Forward," *The Diplomat*, April 18, 2019, https://thediplomat.com/2019/04/pakistans-economic-woes-the-way-forward/.
[47] Jeremy Garlick, "Deconstructing the China-Pakistan Economic Corridor: Pipe Dreams versus Geopolitical Realities," *Journal of Contemporary China* 27.112 (2018): 519–533.
[48] Paweł Paszak, "China and the Malacca Dilemma," *China Report*, February 28, 2021, https://warsawinstitute.org/china-malacca-dilemma/.
[49] Claude Rakisits, "A Path to the Sea: China's Pakistan Plan," *World Affairs* 178.3 (2015): 67–74.
[50] Gurpreet S. Khurana, "China's 'String of Pearls' in the Indian Ocean and Its Security Implications," *Strategic Analysis* 32.1 (2008): 1–39; also see Nadège Rolland, Fillipo Boni, Meia Nouwens et al., "Where the Belt Meets the Road: Security in Contested South Asia," *Asia Policy* 14.2 (2019): 1–41.
[51] Terry Mobley, "The Belt and Road Initiative: Insights from China's Backyard," *Strategic Studies Quarterly* 13.3 (2019): 52–72.

and the United States.[52] The process started almost a decade and a half ago when the United States and India finalized the US–India civilian nuclear agreement. Since then successive American administrations have built upon that accord and have expanded the security dimensions of the relationship through military-to-military exercises, arms transfers, and the completion of several foundational agreements that deal with logistics, intelligence cooperation, and communications security.[53] There is little or no question that concerns about the PRC's rise and growing assertiveness in Asia have served as one of the key binding forces in this incipient strategic partnership. Beijing, not surprisingly, has sought to bolster its economic (and military) ties with Pakistan in response to the emergent US–India strategic partnership.

Despite this substantial economic commitment to Pakistan, it is unclear if the country's fraught politics, institutional weaknesses, and lopsided civil–military relations will enable it to absorb the massive investments that the PRC had envisaged. Within less than a decade of the announcement of this mammoth enterprise, initial, dispassionate, assessments have suggested that significant elements of the project were in jeopardy and would have to be scaled down.[54] These vicissitudes notwithstanding, there is little or no reason to believe that the PRC will abandon its long-standing, multifaceted partnership with Pakistan. Since the 1990s the PRC has come to see Pakistan as a strategic surrogate in South Asia. Given that the India–Pakistan rivalry shows no sign of abating and in light of the heightening of the Sino-Indian rivalry, reinforcing the Sino-Pakistan strategic nexus makes sense for the PRC. No other state in South Asia, regardless of the scope of its ties to the PRC, harbors long-standing territorial claims on India and has aspirations to enter into a *positional* rivalry with the regional behemoth. Consequently, maintaining a multidimensional relationship with Pakistan holds considerable appeal for the PRC.

Diplomatic Support

Beyond these issue areas where the PRC has been a significant source of material support to Pakistan, it has also been an important diplomatic ally. To that end, it has sought to shield Pakistan from international censure. Pakistan's dalliance

---

[52] Rakisits, "A Path to the Sea," 71.
[53] Šumit Ganguly and M. Chris Mason (eds.), *The Future of US-India Security Cooperation* (Manchester: Manchester University Press, 2021).
[54] Small, *The China-Pakistan Axis*, 183–212.

with terror is well known.[55] It has harbored a range of terrorist organizations, including the Jaish-e-Mohammed (JeM) and the Lashhkar-e-Taiba (LeT), both primarily dedicated to carrying out attacks on Indian-controlled Kashmir and elsewhere in India. Both the JeM and the LeT have been implicated in major terrorist attacks in India, the JeM on the Indian Parliament in December 2001 and the LeT at multiple sites in Bombay (Mumbai) in November 2008.[56] The leaderships of both these terrorist organizations, Maulana Masood Azhar and Hafiz Mohammed Saeed, are known to live in Pakistan and to enjoy the protection of the country's Inter-Services Intelligence Directorate (ISI-D).[57]

Given their known complicity in these two terror attacks, India has long sought to have them designated as global terrorists under the aegis of the United Nations Security Council's Islamic State in Iraq and the Levant (ISIL/Da'esh) and Al-Qaeda Sanctions Committee. The PRC, however, acting no doubt at the behest of its ally, repeatedly refused to comply. As late as March 2019 it had placed a "technical hold" on including Azhar on the list without specifying any reasons. Since the committee operates on the basis of consensus, the effort had failed. Finally, in May 2019, most likely under pressure from the United States, the PRC relented and Azhar was designated a global terrorist.[58] Hafiz Saeed, the mastermind of the Bombay (Mumbai) attacks, however, was placed on the UN terrorist list as early as December 2008.[59] In his case, the evidence of his complicity in the Bombay (Mumbai) terrorist attacks was presumably so overwhelming that even the PRC could not come to Pakistan's assistance.

India's Termination of Kashmir's Special Status and the Sino-Pakistani Nexus

On August 6, 2019, the Hindu nationalist Bharatiya Janata Party, which had returned to office for a second consecutive term in April 2019, used

[55] S. Paul Kapur, *Jihad as Grand Strategy: Islamist Militancy, National Security and the Pakistani State* (New York: Oxford University Press, 2016).
[56] On the JeM's role in the parliament attack, see Sumit Ganguly and R. Harrison Wagner, "India and Pakistan: Bargaining in the Shadow of Nuclear War," *Journal of Strategic Studies* 27.3 (2004): 479–507; on the LeT's involvement in the Bombay (Mumbai) terrorist attacks, see Cathy Scott-Clark and Adrian Levy, *The Siege: 68 Hours inside the Taj Hotel* (London: Penguin, 2013).
[57] "Pakistan's ISI Trains LeT, JeM Terrorists Parvez Musharraf," *The Hindustan Times*, February 16, 2016; also see Jason Burke, "Pakistan Spy Agency's Alleged Role in Mumbai Terrorist Attacks to Be Revealed," *The Guardian*, May 9, 2011.
[58] Swati Gupta, "Modi Claims Political Win after UN Lists Masood Azhar as a Terrorist," *CNN*, May 2, 2019, www.cnn.com/2019/05/02/india/masood-azhar-un-sanctions-intl/index.html.
[59] "Hafiz Muhammad Saeed," United Nations Security Council, August 19, 2022, www.un.org/securitycouncil/sanctions/1267/aq_sanctions_list/summaries/individual/hafiz-muhammad-saeed.

its parliamentary majority to abrogate the special constitutional provisions that had long governed its relationship between Jammu and Kashmir and the central government in New Delhi.[60] This decision, while of dubious constitutional propriety, effectively undermined Pakistan's legal claim to the portion of the state under India's control.[61] Quite predictably, Pakistan vehemently protested this decision. Beyond Pakistan's obvious frustration with this Indian decision, the PRC also expressed significant reservations about this unilateral action on India's part. A Japanese scholar observed that India's actions amounted to an "unilateral move to change the status quo" and had thereby "forced China into the Kashmir dispute."[62] There were two reasons for the PRC's misgivings. First, the move had obviously undermined its ally's legal standing on the Kashmir issue. Second, since India had formally bifurcated the state, with one portion, Ladakh, converted into a union territory (under the direct rule of New Delhi), it notionally impinged on Chinese-controlled Aksai Chin, thereby technically undermining Chinese sovereignty.[63]

Previously, the PRC's policies toward the Kashmir dispute had waxed and waned over the decades – often reflecting the vicissitudes of Sino-Indian relations.[64] However, as early as the end of the first decade of the twenty-first century its policy toward the dispute had started to shift. The most significant shift, of course, came in the wake of the announcement of the CPEC project in 2015 as it passed through Pakistan-controlled Kashmir. Not surprisingly, it had elicited a strong official reaction from India.[65]

Conclusions

This chapter has sought to demonstrate how the growth of the Sino-Pakistani strategic nexus has impinged on the Sino-Indian rivalry. Owing

[60] Sumit Ganguly, "Modi Crosses the Rubicon in Kashmir," *Foreign Affairs*, August 8, 2019, www.foreignaffairs.com/articles/india/2019-08-08/modi-crosses-rubicon-kashmir.

[61] Sumit Ganguly and Arzan Tarapore, "Kashmir: A Casualty of India's Rising Power Status?," *The National Interest*, October 22, 2019, https://nationalinterest.org/feature/kashmir-casualty-indias-rising-power-status-90311.

[62] Masahiro Kurita, "China's Kashmir Policy since the mid-2010s: Ramifications of CPEC and India's Kashmir Reorganization," *Asian Security* 18.1 (2021): 56–74.

[63] Aijaz Hussain, "AP Explains: India's Kashmir Move Foretold China Standoff," *The Washington Post*, August 19, 2020.

[64] For a detailed account of the ebbs and flows of Chinese policy toward the dispute see Kurita, "China's Kashmir Policy since the mid-2010s."

[65] For a discussion of India's reservations see Lieutenant-General P. K. Singh (retd.), "China-Pakistan Economic Corridor: Connecting the Dots," *United Services of India Journal* (April–June 2017), https://usiofindia.org/publication/usi-journal/china-pakistan-economic-corridor-connecting-the-dots/.

Table 7.1 *India and Pakistan (relative power)*

	Indicator by most recent year	
Indicator/Country	India	Pakistan
Military spending, current[1] USD	$72,887,446,604.30 (2020)	$10,376,381,620.81 (2020)
Per capita GDP[2]	$1,927.708 (2020)	$1,188.86 (2020)
Number of diplomatic personnel	4,297[3] (2021)	2,993[4] (2020)
Social spending	$229,697,067.60[5] (2021)	$10,014,262,500.18[6] (2019)

[1] World Bank, "World Development Indicators," World Bank DataBank, 2022, https://databank.worldbank.org/source/world-development-indicators#.
[2] World Bank, "World Development Indicators."
[3] Ministry of External Affairs (India), "Annual Report: 2020–21," February 25, 2021, www.mea.gov.in/Uploads/PublicationDocs/33569_MEA_annual_Report.pdf, Annexure VII, page 261.
[4] Ministry of Foreign Affairs (Pakistan), "Data and Statistics," April 23, 2020, https://mofa.gov.pk/data-and-statistics/.
[5] "Expenditure on Social Services Rises 12% to Rs 17 Lakh Crore in FY21: Eco Survey," *The Economic Times*, January 29, 2021, https://economictimes.indiatimes.com/news/economy/policy/expenditure-on-social-services-rises-12-to-rs-17-lakh-crore-in-fy21-eco-survey/articleshow/80588326.cms?from=mdr.
[6] World Bank, "World Development Indicators."

to the steady growth of this tacit alliance, the India–Pakistan rivalry has now become closely tied to the Sino-Indian rivalry. Consequently, these two rivalries have now been transformed into a triadic rivalry. The transformation of these two disparate rivalries into a triangular form is likely to contribute to their intensification. In this context, it appears pertinent to mention that the bolstering of the Sino-Pakistani nexus has led a scholar to refer to it as a "quasi-alliance." More to the point, it is apparently the only bilateral relationship that the PRC refers to as an "all-weather" strategic partnership.[66]

Pakistan, on its own, given the growing asymmetries with India along multiple dimensions, would be, for all practical purposes, headed toward losing its rivalry with India. (For the growing asymmetries between India and Pakistan along multiple dimensions see Tables 7.1 and 7.2.) Its irredentist claim to Kashmir would remain but would mostly be notional.

[66] Andrew Scobell, Bonny Lin, Howard J. Shatz et al., *At the Dawn of Belt and Road* (Santa Monica: RAND, 2018).

Table 7.2 *Longitudinal data (military spending, GDP per capita, diplomatic personnel, diplomatic missions, social expenditure, and social spending)*

Military spending, current USD, by country, 2015–2020[1]

Country name/Year	2015	2016	2017	2018	2019	2020
India	$51,295,483,753.94	$56,637,622,640.87	$64,559,435,280.69	$66,257,801,718.28	$71,468,900,524.30	$72,887,446,604.30
Pakistan	$9,483,482,373.09	$9,973,768,058.78	$11,461,253,916.56	$11,732,131,762.05	$10,388,318,164.57	$10,376,381,620.81

GDP per capita, current USD, by country, 2015–2020[2]

Country Name/Year	2015	2016	2017	2018	2019	2020
India	$1,605.605	$1,732.554	$1,980.667	$1,996.915	$2,100.751	$1,927.708
Pakistan	$1,356.668	$1,368.427	$1,464.926	$1,482.213	$1,288.556	$1,188.86

Diplomatic personnel by country, 2016–2021

Country Name/Year	2016	2017	2018	2019	2020	2021
India[3]	4,054[4]	4,194[5]	4,208[6]	4,225[7]	4,261[8]	4,297[9]
Pakistan[10]	NA	NA	NA	NA	2,993[11]	NA

Diplomatic missions by country, 2016–2019[12]

Country Name/Year	2016	2017	2018	2019
India	173	181	NA	186
Pakistan	NA	116	NA	117

Social expenditure in USD, by country, 2016–2021[13]

Country Name/Year	2016	2017	2018	2019	2020	2021
India[14]	NA	NA	NA	NA	204,933,689.10	$229,697,067.60
Pakistan	NA	NA	NA	NA	NA	

Table 7.2 (cont.)

		Total social spending (health + education) as % of GDP, by country, 2014–2019[15]				
Country Name/Year	2014	2015	2016	2017	2018	2019
India	NA	4.208	4.391	-	NA	NA
Pakistan	3.164	3.390	3.866	3.816	NA	3.589

		Estimated total social spending (health + education) by country, 2014–2019[16]				
Country Name/Year	2014	2015	2016	2017	2018	2019
India	NA	$88,511,859,714.28	$100,775,585,358.85	NA	NA	NA
Pakistan	$7,732,414,197.66	$9,171,962,153.11	$10,773,344,523.03	$11,622,930,238.01	NA	$10,014,262,500.18

[1] World Bank, "World Development Indicators."

[2] World Bank, "World Development Indicators."

[3] Data published in Annual Reports of the Ministry of External Affairs. Reports cover part of two years. Data is entered for the year in which the report is published.

[4] Ministry of External Affairs (India), "Annual Report: 2015–16," March 13, 2016, www.mea.gov.in/Uploads/PublicationDocs/26525_26525_External_Affairs_English_AR_2015-16_Final_compressed.pdf, Appendix IX, page 337.

[5] Ministry of External Affairs (India), "Annual Report: 2016–17," February 28, 2017, www.mea.gov.in/Uploads/PublicationDocs/29521_MEA_ANNUAL_REPORT_2016_17_new.pdf, Appendix IX, page 318.

[6] Ministry of External Affairs (India), "Annual Report: 2017–8," April 6, 2018, www.mea.gov.in/Uploads/PublicationDocs/29788_MEA-AR-2017-18-03-02-2018.pdf. Appendix IX, page 334.

[7] Ministry of External Affairs (India), "Annual Report: 2018–19," August 9, 2019, www.mea.gov.in/Uploads/PublicationDocs/31719_MEA_AR8_19.pdf, Appendix V, page 423.

[8] Ministry of External Affairs (India), "Annual Report: 2019–20," March 9, 2020, www.mea.gov.in/Uploads/PublicationDocs/32489_AR_Spread_2020_new.pdf, Appendix IX, pages 475–476.

[9] Ministry of External Affairs (India), "Annual Report: 2020–21."

[10] Pakistan does not publish annual data on the number of diplomatic personnel.

[11] Ministry of Foreign Affairs (Pakistan), "Data and Statistics."

[12] Lowy Institute, "2019 Country comparison." Global Diplomacy Index, 2019, https://globaldiplomacyindex.lowyinstitute.org/country_comparison.html. Some historic data is available on diplomatic missions for India and Pakistan, despite lack of historic data on Pakistani diplomatic personnel.

[13] Reported social expenditure in national media. Only India had recent data. Expenditure originally reported in rupees, converted to US dollars using current exchange rate.

[14] *The Economic Times*, January 29, 2021.

[15] Combines two indicators from the list of World Bank DataBank World Development Indicators: Domestic General Government Health Expenditure (% of GDP) and Government Expenditure on Education, Total (% of GDP). NA values indicate no data available for one or both indicators for a specific country in a given year.

[16] Social spending as a percentage of GDP is multiplied by GDP of India/Pakistan for a given year. GDP figures are from World Bank DataBank World Development Indicators. Totals are estimated and not exact, as there may be some rounding error resulting from rounding decisions made by the World Bank or by limits of Microsoft Excel.

However, with the PRC now linked with Pakistan on the *territorial* element of the rivalry, Islamabad may feel emboldened in its opposition to India. Simultaneously, with the worsening of the *spatial* dimensions of the Sino-Indian rivalry in conjunction with its *positional* features, the PRC will have even greater incentives to rely on Pakistan as a strategic asset in South Asia to deploy against India.

Only under exceptional circumstances is the PRC likely to restrain Pakistan. It may exercise such restraint if Pakistan were to undertake yet another Kargil-like venture as it did in 1999.[67] Alternatively, the PRC may also discourage a future swarming terrorist attack on the order of the one that Islamabad had launched in November 2008 in Bombay (Mumbai). Owing to Indian unpreparedness for the magnitude and daring of the attack as well as other factors, escalation did not ensue.[68] However, in the future such fortuitous circumstances may not exist, especially if there is a jingoistic and risk-prone government in office.

---

[67] Peter R. Lavoy (ed.), *Asymmetric Warfare in South Asia: The Causes and Consequences of the Kargil Conflict* (Cambridge: Cambridge University Press, 2009).

[68] Angel Rabasa, Robert D. Blackwill, Peter Chalk et al., *The Lessons of Mumbai* (Santa Monica: RAND, 2009).

CHAPTER 8

The Sino-Indian Rivalry in Regional and Global Context

Previous chapters have focused on India and China as rivals. Yet we have also noted that the Sino-Indian rivalry has become fused with the Indo-Pakistani rivalry, the premier rivalry of South Asia, and seems to be in the process of becoming fused with the Sino-American rivalry, the premier rivalry of East Asia and perhaps the global system. Three implications follow. First, the Sino-Indian rivalry should not be studied in isolation. Some attention must be paid to its regional and global context. Second, the Indo-Pakistani rivalry cannot be studied in isolation either. Its regional context very much includes the Sino-Indian rivalry. Third, it also follows that the Sino-American rivalry cannot be viewed in isolation any more than the other two rivalries. For instance, most students of the Sino-American rivalry zero in on the independence of Taiwan or clashes in the South China Sea as the or a key to a possible escalation to war. But if these rivalries are becoming fused, Sino-American hostility levels might also be keyed to developments in Kashmir or Sino-Indian clashes in the Indian Ocean. In a similar fashion, Sino-Indian hostility levels might be strongly influenced by a Chinese attempt to capture Taiwan or ships going bump in the night somewhere in the South China Sea.

A recent graphic example was a March 9, 2022, missile that was accidentally launched by India into Pakistan.[1] Surprisingly, it went little noticed by a world focused on the Russian invasion of Ukraine. Fortunately, it did not hit a military target or an urban area. Nor did it trigger an immediate Pakistani response. But imagine the same error if China had accidentally launched a missile on Taiwan. We might expect such an error to not go relatively unnoticed and perhaps to be more likely to have escalatory ramifications. The point of this hypothetical anecdote is that at some future point when an Indian or Pakistani missile is accidentally launched toward

---

[1] "India Says It Accidentally Fired a Missile into Pakistan," *CNN*, March 12, 2022, www.cnn.com/2022/03/11/asia/india-pakistan-missile-hnk/index.html.

its South Asian rival, it might have major repercussions for not only South Asia but also East Asia because of rivalry fusion.

All this means is that security decisions are in the process of becoming more complex. As will be demonstrated later in this chapter, the way in which major power wars have escalated into general or systemic wars is less straightforward than one might think. To be quite blunt, neither the First World War nor the Second World War started as a war between the declining system leader and an ascending challenger. The First World War began in the Balkans, the Second World War in Central Europe. For a variety of reasons, other major powers joined these wars to turn them into systemic wars. The initial grievances in these systemic wars may seem like acorns that become mighty trees. How does a bungled assassination of an Austrian archduke or even an attack on Poland mushroom into war on multiple continents? One answer is in the ways rivalries are linked. A Serbian attack on Austria has links to Russian commitments in the Balkans that in turn are linked to Franco-Russian commitments and German war planning for dealing with its two rivals, France and Russia. Britain might have stayed aloof from the fighting if German planning had not led to an attack through Belgium.

The origins of the First World War have become something of a cliché in international relations. Sophisticated readers groan when these origins are trotted out as generalized blueprints for systemic wars in general. Yet, while it is true that the specifics of each systemic war have unique components, there are also some general features. One is that decision-makers do not tend to see general wars coming. They make decisions based on short-term considerations without necessarily seeing the big picture. That bigger picture includes linked or fused rivalries that blow up relatively local concerns into global wars. Rivalries such as the Sino-Indian rivalry can be conduits to widening the local concerns that have the capability to become transformed into something far greater and more damaging.

No Rivalry Is an Island

One of the dangers in studying rivalries is that we become overly fixated on the two main actors in question. We sometimes forget that two-actor relationships exist in a larger world and that an important question is how exactly that dyad relates to the larger world – whether it be a region or the entire world. Several things stand out in this context. China is the dominant indigenous power in East Asia. It is embroiled in a contest with the United States for hegemony in East Asia. China is the strongest on the mainland.

The United States is stronger at sea and in the Asian rim areas, highlighting the peculiar nature of East Asia as geographically divided between continental and maritime states. Moreover, China has considerable potential for doubling down on the regional contest by becoming a full-fledged global challenger of the United States. To do this it needs to improve its position in the home region, move its economy beyond relatively routine if massive manufacturing production and into the technological leading sectors, and enhance its military capabilities of global reach. All these three areas of concern seem to be something that China is working hard at.

India is the leading power in South Asia. It would be clearly hegemonic in this region if it were not for the repetitive challenges of Pakistan. A second factor is that a greater Asia is forming or perhaps re-forming. In the immediate past, we could identify East Asia, Southeast Asia, Central Asia, and South Asia, and observers would understand that we were talking about overlapping but roughly separate regions that shared a general Asian location. What seems to be happening, however, is that an Asia is coming together in the sense that the boundaries among these four regions have been breaking down. In some respect, they may have been artifactual all along. The Japanese occupation of Asia in the first half of the twentieth century was not focused solely on East Asia. Southeast Asia was also captured, and India might have been conquered if Japan had not attacked Pearl Harbor in 1941.[2]

We have seen something similar to the amalgamation of a greater Asia before. Europe before the 1490s could be divided into the Italian City States, Western Europe (mainly France, England, the Netherlands, Castilian and Catalan Spain, and Portugal), Baltic Scandinavia, and Central/Eastern Europe. In the 1490s, France invaded Italy, drawing in Spanish opposition and merging Western Europe and the Italian City States. Hapsburg family ties contributed mightily to parts of Central/Eastern Europe being drawn into European conflicts shortly after the French invasion of Naples in 1494. Scandinavia held out longer but was drawn in by Swedish ambitions by the early seventeenth century. Thus, the initial integration of Europe was characterized and augmented by considerable conflict, which continued in various ways to 1945.

A conflictual European history does not necessarily imply that the integration or reintegration of greater Asia some 500 years later need be equally

---

[2] Alternatively, Japan and the Soviet Union might well have renewed their struggle for control of Asia if the Soviet Union had not been attacked by Germany and if Japan had not attacked the United States.

conflictual. Indeed, it is hard to imagine a similar reoccurrence. But one of the common denominators is that regions tend to have pecking orders. They may be very distinct pecking orders in which every actor knows its place, or they may be rather vague hierarchies in which positions fluctuate from time to time. When multiple regions are brought together for whatever reason, some of the original pecking orders must give way to something new. As two of the leading states in a greater Asia, the odds of India and China butting heads increase. India will resent the increase of Chinese influence in Sri Lanka or Nepal just as China will resent the Indian navy participating in South China Sea maneuvers. The point here is not merely that China and India will have new reasons for perceptions of grievance and conflict but that some of that conflict will be due to issues pertaining to regional hegemony that had not really been on the table before.

Nonetheless, it is far too soon to anticipate a full-fledged Indian challenge to China's Asian lead. China's capability advantages over India are far too evident. India's relative weaknesses, however, imply some likelihood of alliance, formal or informal, with a stronger power that is not close to China. The United States would seem to be the most obvious choice. Even though the advantages of such a pairing might seem quite evident, they by no means guarantees that a US–Indian alignment will come to pass – only that there is some possibility of it occurring.[3] Should this alignment come about, the significance of the Sino-Indian rivalry will be enhanced commensurately since it will become closely bound up with the Sino-American rivalry, which may easily become the planet's most critical rivalry somewhat along the lines of the Soviet–American Cold War. It cannot be a replay of the earlier Cold War. The Soviets brought only military threat to the table; there was no economic threat. Nor was the Soviet Union closely integrated into the world economy. The Chinese threat initially is economic and technological. Yet its military threat is growing quickly while it remains integrated into the world economy.

There are six areas of potential clashes for the Sino-American rivalry: (i) northeast Asia and the two Koreas, (ii) Japan and the East Asian Sea, (iii) Taiwan, (iv) the South China Sea, (v) the Indian Ocean, and (vi) the long-contested border between China and India. The first four are at risk regardless of Indian alignment with the United States and its other allies. The first one is a bit of a wild card given a mercurial

---

[3] The likelihood of an Indo-US alliance is complicated by the path dependency of India's reliance on the Soviet Union as a counter to Pakistan's reliance on China. Now that Russia and China are moving closer together, India may have to make a choice.

North Korean leadership. The Japan–East Asian Sea option seems to depend on someone making a commitment to exploiting gas and petroleum deposits in the waters separating Japan from China. So far, that commitment does not seem to be forthcoming, in part perhaps because of the possibility of violent conflict. Taiwan is always a prime target, but it has only been quite recently that China has made major headway in building up its ability to move military force some 100 miles across the South China Sea. Earlier crises were quite possible even without adequate Chinese capability to make good on its threats of forcing Taiwan to accept mainland authority. But they were far less likely to escalate given Chinese military capability problems. Reduce some of those military capability problems and the probability of a Chinese invasion of Taiwan, other things being equal, becomes more likely.

Naval clashes, intended or accidental, must always be considered probable given the stances maintained by the opposing sides. China views much of the South China Sea as Chinese waters; the Western powers argue for the right of transit through those waters, which they view to be international waters, without interference. Whether a naval clash has a high potential for escalating into a shooting war remains to be seen. So far, the clashes have been minor, if more numerous than is safe.

That leaves the possibility of clashes in the Indian Ocean and the Himalayas. The potential for clashes in the Indian Ocean should increase as China, India, and other states build up their naval presence in that large body of water. To date, China lacks bases on the Indian Ocean except for one far away in Northeast Africa. However, there are several opportunities for the development of Chinese naval bases somewhere between Cambodia and Sri Lanka in coming decades. India is also slowly improving its naval capability in the Indian Ocean.

The disputed Sino-Indian borders in the Himalayas have already led to war once (1962). Since then, both sides have been wary and suspicious about the intentions of the other side of the rivalry. Physical clashes have occurred but largely in the form of fist fights between soldiers. Both sides appear reluctant to see their clashes escalate to a higher level of combat. That could change. Yet the point remains that the last two areas with potential for escalating hostilities hinge on the relationship between India and the United States. If the two states remain unaligned, the Himalayas and the Indian Ocean remain places at which Sino-Indian clashes could occur with some likelihood. Whether other states intervene coercively would probably remain ambiguous. If the two (India and the United States) become aligned, the Himalayas and the Indian Ocean extend the perimeter along which China and the United States and its allies are at loggerheads, especially if the Indo-American alignment is formal. If the alignment is less formal, there is more wiggle room for China's opponents to contemplate whether they should act coercively or diplomatically.

All this can be said without much evidence or the ability to read the future. It is a matter of logic, even if international relations do not always proceed on a logical track. Overall, it can also be said that a formal or informal alignment between the United States and India increases the potential for conflict escalation. One reason is that six areas with escalatory potential are greater than four. A second reason is that the alignment increases the number of actors in play and, therefore, the potential for misperception and escalations without informing allies. That is, escalation(s) could take place by more minor actors, catching the major actors off guard.

But there is also a third reason. Combat between declining system leaders and their challengers rarely take the form of a fight between the declining leader and an ascending challenger per se. Instead, they tend to be caught up in coalitional warfare in which the leader–challenger dyad is but one of several dyads at war. That factor alone can change the escalatory potential of initial clashes into wars that no one wanted. At this point, we need to step back and look at the modern history of regional and global violence. For some, it is just a string of wars with more major power participation than is customary. For others, it has a fundamental rhythm that may or may not be extended into the twenty-first century.

Table 8.1 selectively lists sequentially a series of general wars that have taken place since 1494. They are arrayed in two columns although all the wars have been chosen primarily on the basis of widespread great power participation usually involving all or most of the great power elite. On the left are wars that have had a conclusive outcome relating to global politics. A new phase in the concentration of global power emerged during the war. Just how concentrated global power was at the end of the war is variable, but it must minimally exceed 50 percent to qualify as a "conclusive" outcome. On the right are wars that did not have a conclusive outcome vis-à-vis global politics. Some have demonstrated the successful rise of a regional hegemon, but most are inconclusive even though primarily about the regional pecking order.

The distinction between the global and regional concentration of power is not widely acknowledged in the annals of international relations. It is more customary to treat all wars the same unless they vary on the attributes of major power participation or associated deaths. There are two problems with this approach. The first is that the European theater changed

Table 8.1 *General wars, 1494–1945*

Global wars	Nonglobal wars
Italian/Indian Ocean Wars (1494–1516) (France, Spain, Austria, Venice, Portugal, Ottoman Empire)	
	Franco-Spanish Wars (1521–25, 1526–29, 1536–38, 1542–44, 1552–56, 1556–59) (France, Spain or Hapsburgs, England)
Dutch Independence (1585–1608) (England, Netherlands, France, Spain)	
	Thirty Years War (1618–48) (France, England, Spain, Austria, Netherlands)
	Franco-Spanish War (1648–1659) (France, Spain)
War of the League of Augsburg/Spanish Succession (1688–1713) (France, England, Spain, Austria, Netherlands)	
	War of the Austrian Succession (1739–48) (France, Britain, Spain, Austria, Russia, Prussia)
	Seven Years War (1755–63) (France, Britain, Spain, Austria, Russia, Prussia)
French Revolutionary/Napoleonic Wars (1792–1815) (France, Britain, Spain, Austria, Russia, Prussia)	
	Crimean War (1854–56) (France, Britain, Russia)
	Austro-Prussian War (1866) (Austria, Prussia, Italy)
	Franco-Prussian War (1870–71) (France, Germany)
First World War/Second World War (1914–1945) (France, Britain, Austria-Hungary, Russia, Germany, Italy, United States, Japan)	

Note: Participants are listed in parentheses; the participation of any great power does not necessarily extend to the full duration of the war.

in and around the 1490s. Prior to that decade, in addition to the previously mentioned expansion of the effective European region, the region was more isolated from the rest of the world except in terms of trade. This statement is not meant to dismiss Norse voyages to the New World or the Crusades, but they proved to be relatively temporary projections of European power to other regions. After the 1490s, European power began a more permanent extension of power into the Americas and the Indian Ocean. The region became less insular, and some states benefitted from the resources gained abroad that were subsequently applied to European politics and international relations. Quarrels abroad also managed to resonate and become intertwined with European affairs.

The second problem is that two types of great powers emerged after the 1490s. We tend to treat all great powers, and especially all European great powers, as if they were alike. But some were genuinely regional powers and projected little or no influence beyond Europe. Others specialized in long distance trade exploitation and tried to evade becoming overly committed to squabbles about territorial control in the home region. This latter group were increasingly global powers as evidenced by their commitment to naval resources that provided the global reach necessary to protect their trading and later colonial activities. The former group, which was predominantly preoccupied with defending and advancing their claims in the home region, tended to focus on expanding their armies because that type of armed force provided maximum regional reach. Of course, a few states tried to do both but it proved extremely difficult to pull off. Therefore, their sea and land power efforts "wobbled" back and forth, with the appeal of land power usually winning out as a matter of expedience.

Yet these two "worlds" or spheres of action could become fused at times. When an aspiring regional hegemon in Europe threatened to establish control of the home region, it threatened the home bases of the global powers. They needed to fend off these threats. Since sea powers and land powers found it difficult to fight each other, the leading land power would seek to develop naval power as quickly as possible. The sea powers usually could muster some land power but not enough to stay in the regional game. Their recourse was to ally with large land powers that could supply countervailing troops for regional combat to defeat the aspiring regional hegemon. This pattern becomes increasingly evident in the wars listed in the left-hand column and illustrates the way in which the European balance of power functioned in a rather distinct fashion unmatched in any other region. Consequently, Europe rarely returned to a high level of regional power concentration for long. A Napoleon or a Hitler could seize control for a few years but no more than that.[4]

---

[4] Evidence and elaboration of this interpretation may be found in George Modelski and William R. Thompson, *Sea Power in Global Politics, 1494–1993* (London: Macmillan, 1988); William R. Thompson, *On Global War: Historical-Structural Approaches to World Politics* (Columbia: University of South Carolina Press, 1988); William R. Thompson, "Dehio, Long Cycles and the Geohistorical

Returning to Table 8.1, several additional observations can be made about the activities in the left-hand column. After the sixteenth century, the defending coalition organized and led by a global power always ultimately prevailed. The identification of regional and global challenges was fused because success at the regional level meant that the resources for ongoing and subsequent global challenges could be readily anticipated if they were not already underway. But regional and global challengers were always defeated – even if not conclusively. New leading global powers emerged from the winning coalition. They would begin as junior partners of the declining global leader and end up the senior partner by war's end. In this fashion, the Dutch gave way to the British and the British gave way to the United States after the European region had been eclipsed by economic and technological developments outside the region.

This general process continued in the European region after 1945 with the novelty of a balancing coalition being organized shortly after the conclusion of the last war. Nonetheless, Europe's reign as the central region of the world system had come to an end. The question is whether something similar, that is, regional centrality, has emerged in East Asia. Historically, the Asian region has functioned differently. Whereas both regions experienced high power concentrations two thousand years ago in the form of the Roman and Han Empires, Europe tended toward a post-Roman deconcentration of power while Asia fluctuated back and forth between periods of fragmentation and concentration. The unique land–sea power distinction that characterized Western Europe did not develop in East Asia, at least not in the same way. Concentrated sea power in East Asia tended to be wielded by whoever controlled the mainland of East Asia – if they chose to maintain their sea power resources. Famously, the Ming Dynasty abandoned its overwhelming sea power resources in the early fifteenth century to focus more on land power problems. Earlier Chinese sea power had not been sufficient to conquer Japan. Subsequent Japanese attempts to conquer the mainland were initially insufficient in the early seventeenth century and usually subordinated to the efforts in the first half of the twentieth century.

Context of Structural Transitions," *World Politics* 45 (1992): 127–152; Karen Rasler and William R. Thompson, *The Great Powers and Global Struggle, 1490–1990* (Lexington: University Press of Kentucky, 1994); William R. Thompson and Leila Zakhirova, *Racing to the Top: How Energy Fuels Systemic Leadership* (New York: Oxford University Press, 2019); William R. Thompson, *Power Concentration in World Politics: The Political Economy of Systemic Leadership, Growth and Conflict* (Cham: Springer, 2020); and William R. Thompson, *American Global Pre-eminence: The Development and Erosion of Systemic Leadership* (New York: Oxford University Press, 2022).

But now we have an aspiring regional hegemon that is basically a land power with expanding interests in sea power and developing a technological base that could challenge the world's technological leader. It is confronted by the sea and space power of the technological leader, which leads a coalition of states located in the rimlands of Asia and stretching from South Korea in the north to Australia in the south and possibly India in the west. This development is new and novel and yet it possesses characteristics of the European past. The most salient difference is that nuclear weapons are involved in the Asian setting, and they did not quite come to fruition in the European setting but almost did. We believe nuclear weapons are so devastating that they deter a repetition of the types of wars listed in Table 8.1. Perhaps they will but we really do not know whether that will be the case. It remains a belief and probably a fervent wish. It is also less clear that the fear of nuclear exchange can be depended upon to deter a war fought strictly with agreed-upon conventional means. Beliefs and wishes cannot rule out the potential escalation of conflict to a conventional war, and once a conventional war is underway beliefs and wishes cannot rule out further escalation.[5]

The main question of this chapter thus is, how does India's rivalry with China fit into this confrontational setting? Do past episodes offer any enlightenment? We think they might. Some of the warfare of Table 8.1 was not desired by anyone and yet it escalated anyway. We cannot expect things to work out exactly as before – nor did things always work exactly the same way – but we can look at the way in which escalation occurred and ask whether historical events provide any clues as to how it might work out similarly in the future in an Asian setting.

There are two possible structures to consider. If India joins the US-led coalition formally, we can examine a two-sided confrontation: China versus a US-led coalition. If India balks at joining the US-led coalition in a formal way, we should examine a three-sided confrontation: China versus India, with possible third-party intervention. Fortunately, there are two major power cases from Table 8.1 that correspond to the two structures. The Seven Years War matches an initial two-sided confrontation. The Crimean War fits the three-sided confrontation situation. In both cases, we do not have to reinvent the wheel and can make use of an older escalation analysis conducted by Richard Smoke for other purposes than the specific application we have in mind.[6]

---

[5] Early in the Second World War, adversaries seemed to have agreed that bombing the cities of their rivals was something to be avoided. That understanding did not last long.
[6] Richard Smoke, *War: Controlling Escalation* (Cambridge, MA: Harvard University Press, 1977).

The Seven Years War

The first case is chosen because it is largely bilateral in nature – Britain versus France – albeit complicated by the relationship between the two great powers and their American colonies. If nothing else, colonial interests did not always correspond to the interests perceived in London and Paris. Britain and France had fought each other as recently as 1748 and had hoped to have some respite from intense conflict in Europe and around the globe. In both London and Paris, there existed some initial midcentury ambivalence about the value of the American colonies that had been established to serve the respective metropoles but had irritating tendencies to work in ways that exceeded their ostensible mercantile missions. The ambivalence quickly disappeared as a casualty of misperceptions and escalations in a tit-for-tat exchange between 1752 and 1755. The timeline for this sequence is laid out in Table 8.2.

France had claimed the Ohio River Valley since the seventeenth century but found it difficult to persuade French families to move to North America. Even without many French settlers, the valley was considered crucial to maintaining a river network connection from New France in Canada to the smaller colony centered on New Orleans in the south. In contrast, the British colonies along the Atlantic coast were growing rapidly and considered their land grants to extend from the Atlantic to the Pacific. British traders began to penetrate the Great Lakes area increasingly between the 1730s and early 1750s. The French response was to evict British citizens when captured and to erect small forts in the disputed area. From the onset then, both sides saw themselves in a defensive posture. The French were protecting their north–south lifeline. British colonists saw themselves as protecting their land claims.

In 1752 and 1753, the French destroyed one British colonial trading post in the Ohio River Valley and built two small forts in the vicinity. A British demand that they abandon one of the forts because of its location in disputed territory went unanswered. The Virginia colony was ordered to send colonial forces into the area and to build its own forts. One clash, involving a detachment headed by George Washington, killed nine French soldiers but the French retaliated and evicted the Virginia militia by force. Virginia, in turn, demanded that British regular troops be sent to carry out what the colonial militia had failed to accomplish. Initially, the British government was reluctant to respond positively. It preferred to leave the matter to colonial resources and even proposed to resolve the crisis at least temporarily by neutralizing the Ohio River Valley. British colonists would

Table 8.2 *The initial escalation sequence of the Seven Years War*

Approximate date	Event
Before about 1750	Scattered English and French explorers, predominantly French, enter the area south of the Great Lakes and west of the Appalachian Mountains. The French and Indians establish trade and some simple alliances.
About 1750 and thereafter	Frenchmen and their Indian allies begin to warn Englishmen not to enter the Ohio region. The warnings are ignored, and the number of English explorers and traders in the trans-Appalachian area steadily increases.
1752: June	French forces attack and destroy a British trading post on the Miami River.
1753: spring and summer	Duquesne, governor of New France, begins to have forts erected in the Ohio region.
August	English secretary of state, Lord Holdernesse, orders Virginia and Pennsylvania to defend British interests in the Ohio region.
December	Governor Dinwiddie of Virginia requests the French to leave the Ohio area, asserting that it belongs to England. Montreal gives no reply.
1754: February	Virginians begin construction of a fort at the fork where two tributaries join to form the Ohio River (now Pittsburgh).
April	French forces eject the Virginians from the half-finished fort and continue to construct it under their own flag, renaming it Fort Duquesne.
Late June	A group of Virginians under the command of Major Washington approaches Fort Duquesne and finds it being stalked by Frenchmen and Indians. Opening fire, the Englishmen kill ten Frenchmen, including an officer. When Montreal learns of this attack, reinforcements are immediately sent to Fort Duquesne.
July 3	A strong sortie from Fort Duquesne besieges Washington's force at Fort Necessity and after a day-long battle compels its surrender and retreat across the mountains.
Late July	Governor Dinwiddie requests assistance, including two regiments of regulars, from Great Britain.
1755: February 20	Britain proposes neutralizing the Ohio River Valley. British colonial subjects would be limited to trading activities. Settlements would not be allowed. The French would be banned from using the upper Ohio River as part of its water routes to New Orleans. Instead, rivers farther to the west would be utilized. France rejects the proposal, largely due to its reluctance to encourage British trading activity in the Ohio River Valley. Negotiations appear to be at a standstill.

Table 8.2 *(cont.)*

Approximate date	Event
1755: winter	Responding to the Dinwiddie request, two British regiments, about a thousand men in all, are dispatched under General Braddock.
May	France sends reinforcements to Canada that number three times Braddock's force.
June 10	Admiral Boscawen and a squadron of Royal Navy attempt to intercept the French convoy off Newfoundland but capture only two vessels.
July 9	Braddock's expeditionary force is ambushed and badly defeated before reaching Fort Duquesne, its first target. Braddock himself is killed.
1755: summer (through spring 1756)	Britain and France engage in complex diplomatic maneuvers in search of allies among the other great and middle-range powers in Europe.
1756: May 18	Britain declares war on France.

Source: Richard Smoke, *War: Controlling Escalation* (Cambridge, MA: Harvard University Press, 1977), 206–207.

refrain from settling in the territory but retain trading rights in the larger Great Lakes area. France would abstain from making use of the Ohio River and focus instead on rivers to the west for its river-based linkage between Montreal and New Orleans. The French balked, however, at encouraging British trading activities in what it considered its sphere of influence.

Given the failure of negotiations, the British government responded to the Virginia request for troops by agreeing to secretly send 1,000 men. But the secret did not last very long. The information was leaked by governmental hawks who believed that a renewal of war between Britain and France was inevitable. Attempting to reduce the perception of a military escalation, Britain communicated to France that the Braddock expeditionary force was intended entirely for defensive purposes. Since French decision-makers knew that Braddock had been given orders to take control of the Ohio River Valley, the communication fell on deaf ears. While some negotiations continued between the two great powers, France prepared to send 3,000 troops to New France to counter the Braddock expedition. The British response was to attempt to intercept the troop ships in North American waters in order to reduce European complications of a British attack on a French fleet. The interception effort managed to capture only two of eighteen ships and only a few of the troops being sent. France then ceased participation in negotiations. At about the same time, news that the Braddock expeditionary force had been defeated badly and Braddock killed reached Britain. The die seemed cast for war but it took an additional ten months while the primary adversaries sought allies for the European combat theater.

There are a number of interesting facets to this case that have pertinence for contemporary affairs. As previously noted, at the outset decision-makers in both London and Paris expected an indefinite period of relatively peaceful relations and sought to avoid the possibility of war breaking out in several possible places in which their interests were most at odds. These places included India, West Africa, the Caribbean, and North America.

In North America, both sides had initial doubts about whether North America was worth fighting over. The escalation process that ensued over-whelmed these doubts. Both sides, motivated by defensive perceptions, escalated to deter the other side from further intrusions. The escalations, however, were perceived to be offensive in nature and therefore only encouraged further escalation. What started out as an argument about who controlled the Ohio River Valley ended up as a contest to see who controlled all of North America. One of the ironies is that it is conceivable that something might have been worked out that permitted British use of the territory and French usage of the river network, and it was even pro-posed by the British but without success. On the other hand, such a solu-tion would probably have only been temporary in part because people in the British colonies were convinced, incorrectly, that the geographical ter-rain of the Appalachian Mountains dictated that the only route to access the fertile land in what became the American Midwest was through the Ohio River Valley. Even so, at some point, joint usage of the area would have come to be seen as zero-sum by all parties concerned.

Smoke emphasizes that the parties involved began with a set of future expectations about adversarial relations that could be worked out with-out resorting to war. Events and the tit-for-tat escalation process gradually altered and narrowed those future expectations so that by 1755 war seemed the only recourse despite several asymmetries in the relative capabilities of the main adversaries. The French had something of a local advantage in the sense that their decision-making was more centralized in Paris and New France. The British had some fourteen colonies (counting Nova Scotia) and found it difficult to coordinate their activities. For example, Pennsylvania and Virginia were the colonies most clearly involved with the Ohio River Valley claims. But Pennsylvania was controlled by Quakers who preferred noninvolvement in the crisis, leaving Virginia to act on its own in an inad-equate fashion. France, moreover, maintained regular French troops in

New France while Britain relied entirely on colonial militias. Sending the Braddock expedition of regular troops meant a major escalation by Britain. Contrastingly, Britain was the leading sea power while France maintained the largest European army. The British failure to intercept the 3,000 troops sent by France was regarded as simply bad luck by French decision-makers who recognized that the next time might work out much differently. For the French, to fight in North America meant that combat had to be diffused to Europe where its own military advantage lay. This recognition might have convinced French decision-makers that defending its North American position was a losing proposition in the long run. But decisions to go to war are not usually made from a long-term perspective. If it had been, the British might have realized that removing the main geopolitical threat to the British colonies would only encourage their subsequent rebellion and secession from the Empire a few years later.

The Crimean War

The Crimean War is another case of a war that not only was not anticipated but also probably should never have occurred. That it did was due to two contextual elements that interacted in unexpected ways. One was the long slide of the Ottoman Empire from its heyday in the sixteenth and seventeenth centuries. As it weakened, rivals contemplated how best to divide up the spoils in case of its collapse and disintegration. However, in the mid-nineteenth century the Crimean War broke out largely because the government of one adjacent great power thought that the end game for the Ottomans was near at hand while more distant great powers believed it was not unless, of course, some state hastened its demise by coercion that it would be forced to oppose. Yet the actual run-up to the war was much less neat and more complicated than this simple summary suggests. Table 8.3 offers an overview of the twists and turns leading to war in 1854.

The crisis was initiated by an 1852 French demand that Roman Catholics be given religious privileges in Jerusalem that hitherto had been held by Orthodox Christians who enjoyed Russian support. Louis Napoleon sought ways to generate French domestic support for his government. The new demand appealed to Catholics and to people who hoped to see a more ambitious French foreign policy carried out by another Napoleon and seemed reasonably safe given the weakness of the Ottoman Empire that controlled Jerusalem. Unwittingly, however, this demand upset the precarious balance in the tug of war between Russia and Great Britain over the survival of the Ottoman Empire. One of the Russian imperial expansive

Table 8.3 *The initial escalation sequence of the Crimean War*

Approximate date	Events
1852: February	Earlier low-key French diplomatic efforts to secure Roman Catholic control of the Holy Places are stepped up to a full campaign; the Ottomans make some concessions.
April	The French ambassador returns to Constantinople on the battleship *Charlemagne* with additional demands concerning the Holy Places.
July	Napoleon sends a naval squadron to Tripoli and threatens to bombard the city unless his demands are met.
Late in the year	The Ottomans gradually comply with the French demands.
1853: January	Austria successfully demands that a Turkish involvement in Montenegro be brought to an end, under threat of Austrian military intervention.
Late February	Russia sends Prince Menshikov to Constantinople with demands for Russian protection of the Christians residing within the Ottoman Empire, as well as return of the Holy Places to Greek Orthodox control. Simultaneously two Russian corps are mobilized near the frontier.
Late March	Napoleon sends the French Mediterranean fleet to Salamis in Greece.
April	Stratford Canning, reappointed English ambassador to the Ottoman Empire, arrives in Constantinople.
Early May	The Ottoman Empire agrees to restore the Holy Places to the Orthodox but, partly on the advice of Canning, refuses Menshikov's wider demands.
May 21	Menshikov departs. Russia breaks diplomatic relations with Turkey.
Mid-June	British and French naval squadrons arrive in Besika Bay.
Early July	Russian troops cross the border and seize the Ottoman principalities of Moldova and Wallachia.
August 1	The Vienna Note of Britain, France, Austria, and Prussia proposes a basis for negotiated settlement of the crisis.
Mid-August	The Vienna Note is accepted by Russia but rejected by the Ottomans.
Mid-September	Policymakers in Paris and London authorize the naval squadrons to pass through the Dardanelles and sail to Constantinople at the discretion of local commanders, in violation of an international treaty.
October 4	The Sultan declares war on Russia but takes no immediate military action.
October 8	Paris and London order their squadrons to Constantinople immediately.
October 23	Turkish troops enter the two principalities and open hostilities against the Russians.
End of October	The Ottomans cross the border and attack the Russians in the Caucasus.

Table 8.3   *(cont.)*

Approximate date	Events
November 30	The Russian Black Sea fleet intercepts and destroys a Turkish naval squadron in the harbor at Sinope.
1854: January 3	The French and British fleets enter the Black Sea and protect Turkish vessels.
February	The Russian ambassadors are withdrawn from Paris and London.
March	Britain and France conclude a military alliance with Turkey and demand in an ultimatum that Russia evacuate the principalities: When this ignored, they declare war on Russia.
June 3	Austria demands that Russia evacuate the principalities. The czar subsequently complies.
August	The Russians conclude their withdrawal from the principalities.
Mid-September	Britain and France open operations in Crimea with an amphibious landing, aimed at besieging and seizing Sebastopol.

Source: Based on Richard Smoke, *War: Controlling Escalation* (Cambridge, MA: Harvard University Press, 1977), 156–157.

thrusts was to the south. Competing in Russian grand strategy with imperial thrusts to the east and west, multiple wars with the Ottomans had thwarted a Russian Empire that would have access to the Mediterranean. Possession of Constantinople (now Istanbul) would change that. Britain, however, saw the Ottoman Empire as one useful buffer between Russian and other imperial powers and its crown jewel colonial holding in India. The Eastern Question basically was, which great power would determine the future of the Ottoman Empire? Would Russia eventually occupy Constantinople or would Britain be able to prop up the Ottomans to keep other great powers away from South Asia and the Middle East?

The French gambit introduced a third slant to this question. If the Ottomans yielded, as they did, to the French demand that had been backed up by the visit of a French battleship to Tripoli, it meant that Russian influence over the Ottomans was less than what the British had thought. It did not make the British government very happy either. By 1853, the British recommendation to the Ottoman government that the Orthodox privileges be restored in Jerusalem was accepted and acted upon. Seeing little support for their initiative, the French backed down. That might have been the end of the crisis, but the Russians had already sent Prince Menshikov to Constantinople with demands that Orthodox privileges be reinstated and that the Ottoman foreign minister be replaced by someone more sensitive to Russian preferences. Units of the Russian army had been mobilized on the Ottoman border to reinforce these demands.

While the Russians viewed the Menshikov initiative as vital to restoring the earlier status quo, which was more favorable to Russian interests, the Ottomans, the British, and the French perceived the Menshikov mission as both escalatory and predatory. An increase in Russian influence suggested that Russia intended to hasten the fall of the Ottoman Empire. The French response was to move warships to Salamis in Greece. Britain proceeded to send a squadron of ships to Besika Bay in the Dardanelles, which was joined by the French ships stationed in Greece. When Menshikov left Constantinople with his demands unfulfilled, Russia moved troops into two Ottoman principalities, Moldova and Wallachia, with the intention of remaining there until the Menshikov demands had been satisfied. Presumably, two squadrons of warships in the eastern Mediterranean did not suffice to deter the Russian occupation of Ottoman territory. Since the warships did not arrive before the Russian movement into Ottoman territory, it was even more the case. It also turned out that the Russian reading of the fleet movement was that it was not a serious signal of opposition. Rather, it was viewed as an appeasing sop to more belligerent members of the British cabinet.

The Ottoman interpretation of the Western fleet movement was much different. They viewed it as symbolic of an Anglo-French commitment to their cause and chose not to mount an immediate counterattack against the Russian invasion of their principalities – presumably to allow for more Anglo-French military assistance. Smoke points out that if the Ottoman counterattack had been immediate, a Russian–Ottoman war would have been underway before Britain and France could have done much. Negotiations could have been enacted to stop the warfare without other great power military participation in the fighting. As it was, Britain, France, and Austria did meet in Vienna and prepared a Note that proposed a Russian withdrawal for increased Orthodox privileges in Jerusalem. Russia seems to have been prepared to accept this proposal, but the Ottoman Empire was not so inclined. After rejecting the Note, the Ottoman government requested that the Besika Bay squadrons be moved to Constantinople to show support for an incumbent government that was being threatened by popular unrest over making concessions to the Russians. However, while the unrest had been stimulated by a prowar faction within the Ottoman government and probably did not really presage a government overthrow, the threat of political instability in Constantinople did persuade the British and French governments to agree to another move of the Western naval squadrons, this time to Constantinople as requested.[7] The British government was also aware that Austria and Russia had discussed Ottoman partitioning in a recent meeting of the two states to discuss their mutual positions and there was some concern that the Russians viewed the Vienna Note as tantamount to supporting the Menshikov demands. Something stronger in opposition to Russian gains was needed and supplied by the movement of the joint fleet from Besika Bay to Constantinople. Both the British and French governments were also being pressed by newspapers and public opinion to do something concrete.

One problem was that Britain and France did not clarify to the Ottoman Empire that there were limits to their show of support. The Ottomans viewed it as strong support and attacked the Russians not only in the principalities but also in the Transcaucasus region, thereby escalating the scope of fighting. In response, a Russian fleet destroyed a Turkish fleet that had been resupplying Ottoman troops in the Transcaucasus, but it did it while it was in port at Sinope. The Russians had previously been informed that the British navy would not interfere with a Russian–Ottoman naval battle in the Black Sea but would not permit a Russian attack on Turkish ports. The Russian admiral involved in the Sinope fighting had been ordered to intercept the Turkish fleet before it reached Sinope but misinterpreted the order to encourage unqualified support for an aggressive attack. From an Anglo-French point of view, Sinope represented another escalation of the Russian attack on Turkey.

That it was a successful Russian naval attack seemed to resonate particularly in Britain, which prided itself on naval superiority. Popular demands for a punitive response increased. The British government remained reluctant to move its naval forces into the Black Sea but were stung by Napoleon's demand that the joint squadron move into action. If the British balked, Napoleon claimed the French would either go on the offensive on their own or order their ships to return to France. Either way, the British would look bad. The path of least resistance was to send the fleet into the Black Sea. The British did manage to get Napoleon to agree to further consider attempts at a negotiated peace, but these efforts were still borne because they were never supported by the Ottomans who were winning on the battlefield at that time.

Russia next proposed a ceasefire at sea that would have Britain and France restrict Turkish naval activity in the Black Sea. This proposal was

---

[7] The distance from Besika Bay to Constantinople involved only one day of sailing.

rejected. Russia then moved to withdraw its British and French ambassadors. Austria entered the fray by delivering an ultimatum to Russia to withdraw from Moldova and Wallachia and mobilized some of its army on the border to reinforce the ultimatum. But Russia was aware that Austria would attack only if Prussia agreed, and Prussia was not prepared to endorse an Austrian attack at this time.[8] After the Russian rejection of the Austrian ultimatum, France and Britain declared war but would need some time to organize an expeditionary force that could be landed on Russian soil. In the meantime, Prussia altered its position on the wisdom of an Austrian attack and a second Austrian ultimatum was delivered to Russia. Since Austria had a powerful land force immediately at hand – something that Britain and France did not – Russia backed down and withdrew from the two occupied principalities, which were then occupied by Austria to ensure that Russia did not return.

By this point in 1854, the Russian military occupation of Moldova and Wallachia had ended and its former Orthodox privileges in Jerusalem had been restored. There did not seem much to fight about. However, the strongest faction in the British cabinet favored a continuation of the war to do damage to Russia's military capabilities, which would make it less likely that Russia would be able to capture Constantinople at some point in the future. Popular opinion seemed to support this sentiment as well. As often seems the case, the amphibious landing of Western troops in Russia was not viewed as much of a challenge. Yet it turned out to be something of a logistical quagmire that was compounded by disease and the failure of naval bombardment to stop Russian reinforcement of Sebastopol in the Crimean Peninsula – the main target of the eventual landing.

It had been thought that close-in naval artillery could be brought to bear on controlling the Peninsula from both sides. But the water in question turned out to be too shallow to permit close-in naval operations. Other notorious British command decisions such as the infamous charge of the Light Brigade precluded the quick and easy military victory that had been expected by the Western powers. The war dragged on and saw some further expansion in the Baltic and Pacific before the stalemate on land was ended by the threat of additional states (Austria and Sweden) joining the Western coalition. A Russian seizure of Constantinople did not come to fruition, but it is not clear whether that had ever been intended in the first place.

---

[8] Nonetheless, Russia was caught off guard by the unexpected Austrian hostility to the Russian occupation. Russia had thought Austria was in its debt due to Russian support a few years earlier when the Austrian government was threatened by the 1848 domestic turmoil.

Recapitulation

We did not invoke the Seven Years War or the Crimean War because we thought they might be fought again. The Anglo-French contest over the control of North America has been resolved. The Crimean Peninsula still gets invaded from time to time but now it is Russians fighting Ukrainians, and Crimea turned out to be much easier to seize in 2014 than in 1854. These were also wars that took place in times in which communication between adversaries was relatively slow and preparations for combat took more time to prepare. But it is their general escalatory patterns that endure. In neither case did one or both sides welcome military conflict or the type of major power war that did emerge. Yet the major power wars emerged nonetheless, not inevitably but perhaps with some probability once escalation began. Nor are these escalatory patterns so rare that other cases could not be trotted out for further inspection. The First World War is the most famous case of the war no one sought. We have avoided its application in this chapter only because its effects have been dulled by overuse. Still, the more general point is that major power warfare is often the product of processes that escape the full control of the participants. This can be due to asymmetries of capabilities, misperceptions, and/or domestic and interallied politics.

Asymmetries shape the alternatives that are available to adversaries. Maritime powers confronting land powers cannot always replicate the maneuvers that land powers can produce. The reverse holds equally well. Maritime counters to land moves can be viewed as inadequate or weak. Land counters to maritime moves can be viewed as escalatory. In both cases, actors tend to rely on the tool kits that (i) they are most used to and (ii) the ones that are readily available. It does not matter that these tool kits are not always ideal for the problem at hand. It is what it is. One works with what one has. Elephants and whales grapple awkwardly.

Misperceptions are quite common. How does an adversary know what a rival wants or might do if confronted with resistance? If the estimation of intentions is off, it becomes all the more difficult to accurately gauge likely responses. In both cases discussed in this chapter, neither side had accurate interpretations of what the other side intended or desired. It made a great difference to how they responded. At the same time, neither side spent a great deal of time contemplating how their own moves might appear to the enemy.

Domestic politics did not make the adversaries go to war in either case. It was simply a factor encouraging warfare or at least more vigorous responses. Domestic costs can seem high if inaction or failure is perceived. At times, allies can stimulate more aggression to appease them and keep them as allies. Presumably, the opposite can also happen – weaker responses than felt desirable can be generated by a reluctance to offend allies with different interpretations of what is most desirable.

None of these observations are particularly novel but they go some way in explaining how it is that major power warfare rarely involves the simplicity of one major power attacking another one. It is far more likely to come about in the more complicated context of multiple actors stumbling toward the possibility of escalated conflict. Given multiple actors of different power levels, asymmetrical capabilities, and preferences, some tendency toward escalation may seem more probable than improbable because it is very difficult to manage without omniscience and hindsight. There is no necessity to invoke the need to act quickly with little information – another common attribute of crisis situations – to account for escalatory propensities. They tend to be baked into the processes of interacting rivalries when they become focused on expectations of strongly preferred outcomes. This can be the case when the initial confrontations are over relatively trivial values. Somehow, the objects at stake can too easily balloon into struggles of life and death without fully realizing how one got to that point.

The problem is all the more acute in the case of the Sino-Indian rivalry because whatever its own potential for escalation might be it is becoming embedded in the East Asian rivalry field given the mutual attractiveness of India and the US-led coalition in the context of the Sino-American rivalry. They share a common rival and decision-makers perceive advantages in augmenting capabilities in the South China Sea and the Indian Ocean. This is not simply a matter of declining system leaders and their challengers butting heads in an isolated fashion. The Sino-American rivalry, either as the regional clash it is now or as the global-regional contest it seems to be becoming (or some combination of both structured confrontations), is the heavy weight rivalry in the East Asian field, which includes the two Koreas, China–Japan, China–Taiwan, and now China–India. By extension, the India–Pakistan rivalry is also in play in this field and it has already been fused with the Sino-Indian rivalry. As the rivalries become increasingly interdependent, which is what tends to happen in a rivalry field as tensions increase, escalation in one rivalry is apt to be communicated to, or forced on, other, linked, rivalries.

Earlier we chose not to dwell on the trivial catalyst for the First World War (the assassination of Archduke Ferdinand) but it can be argued that the war became increasingly likely because of a chain of developments in several rivalry fields that became interconnected.[9] No one argues anymore that the Anglo-German rivalry was the main cause of the First World War. It was a meaningful part of a multifaceted set of rivalries that spanned the Balkans, the eastern Mediterranean, Central and Western Europe (most prominently, the Russo-German, Austro-Russian, and Franco-German rivalries), and even the Russo-Japanese rivalry.[10] Rivalries themselves are difficult to manage. Multiple rivalries may be impossible for any single set of decision-makers to manage well. Add asymmetrical capabilities, misperceptions, domestic politics, and intransigent allies to this mix and the purported Chinese curse about living in interesting times comes immediately to mind.

Most importantly, however, interconnected rivalries are more danger-ous than rivalries that remain autonomous. Escalations of major power disagreements are not always free of irrational and ill-conceived behav-ior. Interdependent rivalries can make these difficult to control elements more significant and more seemingly escalatory than they might other-wise be. For these reasons, the Sino-India rivalry deserves more attention and "respect" than it has received. As it becomes an integral component of Sino-American rivalry processes, its significance and management are elevated to the top ranks of rivalries in play around the world. The most powerful actors in the global system rarely go directly to war on their own. Instead, they are pulled into the conflicts of other states. The Sino-Indian rivalry, potentially, is a prime conduit for just such an escalation that no one saw coming or desired.

---

[9] See William R. Thompson, "A Streetcar Named Sarajevo: Catalysts, Multiple Causation Chains, and Rivalry Structures," *International Studies Quarterly* 47.3 (2003): 453–474; William R. Thompson, "Powder Kegs, Sparks, and World War I," in Gary Goertz and Jack S. Levy (eds.), *Explaining War and Peace: Case Studies and Necessary Condition Counterfactuals* (London: Routledge, 2007); and Karen Rasler and William R. Thompson, "Strategic Rivalries and Complex Causality in 1914," in Jack S. Levy and John A. Vasquez (eds.), *The War of 1914: Analytic Structure, Politics, and Decision-Making* (Cambridge: Cambridge University Press, 2014), 65–86.

[10] The disappointing outcome of the Russo-Japanese war in 1906 encouraged Russia to return its primary foreign policy focus to the Balkans at a fateful time for Austro-Russian relations.

PART V

Conclusion

CHAPTER 9

Conclusion

The China–India rivalry is thought to be of lesser concern by many, though by no means all scholars as explained in this book. However, despite the growing asymmetries between China and India in recent decades, neither country regards their boundary issue as stalemated. Not only has their *spatial* rivalry intensified in recent years but their *positional* contest has also heightened and expanded into newer domains (such as the naval realm) because of their simultaneous albeit asymmetric rise. Consequently, even as a rising India tries to "carve out a more independent role, ... India may struggle to balance its long-term commitment to strategic autonomy from Western powers with the need to embed itself more deeply into multilateral security architectures to counter a rising China," according to the US National Intelligence Council.[1] In other words, the Sino-Indian rivalry is one of the most consequential geopolitical contests in Asia today since China and India are rising powers and because they have very different relationships with the United States.

In fact, the rise of China and India may even lead to the reemergence of Asia at the center of global politics and economics, thus heralding a significant structural shift in world affairs given that Europe and North America have been the primary world regions for a few centuries now.[2] However, such dramatic shifts have usually been associated with conflict and even global wars. Nevertheless, as argued in this book, there is no reason to emphasize the global at the expense of the regional (Asian) in this looming

---

[1] United States National Intelligence Council. *Global Trends 2040: A More Contested World*, National Intelligence Council, Office of the Director of National Intelligence. March 2021, 96, www.dni.gov/files/ODNI/documents/assessments/GlobalTrends_2040.pdf.

[2] Jacek Kugler and Ronald L. Tammen, "Implications of Asia's Rise to Global Status," in William R. Thompson (ed.), *Systemic Transitions: Past, Present, and Future* (New York: Palgrave, 2009), 161–186. There is some debate in the academic literature on whether Europe and the North Atlantic emerged at the center of global politics and economics during the European "age of discoveries" (post-1490s) or after the Industrial Revolution (post-1750).

power shift. Even the power transition theory has been criticized for placing "too much emphasis" on "the global hierarchy and not enough on the Asian regional hierarchy."[3] Given the Sino-Indian *positional* rivalry as well as the United States' growing ties with India, the Sino-Indian rivalry is rife with systemic implications. Extrapolating from these findings, the China–India rivalry could be the key to global stability given its interactions with the US–China rivalry.

The traditional foci of analyses of the First World War often center on the Anglo-German rivalry. Britain was the declining global leader while Germany was its principal continental challenger. This facet is one of the reasons why the First World War seems pertinent to a more recent Chinese challenge to a declining US global hegemony.[4] The irony is that the Anglo-German rivalry was almost diffused when Germany chose to back down from its challenge to British naval supremacy a few years prior to 1914. By itself then, the Anglo-German rivalry was unlikely to have led to the war. But this rivalry was also embedded in other European rivalries.[5] One of these rivalries involved Germany and Russia. For Germany to win against the Franco-Russian alliance, German decision-makers felt that they needed to knock France out of the combat quickly so that they could concentrate on the greater Russian threat. They also thought that the longer they waited the greater Russian capabilities would become. As a consequence, the Germans attacked the French in the west and chose to do so by moving through Belgium. This threat to the English Channel encouraged British entry in the war on the side of the French and Russian alliance. All of a sudden, most of the major powers were at war.

The moral of this particular dimension of the First World War story is that (i) it can be a mistake to focus too strongly on the most obvious rivalry – that between a rising challenger and a declining leader when (ii) other rivalries can prove to be more important to the escalation to a wider war. While most analyses of systemic change and order transition tend to focus on US–China

---

[3] Jack S. Levy, "Power Transition Theory and the Rise of China," in Robert S. Ross and Zhu Feng (eds.), *China's Ascent: Power, Security, and the Future of International Politics* (Ithaca: Cornell University Press, 2008), 32.

[4] Richard N. Rosecrance and Steven E. Miller (eds.), *The Next Great War? The Roots of World War I and the Risk of U.S.-China Conflict* (Cambridge, MA: The MIT Press, 2014).

[5] William R. Thompson, "A Streetcar Named Sarajevo: Catalysts, Multiple Causation Chains, and Rivalry Structures," *International Studies Quarterly* 47.3 (2003): 453–474; and Karen Rasler and William R. Thompson, "Strategic Rivalries and Complex Causality in 1914," in Jack S. Levy and John A. Vasquez (eds.), *The Outbreak of the First World War: Structure, Politics, and Decision-Making* (New York: Cambridge University Press, 2014), 65–86.

contingencies in East Asia[6] – the Korean Peninsula, the East China Sea/
Japan, Taiwan, and the South China Sea – it is equally possible that it is a
China–India conflict (whether in the Himalayas or in the Indian Ocean)
that leads to America's participation. Not only does the United States fear
that China seeks Indo-Pacific hegemony but the Pentagon also believes that
the "PLA's evolving capabilities and concepts continue to strengthen the
PRC's ability to counter an intervention by an adversary in the Indo-Pacific
region and project power globally."[7] Given the growing strategic partnership between the United States and India, a Sino-Indian regional war may
precipitate a systemic crisis by involving the United States.

Therefore, as argued in this book, the Sino-Indian rivalry is more
important than is generally believed. Furthermore, even though the *spatial*
dimension of their rivalry is important and has intensified in recent years,
the Sino-Indian *positional* contest may be of equal or greater consequence.
In fact, even if the spatial element were to disappear, there would still be
a strong Sino-Indian (positional) rivalry. These findings hold despite their
various asymmetries. In fact, any Indian attempt to close the gap with
China will escalate the tempo of the Sino-Indian rivalry. Furthermore,
the interconnections between the Sino-Indian and Indo-Pakistani rivalries
and China's strategic alignment with Pakistan also mean that if the power
balance in the subcontinent were to tilt further in India's favor (as it has
been since the end of the Cold War) it will heighten Beijing's concerns
and escalate the Sino-Indian contest.

Consequently, not only has the Sino-Indian rivalry fused with the
Indo-Pakistani rivalry but it is also in the process of becoming entangled
with the Sino-American rivalry given the growing alignment between the
United States and India. While India's quest for strategic autonomy may
affect the pace of the growing US–India strategic partnership, the history
of Sino-Indian conflicts demonstrates that the United States has always

---

[6] There is a vast literature on these issues. Important contributions include Eric Heginbotham,
Michael Nixon, Forrest E. Morgan et al., *The U.S.-China Military Scorecard: Forces, Geography, and
the Evolving Balance of Power, 1996–2017* (Santa Monica: RAND, 2015); Evan Braden Montgomery,
"Contested Primacy in the Western Pacific: China's Rise and the Future of U.S. Power Projection,"
International Security 38.4 (2014): 115–149; Charles L. Glaser, "A U.S.-China Grand Bargain? The
Hard Choice between Military Competition and Accommodation," *International Security* 39.4
(2015): 49–90; Sheila A. Smith, *Japan Rearmed: The Politics of Military Power* (Cambridge, MA:
Harvard University Press, 2019); Robert Ayson and Desmond Ball, "Can a Sino-Japanese War Be
Controlled?," *Survival* 56.6 (2014): 135–166; and Bruce W. Bennett and Jennifer Lind, "The Collapse
of North Korea: Military Missions and Requirements," *International Security* 36.2 (2011): 84–119.

[7] "Military and Security Developments Involving the People's Republic of China 2020, Annual
Report to the Congress," Office of the Secretary of Defense, vi, https://media.defense.gov/2020/
Sep/01/2002488689/-1/-1/1/2020-DOD-CHINA-MILITARY-POWER-REPORT-FINAL.PDF.

had a stake in this rivalry. Not only had the United States aided "non-aligned" India during the 1962 Sino-Indian War but it had even threatened to strike China in East Asia "if China intervened in support of Pakistan" after Beijing issued a threat to open a second front against India during the 1965 India–Pakistan War.[8] Though the United States sided with Beijing and even prodded China to attack India during the 1971 Bangladesh War due to the changed Cold War geopolitics,[9] our larger point is that any Sino-Indian conflict has the propensity to involve the United States in some capacity, India's "strategic autonomy" notwithstanding.

According to Admiral Philips Davidson, Commander of the US Indo-Pacific Command, even if India remains "committed" to its "nonaligned approach," it is likely to "deepen" its engagement with the Quad, and this is "an opportunity" for the United States given the Chinese challenge.[10] This dramatic transformation in US–India relations after the Cold War has not gone unnoticed in China, and Chinese scholars worry whether India's "new" strategy is to pursue "selective alliances" on certain issues with the United States and that it remains "unknown whether India can adhere to strategic autonomy."[11] Not surprisingly, despite asymmetries, China has begun to take India more seriously because of its gradual ascent and the growing US–India alignment.

The China–India rivalry for power and influence at the regional level in Asia is in the process of fusing with the US–China rivalry in Asia and consequently at the global level. What is also noteworthy is that the *spatial* and *positional* dimensions of the Sino-Indian rivalry are also intertwined. Any potential de-escalation (let alone resolution) of the military tensions along the Sino-Indian border will enable India to pour more resources into projecting power into the Indian Ocean and into Looking/Acting East. These developments will also have the ability to undermine any Chinese bid for regional hegemony, whether at the East Asian level or at the pan-Asian level, especially if India works in tandem with the United States (and America's Asian allies, especially Japan and Australia).[12]

---

[8] John W. Garver, *Protracted Contest: Sino-Indian Rivalry in the Twentieth Century* (Seattle: University of Washington Press, 2001), 202.

[9] Sumit Ganguly, *Conflict Unending: India-Pakistan Tensions since 1947* (New York: Columbia University Press, 2002), 51–78.

[10] Press Trust of India, "US Provided Info, Equipment to India during China Border Crisis: Pentagon Commander," *NDTV*, March 10, 2021, www.ndtv.com/india-news/us-provided-info-equipment-to-india-during-china-border-crisis-pentagon-commander-2388015.

[11] Li Li, "The New Trend of India's Rising as a Great Power," *Contemporary International Relations* 28.2 (2018): 46, 49.

[12] Manjeet S. Pardesi, "American Global Primacy and the Rise of India," *AsiaPacific Issues* No. 129 (2017), www.eastwestcenter.org/publications/american-global-primacy-and-the-rise-india.

Not surprisingly, one noteworthy dimension of America's response to the rise of China has been "region expansion" – expanding its definition of the region in question from East Asia to the Indo-Pacific.[13] Focusing on East Asia alone may favor the prospects for Chinese hegemony. At least doubling the size of the region at stake dilutes China's growing power because China now has a much larger region to dominate and show some form of leadership. Simultaneously, it augments India's power as the United States and its Asian allies are now favorably disposed toward India.

In other words, the China–India rivalry has implications for the United States' position as the system leader, and a China–India war has the potential to become a much larger regional war in Asia, and potentially a systemic war with the participation of the United States. In addition to Korea, Taiwan, the South China Sea, and the East China Sea, India and the Indian Ocean is now a fifth potential flashpoint in US–China relations. If one were looking for the best place for an accidental escalation of conflict, the disputed Sino-Indian border in the Himalayas or a Sino-Indian naval showdown in the Indian Ocean would seem like a reasonable bet. The Sino-Indian rivalry is now a part of the larger mosaic of regional and global power competition.

---

[13] Manjeet S. Pardesi, "The Indo-Pacific: A 'New' Region or the Return of History?," *Australian Journal of International Affairs* 74.2 (2020): 124–146.

Bibliography

Abhyankar, Rajendra M. "Assuring India's Water Security." In P. R. Kumaraswamy (ed.), *Facets of India's Security: Essays for C. Uday Bhaskar* (London: Routledge, 2022), 233–248.

"About India Economy Growth Rate & Statistics." India Brand Equity Foundation. October 2021. www.ibef.org/economy/indian-economy-overview.

Acharya, Amitav. *East of India, South of China: Sino-Indian Encounters in Southeast Asia* (New Delhi: Oxford University Press, 2017). https://doi.org/10.1093/acprof:oso/9780199461141.003.0003.

Allison, Graham. *Destined for War? Can America and China Escape Thucydides' Trap* (Boston: Harcourt, 2018).

Ang, Cheng Guan. *The Southeast Asia Treaty Organization* (London: Routledge, 2022).

Angell, Norman. *The Great Illusion*, 2nd ed. (New York: Putnam's, 1933).

Arpi, Claude. "Major Bob Khathing, the Indian Hero Who Secured Tawang." *The Daily Guardian*, February 20, 2021.

"Asian Conference and Asia's Future." *China Digest*, February 8, 1949, 13.

Asian Relations: Being Report of the Proceedings and Documentation of the First Asian Relations Conference, New Delhi, March–April 1947 (New Delhi: Asian Relations Organization, 1948).

Associated Press, "China Objects to Ladakh Status, Indian Border Activities." September 29, 2020. https://news.yahoo.com/china-objects-ladakh-status-indian-095814241.html?fr=yhssrp_catchall.

Ayson, Robert, and Desmond Ball. "Can a Sino-Japanese War Be Controlled?" *Survival* 56:6 (2014): 135–166. https://news.yahoo.com/china-objects-ladakh-status-indian-095814241.html?fr=yhssrp_catchall.

Bagchi, Indrani. "India Should Bond with Japan and Stop Looking over Its Shoulder at China." *The Economic Times*, May 27, 2013. https://economictimes.indiatimes.com/opinion/et-commentary/india-should-bond-with-japan-and-stop-looking-over-its-shoulder-at-china/articleshow/20281787.cms?from=mdr.

Bagchi, Indrani. "India Wary as Japan, US Seek Quadrilateral with Australia." *The Times of India*, October 28, 2017. https://timesofindia.indiatimes.com/india/india-wary-as-japan-us-seek-quadrilateral-with-australia/articleshow/61281250.cms.

Bajpai, Kanti P. *India versus China: Why They Are Not Friends* (New Delhi: Juggernaut, 2021).

Bajpai, Kanti P., Pervaiz Iqbal Cheema, P. R. Chari, Stephen P. Cohen, and Sumit Ganguly. *Brasstacks and Beyond: Perception and the Management of Crisis in South Asia* (New Delhi: Manohar, 1995).

Bambawale, Gautam, Vijay Kelkar, and Raghunath Mashelkar et al. "Strategic Patience and Flexible Policies: How India Can Rise to the China Challenge." Pune International Centre. March 16, 2021. https://xkdr.org/paper/bambawaleeteal2021_strategicPatienceand Flexiblepolicies.pdf.

Barbieri, Katherine. *The Liberal Illusion* (Ann Arbor: University of Michigan Press, 2002).

Barnds, William J. "China's Relations with Pakistan: Durability amidst Discontinuity." *The China Quarterly* 63 (1975): 463–489.

Barnes, Robert. "Between the Blocs: India, the United Nations, and Ending the Korean War." *The Journal of Korean Studies* 18:2 (2013): 263–286.

Barua, Pradeep P. *The State of War in South Asia* (Lincoln: University of Nebraska Press, 2005).

Basrur, Rajesh. "India and China: A Managed Nuclear Rivalry?" *The Washington Quarterly* 42:3 (2019): 151–170.

Bayly, Christopher, and Tim Harper. *Forgotten Armies: The Fall of British Asia, 1941–1945* (Cambridge, MA: Harvard University Press, 2005).

Bayly, Christopher, and Tim Harper. *Forgotten Wars: Freedom and Revolution in Southeast Asia* (Cambridge, MA: Harvard University Press, 2007).

Bennett, Bruce W., and Jennifer Lind. "The Collapse of North Korea: Military Missions and Requirements." *International Security* 36:2 (2011): 84–119.

Bhasin, Avtar Singh (ed.). *India-China Relations 1947–2000: A Documentary Study*, 5 Vols. (New Delhi: Geetika, 2018).

Bhasin, Avtar Singh. *Nehru, Tibet, and China* (Gurugram: Penguin, 2021).

Blackwill, Robert D., and Ashley J. Tellis. "The India Dividend: New Delhi Remains Washington's Best Hope in Asia." *Foreign Affairs* 98:5 (2019): 173–183.

Bland, Ben, and Girija Shivakumar. "China Confronts Indian Navy Vessel." *Financial Times*, September 1, 2011. www.ft.com/content/883003ec-d3f6-11e0-b7eb-00144feab49a.

Brecher, Michael. "International Relations and Asian Studies: The Subordinate State System of Southern Asia." *World Politics* 15:2 (1963): 213–235.

Brecher, Michael. *Nehru: A Political Biography* (London: Oxford University Press, 1959).

Brewster, David. "The Red Flag Follows Trade: China's Future as an Indian Ocean Power." In Ashley J. Tellis, Alison Szalwinski, and Michael Wills (eds.), *Strategic Asia 2019: China's Expanding Strategic Ambitions* (Washington, DC: National Bureau of Asian Research, 2019), 174–209.

Brines, Russel. *The Indo-Pakistani Conflict* (New York: Pall Mall, 1968).

Brooks, Stephen G., and William C. Wohlforth. "The Rise and Fall of the Great Powers in the Twenty-First Century: China's Rise and the Fate of America's Global Position." *International Security* 40:3 (2015/16): 7–53.

Buckley, Chris, and Ellen Barry. "China Tells India That It Won't Back Down in Border Dispute." *The New York Times*, August 4, 2017.

Burke, Jason. "Pakistan Spy Agency's Alleged Role in Mumbai Terrorist Attacks to Be Revealed." The Guardian, May 9, 2011.

Buzan, Barry, and Evelyn Goh. *Rethinking Sino-Japanese Alienation: History Problems and Historical Opportunities* (Oxford: Oxford University Press, 2020).

"Cable from the Chinese Foreign Ministry, 'Report on Negotiations Regarding the Tibet Issue between China and India'." November 24, 1950. History and Public Policy Program Digital Archive, PRC FMA 105-00011-02, 42–44. Obtained by Dai Chaowu and translated by 7Brands. https://digitalarchive .wilsoncenter.org/document/114749.

Caussat, Paul. "Facing Political Issues and Protecting National Sovereignty: The Sino-Indian Economic Relation since 1947." In Young-Chan Kim (ed.), *China-India Relations: Geopolitical Competition, Economic Cooperation, Cultural Exchange, and Business Ties* (Cham: Springer, 2020), 81–98.

Chakradeo, Saneet. "How Does the India-China Rivalry Affect Secondary State Behaviour in South Asia?" Brookings Institution Blog. April 28, 2020. www .brookings.edu/blog/up-front/2020/04/28/sambandh-blog-how-does-the-india-china-rivalry-affect-secondary-state-behaviour-in-south-asia/.

Chan, Steve. *Thucydides's Trap? Historical Interpretation, Logic of Inquiry, and the Future of Sino-American Relations* (Ann Arbor: University of Michigan Press, 2020).

Chang, Gordon G. "The Real Threat from China's Military: Going Rogue." The National Interest, September 26, 2014. https://nationalinterest.org/feature/ the-real-threat-chinas-military-going-rogue-11356.

Chansoria, Monika. "India-China Unsettled Boundary and Territorial Dispute: Institutionalized Border Mechanisms since 39 years, sans Resolution." Policy Brief, The Japan Institute of International Affairs, July 31, 2020. www.jiia-jie.jp/ en/policybrief/pdf/PolicyBrief_Chansoira_2020731.pdf.

Chellaney, Brahma. *Water: Asia's New Battleground* (Washington, DC: Georgetown University Press, 2011).

Chen, Jian. "The Chinese Communist 'Liberation' of Tibet, 1949–51." In Jeremy Brown and Paul G. Pickowicz (eds.), *Dilemmas of Victory: The Early Years of the People's Republic of China* (Cambridge, MA: Harvard University Press, 2007), 130–159.

Chen, Jian. "The Tibetan Rebellion of 1959 and China's Changing Relations with India and the Soviet Union." *Journal of Cold War Studies* 8:3 (2006): 54–101.

Chen, Yifeng. "Bandung, China, and the Making of World Order in East Asia." In Luis Eslava, Michael Fakhri, and Vasuki Nesiah (eds.), *Bandung, Global History, and International Law* (Cambridge: Cambridge University Press, 2017), 177–195.

Chen, Zhimin. "China's Power from a Chinese Perspective (II): Back to the Center Stage." In Jae Ho Chung (ed.), *Assessing China's Power* (New York: Palgrave Macmillan, 2015), 271–289.

Cheng, Joey T., and Jessica L. Tracy. "Toward a Unified Science of Hierarchy: Dominance and Prestige Are Two Fundamental Pathways to Human Social

Rank." In Joey T. Cheng, Jessica L. Tracy, and Cameron Anderson (eds.), *The Psychology of Social Status* (New York: Springer, 2014), 3–28.

Chhina, Man Aman Singh. "Army Rushes More Troops to Ladakh after Galwan Clash." *The Indian Express*, June 20, 2020.

Childs, Nick, and Tom Waldwyn. "China's Naval Shipbuilding: Delivering on Its Ambition in a Big Way." Military Balance Blog, May 1, 2018. www.iiss.org/blogs/military-balance/2018/05/china-naval-shipbuilding.

"China Regains Slot as India's Top Trade Partner Despite Tensions." BBC News, February 23, 2021. www.bbc.com/news/business-56164154.

"China Would Consider Resuming Tests if the Nuclear Arms Tension [sic]." *South China Morning Post*, June 2, 1998. 11.

China Power Team, "How Dominant Is China in the Global Arms Trade?" China Power, April 26, 2018 (updated 27 May 2021). https://chinapower.csis.org/china-global-arms-trade/.

Choudhury, G. W. "China's Policy toward South Asia." *Asian Perspective* 14:2 (1990): 127–156.

Clary, Christopher, and Vipin Narang. "India's Counterforce Temptations: Strategic Dilemmas, Doctrine, and Capabilities." *International Security* 43:3 (2018/2019): 7–52.

Cohen, Stephen P. *India: Emerging Power* (Washington, DC: Brookings, 2002).

Cohen, Stephen P. *The Indian Army: Its Contribution to the Development of a Nation* (Delhi: Oxford University Press, 1990).

Cohen, Warren I. *America's Response to China: A History of Sino-American Relations*, 5th ed. (New York: Columbia University Press, 2010).

Colaresi, Michael. "When Doves Cry: International Rivalry, Unrecognized Cooperation, and Leadership Turnover." *American Journal of Political Science* 48:3 (2004): 555–570.

Colaresi, Michael P., Karen Rasler, and William R. Thompson. *Strategic Rivalries in World Politics: Position, Space, and Conflict Escalation* (Cambridge: Cambridge University Press, 2007).

Colley, Christopher. "A Future Chinese Indian Ocean Fleet?" *War on the Rocks*, April 2, 2021. https://warontherocks.com/2021/04/q-future-chinese-indian-ocean-fleet/.

Collin, Koh Swee Lean. "China-India Rivalry at Sea: Capability, Trends, and Challenges." *Asian Security* 15:1 (2019): 5–24.

Collins, Gabriel B., and William S. Murray. "No Oil for the Lamps of China?" *Naval War College Review* 61:2 (2008): 79–95.

Conboy, Kenneth, and James Morrison. *The CIA's Secret War in Tibet* (Lawrence: University Press of Kansas, 2002).

Converse, Benjamin A., and David A. Reinhard. "On Rivalry and Goal Pursuit: Shared Competitive History, Legacy Concerns, and Strategy Selection." *Journal of Personality and Social Psychology* 110:2 (2016): 193–207.

Copeland, Dale. *Economic Interdependence and War* (Princeton: Princeton University Press, 2015).

Copland, Ian. *The Princes of India in the Endgame of Empire, 1917–1947* (Cambridge: Cambridge University Press, 1997).

Cunningham, Fiona, and Rory Medcalf. "The Dangers of Denial: Nuclear Weapons in China-India Relations." Lowy Institute for International Policy, October 2011. www.lowyinstitute.org/sites/default/files/pubfiles/Cunningham_and_Medcalf%2C_The_dangers_of_denial_web_1.pdf.

Cunningham, Fiona S., and M. Taylor Fravel. "Assuring Assured Retaliation: China's Nuclear Posture and U.S.-China Strategic Stability." *International Security* 40:2 (2015): 7–50.

Dai, Chaowu. "China's Strategy for Sino-Indian Boundary Disputes, 1950–1962." *Asian Perspective* 43:3 (2019): 435–457.

Dai, Chaowu. "From 'Hindi-Chini Bhai-Bhai' to 'International Class Struggle' against Nehru: China's India Policy and the Frontier Dispute, 1950–62." In Amit Das Gupta and Lorenz Lüthi (eds.), *The Sino-Indian War of 1962: New Perspectives* (London: Routledge, 2017), 68–84.

Dalton, Toby, and Tong Zhao. "At a Crossroads: China-India Nuclear Relations after the Border Clash." Working Paper, Carnegie Endowment for International Peace. August 2020. https://carnegieendowment.org/2020/08/19/at-crossroads-china-india-nuclear-relations-after-border-clash-pub-82489.

Dalvi, J. P. *Himalayan Blunder: The Curtain-Raiser to the Sino-Indian War of 1962* (Dehradun: Natraj, 1969).

Darwin, John. *The Empire Project: The Rise and Fall of the British World System, 1830–1970* (Cambridge: Cambridge University Press, 2009).

Das Gupta, Amit R. "Pakistan and 1962." In Amit R. Das Gupta and Lorenz Lüthi (eds.), *The Sino-Indian War of 1962: New Perspectives* (London: Routledge, 2017), 124–140.

Dasgupta, Probal. *Watershed 1967: India's Forgotten Victory over China* (New Delhi: Juggernaut, 2020).

Dasgupta, Saibal. "PM Modi, Xi Jinping Meet on April 27–28, to "Reset" Ties after Doklam Standoff." *The Times of India*, April 23, 2017.

Denyer, Simon, and Annie Gowen. "India, China Agree to Pull Back Troops to Resolve Tense Border Dispute." *The Washington Post*, August 28, 2017.

Devare, Sudhir. *India & Southeast Asia: Towards Security Convergence* (Singapore: Institute of Southeast Asian Studies, 2006).

Dibb, Paul. "The Return of Geography." In Russell W. Glenn (ed.), *New Directions in Strategic Thinking 2.0* (Canberra: Australian National University Press, 2018), 91–104.

Diehl, Paul F. "Whither Rivalry or Withered Rivalry?" In T. V. Paul (ed.), *The China-India Rivalry in the Globalization Era* (Washington, DC: Georgetown University Press, 2018), 253–272.

Diehl, Paul F., and Gary Goertz. *War and Peace in International Rivalry* (Ann Arbor: University of Michigan Press, 2000).

Dikötter, Frank. *The Cultural Revolution: A People's History, 1962–1976* (Pittsburgh: Bloomsbury, 2017).

Dittmer, Lowell. "The Strategic Triangle: An Elementary Game-Theoretical Analysis." *World Politics* 33:4 (1981): 485–575.

Doctornoff, Mark H. (trans.). "From the Journal of Ambassador S. F. Antonov, Summary of a Conversation with the Chairman of the CC CPC Mao Zedong." October 14, 1959. History and Public Policy Program Digital Archive, SCCD, Fond 5, Opis 49, Delo 235, Listy 89–96. https://digitalarchive.wilsoncenter.org/document/114788.

Donaldson, Robert. *Soviet Policy toward India: Ideology and Strategy* (Cambridge, MA: Harvard University Press, 1974).

Doran, Charles F. "Living with Asymmetry." *Mershon International Studies Review* 38:2 (1994): 260–264.

Doshi, Rush. *The Long Game: China's Grand Strategy to Displace American Order* (New York: Oxford University Press, 2021).

Doyle, Michael. *Ways of War and Peace* (New York: Norton, 1997).

Dreyer, David R. "Foundations of Rivalry Research." In William R. Thompson (ed.), *The Oxford Encyclopedia of Empirical International Relations Theory*, Volume 2 (Oxford: Oxford University Press, 2018), 65–80.

Ellen, Barry. "U.S. Proposes a Naval Coalition." *The New York Times*, March 3, 2016. www.nytimes.com/2016/03/03/world/asia/us-proposes-india-naval-coalition-balance-china-expansion.html.

Erickson, Andrew S., Walter C. Ladwig III, and Justin D. Mikolay. "Diego Garcia and the United States' Emerging Indian Ocean Strategy." *Asian Security* 6:3 (2010): 214–237.

Fang, Tien-sze. *Asymmetrical Threat Perceptions in India-China Relations* (New Delhi: Oxford University Press, 2013).

Farley, Robert. "How China Defeated India in a Terrifying 1962 War." The National Interest, February 11, 2020. https://nationalinterest.org/blog/buzz/how-china-defeated-india-terrifying-1962-war-122406.

Feigenbaum, Evan A. "India's Rise, America's Interest: The Fate of the U.S.-Indian Partnership." *Foreign Affairs* 89:2 (2010): 76–91.

Finlay, David James, Richard R. Fagen, and Ole R. Holsti. *Enemies in Politics* (Chicago: Rand McNally, 1967).

Fishel, Wesley R. *The End of Extraterritoriality in China* (Berkeley: University of California Press, 1952).

Fletcher, Joseph. "The Heyday of the Ch'ing Order in Mongolia, Sinkiang, and Tibet." In John Fairbank (ed.), *The Cambridge History of China, Volume 10, Late Ch'ing, 1800–1911, Part 1* (New York: Cambridge University Press, 1995), 351–408.

Fournier, Marc A., D. S. Moskowitz, and David C. Zuroff. "Social Rank Strategies in Hierarchical Relationships." *Journal of Personality and Social Psychology* 83:2 (2002): 425–433.

Frankel, Francine R. "The Breakout of the China-India Strategic Rivalry in Asia and the Indian Ocean." *Journal of International Affairs* 64:2 (2011): 1–17.

Frankel, Francine R. *When Nehru Looked East: Origins of India-US Suspicion and India-China Rivalry* (New York: Oxford University Press, 2020).

Frankel, Francine R., and Harry Harding (eds.), *The Indo-China Relationship: What the United States Needs to Know* (New York: Columbia University Press, 2004).

Fravel, M. Taylor. *Active Defense: China's Military Strategy since 1949* (Princeton: Princeton University Press, 2019).

Fravel, M. Taylor. "Stability in a Secondary Strategic Direction: China and the Border Dispute with India after 1962." In Kanti P. Bajpai, Selina Ho, and Manjari Chatterjee Miller (eds.). *Routledge Handbook of China-India Relations* (London: Routledge, 2020), 169–179.

Fravel, M. Taylor. *Strong Borders, Secure Nation: Cooperation and Conflict in China's Territorial Disputes* (Princeton: Princeton University Press, 2008).

Friedberg, Aaron. "Competing with China." *Survival* 60:3 (2018): 7–64.

Gall, Carlotta. *The Wrong Enemy: America in Afghanistan, 2001–2014* (New York: Houghton Mifflin, 2014).

Ganguly, Sumit. *Conflict Unending: India-Pakistan Tensions since 1947* (New York: Columbia University Press, 2002).

Ganguly, Sumit. *Deadly Impasse: Indo-Pakistani Relations at the Dawn of a New Century* (Cambridge: Cambridge University Press, 2016).

Ganguly, Sumit. "India's Pathway to Pokhran II: The Prospect and Sources of New Delhi's Nuclear Weapons Program." *International Security* 23:4 (1999): 148–177.

Ganguly, Sumit. "Modi Crosses the Rubicon in Kashmir." *Foreign Affairs*, August 8, 2019. www.foreignaffairs.com/articles/india/2019-08-08/modi-crosses-rubicon-kashmir.

Ganguly, Sumit. "The Sino-Indian Border Talks: A View from New Delhi." *Asian Survey* 29:12 (1989): 1123–1135.

Ganguly, Sumit, and Andrew Scobell. "The Himalayan Impasse: Sino-Indian Rivalry in the Wake of Doklam." *The Washington Quarterly* 41:3 (2018): 177–190.

Ganguly, Sumit, and Arzan Tarapore. "Kashmir: A Casualty of India's Rising Power Status?" *The National Interest*, October 22, 2019. https://nationalinterest.org/feature/kashmir-casualty-indias-rising-power-status-90311.

Ganguly, Sumit, and M. Chris Mason, *An Unnatural Partnership? The Future of U.S.-India Strategic Cooperation* (Carlisle, PA: Strategic Studies Institute, 2019).

Ganguly, Sumit, and M. Chris Mason (eds.). *The Future of US-India Security Cooperation* (Manchester: Manchester University Press, 2021).

Ganguly, Sumit, and William R. Thompson. *Ascending India and Its State Capacity: Extraction, Violence, and Legitimacy* (New Haven: Yale University Press, 2011).

Ganguly, Sumit, and William R. Thompson. "Conflict Propensities in Asian Rivalries." In Sumit Ganguly and William R. Thompson (eds.), *Asian Rivalries: Conflict, Escalation, and Limitations on Two-Level Games* (Stanford: Stanford University Press, 2011), 1–25.

Ganguly, Sumit, and R. Harrison Wagner. "India and Pakistan: Bargaining in the Shadow of Nuclear War." *Journal of Strategic Studies* 27:3 (2004): 479–507.

Gardner, Kyle J. *The Frontier Complex: Geopolitics and the Making of the India-China Border, 1846–1962* (Cambridge: Cambridge University Press, 2021).

Garlick, Jeremy. "Deconstructing the China-Pakistan Economic Corridor: Pipe Dreams versus Geopolitical Realities." *Journal of Contemporary China* 27:112 (2018): 519–533.

Gartzke, Erik, Quan Li, and Charles Boehmer. "Investing in Peace: Economic Interdependence and International Conflict." *International Organization* 55:2 (2001): 391–438.

Garver, John W. "Asymmetrical Indian and Chinese Threat Perceptions." *Journal of Strategic Studies* 25:4 (2002): 109–134.

Garver, John W. "Calculus of a Chinese Decision for Local War with India." In Jagannath P. Panda (ed.), *India and China in Asia: Between Equilibrium and Equations* (London: Routledge, 2019), 85–105.

Garver, John W. "China's Decision for War with India in 1962." In Alastair Iain Johnston and Robert S. Ross (eds.), *New Directions in the Study of China's Foreign Policy* (Stanford: Stanford University Press, 2006), 86–130.

Garver, John W. *China's Quest: The History of the Foreign Relations of the People's Republic of China* (New York: Oxford University Press, 2016).

Garver, John W. *Protracted Contest: Sino-Indian Rivalry in the Twentieth Century* (Seattle: University of Washington Press, 2001).

Geller, Daniel S. "Power Differential and War in Rival Dyads." *International Studies Quarterly* 37:2 (1993): 173–193.

George, Alexander, and Richard Smoke. *Deterrence in American Foreign Policy* (New York: Columbia University Press, 1975).

Gettleman, Jeffrey, and Javier C. Hernández. "China and India Ease Tensions in Border Dispute." *The New York Times*, August 29, 2017.

Gewirtz, Julian Baird. "China's Long March to Technological Supremacy." *Foreign Affairs*, August 27, 2019. www.foreignaffairs.com/articles/china/2019-08-27/chinas-long-march-technological-supremacy.

Gill, Mehul Singh. "Aksai Chin: From Napoleon to Nehru." *Indian Defence Review*, January 4, 2022. www.indiandefencereview.com/spotlights/aksai-chin-from-napoleon-to-nehru/.

Gilpin, Robert. *War and Change in World Politics* (Cambridge: Cambridge University Press, 1981).

Glaser, Charles L. "A U.S.-China Grand Bargain? The Hard Choice between Military Competition and Accommodation." *International Security* 39:4 (2015): 49–90.

Goertz, Gary, Paul F. Diehl, and Alexandru Balas. *The Evolution of Peace in the International System* (New York: Oxford University Press, 2016).

Goh, Evelyn. *Constructing the U.S. Rapprochement with China, 1961–1974: From "Red Menace" to "Tacit Ally"* (New York: Cambridge University Press, 2005).

Goh, Evelyn. "Great Powers and Hierarchical Order in Southeast Asia: Analyzing Regional Security Strategies." *International Security* 32:3 (2008): 1113–1157.

Gokhale, Vijay. *Long Game: How the Chinese Negotiate with India* (New Delhi: Vintage Books, 2021).

Gokhale, Vijay. *The Road from Galwan: The Future of India-China Relations* (Washington, DC: Carnegie Endowment for International Peace, 2021).

Goldman, Russell. "India-China Border Dispute: A Conflict Explained." *The New York Times*, June 17, 2020.

Goldstein, Avery. "US-China Rivalry in the Twenty-First Century: Déjà Vu and Cold War II." *China International Strategy Review* 2 (2020): 48–62.

Goldstein, Joshua, Jon C. Pevehouse, Deborah J. Gerner, and Shibley Telhami. "Reciprocity, Triangularity, and Cooperation in the Middle East, 1979–97." *Journal of Conflict Resolution* 45:5 (2001): 594–620.

Goldstein, Melvyn C. *A History of Modern Tibet, Volume 1, 1913–1951* (Berkeley: University of California Press, 1989).

Goldstein, Melvyn C. *A History of Modern Tibet, Volume 2, 1951–1955* (Berkeley: University of California Press, 2007).

Goldstein, Melvyn C. *A History of Modern Tibet, Volume 4, 1957–1959* (Berkeley: University of California Press, 2019).

Gopal, Sarvepalli. *Jawaharlal Nehru: A Biography, Volume 2, 1947–1956* (Delhi: Oxford University Press, 1979).

Gopal, Sarvepalli. *Jawaharlal Nehru: A Biography, Volume 3, 1956–1964* (London: Jonathan Cape, 1984).

Grare, Frédéric, and Jean-Loup Samaan. *The Indian Ocean as a New Political and Security Region* (Cham: Springer, 2022).

Gries, Peter Hays. *China's New Nationalism: Pride, Politics, and Diplomacy* (Berkeley: University of California Press, 2004).

Grimes, Paul. "Nehru Promises to Defend Nepal; Wins House Vote." *The New York Times*, November 28, 1959.

Gross, Samantha. "The Global Energy Trade's New Center of Gravity." In Tarun Chhabra, Rush Doshi, Ryan Haas, and Emilie Kimball (eds.), *Global China: Assessing China's Growing Role in the World* (Washington, DC: Brookings, 2021), 319–325.

Guan, Ang Cheng. *Southeast Asia's Cold War: An Interpretive History* (Honolulu: University of Hawaiʻi Press, 2018).

Gupta, Anil. "Karakoram Highway: A Security Challenge for India." *Indian Defence Review*, October 2, 2015. www.indiandefencereview.com/news/karakoram-highway-a-security-challenge-for-india/.

Gupta, Karunakar. "The McMahon Line 1911–1945: The British Legacy." *The China Quarterly* 47 (July–September1971): 521–545.

Gupta, Shekhar. "General Krishnaswami Sundarji, 'Soldier of the Mind,' Who Rewrote India's Military Doctrine." *The Print*, February 8, 2018. https://theprint.in/opinion/general-krishnaswamy-sundarji-soldier-mind-rewrote-indias-military-doctrine/34227/.

Gupta, Shishir. "China Supplies Mounted Howitzers to Pak to Maintain Arms Parity with India." *The Hindustan Times*, January 27, 2022.

Gupta, Sisir. "The Indian Dilemma." In Alastair Buchan (ed.) *A World of Nuclear Powers?* (Englewood Cliffs: Prentice Hall, 1966), 55–67.

Gupta, Swati. "Modi Claims Political Win after UN Lists Masood Azhar as a Terrorist." CNN, May 2, 2019. www.cnn.com/2019/05/02/india/masood-azhar-un-sanctions-intl/index.html.

Guruswamy, Mohan. "A Rajah's Whims and Aksai Chin." *The Asian Age*, September 15, 2015. www.asianage.com/columnists/raja-s-whim-and-aksai-chin-189.

Guyot-Réchard, Berenice. *Shadow States: India, China, and the Himalayas, 1910–1962* (Cambridge: Cambridge University Press, 2017).

"Hafiz Muhammad Saed." United Nations Security Council. www.un.org/securitycouncil/sanctions/1267/aq_sanctions_list/summaries/individual/hafiz-muhammad-saeed.

Hagerty, Devin T. "India's Regional Security Doctrine." *Asian Survey* 31:4 (1991): 351–363.

Hall, Ian. *Modi and the Reinvention of Indian Foreign Policy* (Bristol: Bristol University Press, 2019).

Han, Suyin. *Eldest Son: Zhou Enlai and the Making of Modern China, 1898–1976* (New York: Hill and Wang, 1994).

Harder, Anton. "Not at the Cost of China: New Evidence Regarding US Proposals to Nehru for Joining the United Nations Security Council." Cold War International History Project, Working Paper #76, Woodrow Wilson International Center for Scholars. March 2015. www.wilsoncenter.org/publication/not-the-cost-china-india-and-the-united-nations-security-council-1950.

Hardgrave, Robert L., Jr. "The Challenge of Ethnic Conflict: India – The Dilemmas of Diversity." *Journal of Democracy* 4:4 (1993): 54–68.

Harrison, Selig S. "Trouble India and Her Neighbors." *Foreign Affairs* 43:2 (1965): 312–330.

Heginbotham, Eric, Michael S. Chase, Jacob L. Heim, et al. *China's Evolving Nuclear Deterrent: Major Drivers and Issues for the United States* (Santa Monica: RAND, 2017).

Heginbotham, Eric, Michael Nixon, Forrest E. Morgan, et al. *The U.S.-China Military Scorecard: Forces, Geography, and the Evolving Balance of Power, 1996–2017* (Santa Monica: RAND, 2015).

Heimsath, Charles H., and Surjit Mansingh. *A Diplomatic History of Modern India* (Bombay: Allied, 1971).

Hiim, Henrik Stålhane. *China and International Nuclear Weapons Proliferation: Strategic Assistance* (London: Routledge, 2019).

Hilger, Andreas. "The Soviet Union and the Sino-Indian Border War, 1962." In Amit R. Das Gupta and Lorenz Lüthi (eds.), *The Sino-Indian War of 1962: New Perspectives* (London: Routledge, 2017), 142–158.

Hinton, Harold C. *China's Turbulent Quest: An Analysis of China's Foreign Relations since 1949* (Bloomington: Indiana University Press, 1970).

Ho, Selina. "Power Asymmetry and the China-India Water Dispute." In T. V. Paul (ed.), *The China-India Rivalry in the Era of Globalization* (Washington, DC: Georgetown University Press, 2018), 137–162.

Ho, Selina, Qian Neng, and Yan Yifei. "The Role of Ideas in the China-India Water Dispute." *The Chinese Journal of International Politics* 12:2 (2019): 263–294.

Hoffmann, Steven A. "Anticipation, Disaster, and Victory: India 1962–71." *Asian Survey* 12:11 (1972): 960–979.

Hoffmann, Steven A. *India and the China Crisis* (Delhi: Oxford University Press, 1990).

Holmes, James R., and Toshi Yoshihara. "Redlines for Sino-Indian Naval Rivalry." In John Garofano and Andrew J. Dew (eds.), *Deep Currents and Rising Tides:*

The Indian Ocean and International Security (Washington, DC: Georgetown University Press, 2013), 185–209.

Horelick, Arnold L. "The Soviet Union's Asian Collective Security Proposal: A Club in Search of Members." *Pacific Affairs* 47:3 (1974): 269–285.

Horsburgh, Nicola. *China and the Global Nuclear Order: From Estrangement to Active Engagement* (Oxford: Oxford University Press, 2015).

HT Correspondent. "Pakistan's ISI trains LeT, JeM terrorists: Parvez Musharraf." *The Hindustan Times*, February 16, 2016.

HT Correspondent. "Blow by Blow: A Timeline of India, China Face-off Over Doklam." *The Hindustan Times*, August 28, 2017.

HT Correspondent. "1,600 Chinese Troops Still Hold Position Near Doklam Faceoff Site." *The Hindustan Times*, December 12, 2017.

Hu, Shisheng. "Competitive Cooperation in Trade: A Chinese Perspective." In Kanti P. Bajpai, Jing Huang, and Kishore Mahbubani (eds.), *China-India Relations: Cooperation and Conflict* (London: Routledge, 2015), 67–90.

Hunt, Michael H. *The Genesis of Chinese Communist Foreign Policy* (New York: Columbia University Press, 1996).

Hussain, Alijaz. "AP Explains: India's Kashmir Move Foretold China Standoff." The Washington Post, August 19, 2020.

Huttenback, R. A. "A Historical Note on the Sino-Indian Dispute over the Aksai Chin." *The China Quarterly* 18 (April–June 1964): 201–207.

Hyer, Eric. *The Pragmatic Dragon: China's Grand Strategy and Boundary Settlements* (Vancouver: UBC Press, 2015).

"India – A New Great Power." *The Economist*. October 23, 1948.

"India: Anchor for Asia." *Time*. October 17, 1949.

"India-China Ties 'At Crossroads': Foreign Minister S. Jaishankar." NDTV, May 20, 2021. www.ndtv.com/india-news/india-china-ties-at-crossroads-foreign-minister-s-jaishankar-2446060.

"India Gets a High-tech Boost as US Elevates India to Most-important Allies List." *The Economic Times*, July 31, 2018. https://economictimes.indiatimes.com/news/politics-and-nation/india-gets-a-high-tech-boost-as-us-elevates-india-to-most-important-ally-list/articleshow/65209391.cms.

"India vs. Pakistan: A Tale of Two Economies." *The Times of India*, November 27, 2020. https://timesofindia.indiatimes.com/business/india-business/india-vs-pakistan-a-tale-of-two-economies/articleshow/79450051.cms.

"India Withdraws from Post on NEFA Border." *The Times of India*, September 29, 1959.

Indian Parliament on the Issue of Tibet: Rajya Sabha Debates, 1952–2005 (New Delhi: Tibetan Parliamentary and Policy Research Centre, 2006).

"Indo-Pacific Strategy of the United States." The White House, February 2022. www.whitehouse.gov/wp-content/uploads/2022/02/U.S.-Indo-Pacific-Strategy.pdf.

"Indo-Pacific Strategy Report." United States Department of Defense. June 1, 2019. https://media.defense.gov/2019/Jul/01/2002152311/-1/-1/1/DEPARTMENT-OF-DEFENSE-INDO-PACIFIC-STRATEGY-REPORT-2019.PDF.

Inman, Phillip. "China Overtakes US in World Trade." *The Guardian*, February 11, 2013. www.theguardian.com/business/2013/feb/11/china-worlds-largest-trading-nation.

Ispahani, Mahnaz Z. *Roads and Rivals: The Political Uses of Access in the Borderlands of Asia* (Ithaca: Cornell University Press, 1989).

Jackson, Van. "America's Indo-Pacific Folly: Adding New Commitments in Asia Will Only Invite Disaster." *Foreign Affairs*. March 12, 2021. www.foreignaffairs.com/articles/asia/2021-03-12/americas-indo-pacific-folly.

Jacob, J. F. R. *An Odyssey in War and Peace: An Autobiography* (New Delhi: Roli, 2011).

Jacob, Jabin T. "China, India, and Asian Connectivity: India's View." In Kanti Bajpai, Selina Ho, and Manarji Chatterjee Miller (eds.), *Routledge Handbook of China-India Relations* (London: Routledge, 2020), 315–332.

Jain, R. K. (ed.). *China South Asian Relations 1947–1980, Volume 2* (Brighton: The Harvester Press, 1981).

Jaishankar, S. *The India Way: Strategies for an Uncertain World* (Noida: HarperCollins, 2020).

Jaishankar, S., and Wang Gungwu. "Asia in the New World Order." HT-MintAsia Leadership Summit, May 2, 2018, Singapore. www.channelnewsasia.com/watch/asia-new-world-order-1545236.

Jervis, Robert. "The Impact of the Korean War on the Cold War." *Journal of Conflict Resolution* 24:4 (1980): 563–592.

Jetly, Nancy. *India China Relations, 1947–1977: A Study of Parliament's Role in the Making of Foreign Policy* (New Delhi: Radiant, 1979).

Johnston, Alastair Iain. "How New and Assertive Is China's New Assertiveness?" *International Security* 37:4 (2013): 7–48.

Joseph, Josy. "What Is the Doklam Issue All About?" The Hindu, January 27, 2018.

Joshi, Manoj. *China's 2021 White Paper on Tibet: Implications for India's China Strategy* (New Delhi: Observer Research Foundation, 2021).

Joshi, Manoj. "Eastern Ladakh, the Longer Perspective." ORF Occasional Paper, Number 319. June 2021.

Joshi, Manoj. "Operation Falcon: When Gen Sundarji Took the Chinese by Surprise." The Quint, March 14, 2017. www.thequint.com/voices/opinion/operation-falcon-sundarji-took-china-by-surprise.

Joshi, Shashank. "Can India Blockade China?" *The Diplomat*, August 12, 2013. https://thediplomat.com/2013/08/can-india-blockade-china/.

Joshi, Yogesh, and Anit Mukherjee. "Offensive Defense: India's Strategic Response to the Rise of China." In Kanti Bajpai, Selina Ho, and Manjari Chatterjee Miller (eds.), *Routledge Handbook of China-India Relations* (London: Routledge, 2020), 227–239.

Kampani, Gaurav. "China-India Nuclear Rivalry in the 'Second Nuclear Age'." IFS Insights 3, November 2014. http://hdl.handle.net/11250/226454.

Kapur, S. Paul. *Jihad as Grand Strategy: Islamist Militancy, National Security and the Pakistani State* (New York: Oxford University Press, 2016).

Karl, Rebecca E. *Staging the World: Chinese Nationalism at the Turn of the Twentieth Century* (Durham: Duke University Press, 2002).

Kavic, Lorne J. *India's Quest for Security: Defence Policies, 1947–1965* (Berkeley: University of California Press, 1967).

Keat, James S. "India, China Troops Swap Border Fire." *The Baltimore Sun*, September 12, 1967.

Keenleyside, T. A. "Nationalist Indian Ideas towards Asia: A Troublesome Legacy for Post-independence Indian Foreign Policy." *Pacific Affairs* 55:2 (1982): 210–230.

Kennedy, Andrew B. "Powerhouses or Pretenders? Debating China's and India's Emergence as Technological Powers." *The Pacific Review* 28:2 (2015): 281–302.

Kennedy, John F. "Remarks of Senator John F. Kennedy, Conference on India and the United States, Washington, D. C." John F. Kennedy Presidential Library and Museum. May 4, 1959. www.jfklibrary.org/archives/other-resources/john-f-kennedy-speeches/india-and-the-us-conference-washington-dc-19590504.

Keohane, Robert, and Joseph Nye. *Power and Interdependence*, 4th ed. (Boston: Longman, 2012).

Keshk, Omar, Brian Pollins, and Rafael Reuveny. "Trade Still Follows the Flag: The Primacy of Politics in a Simultaneous Model of Interdependence and Armed Conflict." *Journal of Politics* 66:4 (2004): 1155–1179.

Khan, Sulmaan Wasif. "Cold War Co-operation: New Chinese Evidence on Jawaharlal Nehru's 1954 Visit to Beijing." *Cold War History* 11:2 (2011): 197–222.

Khan, Sulmaan Wasif. *Muslim, Trader, Nomad, Spy: China's Cold War and the People of the Tibetan Borderlands* (Chapel Hill: University of North Carolina Press, 2015).

Khong, Yuen Foong. "Power as Prestige in World Politics." *International Affairs* 95:1 (2019): 119–142.

Khurana, Gurpreet S. "China's 'String of Pearls' in the Indian Ocean and Its Security Implications." *Strategic Analysis* 32:1 (2008): 1–39.

Kim, ChanWahn. "The Role of India in the Korean War." *International Area Studies Review* 13:2 (2010): 21–37.

Knaus, John Kenneth. *Orphans of the Cold War: America and the Tibetan Struggle for Survival* (New York: PublicAffairs, 1999).

Kondapalli, Srikanth. "Perception and Strategic Reality in India-China Relations." In Thomas Fingar (ed.), *The New Great Game: China and South and Central Asia in the Era of Reform* (Stanford: Stanford University Press, 2016), 93–115.

Kondapalli, Srikanth. "Revisiting No First Use and Minimum Deterrence: The View from India." In Lora Saalman (ed.), *The China-India Nuclear Crossroads* (Washington, DC: Carnegie Endowment for International Peace, 2012), 47–67.

Korhonen, Pekka. "Monopolizing Asia: The Politics of a Metaphor." *The Pacific Review* 10:3 (1997): 347–365.

Krishnan, Ananth. "Following the Money: China Inc's Growing Stake in India-China Relations." Impact Series, Brookings India. March 2020. www.brookings.edu/research/following-the-money-china-incs-growing-stake-in-india-china-relations/.

Krishnan, Ananth. "India's Trade with China Crosses $125 Billion, Imports near $100 Billion." *The Hindu*, January 15, 2022. www.thehindu.com/business/Economy/indias-trade-with-china-crosses-125-billion-imports-near-100-billion/article38272914.ece.

Krishnan, Ananth, and Raj Chengappa. "India-China Standoff: All You Need to Know about Doklam Dispute." India Today, July 17, 2017.

Kristensen, Hans M., and Matt Korda. "Chinese Nuclear Weapons, 2021." *Bulletin of the Atomic Scientists* 77:6 (2021): 318–336.

Kristensen, Hans M., and Matt Korda. "Indian Nuclear Forces, 2020." *Bulletin of the Atomic Scientists* 76:4 (2020): 217–225.

Kristensen, Hans M., and Matt Korda. "United States Nuclear Weapons, 2021." *Bulletin of the Atomic Scientists* 77:1 (2021): 43–63.

Kugelman, Michael. "Imran Khan's Silence on Uighurs Undercuts His Defense of Muslims Worldwide." *Foreign Policy*, January 29, 2021. https://foreignpolicy.com/2021/01/29/imran-khan-uighurs-muslims-china/.

Kugler, Jacek, and Ronald L. Tammen. "Implications of Asia's Rise to Global Status." In William R. Thompson (ed.), *Systemic Transitions: Past, Present, and Future* (New York: Palgrave Macmillan 2009), 161–186.

Kuo, Lily. "Satellite Images Show Chinese Construction Near Site of Border Clash; Images of Potential New Camp in Disputed Territory Raise Fears of Further Conflict." The Guardian, June 25, 2020.

Kupchan, Charles A. *How Enemies Become Friends: The Sources of Stable Peace* (Princeton: Princeton University Press, 2010).

Kurita, Masahiro. "China's Kashmir Policy since the mid-2010s: Ramifications of CPEC and India's Kashmir Reorganization." *Asian Security* 18:1 (2021): 56–74.

Lake, David A. "Great Power Hierarchies and Strategies in Twenty-First Century World Politics." In Walter Carlsnaes, Thomas Risse, and Beth A. Simmons (eds.), *Handbook of International Relations*, 2nd ed. (Los Angeles: SAGE, 2013), 555–577.

Lamb, Alastair. *The McMahon Line: A Study in the Relationship between India, China, and Tibet, 1904 to 1914*, 2 vols (London: Routledge & Kegan Paul, 1966).

Lamb, Alastair Lamb. *The Sino-Indian Border in Ladakh* (Columbia: University of South Carolina Press, 1973).

Lavoy, Peter R. (ed.). *Asymmetric Warfare in South Asia: The Causes and Consequences of the Kargil Conflict* (Cambridge: Cambridge University Press, 2009).

Leung, John K., and Michael Y. M. Kau (eds.). *The Writings of Mao Zedong, 1949–1976, Volume II – January 1956–December 1957* (Armonk, NY: M. E. Sharpe, 1992).

Leveringhaus, Nicola. "Beyond 'Hangovers': The New Parameters of Post-Cold War Nuclear Strategy." In Russell W. Glenn (ed.), *New Directions in Strategic Thinking 2.0* (Canberra: Australian National University Press, 2018), 77–90.

Levi, Werner. *Free India in Asia* (Minneapolis: The University of Minnesota Press, 1952).

Levi, Werner. *Modern China's Foreign Policy* (Minneapolis: The University of Minnesota Press, 1953).

Levy, Jack S. "Power Transition Theory and the Rise of China." In Robert S. Ross and Zhu Feng (eds.), *China's Ascent: Power, Security, and the Future of International Politics* (Ithaca: Cornell University Press, 2008), 11–33.

Levy, Jack S. *War in the Modern Great Power System, 1495–1975* (Lexington: University Press of Kentucky, 1983).

Levy, Jack S., and William R. Thompson. *Causes of War* (Malden: Wiley-Blackwell, 2010).

Lewis, Jeffrey. "China's Nuclear Modernization: Surprise, Restraint, and Uncertainty." In Ashley J. Tellis, Abraham M. Denmark, and Travis Tanner (eds.), *Strategic Asia 2013–14: Asia in the Second Nuclear Age* (Washington, DC: National Bureau of Asian Research, 2013), 66–97.

Lewis, John Wilson, and Xue Litai. *China Builds the Bomb* (Stanford: Stanford University Press, 1988).

Lewis Martin, W., and Kären Wigen. *The Myth of Continents: A Critique of Metageography* (Berkeley: University of California Press, 1997).

Li, Hong. "Shoring Up the Nuclear Proliferation Regime: The View from China." In Lora Saalman (ed.), *The China-India Nuclear Crossroads* (Washington, DC: Carnegie Endowment for International Peace, 2012), 121–136.

Li, Jianglin. *Tibet in Agony, Lhasa 1959* (Cambridge, MA: Harvard University Press, 2016).

Li, Laura Tyson. *Madame Chiang Kai-shek: China's Eternal First Lady* (New York: Atlantic Monthly Press, 2006).

Li, Li. "The New Trend of India's Rising as a Great Power." *Contemporary International Relations* 28:2 (2018): 43–48.

Lieberman, Patrick. *Does Conquest Pay* (Princeton: Princeton University Press, 1998).

Lim, Darren J., and Rohan Mukherjee. "Hedging in South Asia: Balancing Economic and Security Interests amid Sino-Indian Competition." *International Relations of the Asia-Pacific* 19:3 (2019): 493–522.

Lin, Hsiao-ting. *Tibet and Nationalist China's Frontier: Intrigues and Ethnopolitics, 1928–1949* (Vancouver: University of British Columbia Press, 2006).

Lin, Minwang. "China, India, and Asian Connectivity: China's View." In Kanti Bajpai, Selina Ho, and Manarji Chatterjee Miller (eds.), *Routledge Handbook of China-India Relations* (London: Routledge, 2020), 303–314.

Lintner, Bertil. *China's India War: Collision Course on the Roof of the World* (New Delhi: Oxford University Press, 2018).

Liu, Xiaoyuan. "Friend or Foe: India as Perceived by Beijing's Foreign Policy Analysts in the 1950s." *China Review* 15:1 (2015): 117–173.

Liu, Xiaoyuan. *To the End of Revolution: The Chinese Communist Party and Tibet, 1949–1959* (New York: Columbia University Press, 2020).

Liu, Xuecheng. *The Sino-Indian Border Dispute and Sino-Indian Relations* (Lanham, MD: University Press of America, 1994).

"Long-Term Macroeconomic Forecasts: Key Trends to 2050." The Economist Intelligence Unit. 2015. https://espas.secure.europa/europa.eu/orbis/sites/default/files/generated/document/en/Long-termMacroeconomicForecasts_KeyTrends.pdf.

Luce, Edward. "The New Era of US-China Decoupling." *Financial Times*, December 21, 2018. www.ft.com/content/019b1856-03c0-11e9-99df-6183d3002ee1.

Lüthi, Lorenz M. *Cold Wars: Asia, the Middle East, Europe* (Cambridge: Cambridge University Press, 2020).

Lüthi, Lorenz M. "India's Relations with China, 1945–74." In Amit R. Das Gupta and Lorenz Lüthi (eds.), *The Sino-Indian War of 1962* (London: Routledge, 2017), 29–47.

Lüthi, Lorenz M. "Non-alignment, 1946–1965: Its Establishment and Struggle against Afro-Asianism." *Humanity* 7:2 (2016): 201–223.

Lüthi, Lorenz M., and Amit R. Das Gupta. "Introduction." In Amit R. Das Gupta and Lorenz M. Lüthi (eds.), *The Sino-Indian War of 1962: New Perspectives* (London: Routledge, 2017), 12–17.

MacFarquhar, Roderick. *The Origins of the Cultural Revolution, Volume 3: The Coming of the Cataclysm, 1961–1966* (New York: Columbia University Press, 1997).

Madan, Tanvi. *Fateful Triangle: How China Shaped U.S.-India Relations during the Cold War* (Washington, DC: Brookings, 2020).

Madan, Tanvi. "Managing China: Competitive Engagement, with Indian Characteristics." In Tarun Chhabra, Rush Doshi, Ryan Haas, and Emilie Kimball (eds.), *Global China: Assessing China's Growing Role in the World* (Washington, DC: Brookings, 2021), 120–131.

Majundar, Rumki. "India: Into the Light, but with Overcast Skies." *Deloitte Insights*, January 7, 2022. www.deloitte.com/us/en/insights/economy/asia-pacific/india-economic-outlook.html.

Malik, Mohan. "The China Factor in the India-Pakistan Conflict." *Parameters* 33:1 (2003): 35–50.

Malik, Shahroo. "Pakistan's Economic Woes: The Way Forward." *The Diplomat*, April 18, 2019. https://thediplomat.com/2019/04/pakistans-economic-woes-the-way-forward/.

Mankekar, D. R. *The Guilty Men of 1962* (Bombay: Tulsi Shah Enterprises, 1968).

Markovits, Claude. "Indian Communities in China, c. 1842–1949." In Robert Bickers and Christian Henriot (eds.), *New Frontiers: Imperialism's New Communities in East Asia, 1842–1953* (Manchester: Manchester University Press, 2000), 55–74.

Mandhana, Niharika, Rajesh Roy, and Chun Han Wong. "The Deadly India-China Clash: Spiked Face-to-Face for Four Hours in the Dark, Some Falling off Cliffs, Indian Officials Said." *The Wall Street Journal*, June 17, 2020. www.wsj.com/articles/spiked-clubs-and-fists-at-14-000-feet-the-deadly-india-china-clash-11592418242.

Mansfield, Edward, and Brian Pollins (eds.). *Economic Interdependence and International Conflict* (Ann Arbor: University of Michigan Press, 2003).

Mansour, Imad, and William R. Thompson (eds.). *Shocks and Rivalries in the Middle East and North Africa* (Washington, DC: Georgetown University Press, 2020).

Manyika, James, Michael Chui, Jacques Bughin, et al. "Disruptive Technologies: Advances That Will Transform Life, Business, and the Global Economy."

McKinsey Global Institute. May 2013. www.mckinsey.com/business-functions/mckinsey-digital/our-insights/disruptive-technologies.

Mao, Tsetung. *Selected Works of Mao-Tsetung*, Volume II (Oxford: Pergamon Press, 1975).

Maoz, Zeev, and Ben D. Mor. *Bound by Struggle: The Strategic Evolution of Enduring International Rivalries* (Ann Arbor: University of Michigan Press, 2002).

Mastro, Oriana Skylar. "Why Chinese Assertiveness Is Here to Stay." *The Washington Quarterly* 37:4 (2015): 151–170.

Mastro, Oriana Skylar, and Arzan Tarapore. "Asymmetric but Uneven: The China-India Conventional Military Balance." In Kanti Bajpai, Selina Ho and Manjari Chatterjee Miller (eds.), *Routledge Handbook of China-India Relations* (London: Routledge, 2020), 240–251.

Mathou, Therry. "Bhutan-China Relations: Towards a New Step in Himalayan Politics." In Karma Ura and Sonam Kinga (eds.), *The Spider and the Piglet: Proceedings of the First International Seminar on Bhutan Studies* (Thimpu: The Centre for Bhutan Studies, 2004), 388–412.

Maxwell, Neville. *India's China War* (London: Jonathan Cape, 1970).

McDonald, Patrick, and Kevin Sweeney. "The Achilles' Heel of Liberal IR Theory." *World Politics* 59:3 (2007): 370–403.

McGarr, Paul M. *The Cold War in South Asia: Britain, the United States and the Indian Subcontinent, 1945–1965* (Cambridge: Cambridge University Press, 2013).

McGarr, Paul M. "The United States, Britain, and the Sino-Indian Border War." In Amit R. Das Gupta and Lorenz Lüthi (eds.), *The Sino-Indian War of 1962: New Perspectives* (London: Routledge, 2017), 105–123.

McGranahan, Carole. *Arrested Histories: Tibet, the CIA, and Memories of a Forgotten War* (Durham: Duke University Press, 2010).

McGranahan, Carole. "Tibet's Cold War: The CIA and the Chushi Gangdrug Resistance, 1956–1974." *Journal of Cold War Studies* 8:3 (2006): 102–130.

Mearsheimer, John J. "Bound to Fail: The Rise and Fall of the Liberal International Order." *International Security* 43:4 (2019): 7–50.

Medcalf, Rory. "India and China: Terms of Engagement in the Western Indo-Pacific." In David Brewster (ed.), *India and China at Sea: Competition for Naval Dominance in the Indian Ocean* (Oxford: Oxford Scholarship Online, 2018), https://doi.org//10.1093/oso/9780199479337.003.0014.

Medeiros, Evan S. *Reluctant Restraint: The Evolution of China's Nonproliferation Policies and Practices, 1980–2004* (Stanford: Stanford University Press, 2007).

"Memorandum of Conversation between Director Zhang Wenji and Indian Ambassador Parthasarathy (1)." July 17, 1961. History and Public Policy Digital Archive, PRC FMA 105-01056-03, 51–59. Obtained by Sulmaan Khan and translated by Anna Beth Keim. https://digitalarchive.wilsoncenter.org/document/121625.

"Memorandum of Conversation between Mao Zedong and Henry Kissinger." November 12, 1973. History and Public Policy Program Digital Archive, Gerald R. Ford Presidential Library, National Security Adviser Trip Briefing Books and Cables for President Ford, 1974–1976 (Box 19), https://digitalarchive.wilsoncenter.org/document/118069.

Menon, Shivshankar. "Economic Decoupling to Self-Strengthening: How India Can Rise to China Challenge." *The Times of India*, October 16, 2021. https://timesofindia.indiatimes.com/blogs/voices/economic-decoupling-to-self-strengthening-how-india-can-rise-to-china-challenge/.

Menon, Shivshankar. *India and Asian Geopolitics: The Past, Present* (Washington, DC: Brookings, 2021).

Menon, Shivshankar. "Some Consequences of the India-China Crisis of 2020." In Leah Bitounis and Niamh King (eds.), *Domestic and International (Dis)Order: A Strategic Response* (Washington, DC: The Aspen Institute, 2020), 77–82, www.aspeninstitute.org/wp-content/uploads/2020/10/Foreign-Policy-2021-ePub_FINAL.pdf.

Miglani, Sanjeev, and Fayaz Bukhari. "New Indian Roads, Airstrips, Sparked Standoff with China, Observers Say." NTD, May 25, 2020. https://ntdca.com/new-indian-roads-airstrips-sparked-border-standoff-with-china-india-observers-say/.

Miller, Manjari Chatterjee. *Wronged by Empire: Post-Imperial Ideology in India and China* (Stanford: Stanford University Press, 2013).

"Minister Says India Will Aid Java Fight." *The New York Times*, December 14, 1948.

Mitchell, Sara McLaughlin, and John A. Vasquez. "What Do We Know about War?" In Sara McLaughlin Mitchell and John A. Vasquez (eds.), *What Do We Know about War?* 3rd ed. (Lanham, MD: Rowman & Littlefield, 2021), 319–342.

Mitter, Rana. *Forgotten Ally: China's World War II, 1937–1945* (Boston: Houghton Mifflin Harcourt, 2013).

Mobley, Terry. "The Belt and Road Initiative: Insights from China's Backyard." *Strategic Studies Quarterly* 13:3 (2019): 52–72.

Modelski, George, and William R. Thompson. *Leading Sectors and World Powers: The Coevolution of Global Politics and Economics* (Columbia: University of South Carolina Press, 1996).

Modelski, George, and William R. Thompson. *Sea Power in Global Politics, 1494–1993* (London: Macmillan, 1988).

Moe, Espen. "Mancur Olson and Structural Economic Change: Vested Interests and the Industrial Rise and Fall of the Great Powers." *Review of International Political Economy* 16:2 (2009): 202–220.

Mohan, C. Raja. "Mind the Power Gap." *Indian Express*, August 2, 2017. https://indianexpress.com/article/opinion/columns/india-china-standoff-mind-the-power-gap-4777926/.

Mohan, C. Raja. *Samudra Manthan: Sino-Indian Rivalry in the Indo-Pacific* (Washington, DC: Carnegie Endowment for International Peace, 2012).

Montgomery, Evan Braden. "Contested Primacy in the Western Pacific: China's Rise and the Future of U.S. Power Projection." *International Security* 38:4 (2014): 115–149.

Mosca, Matthew. *From Frontier to Foreign Policy: The Question of India and the Transformation of Geopolitics in Qing China* (Stanford: Stanford University Press, 2013).

Mukherjee, Anit. "India as a Net Security Provider: Concepts and Impediments." Policy Brief, S. Rajaratnam School of International Studies. August 2014. www.rsis.edu.sg/wp-content/uploads/2014/09/PB_140903_India-Net-Security.pdf.

Mullik, B. N. *My Years with Nehru: The Chinese Betrayal* (New Delhi: Allied, 1971).

"Multipolar World Should Include Multipolar Asia: Jaishankar." *The Hindu*, September 19, 2020. www.thehindu.com/news/national/multipolar-world-should-include-multipolar-asia-jaishankar/article32644407.ece.

Musgrave, Paul. "Asymmetry, Hierarchy, and the Ecclesiastes Trap." *International Studies Review* 21:2 (2019): 284–300.

Musumeci, Natalie. "India Says It Accidentally Fired a Missile into Pakistan." *Business Insider*, March 11, 2022. www.businessinsider.com/india-says-it-accidentally-fired-missile-into-pakistan-during-maintenance-2022-3#:~:text=India%20said%20on%20Friday%20that%20a%20%22technical%20malfunction%22,to%20a%20statement%20from%20India%27s%20Ministry%20of%20Defense.

Narang, Vipin. "Nuclear Deterrence in the China-India Dyad." In T. V. Paul (ed.), *The China-India Rivalry in the Globalization Era* (Washington, DC: Georgetown University Press, 2018), 187–202.

Nathan, Andrew J., and Andrew Scobell. *China's Search for Security* (New York: Columbia University Press, 2012).

Nayar, Baldev Raj, and T. V. Paul. *India in the World Order: Searching for Major Power Status* (Cambridge: Cambridge University Press, 2002).

"Nehru Correspondence, November 1962: 11–19." John F. Kennedy Presidential Library and Museum. www.jfklibrary.org/asset-viewer/archives/JFKNSF/111/JFKNSF-111-016.

Nehru, Jawaharlal. *Independence and After: A Collection of Speeches, 1946–1949* (New York: The John Day Company, 1950).

Nehru, Jawaharlal. "Inter-Asian Relations." *India Quarterly* 2:4 (1946): 323–327.

Nehru, Jawaharlal. *Selected Works of Jawaharlal Nehru (SWJN)*, Series 2, Volume 1 (New Delhi: Jawaharlal Nehru Memorial Fund). https://nehruselectedworks.com/.

Nehru, Jawaharlal. *The Discovery of India*, centenary edition (Delhi: Oxford University Press, 1989 [1946]).

Niu, Jun. "1962: The Eve of the Left Turn in China's Foreign Policy." Cold War International History Project, Working Paper No. 48, Woodrow Wilson International Center for Scholars. October 2005. www.wilsoncenter.org/publication/1962-the-eve-the-left-turn-chinas-foreign-policy.

Noorani, A. G. *India-China Boundary Problems, 1846–1947: History and Diplomacy* (New Delhi: Oxford University Press, 2011).

Norris, William J. "Economic Statecraft as a Tool of Peacemaking? China's Relationships with India and Russia." In Steven E. Lobell and Norrin M. Ripsman (eds.), *The Political Economy of Regional Peacemaking* (Ann Arbor: University of Michigan Press, 2016), 169–191.

Norris, William J. "Geostrategic Implications of China's Twin Economic Challenges." Discussion Paper, Council on Foreign Relations. June 2017. www.cfr.org/report/geostrategic-implications-chinas-twin-economic-challenges.

Nossiter, Bernard. "China, India Troops Renew Border Clash." *The Boston Globe*, September 14, 1967.

Notes, Memoranda and Letters Exchanged between the Governments of India and China, October 1962–January 1963, White Paper No. VIII (New Delhi: Indian Ministry of External Affairs, 1963).

O'Connor, Tom. "China Warns of 'Cold War' after US-India Talks, Pakistan Protests Terror Accusations." *Newsweek*, October 28, 2020. www.newsweek.com/china-cold-war-us-india-talks-pakistan-protests-terror-accusations-1543078.

Office of the Secretary of Defense. "Annual Report to the Congress, Military and Security Developments Involving the People's Republic of China 2016." United States Department of Defense. 2016. https://dod.defense.gov/Portals/1/Documents/pubs/2016%20China%20Military%20Power%20Report.pdf.

Office of the Secretary of Defense. "Military and Security Developments Involving the People's Republic of China 2020, Annual Report to the Congress." United States Department of Defense. 2020. https://media.defense.gov/2020/Sep/01/2002488689/-1/-1/1/2020-DOD-CHINA-MILITARY-POWER-REPORT-FINAL.PDF.

Office of the Secretary of Defense. *Annual Report to Congress, Military and Security Developments Involving the PRC* (Washington, DC: United States Department of Defense, November 2021).

Ollapally, Deepa M. "China and India: Economic Ties and Strategic Rivalry." *Orbis* 58:3 (2014): 342–357.

O'Rourke, Ronald. "China Naval Modernization: Implications for US Navy Capabilities – Background and Issues for Congress." Congressional Research Service. December 2, 2021. https://sgp.fas.org/crs/row/RL33153.pdf.

Padmanabhan, S. G. *Next China-India War – World's First Water War – 2029* (New Delhi: Manas Publications, 2014).

Palmer, Norman D. "China's Relations with India and Pakistan." *Current History* 61:361 (1971): 148–153.

Pan, Zhenqiang. "Thinking beyond Nuclear Doctrine and Strategy: The View from China." In Lora Saalman (ed.), *The China-India Nuclear Crossroads* (Washington, DC: Carnegie Endowment for International Peace, 2012), 25–34.

Pandit, Rajat. "In First Winter Stay, 1,800 Chinese Troops Camping at Doklam." *The Times of India*, December 11, 2017.

Pandit, Rajat. "India Asks China to Retreat from Doklam." *The Times of India*, July 6, 2017.

Panikkar, K. M. *In Two Chinas: Memoirs of a Diplomat* (London: George Allen & Unwin, 1955).

Panikkar, K. M. *The Basis of an Indo-British Treaty* (New Delhi: Indian Council of World Affairs, 1946).

Panikkar, K. M. *The Future of Southeast Asia* (London: George Allen & Unwin, 1943).

Panikkar, K. M. "The Himalayas and Indian Defence." *India Quarterly* 55:3/4 (1999 [1947]): 73–90.

Pardesi, Manjeet S. "American Global Primacy and the Rise of India." *Asia Pacific Issues*, No. 129 (2017). www.eastwestcenter.org/publications/american-global-primacy-and-the-rise-india.

Pardesi, Manjeet S. "China's Nuclear Forces and Their Significance to India." *The Nonproliferation Review* 21:3–4 (2014): 337–354.

Pardesi, Manjeet S. "Explaining the Asymmetry in the Sino-Indian Strategic Rivalry." *Australian Journal of International Affairs* 75:3 (2021): 341–365.

Pardesi, Manjeet S. "Image Theory and the Initiation of Strategic Rivalries." In William R. Thompson (ed.), *The Oxford Encyclopedia of Empirical International Relations Theory*, Volume 2 (Oxford: Oxford University Press, 2018), 225–244.

Pardesi, Manjeet S. "India's Conventional Military Strategy." In Sumit Ganguly, Nicolas Blarel, and Manjeet S. Pardesi (eds.), *The Oxford Handbook of India's National Security* (New Delhi: Oxford University Press, 2018), 114–131.

Pardesi, Manjeet S. "Is India a Great Power? Understanding Great Power Status in Contemporary International Relations." *Asian Security* 11:1 (2015): 1–30.

Pardesi, Manjeet S. "Managing the 1986–87 Sino-Indian Sumdorong Chu Crisis." *The India Review* 18:5 (2019): 534–551.

Pardesi, Manjeet S. "The Indo-Pacific: A 'New' Region or the Return of History?" *Australian Journal of International Affairs* 74:2 (2020): 124–146.

Pardesi, Manjeet S. "The Initiation of the Sino-Indian Rivalry." *Asian Security* 15: 3 (2019): 253–284.

Parthasarathi, G. (ed.). *Jawaharlal Nehru: Letters to Chief Ministers, 1947–1964, Volume 2, 1950–1952* (New Delhi: Jawaharlal Nehru Memorial Fund, 1986).

Parthasarathi, G. (ed.). *Jawaharlal Nehru: Letters to Chief Ministers, 1947–1964, Volume 5: 1958–1964* (New Delhi: Oxford University Press, 1989).

Paszak, Paweł. "China and the Malacca Dilemma." *China Report*, February 28, 2021. https://warsawinstitute.org/china-malacca-dilemma/.

Paul, T. V. *Asymmetric Conflicts: War Initiation by Weaker Powers* (New York: Cambridge University Press, 1994).

Paul, T. V. "Chinese-Pakistani Nuclear/Missile Ties and Balance of Power Politics." *The Nonproliferation Review* 10:2 (2003): 21–29.

Paul, T. V. "Explaining Conflict and Cooperation in the China-India Rivalry." In T. V. Paul (ed.), *The China-India Rivalry in the Globalization Era* (Washington, DC: Georgetown University Press, 2018), 3–24.

Paul, T. V. "The Causes and Consequences of China-Pakistani Nuclear/Missile Collaboration." In Lowell Dittmer (ed.), *South Asia Nuclear Security Dilemma: India, Pakistan and China* (London: Routledge, 2015), 175–188.

Paul, T. V. "The Rise of China and the Emerging Order in the Indo-Pacific Region." In Huiyun Feng and Kai He (eds.), *China's Challenges and International Order Transition: Beyond Thucydides's Trap* (Ann Arbor: University of Michigan Press, 2020), 71–94.

Paul, T. V. "When Balance of Power Meets Globalization: China, India, and the Small States of South Asia." *Politics* 39:1 (2019): 50–63.

Paul, T. V. (ed.). *The China-India Rivalry in the Globalization Era* (Washington, DC: Georgetown University Press, 2018).

Paul, T. V. (ed.). *The India-Pakistan Conflict: An Enduring Rivalry* (Cambridge: Cambridge University Press, 2005).

Paul, T. V., and Mahesh Shankar. "Status Accommodation through Institutional Means: India's Rise and the Global Order." In T. V. Paul, Deborah Welch Larson, and William C. Wohlforth (eds.), *Status in World Politics* (New York: Cambridge University Press, 2014), 165–191.

Perdue, Peter C. "China and Other Colonial Empires." *The Journal of American-East Asian Relations* 16:1/2 (2009): 85–103.

Perkovich, George. *India's Nuclear Bomb: The Impact on Global Proliferation* (Berkeley: University of California Press, 1999).

Pettyjohn, Stacie L. "War with China: Five Scenarios." *Survival* 64:1 (2022): 57–66.

Pham, Sherisse. "India Bans More Chinese Apps as Tensions Remain High." *CNN*, November 25, 2020. https://edition.cnn.com/2020/11/25/tech/india-bans-chinese-apps-hnk-intl/index.html

Pomeranz, Kenneth. "The Great Himalayan Watershed: Water Shortages, Mega-Projects and Environmental Politics in China, India, and Southeast Asia." *The Asia-Pacific Journal* 7:30 (2009): 2.

Prados, John. *Safe for Democracy: The Secret Wars of the CIA* (Chicago: Ivan R. Dee, 2006).

Prasad, Bimla. *The Origins of Indian Foreign Policy: The Indian National Congress and World Affairs, 1885–1947*, 2nd ed. (Calcutta: Bookland, 1962).

Prasad, Birendra. *Indian Nationalism and Asia (1900–1947)* (Delhi: B. R. Publishing Corporation, 1979).

Prime Minister on Chinese Aggression (New Delhi: Ministry of External Affairs, n.d.)

"Preventative Priorities Survey." Council on Foreign Relations. www.cfr.org/preventive-priorities-survey.

Press Trust of India. "US provided Info, Equipment to India during China Border Crisis: Pentagon Commander." NDTV, March 10, 2021. www.ndtv.com/india-news/us-provided-info-equipment-to-india-during-china-border-crisis-pentagon-commander-2388015.

Preston, Andrew. *The War Council: McGeorge Bundy, the NSC and Vietnam* (Cambridge, MA: Harvard University Press, 2006).

Pringsheim, Klaus H. "China's Role in the Indo-Pakistani Conflict." *The China Quarterly* 24 (1965): 170–175.

Pollpeter, Kevin. "Controlling the Information Domain: Space, Cyber, and Electronic Warfare." In Ashley Tellis and Travis Tanner (eds.), *Strategic Asia 2012–13: China's Military Challenge* (Washington, DC: National Bureau of Asian Research, 2012), Kindle Loc. 2787–3452.

Pu, Xiaoyu. "Ambivalent Accommodation: Status Signaling of a Rising India and China's Response." *International Affairs* 93:1 (2017): 155–156.

Pubby, Manu. "Don't Believe in Hindi-Chini bhai-bhai, Nehru Told Envoy." *Indian Express*, January 22, 2010. https://indianexpress.com/article/news-archive/web/dont-believe-in-hindichini-bhaibhai-nehru-told-envoy/.

Rabasa, Angel, Robert D. Blackwill, Peter Chalk, et al. *The Lessons of Mumbai* (Santa Monica: RAND, 2009).

Radchenko, Sergey. *Two Suns in the Heavens: The Sino-Soviet Struggle for Supremacy, 1962–1967* (Stanford: Stanford University Press, 2009).

Raghavan, Srinath. "The Security Dilemma and India-China Relations." *Asian Security* 15:1 (2019): 60–72.

Raghavan, Srinath. *War and Peace in Modern India: A Strategic History of the Nehru Years* (Ranikhet: Permanent Black, 2010).

Rajagopalan, Rajesh. "Evasive Balancing: India's Unviable Indo-Pacific Strategy." *International Affairs* 96:1 (2020): 75–93.

Rajagopalan, Rajeswari Pillai. "An Indian Perspective on China's Military Modernization." In Bates Gill (ed.), *Meeting China's Military Challenge: Collective Responses of U.S. Allies and Security Partners* (Washington, DC: National Bureau of Asian Research, 2022), NBR Special Report #96, 37–48. www.nbr.org/publication/meeting-chinas-military-challenge-collective-responses-of-u-s-allies-and-partners/.

Rajagopalan, Rajeswari Pillai. "Linking Strategic Stability and Ballistic Missile Defense: The View from India." In Lora Saalman (ed.), *The China-India Nuclear Crossroads* (Washington, DC: Carnegie Endowment for International Peace), 65–76.

Rajagopalan, Rajeswari Pillai. "Sino-Indian Competition in South Asia: Another Round." *The Diplomat*, December 3, 2021. https://thediplomat.com/2021/12/sino-indian-competition-in-south-asia-another-round/.

Rakisits, Claude. "A Path to the Sea: China's Pakistan Plan." *World Affairs* 178:3 (2015): 67–74.

Rakisits, Claude. "Pakistan-China Bilateral Relations 2001–2011: A Deepening but Cautious Partnership." *Security Challenges* 8:3 (2012): 83–102.

Rana, A. P. *The Imperatives of Nonalignment: A Conceptual Study of India's Foreign Policy Strategy in the Nehru Period* (Delhi: Macmillan, 1979).

Rao, Nirupama Menon. *The Fractured Himalaya: India, Tibet, China, 1949–62* (New Delhi: India Viking, 2022).

Rasler, Karen, and William R. Thompson. "Assessing Inducements and Suppressors of Interstate Conflict Escalation." Paper presented at the Annual Meeting of the International Studies Association, San Diego, March 22–25, 2006.

Rasler, Karen, and William R. Thompson. "Strategic Rivalries and Complex Causality in 1914." In Jack S. Levy and John A. Vasquez (eds.), *The Outbreak of the First World War: Structure, Politics, and Decision-Making* (New York: Cambridge University Press, 2014), 65–86.

Rasler, Karen, and William R. Thompson. *The Great Powers and Global Struggle, 1490–1990* (Lexington: University Press of Kentucky, 1994).

Rasler, Karen A., William R. Thompson, and Sumit Ganguly. *How Rivalries End* (Philadelphia: University of Pennsylvania Press, 2013).

Ravenhill, John. "Economic Interdependence, Globalization, and Peaceful Change." In T. V. Paul, Deborah Welch Larson, Harold A. Trinkunas, Anders

Wivel, and Ralf Emmers (eds.), *The Oxford Handbook of Peaceful Change in International Relations* (New York: Oxford University Press, 2021), 147–168. https://doi.org//10.1093/oxfordhb/9780190097356.013.9.

"Report from the PLA General Staff Department, 'Behind India's Second Anti-China Wave'." October 29, 1959. History and Public Policy Program Digital Archive, PRC FMA 105-00944-07, 84–90. Translated by 7Brands, https://digitalarchive.wilsoncenter.org/document/114758.

Reuveny, Rafael, and William R. Thompson. *Growth, Trade, and Systemic Leadership* (Ann Arbor: University of Michigan Press, 2004).

Rice, Condoleezza. "Promoting the National Interest." *Foreign Affairs* 79:1 (2000): 45–62.

Richardson, Hugh. *Tibet and Its History* (Boulder: Shambala, 1984).

Richardson, Sophie. *China, Cambodia, and the Five Principles of Peaceful Coexistence* (New York: Columbia University Press, 2009).

Riedel, Bruce. *JFK's Forgotten Crisis: Tibet, the CIA, and the Sino-Indian War* (Washington, DC: Brookings, 2015).

Rikhye, Ravi. "China's Border Build-up." *The Times of India*, April 16, 1987.

Roemer, Stephanie. *The Tibetan Government-in-Exile: Politics at Large* (London: Routledge, 2008).

Rolland, Nadège, Fillipo Boni, Meia Nouwens, et al. "Where the Belt Meets the Road: Security in Contested South Asia." *Asia Policy* 14:2 (2019): 1–41.

Rose, Leo E. *Nepal: Strategy for Survival* (Berkeley: University of California Press, 1971).

Rose, Leo E. *The Politics of Bhutan* (Ithaca: Cornell University Press, 1977).

Rosecrance, Richard. *The Rise of the Trading State* (New York: Basic, 1986).

Rosecrance, Richard N., and Steven E. Miller (eds.). *The Next Great War? The Roots of World War I and the Risk of U.S.-China Conflict* (Cambridge, MA: The MIT Press, 2014).

Roy-Chaudhury, Rahul, and Kate Sullivan de Estrada. "India, the Indo-Pacific, and the Quad." *Survival*, 60:3 (2018): 181–194.

Roy-Chaudhury, Shantanu. "Analysing China's Arms Sales to South Asia." *India Foundation Journal* (July–August 2020): 39–48.

Saalman, Lora. "China's Detachment from the South Asian Nuclear Triangle." SIPRI Commentary, September 8, 2020. www.sipri.org/commentary/blog/2020/chinas-detachment-south-asian-nuclear-triangle.

Saalman, Lora. "Divergence, Similarity, and Symmetry in Sino-Indian Threat Perceptions." *Journal of International Affairs* 64:2 (2011): 169–194.

Saalman, Lora. "Introduction." In Lora Saalman (ed.), *The China-India Nuclear Crossroads* (Washington, DC: Carnegie Endowment for International Peace, 2012), 1–14.

Safi, Michael, and Hannah Ellis-Petersen. "India Says 20 Soldiers Killed on Disputed Himalayan Border with China; First Loss of Life in Area in at least 45 Years Comes amid Renewed Dispute." *The Guardian*, June 16, 2020.

Salisbury, Harrison E. *The Coming War between China and Russia* (London: Martin Secker and Warburg, 1969).

Samaranayake, Nilanthi. "Securing the Maritime Silk Road in South Asia and the Indian Ocean." *Asia Policy* 14:2 (2019): 21–26.

Sample, Susan G. "Arms Races." In Sara McLaughlin Mitchell and John A. Vasquez (eds.), *What Do We Know about War?* 3rd ed. (Lanham, MD: Rowman & Littlefield, 2021), 63–80.

Saran, Shyam. *How China Sees India and the World* (New Delhi: Juggernaut, 2022).

SarDesai, D. R. *Indian Foreign Policy in Cambodia, Laos, and Vietnam, 1947–1964* (Berkeley: University of California Press, 1968).

Schaffer, Teresita C., and Howard B. Schaffer. *India at the Global High Table: The Quest for Regional Primacy and Strategic Autonomy* (Washington, DC: Brookings, 2016).

Schelling, Thomas. *Arms and Influence* (New Haven: Yale University Press, 2008).

Schleicher, Charles P. "Review of India's China War by Neville Maxwell." *American Political Science Review* 66:2 (1972): 682–684.

"Science, Technology, and Innovation Policy 2013." Ministry of Science and Technology. http://dst.gov.in/sites/default/files/STI%20Policy%202013-English.pdf.

Science of Military Strategy. The full text of this document, which was prepared by China's Academy of Military Sciences, was translated into English and published under the auspices of Project Everest and the China Aerospace Studies Institute on February 8, 2021, 2013. www.airuniversity.af.edu/CASI/Display/Article/2485204/plas-science-of-military-strategy-2013/.

"Science, Technology, and Innovation Policy 2020 (Draft)." Ministry of Science and Technology. www.psa.gov.in/psa-prod/psa_custom_files/STIP_Doc_1.4_Dec2020.pdf.

Scobell, Andrew. "Himalayan Standoff: Strategic Culture and the China-India Rivalry." In T. V. Paul (ed.), *The China-India Rivalry in the Globalization Era* (Washington, DC: Georgetown University Press, 2018), 165–186.

Scobell, Andrew, Bonny Lin, Howard J. Shatz, et al. *At the Dawn of Belt and Road* (Santa Monica: RAND, 2018).

Scott-Clark, Cathy, and Adrian Levy. *The Siege: 68 Hours inside the Taj Hotel* (London: Penguin, 2013).

See, Chak Mun. "Singapore-India Strategic Relations – Singapore's Perspective." In Anit Mukherjee (ed.), *The Merlion and the Ashoka: Singapore-India Strategic Ties* (Singapore: World Scientific, 2016), 45–62.

Sen, Tansen. *Buddhism, Diplomacy and Trade: The Realignment of Sino-Indian Relations, 600–1400* (Honolulu: University of Hawai'i Press, 2004).

Sen, Tansen. "The Chinese Intrigue in Kalimpong: Intelligence Gathering and the 'Spies' in a Contact Zone." In Tansen Sen and Brian Tsui (eds.), *Beyond Pan-Asianism: Connecting China and India, 1840s–1960s* (New Delhi: Oxford University Press, 2021), 410–459.

Shafiq, Nadeem. "India versus China: A Review of the Aksai Chin Border Dispute." *Journal of Political Studies* 18:2 (2011): 207–223.

Shakya, Tsering. *The Dragon in the Land of Snows* (New York: Penguin, 1999).

Shakya, Tsering. "The Genesis of the 17 Point Agreement: An Analysis of the Sino-Tibetan Agreement of 1951." In Per Kvaerne (ed.), *Tibetan Studies: Proceedings of the*

Papers Presented at the 6th Seminar of the International Association for Tibetan Studies (Oslo: The Institute of Comparative Research in Human Culture, 1994), 754–793.

Shambaugh, David. "China's International Relations Think Tanks: Evolving Structure and Process." *The China Quarterly* 171 (2002): 579–590.

Shambaugh, David. "The Insecurity of Security: The PLA's Evolving Doctrine and Threat Perceptions towards 2000." *Journal of Northeast Asian Studies* 13 (1994): 3–25.

Shankar, Mahesh. "Territory and the China-India Competition." In T. V. Paul (ed.), *The China-India Rivalry in the Globalization Era* (Washington, DC: Georgetown University Press, 2018), 27–54.

Shankar, Mahesh. *The Reputational Imperative: Nehru's India in Territorial Conflict* (Stanford: Stanford University Press, 2022).

Shen, Dingli. "A Chinese Perspective on India-U.S. Strategic Partnership and Its Implications for China." In Rajiv Narayanan and Qiu Yonghui (eds.), *India and China: Building Strategic Trust* (New Delhi: United Service Institution of India, 2020), 323–338.

Sheng, Michael M. "Mao, Tibet, and the Korean War." *Journal of Cold War Studies* 8:3 (2006): 15–33.

Shi, Zhe. Chen Jian (trans.). "With Mao and Stalin: The Reminiscences of a Chinese Interpreter." *Chinese Historians* 5:1 (1992): 35–46.

Shifrinson, Joshua. *Rising Titans, Falling Giants: How Great Powers Exploit Power Shifts* (Ithaca: Cornell University Press, 2018).

Shirk, Susan. "One-Sided Rivalry: China's Perceptions and Policies toward India." In Francine R. Frankel and Harry Harding (eds.), *The India-China Relationship: What the United States Needs to Know* (New York: Columbia University Press, 2004), 75–100.

Shukla, Ajai. "How China and India Came to Lethal Blows." *The New York Times*, June 19, 2020. Siddiqui, Kalim. "A Comparative Political Economy of China and India: A Critical Review." In Young-Chan Kim (ed.), *China-India Relations: Geo-political Competition, Economic Cooperation, Cultural Exchange and Business Ties* (Cham: Springer, 2020), 31–58.

Sidky, Mohammad Habib. "Chinese World Strategy and South Asia: The China Factor in Indo-Pakistani relations." *Asian Survey* 16:10 (1976): 965–980.

Sikri, Veena. *India and Malaysia: Intertwined Strands* (New Delhi: Manohar, 2013).

Singh, Abhijit. "India's Naval Interests in the Pacific." In David Brewster (ed.), *India and China at Sea* (Oxford: Oxford Scholarship Online, 2018), https://doi .org/10.1093/oso/9780199479337.003.0011.

Singh, Ameya Pratap, and Urvi Tembey. "India-China Relations and the Geopolitics of Water." *The Interpreter*, July 23, 2020. www.lowinstitute.org/ the-interpreter/india-china-relations-and-geopolitics-water.

Singh, C. P. "Indian Navy: The Guardians of the Indian Ocean." *Indian Defence Review*. January 6, 2022. www.indiandefencereview.com/spotlights/ india-navy-the-guardians-of-the-indian-ocean/.

Singh, J. D. "Nathu La Border I: The Chinese Threat." *The Times of India*, October 14, 1967.

Singh, J. D. "Nathu La Border II: Enemy Intentions." *The Times of India*, October 16, 1967.

Singh, L. P. "Dynamics of Indian-Indonesian Relations." *Asian Survey* 7:9 (1967): 655–666.

Singh, P. K. "China-Pakistan Economic Corridor: Connecting the Dots." *United Services of India Journal* (April–June 2017). https://usiofindia.org/publication/usi-journal/china-pakistan-economic-corridor-connecting-the-dots/.

Singh, Sinderpal. "India-China Maritime Competition: Southeast Asia and the Dilemma of Regional States." In Rajesh Basrur, Anit Mukherjee, and T. V. Paul (eds.), *India-China Maritime Competition: The Security Dilemma at Sea* (London: Routledge, 2019), 137–160.

Singh, Swaran. "China and India: Coping with Growing Asymmetry." The Asan Forum, December 19, 2014. https://theasanforum.org/china-and-india-coping-with-growing-asymmetry/.

Singh, Vishal. "The Reactions of South-East Asian Countries." *International Studies* 5:1–2 (1963): 80–84.

Sinha, Aseema. "Partial Accommodation without Conflict: India as a Rising Link Power." In T. V. Paul (ed.), *Accommodating Rising Powers: Past, Present, and Future* (Cambridge: Cambridge University Press, 2016), 222–245.

Sinha, P. B., and A. A. Athale. *History of the Conflict with China, 1962* (New Delhi: History Division, Ministry of Defence, 1992).

"SIPRI Military Expenditure Database." Stockholm International Peace Research Institute. www.sipri.org/databases/milex.

Slater, Joanna, and Gerry Shih. "India and China Trade Barbs after 'Gang War' High in the Himalayas." *The Washington Post*, June 17, 2020.

Small, Andrew. *The China-Pakistan Axis: Asia's New Geopolitics* (New York: Oxford University Press, 2015).

Smith, Jeff M. *Cold Peace: Sino-Indian Rivalry in the Twenty-First Century* (Lanham, MD: Lexington Books, 2014).

Smith, Paul J. "The Tilting Triangle: Geopolitics of the China-India-Pakistan Relationship." *Comparative Strategy* 32:4 (2012): 313–330.

Smith, Sheila A. *Japan Rearmed: The Politics of Military Power* (Cambridge, MA: Harvard University Press, 2019).

Smoke, Richard. *War: Controlling Escalation* (Cambridge, MA: Harvard University Press, 1977).

Southerland, Daniel. "China Accuses India of Violating Border: New Delhi Rejects Charge of Nibbling." *The Washington Post*, April 23, 1987.

Sperling, Elliot. "Tibet and China: The Interpretation of History since 1950." *China Perspectives* 3 (2009): 25–37.

Stargardt, A. W. "The Emergence of the Asian System of Powers." *Modern Asian Studies* 23:3 (1989): 561–595.

Stolte, Carolien, and Harald Fischer-Tiné. "Imagining Asia in India: Nationalism and Internationalism (ca. 1905–1940)." *Comparative Studies in Society and History* 54:1 (2012): 65–92.

Stuart-Fox, Martin. *A Short History of China and Southeast Asia: Tribute, Trade, and Influence* (Crows Nest: Allen & Unwin, 2003).

Stueck, William. *The Korean War: An International History* (Princeton: Princeton University Press, 1995).

Subramaniam, Arjun. *A Military History of India since 1972* (Lawrence: University of Kansas Press, 2021).

Suruyama, Sumio, and Kengo Tahara. "2060 Digital and Global Economy." Japan Center for Economic Research. January 2020. www.jcer.or.jp/jcer_download_log.php?f=eyJwb3NoZlkIjoiODI5OCwiZmlsZV9wb3NoZlkIjoiODMxOXo=&post_id=58298&file_post_id=58319.

Syed, Anwar H. *China and Pakistan: Diplomacy of an Entente Cordiale* (Amherst: University of Massachusetts Press, 1974).

Talmadge, Caitlin. "The U.S.-China Nuclear Relationship: Why Competition Is Likely to Intensify?" In Tarun Chhabra, Rush Doshi, Ryan Haas, and Emilie Kimball (eds.), *Global China: Assessing China's Growing Role in the World* (Washington, DC: Brookings, 2021), 86–91.

Tao, Shengli, Henry Zhang, Yuhao Feng, et al., "Changes in China's Water Resource in the Early Twenty-First Century." *Frontiers in Ecology and the Environment* 18:4 (2020): 188–193.

Tellis, Ashley J. *India's Emerging Nuclear Posture: between Recessed Deterrent and Ready Arsenal* (Santa Monica: RAND, 2000).

Tellis, Ashley J. "The China-Pakistan Nuclear 'Deal': Separating Fact from Fiction." Policy Outlook, Carnegie Endowment for International Peace. July 16, 2010. https://carnegieendowment.org/2010/07/16/china-pakistan-nuclear-deal-separating-fact-from-fiction.

Tellis, Ashley J. "The Evolution of U.S.-Indian Ties: Missile Defense in an Emerging Strategic Relationship." *International Security* 30:4 (2006): 113–151.

Tellis, Ashley J., and C. Raja Mohan. *The Strategic Rationale for Deeper U.S.-Indian Economic Ties: American and Indian Perspectives* (Washington, DC: Carnegie Endowment for International Peace, 2015).

Tellis, Ashley J., Travis Tanner, and Jessica Keough (eds.). *Strategic Asia 2011–12: Asia Responds to Its Rising Powers, China and India* (Washington, DC: National Bureau of Asian Research, 2011).

Ten Brinke, Leanne, and Dacher Keltner. "Theories of Power: Perceived Strategies for Gaining and Maintaining Power." *Journal of Personality and Social Psychology* 122:1 (2022): 53–72.

"The Long View: How Will the Global Economic Order Change by 2050?" Price Waterhouse Coopers. February 2017. www.pwc.com/gx/en/world-2050/assets/pwc-the-world-in-2050-full-report-feb-2017.pdf.

"The Position of Nehru." *The New York Times*, August 29, 1950.

The Sino-Indian Boundary Question, enlarged edition (Peking: Foreign Languages Press, 1962).

Thomas, Raju G. C. "Nonalignment and Indian Security: Nehru's Rationale and Legacy." *Journal of Strategic Studies* 2:2 (1979): 153–171.

Thomas, Raju G. C. *The Defence of India: A Budgetary Perspective of Strategy and Politics* (Delhi: Macmillan, 1978).

Thompson, William R. "A Streetcar Named Sarajevo: Catalysts, Multiple Causation Chains, and Rivalry Structures." *International Studies Quarterly* 47:3 (2003): 453–474.

Thompson, William R. *American Global Pre-eminence: The Development and Erosion of Systemic Leadership* (New York: Oxford University Press, 2022).

Thompson, William R. "Dehio, Long Cycles and the Geohistorical Context of Structural Transitions." *World Politics* 45 (1992): 127–152.

Thompson, William R. "Economic Incentives, Rivalry Deescalation, and Regional Transformation." In Steven Lobell and Norrin Ripsman (eds.), *The Political Economy of Regional Peacemaking* (Ann Arbor: University of Michigan Press), 96–117.

Thompson, William R. "Introduction: How Might We Know that a Systemic Transition Is Underway? Clues for the Twenty-First Century." In William R. Thompson (ed.), *Systemic Transitions: Past, Present, and Future* (New York: Palgrave Macmillan), 1–6.

Thompson, William R. *On Global War: Historical-Structural Approaches to World Politics* (Columbia: University of South Carolina Press, 1988).

Thompson, William R. "Powder Kegs, Sparks, and World War I." In Gary Goertz and Jack S. Levy (eds.), *Explaining War and Peace: Case Studies and Necessary Condition Counterfactuals* (London: Routledge, 2007), 95–122.

Thompson, William R. *Power Concentration in World Politics: The Political Economy of Systemic Leadership, Growth and Conflict* (Cham: Springer, 2020).

Thompson, William R. "Principal Rivalries." *Journal of Conflict Resolution* 39:2 (1995): 195–223.

Thompson, William R. "Status Conflict, Hierarchies, and Interpretation Dilemmas." In T. V. Paul, Deborah Welch Larson, and William C. Wohlforth (eds.), *Status in World Politics* (New York: Cambridge University Press, 2014), 219–245.

Thompson, William R. "Trends in the Analysis of Interstate Rivalries." In Robert Scott and Stephen Kosslyn (eds.), *Emerging Trends in the Social and Behavioral Sciences* (New York: John Wiley & Sons, 2015). https://doi.org/10.1002/9781118900772.etrds0369.

Thompson, William R., and David R. Dreyer. *Handbook of International Rivalries, 1494–2010* (Washington, DC: CQ Press, 2012).

Thompson, William R., Kentaro Sakuwa, and Prashant Hosur Suhas. *Analyzing Strategic Rivalries in World Politics: Types of Rivalry, Regional Variation, and Escalation/De-escalation* (Singapore: Springer, 2022).

Thompson, William R., and Leila Zakhirova. *Racing to the Top: How Energy Fuels Systemic Leadership* (New York: Oxford University Press, 2019). *Tibet, 1950–1967* (New Delhi: Union Research Institute, 1968).

TNN, "Chinese Incursion in Ladakh: A Little Toothache Can Paralyze Entire Body, Modi Tells Xi Jinping." *The Times of India*, September 20, 2014.

Times of India News Service. "Cease Fire and Start Talks: New Delhi Note." *The Times of India*, September 12, 1967.

Times of India News Service. "Chinese Troops Start and Intense Duel with Indian Troops on Sikkim Border." *The Times of India*, September 12, 1967.

Times of India News Service. "All Quiet on the Nathu La Front." *The Times of India*, September 15, 1967.

Toje, Asle (ed.). *Will China's Rise Be Peaceful? Security, Stability, and Legitimacy* (Oxford: Oxford University Press, 2018).

Ton That, Thien. *India and South East Asia, 1947–1960* (Geneve: Librairie Droz, 1963).

Trachtenberg, Marc. "Assessing Soviet Economic Performance during the Cold War: A Failure of Intelligence." *Texas National Security Review* 1:2 (2018): 76–101.

"Trade and Economic Relations." Embassy of India (Beijing, China). Updated 9 July 2021. www.eoibeijing.gov.in/eoibejing_pages/Mjg.

Trumbull, Robert. "Behind India-China Dispute: Leadership of Asia." *The New York Times*, October 28, 1962.

Trumbull, Robert. "Nehru Said to Sway Peiping toward Moderate Policies." *The New York Times*, October 31, 1954.

Tsui, Brian. "Coming to Terms with the People's Republic of China: Jawaharlal Nehru in the Early 1950s." In Young-Chan Kim (ed.), *China-India Relations: Geo-political Competition, Economic Cooperation, Cultural Exchange and Business Ties* (Cham: Springer, 2020), 13–30.

Twomey, Christopher P. "Asia's Complex Strategic Environment: Nuclear Multipolarity and Other Dangers." *Asia Policy* 11 (January 2011): 51–78.

United States National Intelligence Council. "Global Trends 2030: Alternative Worlds." Office of the Director of National Intelligence. December 2012. www.dni.gov/files/documents/GlobalTrends_2030.pdf.

United States National Intelligence Council. "Global Trends 2040: A More Contested World." Office of the Director of National Intelligence. March 2021. www.dni.gov/files/ODNI/documents/assessments/GlobalTrends_2040.pdf.

Unnithan, Sandeep. "Month after Doklam Withdrawal, More Chinese Troops on Plateau than before." *India Today*, October 9, 2017.

"U.S. Strategic Framework for the Indo-Pacific." The White House, January 5, 2021. https://trumpwhitehouse.archives.gov/wp-content/uploads/2021/01/IPS-Final-Declass.pdf;

Valeriano, Brandon. *Becoming Rivals: The Process of Interstate Rivalry Development* (London: Routledge, 2013).

Valeriano, Brandon, and Matthew Powers. "Complex Interstate Rivals." *Foreign Policy Analysis* 12 (2016): 552–570.

Van Walt van Praag, Michael. *The Status of Tibet: History, Rights, and Prospects in International Law* (Boulder: Westview, 1987).

Vasquez, John and Christopher S. Leskiw. "The Origins and War Proneness of Interstate Rivalries." *Annual Review of Political Science* 4:1 (2001): 295–316.

Vaughn, Bruce. "China-India Great Power Competition in the Pacific Ocean Region: Issues for Congress." Congressional Research Service Report, April 20, 2018. https://sgp.fas.org/crs/row/R45194.pdf.

Vertzberger, Yaacov Y. I. *Misperceptions in Foreign Policymaking: The Sino-Indian Conflict, 1959–1962* (Boulder: Westview, 1984).

Wang, Gungwu. *China and the World since 1949: The Impact of Independence, Modernity and Revolution* (London: Macmillan, 1977).

Wang, Hongwei. Chen Guansheng, and Li Peizhu (trans.). *A Critical Review of the Contemporary Sino-Indian Relations* (Beijing: China Tibetology Publishing House, 2011).

Wang, Jisi. "China in the Middle." *The American Interest*, February 2, 2015. www .the-american-interest.com/2015/02/02/china-in-the-middle/.

Wang, Jun. *A Preliminary Study of the New Normal of China's Economy* (Singapore: Springer, 2021).

Wang, Zheng. *Never Forget National Humiliation: Historical Memory in Chinese Politics and Foreign Relations* (New York: Columbia University Press, 2012).

Wei, Julie Lee, Ramon Myers, and Donald Gillin (eds.), Julie Lee Wei, E-su Zen, and Linda Chao (trans.). *Prescriptions for Saving China: Selected Writings of Sun Yat-sen* (Stanford: Hoover Institution Press, 1994).

Weiner, Myron. "The Macedonian Syndrome: An Historical Model of International Relations and Political Development." *World Politics* 23:4 (1971): 665–683

Westad, Odd Arne. *Restless Empire: China and the World since 1750* (New York: Basic Books, 2015).

Westcott, Stephen P. *Armed Coexistence: The Dynamics of the Intractable Sino-Indian Border Dispute* (Singapore: Palgrave Macmillan, 2022).

Whiting, Allen S. *The Chinese Calculus of Deterrence: India and Indochina* (Ann Arbor: University of Michigan Press, 1975).

Wiegand, Krista E. *Enduring Territorial Disputes: Strategies of Bargaining, Coercive Diplomacy, & Settlement* (Athens: The University of Georgia Press, 2011).

Wolff, David (trans.). "Memorandum of Conversation, Soviet Ambassador N. V. Roshchin with CC CCP Secretary Liu Shaoqi." May 6, 1951, History and Public Policy Program Digital Archive, *AVP* RF f. 0100, op. 44, por. 13, pap. 322, II. 17–22. https://digitalarchive.wilsoncenter.org/document/118734.

Wolters, O. W., and Craig J. Reynolds (ed.). *Early Southeast Asia: Selected Essays* (Ithaca: Cornell University Press, 2008).

Womack, Brantly. *Asymmetry and International Relationships* (New York: Cambridge University Press, 2016).

Womack, Brantly. "Mapping the Multinodal Terrain of the Indo-Pacific." Settimana News, February 28, 2018. www.settimananews.it/italia-europa-mondo/mapping-multinodal-terrain-indo-pacific/.

"World Development Indicators," The World Bank, https://databank.world bank.org/source/world-development-indicators.

"World Economic League Table 2021." Centre for Economics and Business Research. December 2020. https://cebr.com/wp-content/uploads/2020/12/welt-2021-final-23.12.pdf.

Wortzel, Larry M. "Concentrating Forces and Audacious Action: PLA Lessons from the Sino-Indian War." In Laurie Burkitt, Andrew Scobell, and Larry M. Wortzel (eds.), *The Lessons of History: The Chinese People's Liberation Army at 75* (Carlisle, PA: Strategic Studies Institute, U.S. Army War College, 2003), 327–352.

Wu, Lin. "India's Perception of and Response to China-US Competition." *China International Studies* 85:6 (2020): 130–133.

Xavier, Constantino. "Across the Himalayas: China in India's Neighborhood." In Kanti Bajpai, Selina Ho, and Manarji Chatterjee Miller (eds.), *Routledge Handbook of China-India Relations* (London: Routledge, 2020), 420–433.

Xi, Jinping. "Speech Delivered at the 19th National Congress of the Communist Party of China." October 18, 2017. www.xinhuanet.com/english/download/ Xi_Jinping%27s_report_at_19th_CPC_National_Congress.pdf.

Yahuda, Michael. "The Limits of Economic Interdependence: Sino-Japanese Relations." In Alastair Iain Johnston and Robert Ross (eds.), *New Directions in the Study of China's Foreign Policy* (Stanford: Stanford University Press, 2006), 162–185.

Yan, Xuetong. Alexander A. Bowe (trans). *Inertia of History: China and the World by 2023* (Newcastle upon Tyne: Cambridge Scholars Publishing, 2019).

Yan, Xuetong. *Leadership and the Rise of Great Powers* (Princeton: Princeton University Press, 2019).

Yang, Yun-Yuan. "Nehru and China, 1927–1949" (PhD Dissertation, University of Virginia, 1974).

Ye, Hailin. "The Strategic Landscape of South Asia and Indian Ocean Region." In Rong Wang and Cuiping Zhu (eds.), *Annual Report on the Development of International Relations in the Indian Ocean Region (2014)* (Heidelberg: Springer, 2015), 27–40.

Ye, Zicheng (trans. Steven I. Levine, and Guoli Liu). *Inside China's Grand Strategy: The Perspective from the People's Republic* (Lexington: University Press of Kentucky, 2011).

You, Ji. *China's Military Transformation: Politics and War Preparation* (Cambridge: Polity, 2016).

You, Ji. "The Indian Ocean: A Grand Sino-Indian Game of 'Go'." In David Brewster (ed.), *India and China at Sea: Competition for Naval Dominance in the Indian Ocean*, Oxford Scholarship Online, May 2018. https://doi.org//10.1093/ oso/9780199479337.003.0006.

Yuan, Jingdong. "Sino-Indian Economic Ties since 1988: Progress, Problems, and Prospects for Future Development." *Journal of Current Chinese Affairs* 45:3 (2016): 31–71.

Zagoria, Donald S. *The Sino-Soviet Conflict, 1956–1961* (Princeton: Princeton University Press, 1962).

Zarakol, Ayse (ed.). *Hierarchies in World Politics* (Cambridge: Cambridge University Press, 2017).

Zhang, Feng. "China's Curious Nonchalance towards the Indo-Pacific." *Survival* 61:3 (2019): 187–212.

Zhang, Feng. "India in China's Strategic Thought." In Kanti P. Bajpai, Selina Ho, and Manjari Chatterjee Miller (eds.), *Routledge Handbook of China-India Relations* (London: Routledge, 2020), 139–148.

Zhang, Hungzhou. "Sino-Indian Water Disputes: The Coming Water Wars?" *WIREs Water* 3:3 (2016): 155–166.

Zhang, Jie. "The Quadrilateral Security Dialogue and Reconstruction of Asia-Pacific Order." *China International Studies* 74:1 (2019): 55–73.

Zheng, Yongnian. "On China-India Border Standoff." *China-US Focus*, July 24, 2017. www.chinausfocus.com/peace-security/on-china-india-border-standoff.

Zhou, Enlai. "Premier Chou En-Lai's [Zhou Enlai's] Letter to the Leaders of Asian and African Countries on the Sino-Indian Boundary Question (November 15, 1962)." November 15, 1962. *History and Public Policy Program Digital Archive* (Peking: Foreign Languages Press, 1973). https://digitalarchive.wilsoncenter.org/document/175946.

Zhou, Enlai (trans. Jeffrey Wang). "Zhou Enlai's Speech at the Political Committee of the Afro-Asian Conference." April 23, 1955. History and Public Policy Digital Program Archive, PRC FMA 207-00006-04, 69–75. https://digitalarchive.wilsoncenter.org/document/114678.

Zhu, Cuiping. "Changes of the International Environment in the Indian Ocean Region and the Strategic Choices for China." In Cuiping Zhu (ed.), *Annual Report on the Development of the Indian Ocean Region (2019)* (Singapore: Springer, 2021), 3–44.

Zubok, Vladislav M. (trans.). "Discussion between N. S. Khrushchev and Mao Zedong." October 2, 1959. History and Public Policy Program Digital Archive, Archive of the President of the Russian Federation (APRF), f. 52, op. 1, d. 499, II. 1–33, copy in Volkogonov Collection, Manuscript Division, Library of Congress, Washington. http://digitalarchive.wilsoncenter.org/document/112088.

Zubok, Vladislav M. "The Mao-Khrushchev Conversations, 31 July–3 August 1958 and 2 October 1959." *Cold War International History Project Bulletin* Issue 12/13 (2001): 248.

Index

For EU product safety concerns, contact us at Calle de José Abascal, 56–1°,
28003 Madrid, Spain or eugpsr@cambridge.org.

www.ingramcontent.com/pod-product-compliance
Ingram Content Group UK Ltd.
Pitfield, Milton Keynes, MK11 3LW, UK
UKHW022330160425
457339UK00017B/311